The McGraw-Hill Language Arts Program

The Series
American Language Today
Secret Hand
Tiger Tree
Emerald Snowflake
Orange Rain
Purple Sand
Flying Free

American English Today
Exploring English
Our Common Language
The Tools of English
The World of English
The Uses of Language
Our Changing Language

AMERICAN ENGLISH TODAY

The World of English

General Editor and Senior Author

HANS P. GUTH

WEBSTER DIVISION/McGRAW-HILL BOOK COMPANY
New York   St. Louis   San Francisco   Dallas   Atlanta

Consultants and Contributors

Creative Writing   **Gabriele Rico,**
   San Jose State University

Cultural Minorities   **Nettye Goddard,**
   San Jose Unified School District

Regional Literature   **Peggy Fisk Paiko,**
   Albuquerque Public Schools

Graphics   **Herbert Zettl,**
   San Francisco State University

Curriculum   **William Slothower,**
   San Jose State University

Linguistics   **Edgar H. Schuster,**
   Allentown (Pa.) Public Schools

Acknowledgment pages 522–525 are an extension of this copyright page.

Editorial Direction: *Charles Packard, Laura Mongello*
Design: *Pedro A. Noa*   Editing and Styling: *Sal Allocco*
Design Supervisor: *Lisa Delgado*   Photo Research: *Rosemary O'Connell*
Production: *Renee Guilmette*

Previous edition and impressions published under the title *The Structure of English.*

Library of Congress Cataloging in Publication Data

Guth, Hans Paul, 1926–
   The world of English.

   (His American English today; [4])
   Published in 1970 under title: The Structure of English.
   SUMMARY: A tenth grade English text offering instruction in the areas of composition, word study, grammar, usage, mechanics, and speech.
   1. English language—Grammar—1950– 2. English language—Composition and exercises. [1. English language—Grammar. 2. English language—Composition and exercises] I. Title.

[PE1408.G933 vol. 4]   [PE1112]   428'.2   75–4775
ISBN 0–07–025320–X

About These Books

American English Today, 7–12, provides a modern program in language and composition. It builds on a synthesis of the best in current teaching and research. It relates theory directly to classroom practice. It appeals directly to the interests and needs of today's students.

Five major themes determine the content and direction of the series as a whole:

(1) THE COMMON CENTER. English is the most basic subject in the student's general education. Each book of the series provides a rich choice of activities and resources in five central areas: word study, sentence building, written expression, oral language, and standard English.

(2) THE INHERENT REWARDS OF ENGLISH. English becomes rewarding when students discover the potential of language, when they experience the satisfaction that comes from the effective and creative use of language. *American English Today* is a positive modern approach that stresses the power of words, the range and variety of American English, the rewards of self-expression and effective two-way communication.

(3) THE FULL RANGE OF ENGLISH. Activities and exercise materials in this series draw on the full range of creative expression through language: Indian legend, African myth, the folklore of the frontier, regional literature, popular humor, science fiction, the literature of adventure and discovery. The student is led to explore the relation between print and other media, between words and other kinds of language—image, gesture, sound.

(4) THE PARTICIPATING STUDENT. In working with *American English Today,* students participate in the process of exploration and discovery. They work with words and sentences to build up their own language repertory. They discover written and oral expression as a means of recording their own observations, formulating their own ideas, developing their own creative potential.

(5) ENGLISH IN THE REAL WORLD. Language is everywhere part of the student's environment. It is the medium of business, politics, entertainment. We see it all around us as headlines, billboards, letters to the editor, instructions, directions, campaign literature, sales talks, posters, commercials, and forms to fill in. *American English Today* treats English as a living thing, to be observed all around us in our everyday world, and serving every kind of human purpose.

TABLE OF CONTENTS

Chapter 2

Chapter 3
COMPOSITION: Why, What, and How   183

Chapter 4
   ORAL LANGUAGE: Making Yourself Heard   325

Chapter 6
MECHANICS: Words on a Page   427

PROSE MODELS

A Word About English

Language is around us everywhere. Without language, life in modern society would be impossible. Business executives use words in planning production and in promoting their products. Politicians use language in discussing the issues, drawing up laws, explaining their stand to the voters. Newspapers keep us informed through words. Teachers, lawyers, ministers—none could do their work without language.

The study of English helps people use language easily and well. The benefits of studying English are of three major kinds:

(1) The study of English helps people *understand the workings of language*. Intelligent voters must know something about the workings of government. Intelligent speakers and listeners must know something about how language works. They must understand why different people use language differently. Before they judge the way other people speak and write, they must know something about the ways of words.

(2) The study of English helps people *speak and write effectively*. No matter what jobs they hold or what people they deal with, people who know how to express themselves have the ad-

vantage. Students who do well in English are learning to say the right thing at the right time. They are learning to say what they mean and to say it in such a way that people will listen. They are learning to express themselves in writing as fluently and as naturally as in speaking.

(3) The study of English helps people *listen and read with profit and pleasure.* When we deal with other people, we want to understand what they are trying to say. When we listen to a commercial or a political speech, we want to understand the techniques being used. When we read a famous novel, we want to respond fully to the characters and events the author has created. Part of the English teacher's job is to help people listen well and read with emotion.

CHAPTER 1

Words: The Range of Meaning

In order to speak and write well, develop a lifelong interest in words.

Success in English requires a knowledge of words. Anyone who wants to do well in English must learn to *study words*—to pay attention to new words, to look them up in a dictionary, to watch for them in future listening and reading. Remember:

—*Words are interesting in themselves.* Our vocabulary is rich and colorful. Even a small-scale dictionary lists thousands of words, covering every possible shade of meaning. Many of these words come to us from the far corners of the world. Many of them have a fascinating history. By studying where they came from, we at the same time learn something about the history of the culture in which we live.

—*Words are the basic building blocks in speech and writing.* No one can communicate without words that convey exact meaning. No matter what their occupations, people who always fumble ·

THE LANGUAGE OF MAGIC AND THE OCCULT

How well do you know the language of mystery and magic? How would you answer the following questions?

1. What is the common meaning of the following: *abracadabra, hocus-pocus, mumbo jumbo*? Are these words in any way different in what they bring to mind?
2. How are the words *telepathy* and *extrasensory* related in meaning?
3. What does a *medium* do at a *séance*?
4. What is the difference between *conjure* and *exorcise*?
5. How many of the following words do you know: *juju, voodoo, revenant, clairvoyant*? What do they mean?
6. What is the difference between a *premonition* and an *apparition*?

for the right expression are at a disadvantage. Both in school and in everyday life, people who want to do well must be *articulate*. They must be able to use words easily and well.

—*Words help us think.* No one can think clearly whose use of words is muddled. No one who attaches only vague notions to major political terms can understand political issues. Often when we say: "I can't quite put it into words," we mean: "I haven't quite thought the matter through."

The following activities may help you become interested in words. They may help you become *word conscious* in your listening and reading:

WHAT'S IN A WORD?

How many of the following words do you know—and how well? Where does each word come from? Where would you expect to find it used? How (and by whom)? Does the word have any special uses or associations? Do you ever use the word yourself—why or why not? Check a dictionary if you can. What does it tell you that you did not already know?

palaver	parasite	persnickety
kibbutz	rhubarb	kickback
do-si-do	spinnaker	wherewithal
habeas corpus		

WHAT'S IN A NAME?

What countries do the following names come from? How do you know?

Magda	Sigrid	Ivan	Octavio
Isaac	Werner	Giuseppe	Joachim
Juan	Giovanni	Golda	Melissa
Stanislaw	Sean	Atsuko	Ian
Giselle	Gail	Deirdre	Elizabeth

PLAYING WITH WORDS

Newspaper reporters and editors are habitual word watchers. They often play games with language. For instance, what is funny about each of the following headlines? Collect a few similar headlines (or make up your own!). Your class may want to vote on a "Headline of the Week."

TARZAN INDUSTRY IN FULL SWING AGAIN

SETBACK FOR THE GREENBACK

WHAT EVERYBODY SAYS

Much of what we say is not original. At least part of the time we say things "that everybody says." How good are you at recognizing "old saws" and familiar sayings? Look at the following garbled proverbs. In each case, what is the popular saying the way we usually hear it? (You may want to make up some garbled proverbs of your own.)

The pen is mightier than the pencil.
Two heads are enough.
A rolling stone plays a guitar.
A fool and his money are very attached.
Early to bed and early to rise makes a man tired.
Half a loaf is better than vegetables.
You can't get blood out of a sick duck.
Fools rush in where people are crowded.
A bird in the hand is warm.
Ask me no questions and I'll tell you the answers.

LANGUAGE IS EVERYWHERE

SOME PEOPLE MAKE SURE
THEY ARE HEARD

SOME MESSAGES ARE IGNORED

BREAKING THE COMMUNICATION BARRIER

If you were an editor, could you help a translator break the communication barrier? Some translations are very *literal*. Could you help bring them closer to everyday English? Some passages merely *sound* as if they were translated from an obscure original. Could you rewrite them to satisfy readers who ask for "Plain English, please"? How would you translate each of the following passages into plain everyday English?

> With great probability, the flying-machine field with horselike speed will announce in words that within not much difference from half an hour a jet plane will take off.
>
> —translation from the Chinese

> Soothlike, when the healer saw the many, he went up on the mount, and where he sat, his learning-men came to him.
>
> —translation from the oldest English Bible

> The quantitative change in people riding motorcycles is reflected in the public mind by the demise of the image of the motorcycle outlaw. Middle-class Americans have taken to motorcycling as a means of recreation, diminishing the social impact of the renegade rider.
>
> —from a magazine article

Bonus: Try your hand at writing an announcement that sounds as if had been translated from the Chinese.

**W1
WORDS IN
CONTEXT**

In learning new words, pay attention to how they are used.

How do we learn new words? When we hear or see a new word, we are often satisfied if we can get a rough idea of what it means. The next time we hear the word, we find that we have forgotten it again. In order to *make a word really your own*, follow these steps:

(1) Get a full **definition** of the word. A good definition sums up in a sentence or two exactly *what the word stands for*. Sometimes writers or speakers will themselves define a difficult or important word. Often you will have to look up the word in a good dictionary. Here are some typical dictionary definitions:

WORDS IN CONTEXT

If you didn't know these words, how could you tell what they mean?

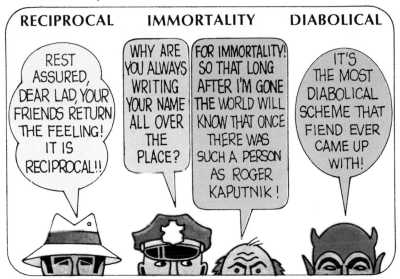

residence	the place where one actually lives as distinguished from a temporary dwelling place
resignation	the act of giving up an office or a position
resilience	the ability to bounce or spring back after being compressed

Make sure you can restate the definition *in your own words*. There is no point in memorizing a definition that you don't fully understand. Restate a dictionary definition something like this:

residence	"My *residence* is my actual home rather than a place I merely visit."
resignation	"Someone who is handing in a *resignation* is quitting a job or retiring from public office."
resilience	"An object has *resilience* if it bounces back to its original form after it has been bent or pressed down."

Look at the following dictionary definitions. In each case, how would you "say it in your own words"?

synchronize | to cause to indicate the same time, as one timepiece with another

equilibrium | a state of rest or balance due to the equal action of opposing forces

unilateral | pertaining to or proceeding from only one of a number of sides or parties in a controversy or transaction

consecutive | following one another in uninterrupted order

prevail | to occur as the most important or conspicuous element; to be or become dominant

(2) Watch how the word you are trying to learn is used in **context.** The context of a word includes the *words that are used with it,* and the situation where it occurs. Pay attention to the expressions in which the word is used. See how it fits into a sentence.

Here are some sentences showing different words in context. Can you tell what each word means from "what goes with it"?

articulate | Senator Graves was an *articulate* and forceful speaker.
| What we need in this campaign is *articulate* discussion of public issues.
| Jim is a thoughtful boy, but I wish he were more *articulate.*

insolent | *Insolent* remarks make Mr. Greene very angry.
| You can criticize something without being *insolent.*
| The editorial used very *insolent* language about our President.

omnipotent | The President of the United States has great power but is not *omnipotent.*
| Unlike the ancient Greeks, the early Christians believed in an *omnipotent* God.

aptitude | He was a lanky, awkward boy with absolutely no *aptitude* for sports.
| The counselor gave us an *aptitude* test to see who would be successful in the program.
| She did not discover her *aptitude* for the creative arts till late in life.

A MISS IS AS GOOD AS A MILE

Sometimes a new word may seem vaguely familiar. But if we are just guessing at the meaning, we may be completely wrong. Which of the meanings given for each of the following words is the right one? (Write the letter after the number of the word.)

1. antidote
   a. a short funny story
   b. counteracts a poison
   c. cuts down your appetite

2. evaporation
   a. evacuates people from a city
   b. helps a bat avoid obstacles
   c. makes water dry up

3. incubator
   a. hatches chickens
   b. incinerates waste materials
   c. puts people to sleep

4. taxidermist
   a. drives a taxi
   b. makes taxicabs
   c. stuffs dead animals

5. astrologist
   a. a space traveler
   b. a space scientist
   c. studies the influence of stars on people

6. mortician
   a. makes mortar
   b. buries people
   c. pronounces people dead

7. cartographer
   a. a maker of maps
   b. a maker of greeting cards
   c. a maker of cartoons

8. optometrist
   a. always hopes for the best
   b. prescribes eyeglasses
   c. favors the metric system

9. philatelist
   a. a stamp collector
   b. a native of Philadelphia
   c. a friend of dogs

10. deterrent
    a. cleans clothes
    b. keeps people from committing a crime
    c. relieves high blood pressure

Context helps us "get the point"—even when a *wrong* word is used by mistake. Can you tell from the context what word should have been used in each of the following sentences?

> We arrived safely at the hotel and *preceded* casually through the fast revolving door.
>
> The stove *omitted* a welcome warmth.
>
> If he mentioned his cousins at all, he would *prefer* to them as traitors.

(3) Try to *tie a new word to something you have read or experienced*. Always try to collect a set of reminders like the following:

exodus   *Exodus* is the word used in the Bible to describe the departure of the Jews from Egypt under the leadership of Moses.

Some years ago, the word *exodus* was used as the title of a movie describing how Jewish survivors of World War II left Europe for what was to become the new state of Israel.

exile   When a king has to flee his native country to live somewhere else, the newspapers say that he has gone into *exile*.

In Roman history, *exile* is used to describe some faraway place to which someone is sent when banished from Rome.

My father joked the other day that he has been *exiled* from the television room.

For which of the following words could you provide some similar "reminders"?

satellite   emancipation   sovereign   omniscient

permissive   collective   contraband

ACTIVITY 1

When the publishers of the original Webster's dictionaries prepared a new dictionary "for the seventies," they included new words such as those below. Pretend you had been the editor in charge of new words and meanings. Write a *one-sentence* definition for each of the words.

air bag	letter bomb	rotary engine
environmentalist	transplant	unisex
noise pollution	bummer	tow-away zone

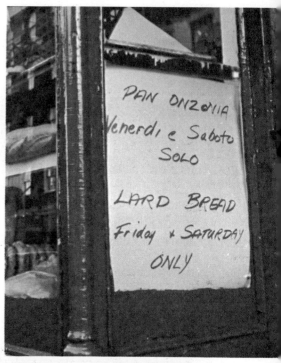

MANY AMERICANS ARE
BILINGUAL (III): CHINATOWN

Explain to someone who has never read any science fiction what these words mean.

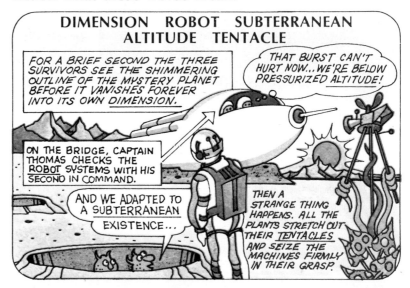

ACTIVITY 2

Each of the following words is used in a sentence that helps explain what the word means. After the number of each word, write down its meaning in your own words. Be prepared to explain to the rest of the class how the *context* helped you find the meaning of words that you did not know.

1. fantasy   Science fiction, with its wildly imaginary adventures, satisfies the modern reader's need for *fantasy*.

2. prototype   *The War of the Worlds,* a novel H. G. Wells published in 1898, became the *prototype* for countless books of science fiction.

3. peril   Many of the early science fiction writers scared their readers by showing the *perils* of uncontrolled scientific experiment.

4. sensational   In the more *sensational* type of book, some unlucky scientist creates a bug-eyed monster that drives everyone hysterical with fear.

5. berserk   Or a robot goes *berserk* and, in an orgy of destruction, kills its master.

6. dominate   Many writers wrote about future societies *dominated* by science, with every detail of life scientifically regulated.

7. totalitarian   In these societies, individual freedom had disappeared under the rule of *totalitarian* governments.

8. technology   Many new inventions and technical appliances had made people completely dependent on *technology*.

9. compulsory   Perfect physical and mental health had become not only possible but *compulsory*, with no room for exceptions.

10. rebel   Sometimes the major character would refuse to be like everyone else and *rebel* against the environment.

11. impetus   A new age dawned for science fiction when the first space flights gave a new *impetus* to the idea of travel to other worlds.

12. utopia   The writers describing imaginary future societies could now locate their *utopias* on distant planets.

13. elaborate   They could describe in great detail the *elaborate* equipment necessary to keep human beings alive on faraway stars.

14. immune   They could describe creatures impossible to hurt with human weapons and *immune* to human diseases.

15. imaginative   The less *imaginative* science fiction writers gave their space creatures an extra set of eyes, or an antenna behind the ears.

16. inhabitable   The bolder writers designed weird new creatures that could live on hot surfaces of bare rock and find them *inhabitable*.

17. migration   Many stories deal with the *migration* of large masses of humans who have to leave our planet after it has been poisoned by atomic warfare.

18. exodus   One novel describes the *exodus* of some people who leave the United States hoping to find a better life on Mars.

19. ethics   In the more serious books, humans sometimes see their own code of *ethics* clash with the moral standards of a different world.

20. leisure   Whether read as entertainment or as food for thought, science fiction is sure to retain its share of the *leisure* hours of the modern reader.

ACTIVITY 3

Follow the same instructions as for Activity 2.

1. flourish   When the European explorers first came to the New World, several great Indian civilizations *flourished* in Central and South America.

2. magnificent   Though all these civilizations are known for splendid cultural achievements, the most *magnificent* of these cultures was probably the Inca culture of Peru.

3. primitive   It would be a big mistake to think of these Indians as *primitive* people living in scattered groups as hunters and warriors.

4. illustrious   When the Spaniards first came to Peru, the Incas looked back with pride on a long *illustrious* past.

5. artifact   They knew how to create glorious *artifacts* in gold, ceramic, and stone.

6. ritual   They performed complicated religious *rituals*.

7. achievement   Compared with the backward state of medicine in Europe, the *achievements* of the Incas in medicine were impressive.

8. legend   The early explorers listened to the *legends* about the heroes of their race and their mysterious white gods.

9. conquest   These Indians lacked the gunpowder and firearms that might have prevented armed *conquest* by the Spanish invaders.

10. formidable   The Indians were divided from the Spaniards by *formidable* barriers of language and religion.

11. possess   They *possessed* untold wealth in gold and jewelry.

12. deteriorate   Though the relations between the natives and their visitors were friendly at first, they soon *deteriorated*.

13. subjugate   In the end, the Indians were *subjugated* and their culture destroyed.

14. subordinate   To this day, many of their descendants live in poverty and play only a *subordinate* role in the culture and economy of their country.

15. élite   For centuries, a relatively small Spanish-speaking *élite* had owned most of the land and set the tone for the political and cultural life of Peru.

16. heritage   Like other South American countries with a similar past, modern Peru is trying to blend its Spanish and its Indian *heritage*.

17. archeologist   In the meantime, *archeologists* will continue to search in the ruins of the old Inca cities for remainders of a vanished culture.

18. implement   Artworks as well as the *implements* of the various crafts and occupations are being preserved for museum showings.

19. extinct   These exhibits will remind visitors of a great culture that once flourished and has now become *extinct*.

20. advent   Visitors will wonder what it was like to live among the Incas long before the *advent* of our industrialized modern civilization.

THE LANGUAGE OF SCIENCE FICTION

FOR FURTHER STUDY

Some science fiction stories show us a future world fallen into poverty and decay. Modern technology is gradually being lost. Science is slowly turning back into magic and legend. In the following excerpt from such a story, the speaker lives in a decaying future world. His job is to scan the heavens for invaders from the stars. Would you have any trouble reading the story? Does the *context* help you with new or difficult words? Read the passage and answer the questions that follow it.

I touched the knobs, made contact with the nodes, monitored the dials. But I did not enter Watchfulness, for I remained aware of Gormon's presence and fearful that he would break into my concentration once again at a painful moment, despite his promise. At length I looked away from the apparatus. Gormon stood at the far side of the road, craning his neck for some sight of Avluela. The moment I turned to him he became aware of me.

"Something wrong, Watcher?"

"No. The moment's not propitious for my work. I'll wait."

"Tell me," he said. "When Earth's enemies really do come from the stars, will your machines let you know it?"

"I trust they will."

"And then?"

"Then I notify the Defenders."

"After which your life's work is over?"

"Perhaps," I said.

"Why a whole guild of you, though? Why not one master center where the Watch is kept? Why a bunch of itinerant Watchers drifting endlessly from place to place?"

"The more vectors of detection," I said, "the greater the chance of early awareness of the invasion."

"Then an individual Watcher might well turn his machines on and not see anything, with an invader already here."

"It could happen. Therefore we practice redundancy."

"You carry it to an extreme, I sometimes think." Gormon laughed. "Do you actually believe an invasion is coming?"

"I do," I said stiffly. "Else my life was a waste."

"And why should the star people want Earth? What do we have here besides the remnants of old empires? What would they do with miserable Roum? With Perris? With Jorslem? Rotting cities! Idiot princes! Come, Watcher, admit it: the invasion's a myth, and you go through meaningless

motions three times a day. Eh?"

"It is my craft and my science to Watch. It is yours to jeer. Each of us to our specialty, Gormon."

"Forgive me," he said with mock humility. "Go, then, and Watch."

"I shall."

Angrily I turned back to my cabinet of instruments, determined now to ignore any interruption, no matter how brutal. The stars were out; I gazed at the glowing constellations, and automatically my mind registered the many worlds. Let us Watch, I thought. Let us keep our vigil despite the mockers.

I entered the state of full Watchfulness.

I clung to the grips and permitted the surge of power to rush through me. I cast my mind to the heavens and searched for hostile entities. What ecstasy! What incredible splendor! I who had never left this small planet roved the black spaces of the void, glided from star to burning star, saw the planets spinning like tops. Faces stared back at me as I journeyed, some without eyes, some with many eyes, all the complexity of the many-peopled galaxy accessible to me. I spied out possible concentrations of inimical force. I inspected drilling-grounds and military encampments. I sought, as I had sought four times daily, for all my adult life, for the invaders who had been promised us, the conquerors who at the end of days were destined to seize our tattered world.

—Robert Silverberg, "Night Wings"

1. What does each of the following words mean in the context of this science fiction story? Find each word in the passage. How does the context help you understand the word?

monitor, apparatus, propitious, itinerant, vectors, detection, redundancy, remnants, constellation, vigil, entities, ecstasy, incredible, rove, complexity, inimical, encampments

2. In other parts of this story, the author names some of the people and objects to be found in this strange future world. What do you think each of the following would have been called in twentieth-century language? Match each word in the column on the left with the right word from the column on the right.

Future	Present
1. outworlders	a. beggars
2. dominators	b. secretaries
3. rememberers	c. prophets
4. changelings	d. astronomers
5. watchers	e. extraterrestrial beings
6. vendors	f. historians
7. mendicants	g. merchants
8. annunciators	h. rulers
9. chronomancers	i. loudspeakers
10. scribes	j. mutants

REVIEW ACTIVITY

The following sentences give you a chance to test your knowledge of words. Many of the words in this activity have appeared in the preceding section. For each word printed in italics, select the word that comes *closest* to it in meaning.

Example: Ours is the only known planet *capable* of supporting human life.
a. able   b. eager   c. willing

(Answer)   *a*

1. The factory *manufactured* refrigerators.
   a. made   b. repaired   c. assembled
2. Americans are proud of their *heritage*.
   a. prosperity   b. traditions   c. hospitality
3. The book described the *migrations* of an Indian tribe.
   a. wanderings   b. wars   c. hardships
4. Some people do not know what to do with their *leisure*.
   a. money   b. health   c. free time
5. He used the attic to store his *elaborate* equipment.
   a. worn-out   b. complicated   c. valuable
6. The book described various kinds of *extinct* animals.
   a. colorful   b. foreign   c. no longer found
7. Foreign languages are not just something for the *élite*.
   a. foreign-born   b. select group   c. immigrants
8. The strikers were rather *belligerent*.
   a. quarrelsome   b. sweet   c. dreamy
9. The coach said I had no *aptitude* for sports.
   a. talent   b. patience   c. liking

10. The mayor has an *urbane* manner.
     a. gentle   b. adult   c. polished
11. The students worked *diligently* on their projects.
     a. steadily   b. off and on   c. reluctantly
12. Our Indian guide told us many *legends* about the tribe's past.
     a. tales   b. complaints   c. facts
13. His aunt's store sold farm *implements*.
     a. products   b. insurance   c. equipment
14. George's role in the firm had always been a *subordinate* one.
     a. important   b. under someone else   c. essential
15. Relations between the two countries have *deteriorated*.
     a. gotten better   b. gotten worse   c. stayed the same
16. *A New Horizon* was intended as a book for *adolescents*.
     a. toddlers   b. teenagers   c. adults
17. The weekly programs were designed to *foster* patriotism.
     a. study   b. discuss   c. promote
18. The designers found the plans quite *baffling*.
     a. encouraging   b. puzzling   c. familiar
19. Television as a news medium has tremendous *potentialities*.
     a. possibilities   b. dangers   c. difficulties
20. Simon has always been a *taciturn* boy.
     a. talkative   b. silent   c. bashful

W2
WORDS AND THEIR
MEANINGS

Remember that words have more than one meaning.

Most words do double duty. In a good dictionary, many words are listed with more than one meaning. The dictionary entry for *hand*, for instance, must list the different meanings of the word as found in the following expressions. (What *are* the different meanings?)

The *hands* of the watch had come loose.
The knight asked for the damsel's *hand* in marriage.
The matter is in the *hands* of my lawyer.
We gave the singer a big *hand*.
We learned the meaning of disaster at first *hand*.

To use a dictionary, we must *select the meaning that fits the context*. We ask: "Who uses this word, and in what connection?"

Here are different meanings of two familiar words as used in typical contexts:

article   The editor of the student newspaper talks about an article she has written. She means a *piece of writing*, usually combining information and opinion.

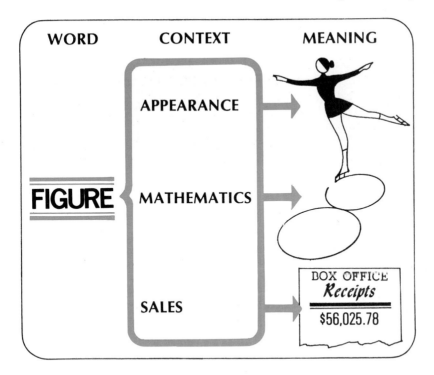

WORD   CONTEXT   MEANING

FIGURE

APPEARANCE

MATHEMATICS

SALES

BOX OFFICE
Receipts
$56,025.78

   A history teacher discusses the articles of the U.S. Constitution. He means the *major points* included in it.

   A salesperson in a department store talks to a customer about articles of clothing carried by the store. The salesperson means *items* of merchandise.

figure   A skater talking about a figure eight means something that looks like the actual *numeral*, the symbol for "8" in writing.

   A used-car dealer who asks a customer to name an "approximate figure" is talking about an approximate *amount*, a suggested price.

   People who are worried about their figures are worried about their shape or physical appearance.

   The more complete a dictionary is, the more information it gives about the different possible meanings of such words. Make sure you understand how dictionary editors *order and present different meanings:*

   (1) In many dictionaries, the *most frequent meaning of a word comes first.* Special uses of the word, rarely encountered by the

DICTIONARY MAKER FOR A DAY

Pretend you are back in the nineteenth century, traveling in some country far from home. A group of missionaries working there has asked you to help them put together a simple dictionary of basic English words. Today's assignment is the word *right*. Could you provide one-sentence definitions for each use of *right* found in the following expressions?

with the right hand
a right angle
in his right mind
the right answer
the right wing of the party
soaked right through
recognized in his own right
civil rights
the railroad right of way
they tried to right the boat

ordinary reader, will come later. If several meanings of a word are common, the *most* common one will head the list. Here, for instance, is part of the entry for *fancy* in the *Thorndike-Barnhart High School Dictionary*:

fan cy (fan'sē), *n., pl.* **-cies**, *v.,* **-cied, -cy ing,** *adj.,* **-ci-er, -ci est.** —*n.* **1.** power to imagine; imagination: *Dragons, fairies, and giants are creatures of fancy.* **2.** thing imagined. **3.** thing supposed; idea; notion. **4.** a liking; fondness: *They took a great fancy to each other.* **5.** a liking that lasts only a short time.

Apparently, the most often used meaning of this word is "the ability to imagine things," as in "His *fancy* ran riot." Less frequent is the use of the word to mean the *idea* we are imagining, as in "a passing *fancy*." Even less frequent is the special meaning of "liking" in "He took a *fancy* to her."

In each of the following examples, do you agree that the *first* meaning listed is the most frequent and familiar one?

humor   ability to see the funny side of things, as in "a good sense of humor."

          mood or temperament, as in "The superintendent was in a good humor."

wit   talent for making clever remarks, as in "The British are
noted for their dry wit."

              intelligence or ability to think, as in "He was at his
wit's end."

credit   privilege of obtaining something on promise of future payment, as in "The store refused to extend credit."

              good name or reputation, as in "Her refusal to accept the
offer is greatly to her credit."

(2) In many dictionaries, the *meanings of a word appear in
their historical order.* Meanings that have been in use the longest
appear first. If a word has acquired a *new* meaning very recently,
that meaning will appear last.

Here, in historical order, are the meanings of *magazine* as
listed in *Webster's New Student Dictionary:*

> **mag·a·zine** \\'mag ə ˌzēn, ˌmag-ə'\\ *n* [MF, fr. Ar *ma-
> khazin,* pl. of *makhzan* storehouse] **1 :** a storehouse
> or warehouse esp. for military supplies **2 :** a place for
> keeping gunpowder in a fort or ship **3 :** a publication
> usu. containing stories, articles, or poems and issued
> periodically (as weekly or monthly) **4 :** a supply
> chamber: as **a :** a chamber in a gun for holding car-
> tridges **b :** a chamber for film on a camera or motion-
> picture projector

Here are some of the ways in which a word may come to cover
several related meanings:

—We often *extend* the meaning of a word, for instance, from
a part to the whole. A "Yankee" originally was someone from
New England. Later the word was used by Southerners to describe
anyone from the North of the United States. Still later, the word
was used by many non-Americans to describe Americans in general.

—We often *transfer* a word from what it originally stood for
to something that resembles it. A "beam" was originally a long,
heavy piece of timber. Later, the word was used for a shaft of light,
or for a collection of rays extending straight like a wooden beam.

—Sometimes we *narrow down* the meaning of a word. Originally, an "accident" was anything that happened merely by chance,
whether good or bad. Thus, we can say that something was a
"lucky accident." Later, the word was narrowed down to undesir-
able accidental happenings, resulting in injury or loss.

AROUND THE WORLD IN YOUR DICTIONARY

JUNK

‡**Ge·sund·heit** (gə zoont′hīt′) *n.* [G.] (your) health: spoken as a toast or as an expression of good wishes to someone who has just sneezed

graf·fi·to (grə fēt′ō) *n., pl.* **-fi′ti** (-ē) [It., a scribbling < *graffio,* a scratch < L. *graphium*: see ff.] an inscription, slogan, drawing, etc. crudely scratched or scribbled on a wall or other public surface

junk[2] (juŋk) *n.* [Sp. & Port. *junco* < Jav. *jon*] a Chinese flat-bottomed ship with battened sails and a high poop

jun·ta (hoon′tə, jun′-) *n.* [Sp. < L. *juncta,* fem. of *junctus,* pp. of *jungere,* to JOIN] **1.** an assembly or council; esp., a Spanish or Latin-American legislative or administrative body **2.** a group of political intriguers; esp., such a group of military men in power after a coup d'état: also **jun·to** (jun′tō), *pl.* **-tos**

ka·ra·te (kə rät′ē) *n.* [Jap., lit., open hand < *kara,* empty + *te,* hand] a Japanese system of self-defense characterized chiefly by chopping blows delivered with the side of the open hand

kay·ak (kī′ak) *n.* [Esk.] **1.** an Eskimo canoe made of skins, esp. sealskins, stretched over a frame of wood to cover it completely except for an opening in the middle for the paddler **2.** any similarly designed canoe for one or two paddlers, made of canvas, plastic, etc.

‡**maz·el tov** (mä′z′l tōv′, tôf′) [Heb. (often via Yid.) < *māzal,* luck + *tōv,* good] good luck: an expression of congratulation: also **maz′el·tov′, maz′zel tov**

☆**voo·doo** (vōō′dōō) *n., pl.* **-doos** [Creole Fr., of WAfr. orig., as in Ewe (Dahomey and Togo) *vodu,* a fetish, demon] **1.** a primitive religion based on a belief in sorcery and in the power of charms, fetishes, etc.: it originated in Africa and is still practiced, chiefly by natives of the West Indies **2.** a person who practices voodoo **3.** a voodoo charm, fetish, etc. —*adj.* of voodoos or voodooism —*vt.* to affect by voodoo magic

KAYAK

from *Webster's New World Dictionary of the American Language,* Second College Edition, copyright © 1970 by The World Publishing Company.

What part of the world does each of these words come from? In your own words, can you explain what each word means and how it is used? In what <u>context</u> are we likely to encounter the word?

(3) Within limits, dictionaries *give the specialized or technical meanings of a word*. Many occupations and hobbies have their own lingo. *Hook* has a specialized technical use when a golfer talks about the difference between a "hook" and a "slice." The word has a different technical meaning when a home economics teacher talks about a "hooked rug" or a device called "hook and eye." Here are some familiar terms with first a general meaning and then a more specialized one:

gear   generally, equipment, as in "fishing gear"
                (automotive) adjustments of an automobile's transmission, as in "Trucks shift into low gear."

fatigue   generally, tiredness or weariness, as in "He was bleary-eyed with fatigue."
                (military) chores assigned to soldiers, as in "fatigue duty" or "fatigue clothes"

notion   generally, view or idea, as in "They have strange notions about our schools."
                (sales) small household articles, found at a "notions counter" in a store

Usually, the more technical meanings *follow* the more general ones. Usually, there is a label indicating the special field, such as "Geology" or "Military Science." Sometimes an abbreviation is used. *Naut.*, for instance, stands for "nautical" and shows how a word is used by sailors. *R.C.* stands for "Roman Catholic" and indicates how a word is used in the teachings or services of the Roman Catholic Church.

Your Turn: For each of the following words, the first meaning given is a fairly common or familiar one. Then there is a blank space for a meaning that is *less common*, or developed *later* in the history of the word, or applies only in a *specialized field*. On a separate sheet of paper, write down the appropriate meaning. (Sum it up as briefly and accurately as you can.)

Your teacher will tell you whether to use the dictionary in working this exercise.

Example: **notice** A "notice" may be any kind of announcement. But when an employee "gives notice," he announces his intention to ———————.

(Answer)   *give up his job*

1. fault   A "fault" may be any kind of defect. When the geologist describes the layers of rock that form the earth's crust, a "fault" is ——————.

2. age   A person's "age" is the number of years lived. In a history class, "Age" with a capital *A* refers to a ——————.

3. favorite   A "favorite" artist is one we prefer. In competitive sports, however, the "favorite" is the competitor who ——————.

4. favor   If we regard something with "favor," we regard it with approval. But when the girl in an old-fashioned love story *wears* a "favor," she is wearing a —————— —.

5. title   A "title" may be the name given to a book or a play. But when someone buys a car or a house, the "title" is ——————.

6. tide   The "tide" is the daily rising and falling of the surface of the ocean. In a combination like "yuletide," we still encounter the earlier meaning of the word, which is ——————.

ACTIVITY 1

In each of the following pairs, the same word is used with two different meanings. Explain how the rest of the sentence makes you choose the meaning that *fits the context*. For each pair, write brief translations of the two meanings.

Example: Rita had always been *modest* about her talents.
(Answer)   *not conceited*

Example: Rita's family had a *modest* income.
(Answer)   *small*

1. Being *homely* has nothing to do with being attractive.
   Honesty and thrift are *homely* virtues.

2. Pierre had worked as a reporter for European *journals*.
   Each night Pierre recorded his thoughts in his *journal*.

3. The postal worker *delivered* the mail.
   The cabdriver *delivered* the baby.

4. The manager's assistant took the *call*.
   Several of the neighbors dropped in for a *call*.

5. Every night Sergeant Gallagher walked the familiar *beat*.
   The Three Simons recorded an album with the familiar *beat*.

6. No one was allowed to leave without a valid *reason*.
   We differ from animals in our use of *reason*.

7. Mr. Wilson *fired* his trusted Winchester rifle.
   The management *fired* Mr. Wilson.

8. A yellowish *film* of plastic protected the material.
   The *film* footage he found was in excellent condition.

9. The little girl was wearing a *plain* cotton shirt.
   He tried hard to make his meaning *plain*.

10. During the spring we have a *fair* amount of rain.
    His partner insisted on a *fair* share of the profits.

11. My friend received us with *open* arms.
    Whether Sam will be disqualified is an *open* question.

12. Many clothing fads soon go out of *fashion*.
    Miss Smith likes to do things in her own *fashion*.

13. All night the election *returns* were coming in.
    The *returns* from the business were disappointing.

14. My brother got his first *taste* of army life at Fort Worth.
    My brother did not find army life to his *taste*.

15. In Hollywood, some famous novels have been *screened* five times.
    All artworks submitted were *screened* by a committee.

ACTIVITY 2

For each of the following words, three possible meanings are listed. *Match the right example* with each of the meanings listed.

Example: **return**
            A. *come back*   a. He *returned* the book to the library.
            B. *hand down*   b. Few customers *returned*.
            C. *bring back*   c. The jury *returned* its verdict.
(Answers)   A. *b*   B. *c*   C. *a*

1. sustain
A. *uphold*   a. Mars probably cannot *sustain* life.
B. *support*   b. The court *sustained* the verdict.
C. *undergo*   c. The victim *sustained* a heavy blow.

2. recover

A. *be compensated for*   a. The patient quickly *recovered*.
B. *get back*   b. None of the stolen jewels has been *recovered*.
C. *get well*   c. The injured went to court and *recovered* damages.

3. pursue

A. *extend*   a. The posse *pursued* the fleeing outlaws.
B. *chase*   b. He wanted to *pursue* this line of conversation further.
C. *practice*   c. He should *pursue* some worthwhile occupation.

4. consume

A. *destroy*   a. The negotiations *consumed* too much time.
B. *use up*   b. The house was *consumed* by fire.
C. *eat or drink*   c. The guests *consumed* great quantities of punch.

5. conduct

A. *behave*   a. The host *conducted* us to the gate.
B. *direct*   b. Ms. Brown *conducts* the school orchestra.
C. *accompany*   c. The accused *conducted* himself with dignity.

6. prevail

A. *win*   a. In battle after battle the Romans *prevailed*.
B. *persuade*   b. She studied *prevailing* trends in the industry.
C. *be common*   c. He finally *prevailed* on the customer to reconsider.

7. assume

A. *suppose*   a. I *assumed* he was a member.
B. *accept*   b. A new government had *assumed* control.
C. *take over*   c. The parents were expected to *assume* responsibility.

8. relate

A. *tell*   a. You should *relate* your ending to the rest of your paper.

B. *refer*

C. *connect*

b. The old prospector *related* his adventures.

c. This statement *relates* to our earlier discussion.

9. **defer**

A. *postpone*

B. *give in*

C. *pass over*

a. Jim had been twice *deferred* by his draft board.

b. The judge *deferred* sentencing.

c. Mr. Smith *deferred* to the judgment of his advisers.

10. **defy**

A. *demand*

B. *go against*

C. *make impossible*

a. I *defy* you to prove your accusations.

b. The prisoners openly *defied* authority.

c. The problem *defied* solution.

REVIEW ACTIVITY

Test your ability to recognize one of the *less familiar meanings* of the words you have studied in this section. For each italicized word, select the meaning that best fits the context. On a separate sheet of paper, write the appropriate letter after the number of the sentence.

Example: Some people wake up in a nasty *humor.*

   a. ability to laugh at things   b. mood   c. situation

(Answer)   *b*

1. Before surrendering the fort, the defenders blew up the *magazine.*
   a. secret tunnel   b. storehouse for gunpowder   c. water tower
2. John was convinced that in the long run the strongest *prevail.*
   a. win out   b. become proud   c. hesitate
3. The family managed to live well on a *modest* income.
   a. small   b. inadequate   c. irregular
4. Uncle Tim hated regulations and preferred to do his work in his own *fashion.*
   a. fad   b. workshop   c. manner
5. The document that sealed the enemy's surrender consisted of thirty-eight *articles.*
   a. major points   b. double pages   c. conditions
6. The prisoners were *delivered* by the arrival of the allied armies.
   a. handed over   b. surprised   c. set free

7. The principal *conducted* the speaker to the auditorium.
   a. sent   b. accompanied   c. directed

8. At our next meeting we can *pursue* this subject further.
   a. postpone   b. explore   c. denounce

9. During the last war, Marie had operated an *intelligence* network in France.
   a. sabotage   b. black market   c. secret information

10. He came from a family of teachers and *divines*.
    a. ministers   b. prophets   c. geniuses

11. The accused had *sustained* a blow with a heavy instrument.
    a. struck   b. received   c. avoided

12. My grandfather loved to *relate* tales about the gold rush.
    a. hear   b. ridicule   c. tell

13. During the rest period, Tony studied the entries in his *journal*.
    a. passport   b. bank book   c. diary

14. The volunteers had worked for eighteen hours without *relief*.
    a. someone to take their place   b. letup   c. pay

15. The controversy had *defied* our attempts at a friendly settlement.
    a. thwarted   b. invited   c. delayed

16. The Andersons acquired *title* to a house down the street.
    a. first choice   b. ownership   c. rental

17. Fred was willing to *defer* to the judgment of more experienced people.
    a. object   b. give in   c. give credit

18. This jury will never be able to *return* a verdict.
    a. overturn   b. hand down   c. change

19. He praised the mountain people for their *homely* virtues.
    a. domestic   b. ungainly   c. religious

20. Mr. Swaithmore approached the familiar desk in a nasty *humor*.
    a. wit   b. temperament   c. mood

W3
WORDS AND THEIR
ROOTS

Recognize the building blocks that help us understand and remember related words.

Learning new words would be a real chore if you had to learn them one by one. Often, however, a new word turns out to be related to words that you already know. For instance, suppose you are checking your dictionary for the meaning of *countermand* in "He countermanded the order." This word appears in your dictionary with others that also start with *counter–*. We have words like *counterspy*, *counterattack*, and *counterclockwise*. All of these show that *counter–* means "against, contrary, opposed to." A "counterattack" is directed *against* an earlier attack by the enemy. A "counterpart" is the "opposite number" of something, as in "The right arm is the counterpart of the left arm." To "countermand" an order means to issue a second order *contrary* to it, in other words an order that *cancels* it out.

Learn to watch for such common building blocks. They often help to explain the meanings of a large group of related words.

Study the way our language uses Latin and Greek roots.

W3a
Latin and Greek Roots

For many centuries, Latin and Greek served as international languages in religion, science, and education. The modern scientist or inventor often draws on Latin or Greek **root words** and uses them in new combinations. To name a device for carrying a conversation across a long distance, the inventor could use the Greek roots for sound ("phon–") and distance ("tele–"). The result was *telephone*. To name a device to carry pictures as well as sounds, the inventor could substitute the Latin root for sight ("visio–"). The result was *television*.

Here are some important Greek and Latin roots:

audi–	*hearing*	An "audience" is a group of people who *listen* or watch.
		A barely "audible" sound can just barely be *heard*.
		At an "audition" singers can be *heard* by someone who might hire them.
		In an "auditorium" we can *listen* to a lecture or concert.
auto–	*self*	Something that is "automatic" works *by itself*.
		"Autographs" are the names of important persons signed *by the persons themselves*.
		An "automobile" is a vehicle that moves *by itself*, that is, without horses.
bio–	*life*	"Biology" is the study of *life*, especially plant and animal life.
		A "biography" is the story of a person's *life*.
		"Antibiotics" destroy the *life* of small organisms that cause disease.
chron–	*time*	"Chronological" order follows the order of events as they happened in *time*.
		A "chronicle" records historical events as they happened in *time*, without giving much explanation.

THE LANGUAGE OF POLITICS

Many of the words used in our political life come to us from or through Latin.

(1) Discuss three of these words and tell us what they bring to your mind.

(2) Trace three of these words back to their roots and report your findings to the class.

GOVERNOR   IDENTIFICATION
CAMPAIGN
Assassination
REPRESSION   CRUSADE
LABOR
VIGILANCE   INFORMATION
INDEPENDENCE
Conservative   FEDERALISM

When we "synchronize" two watches, we make sure they *keep time* exactly alike.

Something is "anachronistic" when it seems out of place in a particular *period*.

cred—   *belief*   A story is "credible" if it can be *believed*.

A "credulous" person is one who *believes* things too easily.

A person's "credo" is the set of principles he or she *believes in*.

graph—   *writing*   A "stenographer" *writes* things down in shorthand.

"Geography" *describes* the different areas of the earth.

SHADOWS OF FORGOTTEN ANCESTORS

If the ancient Romans could come back to life, they would find bits and pieces of their language surviving in many modern languages. The syllables listed below still carry in many instances the same meaning they carried in Latin over two thousand years ago. How many of these "living fossils" do you recognize? Can you find all of the sample words that show each of these syllables put to use? (Write the sample words on a separate sheet of paper.)

min—   *little, less*   An employer who is paying as *little* as is legally possible is paying the _____ wage. A group that is *less* numerous than the majority is a _____. When we want someone to wait only a *little* while, we ask him to wait a _____.

capt—   *take, catch*   When an escaped prisoner is *retaken,* he is re_____. The young of animals that were *caught* and put in a zoo are born in _____.

pop—   *people*   The *people* living in a town are its _____. When wars or diseases kill off people, they de_____ the countryside.

de—   *off*   When you cut something *off* from water, it becomes de_____. When the leaves fall *off* a plant, it becomes de_____. When a military unit is taken *off* active duty, it is de_____.

vit—   *life*   If someone seems very much *alive,* she has a lot of _____. If a dying community has been brought back to *life,* it has been re_____. Important facts about a person's life are part of his or her _____ statistics.

verb—   *word*   Someone protesting in *words* is only making a _____ protest. When we quote something exactly *word for word,*

		we quote it _____. When we cannot put something in *words,* we cannot _____ it.
dis–	*away, opposite*	When police officers take firearms *away* from a suspect, they dis_____ him. When people show the *opposite* of respect, they are dis_____. A jeweler doing the *opposite* of assembling a watch is dis_____ it.
inter–	*between*	An agreement *between* nations is an inter-_____ agreement. When a power source comes between your radio and the station, it may inter_____ with your reception. The space *between* the stars is inter_____ space.
ulti–	*last*	When we give people a *last* chance to surrender, we are issuing an _____. The *last* stop for a train or a plane is its _____ destination.
ten–	*hold*	Someone who temporarily (and for rent) *holds* a piece of land is a _____. People who *hold* on stubbornly are _____. When we can no longer *hold on* to a place or a belief, it becomes un_____.

		A "graph" *traces* changes in such a way that we can see them clearly on paper.
hydr–	*water*	A "hydrant" supplies *water* to firefighters. The *water* has been removed from "dehydrated" food. "Hydraulic" brakes make use of pressure created in a *liquid.* "Hydroelectric" power is electricity produced through *water* power.
man–	*hand*	"Manual" labor is work requiring the exercise of one's *hands,* or, more generally, physical exertion.

"Manufactured" goods are goods made by *hand* or by machinery.

A "manuscript" is the text of an article or book when it is written by *hand* or typed, before it is printed.

psych–	*mind*	"Psychology" is the study of how the human *mind* works.
		"Psychiatry" is concerned with the healing of *mental* illness.
urb–	*city*	"Urban renewal" involves the rebuilding of older sections of a *city*.
		A "suburb" is a residential area outside the central part of a *city*.
		An "urbane" manner is a suave or sophisticated manner that someone might develop by living in a big *city*.

ACTIVITY 1

This activity provides an *additional word for each of the Greek and Latin roots* you have just studied. In the sentence describing its meaning, the last part has been left blank. On a separate sheet of paper, write down the word (or words) that would complete each sentence.

Your teacher will tell you whether or not to check a dictionary in working this exercise.

Example: auto–   An institution has "autonomy" if it has full power to govern ——————.

(Answer)   *itself*

1. audi–   A reply is "inaudible" if it cannot be ——————.

2. auto–   An "autobiography" is the story of a person's life written by ——————.

3. bio–   "Biochemistry" studies the chemical processes that occur in ——————.

4. chron–   A "chronometer" is a device for measuring ——————.

5. cred–   A story that is hard to "credit" is hard to ——————.

6. graph–   "Orthography" is the study of how words are correctly
             _____.

7. hydr–   "Hydrogen" is the gas that combines with oxygen to
             form _____.

8. man–   "Manacles" are used to chain a person's _____.

9. psych–   A "psychopath" is a person suffering from a disturbed
             _____.

10. urb–   An "exurbanite" is a person who lives outside a
             _____.

ACTIVITY 2

Here are some *additional Greek and Latin roots,* each with
several words in which it occurs. Can you tell by studying these
words what each root means? On a separate sheet of paper, write
down the English word that comes closest to summing up the
meaning of each root. Be prepared to explain in class *how* the root
word helps us understand the meaning of each of the words in
which it is used.

Your teacher will tell you whether or not to use a dictionary
in working this exercise.

Example: phon–   phonograph, symphony, telephone
(Answer)   *sound*

1. capit–   capital city, per capita, decapitate

2. cent–   century, percent, centigrade

3. dec–   decade, decimal system, decathlon

4. dupl–   duplicate, duplex, duplicity

5. flor–   flora, florist, florid

6. geo–   geography, geometry, geology

7. jur–   perjure, juror, conjure

8. loqu–   eloquent, loquacious, colloquy

9. magn–   magnify, magnitude, magnanimous

10. port–   portable, portage, transport

11. rupt–   rupture, interrupt, abrupt

12. sect–   intersection, section, insect

13. temp–   temporary, contemporary, tempo

14. voc–   vocal, invocation, vocation

15. vol–   voluntary, volunteer, volition

Study the way prefixes help us understand and remember words.

W3b
Common Prefixes

Many words derived from Latin and Greek consist of a familiar root word and a common **prefix.** A prefix is a syllable (or sometimes two syllables) attached *at the beginning* of a word. For instance, the Latin prefix *sub–* means "below" or "under." "Subsoil" is a layer of soil *below* the surface layer. A "submarine" travels *below* the surface of the sea. A "subterranean" tunnel leads *below* the surface of the earth.

Here are some important Greek and Latin prefixes:

anti–	*against*	"Antifreeze" is put in a radiator as a protection *against* freezing.
		"Antipathy" is a strong feeling we have *against* somebody or something.
		An "antidote" is a remedy that *counteracts* the effects of poison.
bene–	*good*	Something is "beneficial" if it does us *good.*
		A "benevolent" person is someone who wishes us *well.*
		A "benediction" is a saying of *good* words, that is, a blessing.
bi–	*two*	A "bicycle" has *two* wheels.
		A "bilateral" treaty is a treaty between *two* countries.
		A "bipartisan" foreign policy is supported by *both* major parties.
ex–	*out*	To "expel" a person is to drive the person *out.*
		A person who "excels" stands *out* from the rest.
		Results "exceed" expectation if they go *beyond* what we expected.

FOR FUN

FROM THE DICTIONARY OF MAKE-UP WORDS

People who make up new words often use familiar building blocks from Latin and Greek. Suppose ten years from now you had just collected the following newly coined, brand-new words. Can you match the right definition with each made-up word? Can you explain how you know which is which?

1. a very dull speaker	a. millipede
2. a vehicle for getting around in underground mines	b. meliorist
3. a very poor cook	c. trinoculars
4. someone's life story told orally on tape	d. proxivision
5. field glasses for three-eyed space creatures	e. micropolis
6. a home viewer for horror movies	f. vaporarium
7. equipment for transmitting images from close-by	g. decumbent
8. a spray to give frozen fruit back its fruit smell	h. monotonist
9. someone who always hopes for something a little better	i. somniloquist
10. a tank for reptiles that need constant steamy heat	j. subterrine
11. a very small town	k. horrorscope
12. a caterpillar with a thousand tiny legs	l. malnutritionist
13. an incumbent who's been voted out	m. autobiophony
14. someone who talks in his sleep	n. accelerizer
15. a pill that makes slow people speed up	o. reodorant

in–	not	Two friends are "inseparable" if they can*not* be separated.
		Space is "infinite" if it is *un*limited.
		A sentence is "incomprehensible" if it can*not* be understood.
		An "inept" person is one who tends to bungle things because of a *lack* of aptitude.
neo–	new	A "neofascist" represents a *new* version of fascism.
		A "neologism" is a word that has been *recently* coined.

per— *through* In a "percolator," water seeps *through* ground coffee.

An air of optimism "pervades" an organization if it spreads all the way *through* it.

Something is in a state of "perturbation" if it is shaken *through and through*.

pre— *before* A "prehistoric" monster existed *before* the beginning of recorded history.

A "preamble" is an introductory statement that *precedes* a law or similar document.

"Prefabricated" parts were ready-made at a factory *before* the time for assembly or construction.

re— *back* When a gun "recoils," it jumps *back*.

A "rebate" is the part of a purchase price that a customer gets *back*.

When you "reciprocate," you give something *back* for something you received.

trans— *across* A "transcontinental" railroad goes *across* the continent.

A "transition" in a piece of writing carries the reader *across* from one sentence or paragraph to the next.

A radio "transmitter" sends signals *across* the space between sender and receiver.

ACTIVITY 1

This activity provides an *additional word for each of the prefixes* you have just studied. In the sentence describing its meaning, part has been left blank. On a separate sheet of paper, write down the word (or words) that would complete each sentence.

Your teacher will tell you whether or not to check a dictionary in working this exercise.

Example: re— When you "reverse" a procedure, you do the same thing —————.

(Answer) *backward*

1. anti— An "antisocial" person does things that go ————— the welfare of society.

2. bene—   A "benefactor" is someone who does us a —————— turn.

3. bi—   A "bilingual" person speaks —————— languages.

4. ex—   To "exempt" persons is to take them —————— a category where they would normally belong.

5. in—   If a vote has been "invalidated," it has been declared —————— valid.

6. neo—   A "neophyte" is a person who is —————— to a faith or calling.

7. per—   An odor that "permeates" a room is spread —————— it.

8. pre—   The "preface" of a book comes —————— the main part.

9. re—   If invaders are "repelled," they are beaten ——————.

10. trans— "Transoceanic" cables extend —————— the ocean.

ACTIVITY 2

Here are some *additional Greek and Latin prefixes*, each with several words in which it occurs. Can you tell by studying these words what each prefix means? On a separate sheet of paper, write down the English word that comes closest to summing up the meaning of each prefix. Be prepared to explain in class *how* the prefix helps you understand the meaning of each of the words in which it is used.

Your teacher will tell you whether or not to use a dictionary in working this exercise.

Example: pseudo—   pseudoscientific, pseudoclassic, pseudonym
(Answer) *false*

1. ante—   antedate, antediluvian, anterior

2. circum— circumference, circumlocution, circumstance

3. con—   confederate, concurrent, congenial

4. contra— contradict, contraband, contrary

5. extra—   extracurricular, extravagant, extraneous

6. mon—   monologue, monarch, monotone

7. omni–   omnipotent, omniscient, omnipresent

8. pan–   Pan-American, panacea, pantheon

9. post–   postpone, postscript, postwar

10. quadr–   quadrangle, quadruped, quadruplicate

11. se–   secede, seclude, separate

12. semi–   semicircle, semifinal, semiformal

13. super–   superhuman, superfluous, supernatural

14. ultra–   ultramodern, ultraconservative, ultraviolet

15. uni–   unilateral, unison, uniform

Study the way suffixes help us understand and remember words.

W3c
Common Suffixes

Many words derived from Latin and Greek consist of a familiar root and a common **suffix.** A suffix is a syllable (or sometimes several syllables) attached *at the end* of a word to add something to its meaning. Greek and Latin suffixes are most common in technical or scientific words. For instance, the student of biology encounters many words ending in –*derm* (for "skin" or "tissue") or –*morph* (for "shape").

A few Latin and Greek suffixes help explain words that are part of our everyday language.

–cide	*killing*	An "insecticide" *kills insects.*
		The police "homicide" squad investigates *killings* of persons.
		"Suicide" is the *killing* of oneself.
–cracy	*rule*	In a "democracy" the people *rule.*
		In a "theocracy" priests *rule* in the name of God.
		An "autocracy" is *government* by a single person.
–ennial	*yearly*	A "centennial" is a one-hundredth *anniversary.*
		A "perennial" plant lasts through the *years.*
–fy	*make*	A "magnifying" glass *makes* things larger.
		An "amplifier" *makes* sound stronger.
		People who "unify" a country *make* it one.

FOR THE WORD
WATCHER

ALL IN THE FAMILY

Look up the following words in your dictionary. Explain what they mean. Can you find all the Latin and Greek building blocks in these "family words"?

fratricide	*matriarchy*	*paternalism*	*nepotism*
maternity	*avuncular*	*affiliate*	*fraternal*
congenital	*matrimony*	*sorority*	

–lateral	*side*	A "unilateral" decision is one-*sided*. "Multilateral" treaties involve several *parties*.
–logue	*speech*	A "monologue" is a *speech* addressed to oneself. In a "dialogue," two people are *speaking* to each other. A "prologue" is a short *speech* introducing a play.
–logy	*study*	"Zoology" is the *study* of animal life. "Meteorology" is the *study* of weather. "Ornithology" is the *study* of birds.
–meter	*measure*	A "thermometer" *measures* temperature. A "barometer" *measures* atmospheric pressure.
–scope	*see*	A "microscope" enables us to *see* very small things. A "telescope" enables us to *see* distant things.
–vorous	*eating*	A "carnivorous" animal is a flesh-*eating* animal; it feeds on other animals. A "herbivorous" animal is a grass-*eating* animal; it feeds on plants.

Your Turn: Look at an additional word for each of the suffixes you have just studied. In the sentence describing its meaning, part has been left blank. On a separate sheet of paper, write down the word (or words) that would complete each sentence.

Your teacher will tell you whether or not to check a dictionary in working this exercise.

Example: –fy   Something that "terrifies" us —————— us afraid.
(Answer)   *makes*

1. –cide   "Fratricide" is the ——————— of a brother.

2. –cracy   "Mobocracy" is ——————— by a mob.

3. –ennial   A "biennial" exhibition takes place every two ———.

4. –fy   We "rectify" an error by ——————— it right.

5. –lateral   A "bilateral" agreement involves two ———————.

6. –logue   An "epilogue" is a short ——————— that follows a play.

7. –logy   "Biology" is the ——————— of living things.

8. –meter   A "pyrometer" ——————— very high temperatures.

9. –scope   A "periscope" enables someone in a submarine to ——————— what is happening on the surface.

10. –vorous   An "omnivorous" animal is one that ——————— everything.

REVIEW ACTIVITY

Test your knowledge of *familiar Greek and Latin roots, as well as of common prefixes and suffixes*. Select the meaning that sums up best the part of the word printed in italics. On a separate sheet of paper, write the appropriate letter after the number of the word.

Example: benefactor   a. good   b. bad   c. beautiful
(Answer) *a*

1. autograph   a. self   b. famous   c. person

2. vitality   a. vigor   b. speed   c. life

3. audition   a. hearing   b. seeing   c. trying

4. excel   a. out   b. up   c. before

5. international   a. without   b. between   c. against

6. psychology   a. body   b. muscle   c. mind

7. suburban   a. country   b. city   c. hill

8. magnify   a. make   b. bring close   c. reverse

9. transition   a. across   b. together   c. in between

10. stenographer   a. hand   b. short   c. write

11. manuscript	a. write	b. hand	c. type
12. telescope	a. distance	b. see	c. turn
13. centennial	a. yearly	b. monthly	c. daily
14. antipathy	a. against	b. with	c. about
15. democracy	a. vote	b. people	c. rule
16. temporary	a. try	b. time	c. short
17. eloquent	a. well	b. speak	c. create
18. credulous	a. belief	b. doubt	c. certainty
19. pervade	a. new	b. before	c. through
20. omnipotent	a. all	b. little	c. nothing
21. contradict	a. together	b. against	c. without
22. semicircle	a. half	b. full	c. double
23. hydraulic	a. pressure	b. steam	c. water
24. chronological	a. order	b. time	c. space
25. geography	a. earth	b. country	c. map

W4
WORDS THAT
MAKE US CHOOSE

Learn to choose the word that says exactly what you mean.

A carpenter uses different kinds of nail-shaped metal pieces to hold together pieces of wood. When at the hardware store, the carpenter asks for "nails" or "screws" or "bolts." There is no need to explain whether or not the requested fasteners should all have a spiral groove. Similarly, the fashion designer needs a word not only for green but also for *different shades* of green. He or she will use words like *turquoise* for bluish green, *olive* for yellowish green. It is hard to talk about building a house or designing a dress if the people involved do not know the exact words.

W4a
Studying Synonyms

Choose the synonym with the right shade of meaning.

Dictionaries help us choose the right word by bringing together words that cover roughly the same ground. Such words are called **synonyms.** Synonyms "mean the same"—but only *roughly* the same. For instance, *fracture* and *rupture* both stand for some kind of a "break." What is the difference?

Here is the discussion of these synonyms that follows the entry for *fracture* in *Webster's New Students Dictionary:*

> **syn** FRACTURE, RUPTURE mean a break in tissue. FRACTURE applies to the cracking of hard substances ⟨*fractured* bones⟩ RUPTURE applies to the tearing or bursting of soft tissues ⟨*ruptured* blood vessel⟩

Often such entries help us distinguish among *three or four* closely related words. In your own words, how would you restate the differences described in the following entry?

> **syn** FORETELL, PREDICT, FORECAST mean to tell or announce beforehand. FORETELL often implies seeing the future through occult or unexplained powers ⟨sorcerers *foretold* his death by drowning⟩ PREDICT implies often exact foretelling through scientific methods ⟨*predict* an eclipse⟩ FORECAST commonly deals in probabilities and eventualities rather than certainties ⟨*forecasting* the week's weather⟩

Study the synonyms in the following sets. For the third word in each set, what explanation would you fill in to help someone tell it apart from the other two?

journey—voyage—excursion
A journey may be any kind of fairly extended trip.
A voyage is usually a journey by ship or sometimes by plane.
An excursion is ――――――.

salary—wage—fee
A salary is a fixed sum paid regularly, often over a long period and for demanding or responsible work.
A wage may be earned by the hour or by the week and is often paid for manual labor.
A fee ――――――.

burn—sear—scorch
We burn something if we expose it to extreme heat; often when we burn something, we destroy it completely.
We sear something by a short and sudden application of heat; when we sear meat, we merely brown the outer surface.
We scorch something if ――――――.

combat—battle—skirmish
Combat is the general term for armed conflict.
A battle is a single major encounter between sizable numbers of troops.
A skirmish is ――――――.

SYNONYMS OVERLAP

COMMON DENOMINATOR: "An automobile is a self-propelled vehicle, usually with four wheels, used to transport passengers."

BUT:

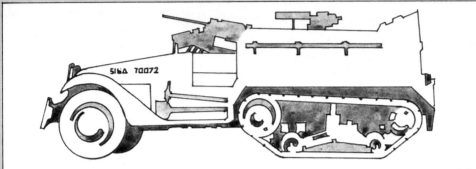

A TROOP CARRIER may move partly on tracks and transports soldiers.

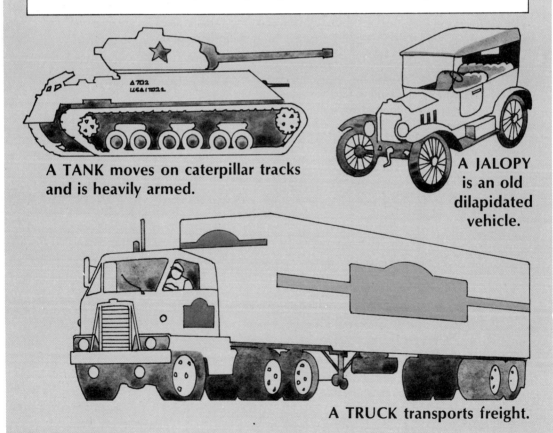

A TANK moves on caterpillar tracks and is heavily armed.

A JALOPY is an old dilapidated vehicle.

A TRUCK transports freight.

A BUS transports many people at the same time.

A LIMOUSINE is often driven by a chauffeur.

A FIRE ENGINE transports fire fighters and their equipment.

YOUR TURN

A JEEP _____

An AMBULANCE _____

A TRACTOR _____

A GOLF CART _____

revolution—insurrection—mutiny

A revolution is usually a large-scale and well-organized attempt to overthrow a government.

An insurrection is usually a more limited uprising, which may have happened on the spur of the moment.

A mutiny is —————.

remedy—alleviate—cure

To remedy a fault is to correct it.

To alleviate an ill is to provide partial and perhaps temporary relief.

To cure an evil is to —————.

nag—reproach—reprimand

We nag someone if we repeatedly find fault with him over fairly petty things.

We reproach someone if we express our disapproval of something he has done, especially if we indicate that we expected something better of him.

We reprimand someone if we —————.

taciturn—laconic—surly

Someone is taciturn if he habitually prefers to keep silent.

Someone is laconic if he says little because he does not want to waste words.

Someone is surly if he —————.

courageous—heroic—gallant

A courageous person overcomes fear and as a result acts bravely.

A heroic person performs outstanding courageous acts for a noble cause.

A gallant person —————.

retreat—withdrawal—rout

A retreat is the moving back of troops after a lost battle.

A withdrawal is a deliberate, perhaps completely voluntary, retreat.

A rout is —————.

ACTIVITY 1

Test your ability to tell apart the *synonyms* you have just studied. In each sentence, a part has been left blank. Of the two words listed at the beginning of the sentence, choose the one that *best fits the context*. Write it on a separate sheet of paper.

Example: **salary—wage**   ————— laborers are often paid a low ————— for exhausting manual work.

(Answer)   *wage*

PLAYING A NAME GAME

Can you match each of the following rhyming phrases with an appropriate synonym from the column on the right? For a bonus, make up some rhyming phrases of your own.

1. top cop
2. terse verse
3. old gold
4. foul owl
5. sad lad
6. crass lass
7. fat cat
8. lanky Yankee
9. big pig
10. sane Dane

a. unclean nocturnal bird
b. melancholy youngster
c. brash girl
d. eminent detective
e. very brief poem
f. very substantial hog
g. ancient treasure
h. chubby feline
i. rational Scandinavian
j. emaciated Northerner

1. voyage—excursion

The Pembertons had just returned from their _____ around the world.

2. salary—fee

Though the operation had been unsuccessful, the surgeon was paid a sizable _____.

3. sear—scorch

The meat had been thoroughly _____ and was unfit to eat.

4. battle—skirmish

The patrol had fought a few _____ with the rearguard of the enemy.

5. revolution—mutiny

The men who had refused to obey the major's order were tried for _____.

6. remedy—alleviate

All the doctor could do was to try to _____ the pain.

7. nag—reprimand

The school board voted to _____ the vandals rather than to expel them.

8. taciturn—surly

Our new neighbor turned out to be a very good-natured but _____ person.

9. courageous—heroic

Among the pirates were many _____ but embittered men.

10. retreat—rout

What had started as an organized withdrawal soon turned into a complete _____.

ACTIVITY 2

Choose three of the following sets of synonyms. For each word, write a sentence that explains its meaning and helps us tell it apart from the other two words in the set. Your teacher will tell you whether or not to use the dictionary in working this exercise.

1. promote—sponsor—endorse
2. detect—discover—invent
3. argument—quarrel—confrontation
4. abolish—repeal—discontinue
5. avenge—retaliate—reciprocate

W4b
Studying Connotations

Become aware of the way words show feelings and attitudes.

Words do not merely name, or point out, or report. They also show approval or disapproval. When we call a group of people a "crowd," we are merely naming it or pointing it out. When we call it a "mob," we show that we *disapprove* of its behavior.

Synonyms may point to roughly the same object but show *different feelings* about that object. Such differences in feeling or attitude are called differences in **connotation.** *Cur* points to the same animal as *dog*; but *cur* has unfavorable connotations. A "cur" is a dog we dislike. Not all connotations are unfavorable. A "cottage" is merely a small frame house, but to most people it has favorable associations. The word makes them think of a cozy little place in the country, ideal for a long, lazy vacation.

There are several ways you can pin down the connotations of a word:

—To decide whether a word is flattering or not, ask whether you would *apply it to yourself.* Would you call yourself a *runt,* a *bookworm,* an *opportunist?* Would you call your dog a *cur?* Would you call a close friend a *yokel* or a *teacher's pet?* (Why not?)

—To confirm your own impressions about a word, see whether it typically occurs in a flattering or an unflattering *context.* What kind of feeling, favorable or unfavorable, is expressed by the words that surround the word you are looking at? For instance, we say: "He was justly *proud*"; we never say: "He was justly *arrogant.*" We say: "That was an inspiring *story*"; we never say: "That was an inspiring *fabrication.*" (Why not?)

—As a final check, find out what your dictionary says. Does it say what the word suggests or *connotes?* A good dictionary does

WHAT'S IN A WORD?
What does each of these words make people feel?
What images or associations does each word bring to mind?

not merely say that the word *scheme* means the same as *plan*. We call a plan a "scheme" to show that we dislike it. The word hints that the people who are doing the planning are incompetent or have the wrong motives.

Study the following pairs of synonyms. The words in each pair point to roughly the same thing or quality. But they imply *different attitudes* on the part of the speaker or writer.

thrifty—stingy

Both words apply to people who hold on to their money. But we *praise* people for thrift; we applaud them for spending no more than necessary and saving something for the future. We call the same people "stingy" to show that we think they *should* be spending more (sometimes for our own benefit).

famous—notorious

Both famous and notorious people are extremely well known, but notorious people are known for the *wrong* things—such as well-executed swindles or attempts to bribe legislators.

FOR LIMBERING UP

WHAT'S IN A NAME?

People who name places or things sometimes make good use of the resources of language—and sometimes they don't. How well would you do if you were asked to name the following? Try to find a striking name for each. Write on a separate sheet of paper.

Example: a smog-ridden valley: Asphyxiation Gulch

a very quiet town: _____
a messy pizza parlor: _____
an overcrowded school: _____
a hangout for motorcycle riders: _____
a day-care center for babies: _____
a very small foreign sports car: _____
a very nosy detective: _____
a very tough neighborhood: _____
a huge administrative building: _____

tenderness—sentimentality

If we approve of the warm emotional feeling a parent shows for a young child, we call it "tenderness." If we disapprove, we call it "sentimentality," hinting that it seems insincere or put on too thick.

strict—rigid

If we call rules "strict," our attitude may be that they are severe but necessary. If we call them "rigid," we imply that they are unreasonable or that they work a hardship on those involved.

curious—inquisitive

In many school subjects, the curious student is likely to learn more than the rest. But when we call someone "inquisitive," we hint that he is curious about things that are none of his business, that he is prying into someone else's affairs.

firmness—obstinacy

We call someone "firm" if we feel that she is sticking to her guns in a good cause. We call her "obstinate" if we feel that she is firm about the wrong thing, that she refuses to change her mind because she is wrongheaded.

conquer—subjugate

Conquest to many people suggests something glorious; "the Spanish conquest of Mexico" sounds inspiring. *Subjugation* calls to mind the

loss of freedom and the suffering of conquered peoples; it is a much
less favorable term.

toil—drudgery

Toil often means hard but useful or even noble work; *drudgery* is
the word for hard work that seems meaningless and boring.

boisterous—rowdy

We call noisy and unruly behavior "boisterous" if we consider it
high-spirited fun; we call it "rowdy" if we consider it rude and a
sign of bad manners.

painstaking—pedantic

We call a job "painstaking" if it was done with careful attention to
every little detail; we call it "pedantic" if we think it was done with
too much attention to details that do not really matter.

Your Turn: Are you sometimes angry or pleased because of a name
you have been called? If so, study the following questions about
names we call people and about words that can make people angry.

1. Do you ever call anyone "Sir"? Do you ever call anyone
   "Ma'am"? When, and why?
2. What is the difference between a "woman," and a "lady," and
   a "dame"?
3. Which of the following would you consider insulting? Why?
   *Yankee, Polack, Dutchman, Chinaman, Swede, hillbilly, cracker,
   wop.*
4. Which of the following do you use? Why? *colored, Negro, black,
   Afro-American, African.*
5. Do the people you know say "d——" or "darn," "h——" or "heck"?
   What difference does it make?

ACTIVITY 1

Test your ability to *choose the word with the right connotations.* In each sentence, a part has been left blank. Of the words
listed at the beginning of a sentence, choose the one that *best fits
the context.* Write it down on a separate sheet of paper after the
number of the sentence.

Example: **toil—drudgery**   The old man looked back with pride on
                               a life of dedicated —————.

(Answer)   *toil*

1. thrifty—stingy

Grandmother always said that she came from a family of God-fearing and _____ people.

2. famous—notorious

The governor refused to rely on the testimony of a _____ liar.

3. tenderness—sentimentality

The play was well acted, but its final scenes were marred by the author's familiar _____.

4. strict—rigid

A school may have _____ discipline and yet respect the student as a person.

5. curious—inquisitive

Movie stars should have the right to tell _____ reporters to mind their own business.

6. firmness—obstinacy

Everyone was impressed by William's _____ in turning down such a tempting offer.

7. conquer—subjugate

The charter said that no nation should have the right to _____ other nations.

8. toil—drudgery

Mr. Smith, who had always complained about the _____ of office work, finally quit his job and hitchhiked to Mexico.

9. boisterous—rowdy

The principal announced that _____ behavior in the halls would no longer be tolerated.

10. painstaking—pedantic

Everyone praised Alexis for the _____ job she had done.

ACTIVITY 2

In each pair, which is the *less favorable or less flattering term?* Write it on a separate sheet of paper. Be prepared to explain the difference in class. Your teacher may ask you to choose five of these pairs and write a sentence about each. The sentence should explain the difference between the two members of the pair in your own words.

Example: bold—reckless
(Answer)   *reckless*

1. easygoing—shiftless
2. clever—intelligent
3. force—violence
4. simple—crude
5. weak—delicate

6. big—husky
7. fat—stout
8. different—odd
9. talk—gossip
10. aggressive—fresh

REVIEW ACTIVITY

Test your knowledge of the words that appeared in the preceding section. For each blank left in a sentence, choose the word that fits the context *best*. Write the letter for that word after the number of the sentence. Write on a separate sheet of paper.

Example: Business firms are always looking for _____ sales-
            persons.
                a. courageous   b. heroic   c. aggressive
(Answer)   *c*

1. Our _____ leader led the troop with a quiet smile and an occasional word of encouragement.
    a. surly   b. rowdy   c. taciturn

2. Our _____ editor was as usual bogged down in unimportant details.
    a. pedantic   b. painstaking   c. laconic

3. Sir Winston Churchill had the _____ gift of giving noble expression to inspiring thoughts.
    a. peculiar   b. eccentric   c. unique

4. Because of the rain, we canceled the _____ that had been planned for the last day of the vacation.
    a. excursion   b. voyage   c. skirmish

5. The legislature voted to _____ the law barring the sale of the merchandise.
    a. repeal   b. reproach   c. discontinue

6. The officer who had given the ill-fated order was _____ by his superiors.
    a. reciprocated   b. reprimanded   c. alleviated

7. On the last day before the election, the local newspaper reluctantly _____ our candidate.
   a. promoted   b. sponsored   c. endorsed

8. The chairman bitterly denounced the committee for its _____ refusal to face the facts.
   a. firm   b. obstinate   c. inquisitive

9. Susan disliked the tearful scenes and gushy dialogue of _____ movies.
   a. sentimental   b. boisterous   c. notorious

10. The principal disapproved of sandals, long hair, or anything else that parents might consider _____.
    a. gallant   b. husky   c. eccentric

11. Martin was always trying to _____ a new eggbeater or a better mousetrap.
    a. detect   b. discover   c. invent

12. Frieda was getting used to the good-natured pranks of her _____ cousins.
    a. boisterous   b. arrogant   c. rowdy

13. Good government depends not only on effective persuasion but also on the effective use of _____.
    a. force   b. violence   c. combat

14. The _____ of a tyrant has often seemed no crime to lovers of liberty.
    a. murder   b. assassination   c. mutiny

15. The Senate refused to _____ the treaty negotiated by the President.
    a. avenge   b. sponsor   c. ratify

16. The teacher was becoming annoyed by Fred's _____ answers.
    a. intelligent   b. clever   c. inquisitive

17. Sports fans admire _____ football players and lean track stars.
    a. husky   b. crude   c. delicate

18. Cut off from all medical supplies, the missionaries could do little to _____ the sufferings of the natives.
    a. retaliate   b. alleviate   c. acclaim

19. People were shocked when the king chose a _____ quack as medical adviser.
    a. notorious   b. famous   c. heroic

20. The regulations do not become oppressive unless they are applied ———————.

    a. intelligently   b. strictly   c. rigidly

Learn to use words that make language real and colorful.

Effective speakers and writers use words that seem clear, vigorous, alive. They use **concrete** words—words that make us *see*, *hear*, or *feel*. "Office worker" is a colorless expression. "White-collar worker" is more likely to make us imagine someone wearing a white shirt and tie and working at a desk. "Portable chair" has an indefinite, all-purpose quality. "Camp stool" is more likely to make us visualize an actual piece of furniture, used in its appropriate surroundings.

To make your use of language more concrete, learn to ask yourself: "What does this word make me see? What does it bring to mind? Would this word help someone get a vivid mental picture of what I am trying to say?"

Learn to use specific, accurate labels.

To give a listener or a reader a mental picture of an actual shape, we have to learn specific words like *column, pyramid, oval, coil, spiral,* or *cone.* We have to do without vague words like *gadget* and use instead words bringing to mind a quite specific

W5
WORDS THAT
MAKE US SEE

W5a
Using Specific Language

WORDS
THAT SHOW
MOVEMENT

flap,
flutter,
peck,
swoop,
soar,
dart,
hop

function: *lever, valve, swivel, pivot, scalpel.* When we describe a lakeside picnic, we have to use words that accurately label the various sights and sounds: the lights *bobbing* on the water; the *swirling* smoke rising from the barbecue pits; the wind *rustling* in the trees.

Here is a choice of concrete synonyms for some of the colorless, all-purpose words describing everyday actions. What explanation would you fill in for the fourth word in each set?

walk

stride	walk with long, firm steps
shuffle	walk while dragging or sliding one's feet
stalk	walk stiffly or pompously
ramble	——————

speak

mumble	speak indistinctly, with lips almost closed
blurt	speak suddenly and excitedly
declaim	speak as though one were making a very solemn speech
rant	——————

look

glance	look in passing
stare	look long and in amazement
gaze	look long and thoughtfully
glare	——————

touch

tap	touch lightly, often repeatedly
rap	touch quickly and sharply
dab	touch lightly, usually applying or removing something
pat	——————

move

scoot	move suddenly and swiftly
drift	move without much effort and without definite direction, as if carried by a current
meander	move in a winding pattern, like a stream
slither	——————

strike

batter	strike violently and repeatedly
pelt	strike with small objects, like snowballs or hail
swipe	strike with a sweeping motion
pound	——————

seize

snatch	seize suddenly
pounce	seize on suddenly from above
grab	seize in a hurry
scoop	————

THERE MUST BE A WORD FOR IT   FOR LIMBERING UP

How complete is your repertory of *specific, concrete words?* How many words do you know that would fill the blank spaces in the following passages? Find words that bring to mind specific sights and sounds. Write them down on a separate sheet of paper after the number of the sentence.

Example: A piece of rope can assume many different shapes. Depending on how it is stretched or arranged, it may be *taut,* ————, ————, ...

(Answer)   *slack, coiled, looped, knotted, tangled.*

1. We have many different words for the sounds made by birds. If we were listening to the cries of a large collection of birds in a zoo, we could hear them *chatter,* ————, ———— . . . .
2. Some fires burn more brightly than others. Fires *flare,* ————, ———— . . . .
3. We have different words to show that something has been exposed to moisture or water. Clothes that were exposed to rain may be *wet,* ————, ———— . . . .
4. How many words do you have for different kinds of smiles? Someone's smile may be *sweet,* ————, ———— . . . .
5. We use different words to describe what happens when a vase breaks, or a wire, or a twig. When something breaks or comes apart, it may *burst,* ————, ———— . . . .

ACTIVITY 1

Test your ability to choose the *word that creates the right picture in the reader's mind.* In each sentence, a part has been left blank. Of the words listed at the beginning of the sentence, choose the one that *fits the context best.* Write it on a separate sheet of paper after the sentence number.

Example: **rap—dab**   There was an impatient ———— on the door.

(Answer)   *rap*

1. stride—shuffle   We saw the colonel _____ into the room like someone long used to command.

2. glance—gaze   He gave the papers only a passing _____.

3. meander—drift   From the plane, we could see the river _____ through the green valley.

4. mumble—blurt   Theron rushed into the room, ready to _____ out everything he had just been told.

5. scoot—slither   The two youngest children had seen the brightly colored snake _____ through the wet grass.

6. declaim—rant   In his familiar soothing voice, Mr. Richards began to _____ about the high goals of the club.

7. stalk—ramble   Her face pale with anger, the ambassador had begun to _____ from the meeting room.

8. pelt—batter   In earlier days, hostile audiences would _____ an opposition candidate with rotten eggs and tomatoes.

9. pounce—scoop   From our hiding place, we could see the animal get ready to _____.

10. tap—pat   Waiting at the bus stop, I have often had a stranger _____ me on the shoulder and ask for directions.

ACTIVITY 2

Each of the following pairs contains *concrete words with similar or related meanings*. Can you explain the difference? Choose three of these pairs. For each pair, write a sentence or two in which you explain what the words mean and how they differ.

Your teacher will tell you whether or not to use a dictionary in working this exercise.

1. swerve—veer
2. whine—whimper
3. gallop—trot
4. loiter—linger
5. slink—sneak

6. sling—hurl
7. glisten—glitter
8. glide—slide
9. scoff—sneer
10. jolt—jerk

Use effective figurative language.

To make language come to life, we can use labels accurate enough to create a vivid picture in our minds. Words that provide an accurate label for an action or object are called **literal** words. Or, we can use words that create a vivid picture of something *similar* to the object or action we want to describe. Words that create a picture of something similar are called **figurative** words. "The President was reelected by a *large majority*" is a literal statement. "The President was reelected by a *landslide*" is a figurative statement. The second statement *compares* the election results to a landslide. It creates a picture of a large mass moving on irresistibly to bury whatever is in its way.

Every day we encounter numerous figurative expressions that help speakers and writers make their meaning clear and concrete:

Literal: Fred always manages to get a conversation off the subject.

Figurative: Fred always manages to *sidetrack* a conversation.
              (Like a railroad car shunted off the main track)

Literal: In our committee meetings, Sue used to cause controversy.

Figurative: In our committee meetings, Sue used to act the *gadfly*.
              (Like a fly pestering and stirring up cattle that might otherwise go to sleep)

Literal: All around the corral, spectators were sitting on the fence.

Figurative: All around the corral, spectators were *perched* on the fence.
              (Balanced on a narrow support like birds)

Look at the following examples of figurative language. What *picture* does each make you see?

No real *dent* has been made in the problem of smog control.

He was *sweating* out his promotion.

Our intelligence agents had *outfoxed* the Germans with great success.

Our teachers tried in vain to *pound* arithmetic into our heads.

The new principal always *talked down* to the students.

Marvin has been in a batting *slump*.

He *nursed* his drink so it would last the evening.

They had never tried to *crash* a party before.

His enemies *crowed*, "I told you so!"

Her investigation finally hit *pay dirt*.

THE LANGUAGE OF SPORTS

How many examples of figurative language can you find in the following sports headlines?

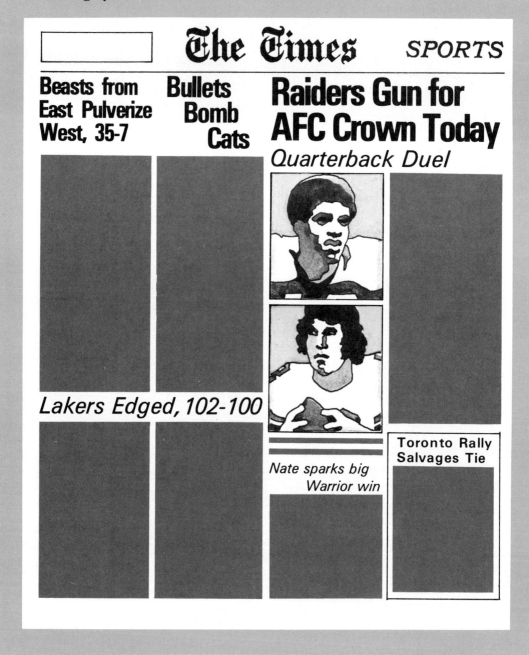

The Times — *SPORTS*

Beasts from East Pulverize West, 35-7

Bullets Bomb Cats

Raiders Gun for AFC Crown Today

Quarterback Duel

Lakers Edged, 102-100

Nate sparks big Warrior win

Toronto Rally Salvages Tie

CAN YOU TOP THAT?

Many folk sayings are earthy and to the point. Would you agree that each of the following comparisons gives us a striking picture to think about? For each, write down a fresh comparison of your own that gives us a similar striking picture. (Write on a separate sheet of paper.)

1. He's as awkward as a cow with a musket.
   He's (She's) as awkward as _____.

2. He's so mean he would steal a fly from a blind spider.
   He's (She's) so mean _____.

3. They were as happy as pigs in a peanut patch.
   They were as happy as _____.

4. He was as handy as a hog with a fiddle.
   He (She) was as handy as _____.

5. It fits like a saddle on a sow.
   It fits like _____.

6. He's so green that when it rains he'll sprout.
   He's so green that _____.

7. He doesn't know enough to pull in his head when he shuts the window.
   He (She) doesn't know enough to _____.

8. He looks like the tail end of bad luck.
   He looks like _____.

9. He's all vine and no potatoes.
   He's (She's) all _____.

10. It was all mixed up worse than a dog's breakfast.
    It was all mixed up _____.

We usually distinguish *two kinds of figurative expressions*. The first is actually *stated* as a comparison and uses words like "like" or "as." Such an expression is called a **simile.** The following are all similes:

The first-graders sitting around the table were chattering *like monkeys*.
He's *as nutty as a fruitcake*.
The storm had snapped the big trees *like matches*.
The roof had been ripped off *as if by giant hands*.

The second kind of figurative expression simply *makes* the comparison; the listener or reader has to supply the "as if" for himself. Such an expression is called a **metaphor.** The following expressions are all metaphors:

Her little brother *parroted* everything she said.
The cars of the derailed train had *jackknifed.*
Television antennas had *sprouted* on the roof of every cottage.

ACTIVITY 1

Test your ability to tell literal and figurative expressions apart. Which is the *figurative* one of the two sentences in each of the following pairs? On a separate sheet of paper, write down the appropriate letter after the number of the pair.

Be prepared to explain in class *what comparison is used* in each figurative expression.

Example: a. The performers looked *disappointed.*
           b. The performers looked *crestfallen.*
(Answer)   *b*

1. a. The students were studying the *procedures* of government.
   b. The students were studying the *mechanism* of government.

2. a. Her grandfather had a fortune *tucked away* in stocks.
   b. Her grandfather had a fortune *invested* in stocks.

3. a. Irma knew how to *sidestep* embarrassing questions.
   b. Irma knew how to *evade* embarrassing questions.

4. a. All night, the *noise* of the engines kept us awake.
   b. All night, the *roar* of the engines kept us awake.

5. a. After the game, the spectators *swarmed* onto the field.
   b. After the game, the spectators *ran* onto the field.

6. a. The speaker praised the moral *fiber* of the pioneers.
   b. The speaker praised the moral *strength* of the pioneers.

7. a. The camping ground was surrounded by *huge* trees.
   b. The camping ground was surrounded by *towering* trees.

8. a. We could do nothing but *grit our teeth* and wait.
   b. We could do nothing but *be patient* and wait.

9. a. The law was designed to *close loopholes.*
   b. The law was designed to *correct* omissions.

10. a. John did not want to spend his life *working at* a desk.
    b. John did not want to spend his life *chained to* a desk.

11. a. The committee was *accomplishing nothing*.
    b. The committee was merely *treading water*.

12. a. She left the organization to form an *independent* group.
    b. She left the organization to form a *splinter* group.

13. a. Our group decided to *swallow* the insult.
    b. Our group decided *not to react* to the insult.

14. a. No one had predicted Sheilah's *meteoric* rise to fame.
    b. No one had predicted Sheilah's *rapid* rise to fame.

15. a. Everyone was afraid of Robert's *cutting* remarks.
    b. Everyone was afraid of Robert's *sarcastic* remarks.

ACTIVITY 2

Our everyday language uses many figurative expressions for *familiar* situations. Do you know one or more figurative expressions that would fill the blank spaces left in the following passages? Write them down on a separate sheet of paper.

Example: When people are almost ready to lose their tempers during a quarrel, we say that their tempers are reaching ————.

(Answer) *the boiling point*

1. When we unexpectedly receive money as the result of a lucky break, we call it a ————.

2. When people have a hard time trying to pay attention, we say that their minds ————.

3. When the wind stops after a storm, we say that it ————.

4. When interest in a sport or a form of music has reached a low point, we say interest in it is at a low ————.

5. When someone constantly tries to stir us to action by pointed remarks, we say she is ———— us.

6. When someone agrees to weaken an originally strongly worded proposal, we say he has ———— it down.

7. When a rumor has been deliberately started by someone, we say that it has been ————.

8. When a project has been indefinitely postponed, we say it has been —————.

9. When a proposed budget seems excessive, we say that it needs to be —————.

10. When people go against current popular trends, we say they are going against the —————.

FOR FURTHER
STUDY

THE POWER OF WORDS

The speeches of the Reverend Martin Luther King, Jr., stirred the minds and hearts of his listeners. He used powerful figurative language to make people see and feel. How many figurative expressions can you find in the following passages from a famous speech? What does each make you see? What does each make you hear?

Five score years ago, a great American, in whose symbolic shadow we stand today, signed the Emancipation Proclamation. This momentous decree came as a great beacon of light of hope to millions of Negro slaves who had been seared in the flames of withering injustice. It came as a joyous daybreak to end the long night of their captivity.

But one hundred years later, the Negro still is not free. One hundred years later, the life of the Negro is still sadly crippled by the manacles of segregation and the chains of discrimination. One hundred years later, the Negro lives on a lonely island of poverty in the midst of a vast ocean of material prosperity. . . .

There will be neither rest nor tranquility in America until the Negro is granted his citizenship rights. The whirlwinds of revolt will continue to shake the foundations of our nation until the bright day of justice emerges.

But there is something that I must say to my people who stand on the warm threshold which leads into the palace of justice. . . . Let us not seek to satisfy our thirst for freedom by drinking from the cup of bitterness and hatred. We must forever conduct our struggle on the high plane of dignity and discipline. We must not allow our creative protest to degenerate into physical violence. Again and again we must rise to the majestic heights of meeting physical force with soul force.

—Martin Luther King, Jr., "I Have a Dream"

Think about what it takes to give specific meaning to general words.

Some words cover more ground than others. When we say that some people have "bad manners," we may mean a number of things. Perhaps they are quarrelsome and frequently call people names. Perhaps they are otherwise well-behaved but rest their elbows on the table when eating soup. Perhaps they habitually use profane, offensive language. The label "bad manners" is *very general*; it does not tell us *specifically* enough what kind of bad manners the speaker has in mind.

Words like *expensive, poor,* or *hot* are elastic; they can be stretched to cover a whole range of different situations. To one person an "expensive" gift may be something costing thirty or forty dollars; to a student on a small allowance anything costing over a dollar may seem "expensive."

There are several things you can do to keep your general words from becoming *too* general:

(1) *Follow up a general word with a concrete example.* Many successful professional writers do this almost automatically. "Give an example!" is the war cry of English teachers both in high school and college.

WORDS THAT MAKE US THINK
**Choose one of these words. Take a minute
or two to tell us what it brings to mind.**

REASON   MEMORY

ATTENTION   INTUITION

IMAGINATION   MEDITATION

Notice how the concrete examples in the following passages help to pin down a general word. Choose two or three of these words and give a concrete example from *your* experience.

poor	His parents were *so poor* they lacked money to buy milk for the baby, let alone shoes for three growing boys.
shy	She assured me that she grew up a very *shy* girl, who had to be plucked from under the sofas whenever friends came to call.
respectable	His mother came of highly *respectable* New England stock, so highly respectable indeed that one of her distinguished forebears, the Reverend Pitt Clarke, withdrew his grown son by the ear from what we should consider a painfully decorous dance.
interesting	Librarians should do something to make their bookshelves more *interesting*, like pasting a skull and crossbones on the spine of each volume in the mystery-book section.
natural	Writing a paper should be something you do *naturally*, like riding a bicycle without constantly thinking of your feet.

(2) *Narrow down a general word by supplying a definition.* If a word might be misunderstood, a **definition** spells out and clearly *limits* its meaning. A typical definition first places the thing to be defined in a general category. For instance, a "patriot" is "a dedicated citizen." Then the typical definition shows how the thing to be defined is *different* from other things in the same category. For instance, a "patriot" is a dedicated citizen "who does what is best for his or her country."

All the following definitions fit this general scheme:

Word to Be Defined	What General Category?	How Is It Different?
The honor system	is a way of promoting honesty in the students' work	by removing all supervision and appealing only to the students' conscience.

Free enterprise	is a way of running business and industry	with as little government regulation as possible.
Integrity	is a standard of conduct	that requires us to live up to our ideals and principles.

The best way of making the meaning of a word clear is to *combine definition and example:*

integrity   Integrity is a standard of conduct that requires us to live up to our ideals and principles. If officials strongly believe in honesty in government, integrity requires that they make no exception for friends or relatives guilty of dishonest acts.

tolerance   Tolerance is the attitude that enables us to respect people who disagree with our views. A minister is tolerant if able to befriend people of a different religious view.

impartiality   Impartiality is the attitude that enables us to make just decisions even when our interests or prejudices are at stake. A jury is impartial if it carefully weighs the evidence even when the accused is the type of person each member intensely dislikes.

ACTIVITY 1

How rude does an action have to be before you call it rude? What is your idea of "hard work"? At what point does discipline cease to be "lax" and begin to become "strict"? For *three* of the following words or expressions, write *two or three sentences* that provide a specific example.

Example: *rude*   The other day I saw a newcomer to our school walk up to say something to a classmate. The other student simply turned around and walked away. I would call such an action very rude.

1. rude
2. hard work
3. lax discipline
4. strict discipline
5. sense of humor
6. modesty

YOUR TURN

I SEE WHAT YOU MEAN

To show what a general feeling is like or what a general idea stands for, we can use one striking example. Or we can use several striking examples in a row. Look at the following poems. Do you agree that they would make the reader say: "I see what you mean"?

Sorrow

Sorrow is a flat tire five minutes
    after the last one.
Sorrow is shutting and locking the car
    door with your keys on the inside.
Sorrow is trying to sleep and listen
    to your older brother talk.
Sorrow is baking a cake, icing it and
    then dropping it on the floor.

Murder

A fish hooked for sport,
Leaping blindly for his life,
Drowning in the air.

Write a poem of your own about some general feeling, quality, or idea. For instance, you might choose one of the following for a subject: meanness, loneliness, anger, fairness, patience, crime. For limbering up, complete the following poems:

Meanness

Meanness is
    cheating the little girl selling Girl Scout cookies.
Meanness is
    _____.

Meanness is
    _____.

Meanness is
    _____.

—Poems from South Hagerstown High School

ACTIVITY 2

Choose *one* of the following words. Write a short paragraph that shows what you mean by the word and how you would use it. Provide first a *definition* and then an example.

Example: *modesty*   Modesty is a character trait that makes people reluctant to advertise their good points
or to accept praise. I once knew a boy who
spent many hours helping our drama club
get ready for a play. Nevertheless, he refused to let his name appear in the printed
program.

1. conformity
2. optimism
3. hypocrisy
4. compassion
5. expediency

REVIEW ACTIVITY

Choose the general word that *best fits the example.* Write the letter for that word after the number of the sentence. Write on a separate sheet of paper.

Example: Fred does not like to be praised in front of other students.
a. modesty   b. integrity   c. optimism
(Answer)   *a*

1. Mr. Brown resigned rather than follow policies that he considered harmful.
a. integrity   b. modesty   c. tolerance

2. Sheilah voted for Paul even though the other candidate was a
close friend of hers.
a. tolerance   b. respectability   c. impartiality

3. Even in apparently hopeless situations, Mr. Micawber was sure
that something would turn up.
a. hypocrisy   b. optimism   c. impartiality

4. Mr. Smith had made sure that there could never be a breath of
scandal about his family.
a. modesty   b. respectability   c. tolerance

5. Though Martha is a strongly religious person, she respectfully listens to views different from her own.
   a. tolerance   b. integrity   c. optimism

6. Though the editor of our hometown newspaper frequently printed editorials praising freedom of speech, he seldom printed views differing from his own.
   a. hypocrisy   b. impartiality   c. integrity

7. Francis is the kind of person who will wear a pink shirt if everybody else wears a pink shirt.
   a. hypocrisy   b. conformity   c. respectability

8. A woman judge does not judge women more leniently than men.
   a. conformity   b. respectability   c. impartiality

9. Fred told the truth even though he knew he would lose the respect of his friends.
   a. integrity   b. conformity   c. respectability

10. When my aunt was in school, a teacher's wife would have sooner died than be seen on a public beach in a two-piece bathing suit.
    a. respectability   b. tolerance   c. optimism

FURTHER STUDY

WORD-WATCHING

In this chapter, you have taken a look at some of the things that are important in the study of words. However, such study will bear fruit only if you *make word-watching a habit*. Pay attention to new and different words in an article or a speech. Spend some time every week browsing in a dictionary. The following assignments raise the kind of questions in which a word watcher should take an interest.

Assignment 1: The following twenty words were selected from an inaugural address by a U.S. President. For each word give its most common or familiar meaning. Then show how the word would be *used in a typical context*. (Your teacher will tell you whether or not to use a dictionary in working this assignment.)

destiny, covenant, flourish, resources, forebears, rejoice, liberation, mission, isolation, incredible, fragile, dominion, tyranny, wilderness, bounty, abiding, heritage, abundance, clamor, ancient

Assignment 2: In the following paragraphs, a well-known authority on the English language discusses our attitudes toward languages spoken by so-called primitive peoples. How well do you understand what he is saying? Some of the words printed in italics are words in *general* use. Others are *technical* words used mainly by students of language. One or two are familiar words used here in a special technical sense.

Select *ten* of the italicized words. For each, give the meaning that best fits the context. Your teacher will tell you whether or not to use a dictionary in working this assignment.

Savages have long been thought to be almost *devoid* of language. The American Indian, in most popular representations, communicates entirely by means of grunts and a few verbs in the *present indicative.* The Greeks assumed that anyone who was not speaking Greek was merely making an idiotic repetition of the sound "bar-bar," and hence *dismissed* him from consideration as a bar-bar-ian. The name Hottentot is *cognate* with the Dutch word for stutterer, and reflects the conviction of the early Dutch travelers that the black people were not speaking but only trying to speak.

Pidgin English (a *corruption* of "business" English), composed mainly of *debased* English words following Chinese *idiomatic* usage, has done a great deal to encourage the *delusion* that *primitive* peoples talk like half-witted children with cleft palates. The gaiety of nations has been much *enhanced* by *innumerable* cartoons *depicting* a fuzzy savage speaking this outlandish *gibberish* to some stranded sailor or aviator. But it is rarely considered that of the two men pictured it is the savage who is the *linguist.* Poor English though pidgin may be, it is, after all, a form of the white man's language, and it is the savage who has had the intelligence and enterprise to master it. It probably seems silly to him, too, but since it is the only talk that white men *comprehend*, he has to use it.

Among his own people, he is likely to speak an exceedingly *complex* language, with elaborate *declensions, conjugations,* tenses, numbers, and moods. Stefansson says that one Eskimo verb may be used ten thousand different ways. Driberg believes that the Didinga have a much larger vocabulary than most English-speaking people and denies that savages cannot express *abstractions.* In all of the Bantu languages, he says, by way of specific illustration, there is a whole class of words devoted to the abstract.

Primitive people are more likely to be *precise* than civilized people. Thus where a white man might say that he hears a dog barking, a Dakota Indian would be inclined to say that he hears a brown dog, which is about two hundred yards away and running in a northeasterly direction, barking loudly. The white man would, no doubt, regard the Indian as *tedious*, but the Indian would probably regard the white man as vague.

—Bergen Evans, *The Natural History of Nonsense*

Assignment 3: For many common words, we have *related words* that express the same basic meaning but are *derived from a different root*. Often that different root turns out to be Latin or Greek. For instance, a question of *law* is a *legal* question. *Legal* is derived from the same Latin root as *legitimate* and *legislation*.

In each of the following sentences, a blank space has been left for a related word from a Latin or Greek root. Write down the missing words on a separate sheet of paper.

Example: A person who gives advice on questions of *law* is a —————— adviser.

(Answer)   *legal*

1. The *King* and Queen of a country belong to its —————— family.
2. The *Middle Ages* are also called the —————— period.
3. Something that causes *sleep* is called ——————.
4. A plot that seems *devil*ish is called a —————— plot.
5. Someone who is in danger of *death* is in —————— danger.
6. Earth*quakes* cause —————— shocks.
7. *Above*-average goods are of —————— quality.
8. *Below*-average goods are of —————— quality
9. Subjects commonly taught in the *schools* are —————— subjects.
10. The *first* few years of a student's schooling are known as the —————— grades.
11. *Cats* are said to have a —————— grace.
12. A statue showing someone on *horseback* is an —————— statue.

13. A blade that turns around an axis like a *wheel* is a
—————— blade.
14. Soil that can be worked by the farmer's *plow* is ——————
soil.
15. Someone who welcomes *guests* is a —————— person.

Assignment 4: Look up the following words in your dictionary. What does each word mean? What does the italicized
part of the word add to its meaning? For each word, try to
find *one* additional word using the *same Greek or Latin
element*.

eulogy, sym*pathy*, *poly*theistic, *matri*archy, *hyper*sensitive, *penta*-
gon, *dema*gogue, *naut*ical, *hetero*geneous, *ambi*dextrous, *pseudo*-
nym, *an*archy, *mono*gram, *culp*rit, *in*carnation

Assignment 5: In each of the following groups of words, the
same root is used with three *different prefixes*. Can you distinguish the three words in each group? What is the basic
meaning of the common root? In which of the words can you
see how a prefix changes the meaning?

1. describe, prescribe, proscribe
2. reduce, induce, produce
3. prefer, transfer, confer
4. transmit, remit, admit
5. receive, deceive, perceive
6. inject, project, reject
7. inherent, coherent, adherent
8. discriminate, incriminate, recriminate
9. interrupt, disrupt, corrupt
10. allocate, dislocate, relocate

Assignment 6: What is the difference between the two words
in each of the following pairs?

1. drinker, drunkard
2. childish, childlike
3. human, humane
4. female, feminine
5. practical, practicable
6. national, nationalistic
7. womanish, womanly
8. judicial, judicious
9. credible, creditable
10. German, Germanic

Assignment 7: What is meant by the following figurative expressions? Write one or two sentences about each, explaining what it means and how it is used.

ugly duckling; lame duck; dark horse; gild the lily; burn one's bridges behind him; beat around the bush; white lie; cut one's losses; steal a march on someone; go out on a limb

Assignment 8: Many words that were at first figurative *have now become literal.* By studying the history of each of the following words in your dictionary, can you find out what picture the word originally brought to mind?

1. recalcitrant	6. interval
2. supercilious	7. disaster
3. blitzkrieg	8. expire
4. eliminate	9. segregate
5. intramural	10. influence

CHAPTER 2

Sentences: Putting Words to Work

Study and practice the way we put words to work in a sentence.

Language is more than just words. People who learn English as a foreign language early pick up words like *car, park, restaurant, buy, ticket, plane, eat, go,* and *have*. However, their first attempts to say something in English may be hard to puzzle out. At first, what they say may be just strings of words:

    car—park—restaurant
    buy—ticket—plane
    go—eat

Soon, however, they will learn what *to do* with these words. As their command of the language improves, what they say will sound more *English*. For instance, the first string of words may eventually sound like this:

His car is parked behind the restaurant.

Or like this:

Did you park the car at the restaurant?

The second and third strings of words may turn out like this:

> I bought my plane ticket.
> Did you buy your ticket for the plane?
> Who will buy our plane ticket?
>
> I am going to eat.
> Are you going to eat?
> He went out to eat.

What the speakers have done is taken the single words and put them to work in a sentence. They have learned not only what the words mean, but also how they work together. A sentence is not just a list of words. It is a structure with interlocking parts. When we study sentence structure, we look at the way sentences are put together. We look at what holds them together and enables them to do their work.

There are three main reasons for studying sentences:

(1) *Language is fascinating in itself.* Long before space travel became a possibility, people were studying the stars and the paths of the planets. Some of this interest was practical: The skippers of sailing ships had to chart their courses with the help of the stars in order to find their way back to port. But many studied the stars simply because they *wanted to know.* They tried to understand the world in which they lived. They wanted to find out how the universe was put together—how it works. One main reason men and women study language is that they are fascinated with how it works.

(2) *Understanding language helps us use it better.* Good workers know their tools. Good mechanics not only know how to use a machine; they understand its operation. It is true that some people speak and write well without much understanding of how language operates. But most of us do not have this natural talent. When we try to improve our speaking and writing, we first take a look at what we are working with.

(3) *Practice makes perfect.* As you survey the resources of the English sentence, you will have a chance to practice what you learn. You will have a chance to do the limbering-up exercises that will help you make fuller use of structures you already know. You will do the kind of sentence stretching that will make you try out something new.

THE ENGLISH SENTENCE
A Bird's-Eye View

SEVEN SENTENCE PATTERNS

S–V	Dogs bark.
S–V–O	Dogs chase cats.
S–LV–N	Linda is a sophomore.
S–LV–ADJ	The house is green.
S–V–IO–O	The relatives gave Gertrude money.
S–V–O–OC	The teacher called Einstein a genius.
S–V–O–ADJ	The foreman called Bill lazy.

FOUR SIMPLE TRANSFORMATIONS

Request	*Answer* the phone.
The Passive	The message *had been left* by a survivor.
The Question	*Have* you *lost* your mind?
There-is	There has been *a mistake.*

FOUR KINDS OF MODIFIERS

Adjectives	You are a *wonderful* person.
Adverbs	They loved one another *madly.*
Prep. phrase	I sent my compliments *to the chef.*
Appositive	David, *a little man,* slew Goliath.

FOUR KINDS OF CLAUSES

Independent	Man proposes, *but God disposes.*
Adverbial	Nero fiddled *while Rome burned.*
Relative	The people *who built the city* had disappeared.
Noun clause	He had forgotten *what he had learned.*

THREE KINDS OF VERBALS

Participle	The women left the *burning* city.
Verbal noun	*Wishing* won't make it so.
Infinitive	The eggs had started *to burn.*

The English sentence uses three basic tools: word order, word forms, and function words.

There are many ways of putting an English sentence together. But some very basic features come back again and again, in sentence after sentence. Some basic tools are used over and over again. Start by looking at the three most basic tools we use in constructing the English sentence.

To build an English sentence, put the right words in the right order.

The most basic tool we use in sentence building is **word order.** English words do not make a sentence unless they follow each other in their right order. Each part of the sentence must fit into its proper slot. The following is merely a scrambled list of words: "Cafeteria went lunch to the Jim for." To make it into an English sentence, we have to *rearrange* the words in their proper order: "Jim went to the cafeteria for lunch."

Here are some other English sentences first *without*, and then *with*, their proper word order:

Scrambled: In practice typing their students afternoon the.
In Order: Students practice their typing in the afternoon.

Scrambled: Barely time made Alfred in to it class.
In Order: Alfred barely made it to class in time.

Much of the word order in the typical English sentence is compulsory. Most words *must* be put in a definite position in the sentence. Even a minor change in the order can make nonsense of a group of words:

Sense	*Nonsense*
the new car	new the car
a delicious spaghetti dinner	a spaghetti delicious dinner
no snacks before dinner	snacks no dinner before
express my sincere appreciation	express appreciation my sincere
has been reading	been has reading

Some kinds of word order are very basic to how English sentences operate. For instance, many English sentences are built on the "Agent-first" pattern. They tell us first *who* (or *what*) does something. Then they go on to *what* he or she does. Many sentences then go on to the *target*, or the result, of the action. To show who does what, and with what result, we arrange the words in the

"Actor–Action–Target" order. By merely looking at the order of the words in the following headlines, can you tell who does what—and to whom? (or to what?)

Cold Killing Old Britons

He Survived His Relatives

China Bans Beethoven

Cons Wreck Jail

Crash Injures Flier

Rebels OK Talks

We can often change the meaning of a sentence merely by putting the words in a different order. There is a big difference between "The snake ate the bird" and "The bird ate the snake." (It certainly makes a big difference to the snake.) It's one thing to say, "He offered the girl a chair *with spindly legs*." It's another thing to say, "He offered the girl *with spindly legs* a chair."

Your Turn: How would changes in word order change the meaning of the following sentences? *Rearrange* the words in each sentence to produce another sentence that makes sense.

Kites fly.
Maria lost only the copy.
The batter hit the ball.
The fast train stopped.

The zookeeper called a monkey Albert.
The boy gave the sweet girl a mean look.
Surprisingly, the lean man ate only fat meat.

ACTIVITY

Suppose the year is 2001. Speech machines have been constructed that can turn out simple magazine articles. Look at the following two short pieces "printed out" by one of the machines. Can you see that there is a malfunction in the part of the machine that arranges *words in their right order?* How would you *reorder* the words in each sentence so they will make sense?

Example: The mail were in the lost magazines.
(Answer)   *The magazines were lost in the mail.*

A. Season is the autumn of hunters.
   Man has been a primitive times since hunter.
   To obtain food man in order hunted early.
   Hunting become has a pastime in modern times.
   Without the hunter animals wild would get some too numerous.
   Many farmers about have mixed hunters feelings.
   Some hunters cannot from deer tell cattle stray.
   Some hunters do to the damage farmer's fences.
   For many hunters the shooting least is actually important.
   They enjoy the simply fresh air bracing open of the spaces.

B. Alaska lives in Joan in a small village fishing.
   Has the village long only one street.
   Of the paved are only blocks four street.
   The rocks mud is rest and all.
   In the people village simple at jobs old-fashioned the work.
   Joan's fishing run a parents boat.
   Several work of her many cannery in the relatives.
   Joan's waits brother during tables on his vacations.
   Fresh ship and Seattle from vegetables are brought by fruit.
   Each daily newspapers get their villagers the Monday the whole
     for week.

Use the appropriate word forms to tie a group of words together in a meaningful statement.

S1b
Our Changeable Word
Forms

What happens when one doctor doctors another? Answer: The *doctoring* doctor *doctors* the *doctored* doctor. Notice that the same basic word here appears in four different forms: *doctor—doctors—*

doctored—doctoring. We have to choose the right form of the word to fit it into its place in the sentence and to make it carry the meaning we have in mind. Anyone who wants to speak English has to learn not only words but **word forms** as well.

To change the form of a word, we often simply add an *ending* the way we would attach a handle to a box. For instance, we add *–ing* to change *doctor* to *doctoring, fish* to *fishing, climb* to *climbing, write* to *writing.* The endings spelled *–s, –ed* (sometimes spelled *–t*), and *–ing* account for most of the changes in English word forms. But adding one of these endings is not the only way to change the form of a word. Instead, or in addition, we sometimes change something *in the word itself.* To make it go with a word like *vase* or *glass,* we change *break* to *broken*: "a *broken* vase," "a *broken* glass." We say "*Light* the fuse," but "a *lit* fuse." We say "*Wear* these shoes," but "these *worn* shoes."

Possible changes in word form give us a rough way of sorting out the basic building blocks in the English sentence. Differences in word forms set apart three of the major **word classes** that help us build basic sentences:

(1) With most English *nouns,* we can add the ending *–s* to add the idea of "more than one." Nouns are words like *boy, girl, brother, bird, room, tree, car, garage, motorcycle.* With each of these words, we can add *–s* to change the word from **singular** (one of a kind) to **plural** (more than one of a kind):

Singular:	boy	girl	bird	car
Plural:	boys	girls	birds	cars

With some English nouns, we produce the plural form by a change in the word itself. If we want to add the idea of "more than one" to the word *foot,* we change it to *feet.* We change *tooth* to *teeth.*

(2) With most English verbs, we can add the ending spelled *–ed* to add the idea of "past time." For instance, we attach *–ed* to the word *ask* to get *asked.* This way we keep the basic meaning of the word but add the idea that the asking took place in the past.

Present:	You ask.	I complain.	We try.
Past:	You ask*ed.*	I complain*ed.*	We tri*ed.*

With some English verbs, we produce the past form by a change in the word itself. If we want to add the idea of "past time" to the word *break,* we change it to *broke.* We *dig* now, but we *dug* in the past. We *sing* now, but we *sang* in the past.

A TIME FOR SUPERLATIVES

Sometimes writers get carried away when writing about a place close to their hearts. Everything is bigger, or newer, or more impressive than in other places. Labels like *big, new,* or *impressive* are all adjectives. To help us compare things, they have special forms with *–er* or *more: bigger, more impressive.* We call these "comparative" forms. To help us show that something stands out among everything else, adjectives have special forms with *–est* or *most: biggest, most impressive.* We call these "superlative" forms.

Look at the following passages about the short grass country of the Mississippi Valley. In the first passage, point out all the superlatives. In the second passage, point out all the comparative forms. Can you think of any place, or building, or person that would make *you* reach for superlatives? Write two short descriptions of it. In the first, use as many superlatives as you can. In the second, use as many comparatives as you can.

It grows the shortest grass—and the tallest; has the widest rivers—with the least water in them; the thickest dust and the deepest mud, the least rain and the heaviest downpours; the hottest days and the coolest nights; the brightest sunshine and the blackest clouds; the strongest winds, the most magnificent electrical storms, the longest summers, and the shortest winters, the biggest hail, the loudest thunder, and the brightest moonlight in the whole Mississippi Valley.

The Plains buffalo is bigger than the woods buffalo; the antelope is swifter than anything that runs. . . . The jackrabbit is speedier than any other hare; the centipedes have more legs here, scorpions sharper tails. Rattlesnakes are bigger and more venomous. Wolves are fiercer, coyotes more cunning than in other regions. . . . The mustang, running wild, became swifter, harder, warier than his ancestors.

—from Stanley Vestal, *Short Grass Country*

PUTTING IT TO WORK

SAFEST, FASTEST AND FINEST
TRAINS IN AMERICA

(3) With many English *adjectives,* we can add *–er* or *–est* to add the idea of "more so." Adjectives have word forms that show differences in degree: **plain**—(ordinary, like everybody else); **comparative**—(used in comparisons to show that something is "more

so"); and **superlative**—(used to show that something stands out from all the rest).

Plain:	smart	warm	fast
Comparative:	smarter	warmer	faster
Superlative:	smartest	warmest	fastest

With many other English adjectives, we use the words *more* and *most* instead of these adjective endings: *more* harmful, *most* harmful; *more* important, *most* important.

Some word forms are as different from the plain form of the same word as a caterpillar is from a butterfly or a tadpole from a frog. Still, the word keeps its basic meaning. If we change "I *go*" to the form for the past, we get "I *went*." "He *is* here" changes to "He *was* here." Depending on how it is used in a sentence, the word you apply to yourself will be "I" in one sentence and "me" in another.

Your Turn: In the following pair, word forms make the difference between a mere *list* of words and a meaningful sentence:

Before: The dog follow I to the swim hole.
After: The dog follow*ed me* to the swim*ming* hole.

How many word forms would you have to change to tie together each of the following groups of words into a statement that makes sense?

The howl wind frighten we.
Burglar have break into the desert house.
The trooper give the speed motorist a ticket.
The boy have be drive with an expire license.
Wild cat are big than their domesticate cousin.
Houdini have be call the great escape artist ever.
My late grandfather love Grandmother toast almond pie.

ACTIVITY 1

For each of the following words, write down another form produced by a change *in the word itself*. On a separate sheet of paper, write the new form after the number of the word.

Example: *break*
(Answer) *broke*

1. mouse	4. woman	7. bring	10. take	13. wear
2. swim	5. throw	8. do	11. run	14. come
3. choose	6. man	9. know	12. we	15. her

ACTIVITY 2

Some English words have as many as *five different forms,* produced both by added endings and by changes in the word itself. On a separate sheet of paper, fill in the four remaining forms for each word in the following list. List the forms in the same order as in the first example.

1. break   breaks   broke   broken   breaking
2. freeze
3. draw
4. eat
5. fall
6. see
7. drive
8. blow
9. speak
10. take

ACTIVITY 3

In each of the following sentences, one word form does *not* fit. After the number of the sentence, write the changed form that would fit naturally into the sentence.

1. "The Raven" is a famous poem write by Edgar Allan Poe.
2. It has sent shivers down the spines of many reader.
3. Once upon a midnight a man was nap in his study.
4. The fire in the fireplace had almost die down.
5. During the evening the man had think of his lost Lenore.
6. He was half asleep when he suddenly hear someone knocking.
7. His heart started to beat fast than ever before.
8. He opened the door wide but see nothing but darkness.
9. Soon again he heard the rapping somewhat loud than before.
10. He flung open the shutter and a stately black raven step in.
11. The man thought the bird bring tidings from the beyond.
12. He asked if the soul of lovers would be reunited after death.
13. The bird looked at he with fiery eyes.
14. The right answer would have made his listener the happy of men.
15. But to all question the bird replied, "Nevermore!"

Use function words to help make separate words a part of the whole sentence.

Function words help the parts of a sentence go together. We use them, not so much because of the meaning they have by them-

S1c
What Function Words
Do

selves, but because they *perform a function in the sentence.* Some words have meaning even when they appear as single words: *car, church, run, beautiful, rapidly.* They point to things or actions or qualities that we can think of one at a time. They furnish the *content* for our conversation and writing. We could in fact call them "content words." But other words do not have the same kind of separate meaning. When we see *a* or *the,* we automatically look for something else to go with it. When we see *with* or *for,* we automatically ask "with whom?" or "for what?"

When we look at the structure of a sentence, function words are like the supporting joists and connecting crosspieces rather than the basic beams or pillars that hold up the whole. Three kinds of function words are used over and over even in simple English sentences:

—The "little words" *the, a,* and *an* are called **articles.** They are among the words we use as noun markers. They tell us: "a noun will soon follow." See how the use of these articles turns a jerky, disconnected list of words into a smoothly flowing sentence:

Before: host found guest chair
After: *The* host found *the* guest *a* chair.

Before: teacher gave class assignment
After: *The* teacher gave *the* class *an* assignment.

Before: observer called decision mistake
After: *An* observer called *the* decision *a* mistake.

—Words like *can, may, will,* and *have* are called **auxiliaries.** They help us make up verb forms that consist of more than one word. The different forms of *be (am, are, is, was, were)* are also used as auxiliaries. Look at the way auxiliaries help us hook up the major sentence parts in examples like the following:

Before: The manager see what she do.
After: The manager *will* see what she *can* do.

Before: The relatives of the victim   notified.
After: The relatives of the victim *should have been* notified.

Before: We told why the phone   disconnected.
After: We *were* told why the phone *was* disconnected.

—The function words in the third group are called prepositions. These are words like *at, with, on, by, in, of, to, through, under, about, until,* and *like.* One typical function they perform is to link two things by showing their relation in space or in time:

WHAT IS THE MESSAGE?

When we want to say something, words alone are not enough. We have to show how words *go together* before the listener can get the message. Can you show that the words in each of the following sets might be put together in two different ways? Use the three basic tools of the English sentence: word order, word forms, and function words (as needed). Write two different sentences for each set, using all the words in the set.

Example: work—tire—boy
(Answer)   *Work tired the boy.*
             The tired boy worked.

1. chemistry—teacher—like—student
2. Fred—go—work—farm
3. resentment—visitor—cause—fight
4. class—report—progress—project
5. Jean—dance—twist—ankle

the store *at* the corner	a chat *after* dinner
the cat *on* the roof	the calm *before* the storm
money *in* the bank	a disturbance *during* the concert
a path *through* the woods	darkness *at* noon

In the following examples, prepositions are essential to the smooth functioning of a whole sentence:

Before: The assignment   Monday was written   the blackboard.
After: The assignment *for* Monday was written *on* the blackboard.

Before: The students   our school sat   the far side   the field.
After: The students *from* our school sat *on* the far side *of* the field.

Before: Do not walk   the parking lot   further notice.
After: Do not walk *through* the parking lot *until* further notice.

Your Turn: Newspaper headlines give essential information in a short space. The editor who writes the headline often keeps only the most essential words. He or she is likely to omit many of the function words. *Rewrite the following headlines* in order to make them into ordinary English sentences. Keep all the words in the headline. Add articles and auxiliaries as needed.

Example: JUDGE SENTENCES BANDIT
(Answer)   *A judge sentences a bandit.*

1. PRESIDENT PROCLAIMS HOLIDAY

2. **GARBAGEMEN DENIED RAISE**

3. MASKED BURGLAR ROBS AGED LADY

4. ROAD BLOCKED BY MUDSLIDE

5. ENTERTAINER OWES GOVERNMENT MILLION

6. American Made Cardinal by Pope

7. STOCK MARKET SWEPT BY PANIC

8. PLANE HITS PEAK IN SWISS ALPS

9. KIDNAP VICTIM FOUND IN FARMHOUSE

10. Champion Defends Title in Nation's Capital

ACTIVITY

On a separate sheet of paper, write down the prepositions needed to fill the blank spaces in the following sentences. Are you using any that were not listed in the material you have just studied? If so, be prepared to point them out to the class.

Example: Aunt Martha had sent the package —————— mail.
(Answer)   *by*

1. The men cleared a path —————— the jungle.
2. Fred fell asleep —————— the concert.
3. Belinda fell —————— the horse.
4. Mr. Browne was angry —————— his students.
5. The house —————— the river was swept away.
6. The physician sent the patient —————— a specialist.
7. The boys were preparing the food —————— the picnic.
8. Jim needs a new ribbon —————— his typewriter.
9. The handwriting —————— your new friend is illegible.
10. Fred accepted the offer —————— misgivings.

11. The merchandise —————— the shelves looked dusty.
12. The sun came out —————— the rain.
13. The boys had to leave —————— breakfast.
14. Lucy likes to read —————— bed.
15. The train emerged —————— the tunnel.

REVIEW ACTIVITY

The three basic tools of the English sentence are word order, word forms, and function words. Examine each of the following pairs to see *which* of the three tools has been used to change the meaning of the original sentence. On a separate sheet of paper, put the appropriate abbreviation after the number of the pair: *WO* for word order, *WF* for word form, *FW* for function word. Be prepared to describe in class *how* these tools are being used in these pairs—what changes in meaning they bring about.

Example: Philip brought monkey food.
           Philip brought the monkey the food.
(Answer)   *FW*

1. The realtor called the house a shack.
   The realtor called the shack a house.

2. Her friend was driving to work.
   Her friend was driven to work.

3. The man jumped on the ledge.
   The man on the ledge jumped.

4. Linda found a boy friend.
   Linda found the boy a friend.

5. The mother protected the baby birds.
   The mother protected the baby from birds.

6. The starving explorer found the village.
   The explorer found the village starving.

7. The grandfather left the boys his farm.
   The grandfather left with the boys for his farm.

8. The physician studied burns.
   The physician's study burned.

9. Report the change.
   Change the report.

10. The fire fighters rebelled.
    The fired fighters rebelled.

S2
THE BARE-MINIMUM
SENTENCE

Look at the way subject and predicate make up the bare-minimum sentence.

Some sentences are short; some are long. But regardless of how long a sentence is, there will be a simple underlying structure that supports the whole. There will be a basic structure to which the other parts are attached or from which the other parts are suspended. In the typical English sentence, the subject and the predicate are the two essential parts of that underlying structure. They provide the scaffolding that holds up the rest. They provide the skeleton that the other parts of the sentence flesh out.

In many sentences dealing with actions and events, we can find the subject and predicate by asking "Who does what?"

Complete:	In the fall, our songbirds migrate to Mexico.
Basic:	Our songbirds migrate.
Complete:	The boy turned at the corner for a last look.
Basic:	The boy turned.
Complete:	The rider on the beautiful pale horse disappeared into the sunset.
Basic:	The rider disappeared.

S2a
Filling the Subject Slot

Learn to recognize the words that can fill the subject slot in the typical English sentence.

The **subject** is normally the first of the two basic parts of a sentence. It singles something out or calls it to our attention. Once the subject has identified something, the predicate can go ahead and make a statement about it.

Subject	(Predicate)
Birds	(fly.)
A plane	(was landing.)
The car	(stopped.)
My eyes	(hurt.)
Our lease	(has expired.)
His sister	(had left.)
This neighborhood	(has improved.)
Our organization	(will grow.)

Take a look at what fills the subject slot in these simplified basic sentences. The part of the subject that actually names something is typically a **noun.** Nouns are words like *bird, street, tree, boy, girl, city, courage, illness, organization.* They name things, people, places, animals, ideas. The name of any article you order from a catalog is a noun. The name of any object you see in a shop is a noun.

Here is a capsule review of nouns:

NOUNS: A CAPSULE REVIEW

(1) Most English nouns have different *forms* for singular (one of a kind) and plural (several of a kind). With the great majority of English nouns, we obtain the plural form by adding the ending *–s: birds, eyes, boys, girls, cars, plants, organizations.*

(2) There are several *signals* that can help you spot a noun. Three kinds of function words serve as signals that a noun may soon follow. We call such words **noun markers,** since they prepare us for the appearance of a noun. A more technical term for the noun markers is "determiners."

Here are the three kinds of noun markers:

articles (*the, a, an*)	the car, a plane
possessive pronouns (*my, your, his,* etc.)	my eyes, his sister
demonstrative pronouns	
(*this, these, that, those*)	these plants

You can use these noun markers as a rough test. If you are not sure whether a word can be used as a noun, try to put *the, a, my,* or *this* in front of it: the _____, a _____, my _____, this _____. Remember, however, that in practice the noun may not always *immediately* follow its noun marker. One or more other words may intervene.

(3) In many nouns, the last part of the word is a noun-forming *suffix* like *–ness* or *–hood:*

–ness:	fairness, ugliness, friendliness, illness
–hood:	childhood, boyhood, nationhood
–ation:	organization, invitation, circulation
–ance:	appearance, attendance, performance, tolerance
–ence:	preference, coincidence, independence
–ism:	nationalism, liberalism, imperialism

Several kinds of words may *substitute* for a noun in a sentence. The most important of these noun substitutes are the **personal pronouns:** *I, you, he, she, it, we, they.*

Noun: Birds fly.
Pronoun: *They* fly.

Noun: The car stopped.
Pronoun: *It* stopped.

Noun: His sister had left.
Pronoun: *She* had left.

Nouns perform various other functions in a sentence besides serving as subjects. To help you find the noun that actually serves as a subject, remember the following pointers:

—Most of the time, though not always, the subject *precedes* the predicate:

The boy has left.

—The subject *cannot* be a noun linked to the rest of the sentence by a preposition:

The boy (in the sports car) has left.

—When the predicate changes in **number** (from singular to plural or the other way around), the subject is the noun *that changes along with it:*

The boy in the sports car *has* left.
The boys in the sports car have left.

Your Turn: What noun could you use to fill the subject slot in each of the following bare-minimum sentences? For each blank, write down a single word (but include a noun marker as needed).

——————— migrate.
——————— radiates.
——————— explodes.
——————— ferment.
——————— expire.
——————— erodes.
——————— may abdicate.
——————— has expanded.
——————— will deteriorate.

SHOTS RING OUT AT HIGH NOON

In each of the following sentences, *two* nouns have been italicized. Which is the one that serves as the subject of the sentence? Write the word after the number of the sentence. (Include any noun marker that goes with the noun.) Make sure to choose the noun that is *not* linked to the rest of the sentence by a preposition. Ask: "Who (or what) does what?"

Example: The *audience* of *Westerns* loves gunplay.
(Answer)   *the audience*

1. The *town* in the *Sierras* was broiling in the sun.
2. In the *saloon* the *idlers* were talking.
3. *Hoodlums* from the big *ranch* had killed a farmer.
4. A *witness* to the *murder* had disappeared.
5. In the *distance* a *horse* was neighing.
6. The *avenger* was riding into *town*.
7. The *time* for the *showdown* was approaching.
8. The *people* in their *houses* were whispering.
9. *Shots* from *rifles* rang out.
10. The *glass* in the *windows* was rattling.
11. *Corpses* were sprawling in the *dust*.
12. The *proprietress* of the *saloon* wept.
13. Her *heart* of *gold* was breaking.
14. After the *shootout* our *hero* dies.
15. At the *end* the *villain* repents.

ACTIVITY 1

Which of the following words could normally be used as nouns? Write down the number of each word that meets *at least one* of the following tests:

(1) Can you use it at the end of a sentence right after *the, a* (or *an*), *my,* or *his?*

(2) Could you change it from one to several by adding the plural ending *–s* (or *–es*)?

(3) Could you use it in a sentence and then *replace* it with *he, she,* or *it?*

Example: sister   Test 1   I asked *my* sister.
                          Test 2   He has three sisters.
                          Test 3   My sister came home. *She* came home.

1. cave	11. chapel	21. explain
2. huge	12. goblin	22. armor
3. dragon	13. rain	23. shout
4. expedition	14. meditate	24. besiege
5. threaten	15. light	25. very
6. forest	16. dark	26. inspiration
7. wreath	17. dance	27. gossip
8. maiden	18. not	28. bell
9. slowly	19. forget	20. extremely
10. legend	20. tradition	30. sleep

ACTIVITY 2

Not all nouns pass *all* the tests that we can apply to see whether a word is used as a noun or not. For instance, most nouns add –s (or –es) to form the plural: one box—several box*es*. However, some nouns have quite different plural forms: one mouse—several *mice*. Some nouns have no plural at all. *Rice* is a noun, but we do not normally say "several ric*es*."

Write down the plural form for each noun in the following list. Find the plural by putting "several" or "two" or "three" in front of the word. If the word normally does not have a plural, write *None*.

Example:	car	(Answer) *cars*	(Test: several cars)
	mouse	(Answer) *mice*	(Test: several mice)
	rice	(Answer) *none*	(Test: several rices?)

1. book	11. chaos	21. vehicle
2. child	12. ticket	22. crisis
3. lamp	13. woman	23. warmth
4. weather	14. wealth	24. knife
5. newspaper	15. democracy	25. nation
6. music	16. ocean	26. nationhood
7. darkness	17. poverty	27. concrete
8. invitation	18. liberty	28. blood
9. tooth	19. illness	29. fox
10. man	20. moisture	30. ox

S2b
Filling the Predicate Slot

Learn to recognize the words that can fill the predicate slot in the typical English sentence.

The **predicate** is normally the second of the two basic parts of a sentence. It makes a statement *about* something that the subject has singled out. First the subject calls something to our attention. Then the predicate says something about it.

(Subject)	Predicate
(Dogs)	bark.
(The prisoner)	has escaped.
(The bus)	is leaving.
(The children)	slept.
(Time)	flies.
(Our guide)	will return.
(The champion)	had been training.

Take a look at what fills the predicate slot in these simplified sentences. The essential part of the predicate is always the **verb.** Verbs are words like *ask, read, write, send, dig, arrive, think, choose, complain, expire, improve.* Such words point to *actions and events* as they happen (or could happen) in time. Some verbs point to *conditions* as they exist in time.

Here is a capsule review of verbs:

VERBS: A CAPSULE REVIEW

(1) A verb can signal a difference in time by a simple change in the form of the word itself. "I *ask*" refers to the present; "I *asked*" refers to the past. "I *think*" refers to the present; "I *thought*" refers to the past.

(2) The complete verb may be just one word, like *bark, slept,* or *flies.* But often the complete verb includes one or more **auxiliaries,** or helping verbs. The two most basic ones, used either alone or in combination, are *be* (with its various different forms: *am, are, is, was, were*) and *have* (with its two other forms: *has* and *had*). Other important auxiliaries are *will (would), shall (should), can (could), may (might),* and *must.* Starting from a simple verb like *ask,* we get combinations like the following:

will ask	will have asked
has asked	will be asked
had asked	has been asked
am asking	had been asked
was asking	will be asking
was asked	has been asking
may be asked	might have been asked

Notice that in one way or another all these forms place the action of the verb *in time*—in the past, in the present, or in the future.

(3) In its various uses as a verb, a word like *break* has five different forms: *break, breaks, broke, broken, breaking.* The first three of these can serve as complete verbs by themselves (The waves *break.* Glass *breaks.* The news *broke*). The remaining two serve as complete verbs only in combination with the auxiliaries (The chain *has broken.* The rope *is breaking*). With verbs like *ask,* we have only four different forms: *ask, asks, asked, asking.* The form with *–ed* does double duty: It takes the places of both *broke* and *broken* (The boy *asked.* The boy *had asked*).

(4) In many verbs, the last part of the word is a verb-forming *suffix* like *–en, –ize,* or *–fy.* The following words are typically used as verbs: *soften, blacken, sharpen; organize, baptize, hypnotize; magnify, glorify, clarify.*

Verbs, or parts of verbs, perform various other functions in a sentence besides serving as predicates. To help you find the verb that actually serves as a predicate, remember the following pointers:

—Most of the time (though not always) the predicate *follows* the subject:

The boy *has left.*

—Normally, a verb *cannot* be the predicate unless *one* or *several* would fit in front of it:

(One) *has left.*
(Several) *have left.*

—When the subject changes in number, the predicate frequently changes along with it:

The boy selected by the group *has left.*
The boys selected by the group *have left.*

ACTIVITY 1

Which of the following words could normally be used as verbs? Write down the number of each word that meets *at least one* of the following tests:

(1) Can you change the word from present to past by changing its *form?*

(2) Could the word appear after *may* or *will* at the very end of a sentence?

Example: rain   Test 1   It *rained.*

Test 2   It *may* rain.

(Words that do not *normally* function as verbs may appear as verbs in some very special or rare uses. Select words according to their normal use, but be prepared to discuss any borderline cases in class.)

1. explain	11. cowboy	21. purple
2. history	12. jam	22. much
3. fairly	13. begin	23. boil
4. forget	14. tough	24. teach
5. ceiling	15. sing	25. lamp
6. weak	16. free	26. protest
7. find	17. church	27. gather
8. available	18. mow	28. justice
9. advertise	19. repair	29. freedom
10. shrink	20. develop	30. announce

ACTIVITY 2

In some of the following sentences, a complete verb follows a possible subject. After the number of each such sentence, write C for "complete." In some of the sentences, there is only part of a verb. After the number of each such sentence, fill in an *auxiliary* that would make the verb complete. You may use a single word, like *is, has, had, can, will,* or a combination of several auxiliaries, like *has been* or *will be.*

Examples: The car stopped.   (Answer) *C*
The cable broken.   (Answer) *had*

1. The cord snapped.	11. Jewels stolen.
2. The wheels turning.	12. The coach resigned.
3. The glass broken.	13. Her friends eaten.
4. The crowd booed.	14. My brother knew.
5. The police officers arrived.	15. The customers complaining.
6. Slides shown.	16. The work done.
7. The musicians practiced.	17. Rain fell.
8. Edgar leaving.	18. Disaster struck.
9. His wife drove.	19. The leaves fallen.
10. The fog disappeared.	20. Vacationers swimming.

FOR FURTHER
STUDY

SOME VERBS WITH ALL-PURPOSE FORMS

A few English verbs, such as *hit*, *shut*, and *put*, do not have a separate form for the past. Can you find more in the following list? Normally, the form of the verb changes when the sentence changes from "now" to "then" (at some time in the past). "Now tomatoes *grow*" but "Then tomatoes *grew*." In which of the following sentences would the form of the verb remain unchanged? Write down all the verbs that you find by applying this "now/then" test.

1. Birds fly.	11. Gamblers bet.
2. Knives cut.	12. Salespeople sell.
3. Bullets whistle.	13. Bubbles burst.
4. Goats climb.	14. Lawyers advise.
5. Antelopes jump.	15. Cowards quit.
6. Sun and moon set.	16. Lions roar.
7. Insults hurt.	17. Flowers grow.
8. Teachers teach.	18. Boards split.
9. Fads spread.	19. Carpenters hammer.
10. Scientists think.	20. Doctors heal.

ACTIVITY 3

Some words are used both as nouns and as verbs. This means that in some sentences they may occur as subjects; in other sentences they may occur as predicates. The word *dance* is used as a noun in the sentence "The *dance* started." The same word is used as a verb in the sentence "The guests *dance*." In each of the following sentences, a word used as a noun has been italicized. Write a second short sentence in which the same word is used as a verb. Use the same or a different *form* of the word the second time. (Use sentences that contain *only* subject and predicate. Include noun markers and auxiliaries as needed.)

Example: An *answer* arrived.
(Answer)   *The witness answered.*

1. *Sound* travels.	6. *Shouts* could be heard.
2. The *talk* had ended.	7. His *walks* have stopped.
3. Your *help* is needed.	8. *Rain* fell.
4. His *jokes* have improved.	9. *Sleep* refreshes.
5. Her *cry* echoed.	10. The *hammer* dropped.

REVIEW ACTIVITY

Which of the items in the following list are possible subjects of a sentence? After the appropriate number, put S for "Subject." Which are possible predicates? After the appropriate number, put P for "Predicate." Which are possible complete sentences containing both subject and predicate? After the appropriate number, put SP for "both Subject and Predicate." Be prepared to point out all signals that helped you sort these items out into the three categories.

Examples: was running   (Answer) P
             flowers grow   (Answer) SP

1. these coins
2. was melting
3. happiness
4. frogs croaked
5. collapsed
6. the attempt
7. applications
8. bees sting
9. had been reported
10. their relatives
11. shook
12. appearances deceive
13. has left
14. my collection
15. could have been repaired
16. hid
17. complaints
18. the ball bounced
19. a schedule
20. money helps
21. were traveling
22. had been organized
23. love ennobles
24. may weaken

Know the seven basic patterns of the English sentence and put them to work.

S3
Seven Sentence Patterns

The subject followed only by its verb makes up the basic "bare-minimum" sentence. But in many sentences we need a third part to complete the predicate. The verb alone does not tell the whole story. We add a "completer" to get a statement that makes sense. This completer becomes part of the basic structure. It is as much part of the basic construction as the third wheel of a tricycle:

Incomplete: Columbus discovered ———— (what?)
Complete: Columbus discovered *America.*

Incomplete: Columbus was ———— (what)?
Complete: Columbus was *Italian.*

Some sentences are still incomplete even after a third part has been added. They need *two* completers before thy make a complete statement:

YOUR TURN

WHAT'S MY LINE?

What does each of the following do for a living? After each word, fill in *one* word that states what each person does. The word you fill in will be a verb that can complete an *S–V* pattern. It will be the kind of verb that can "tell the whole story." Write on a separate sheet of paper.

Example: Track stars *run*.

Pilots —————.
Surgeons —————.
Tailors —————.
Janitors —————.
Sopranos —————.
Ballerinas —————.
Chefs —————.
Ministers —————.
Detectives —————.
Chauffeurs —————.
Jockeys —————.
Architects —————.
Contractors —————.
Instructors —————.
Merchants —————.
Laborers —————.
Soldiers —————.
Scientists —————.
Authors —————.
Physicians —————.

Incomplete:	The cashier gave —————.
Still Incomplete:	The cashier gave *Fred* —————.
Complete:	The cashier gave *Fred his money.*
Incomplete:	Bill considered —————.
Still Incomplete:	Bill considered *John* —————.
Complete:	Bill considered *John a friend.*
Incomplete:	The traffic made —————.
Still Incomplete:	The traffic made *the driver* —————.
Complete:	The traffic made *the driver nervous.*

BUILDING THE BASIC PATTERNS

Some verbs
tell the
whole story.

Some verbs
need a completer.

Some verbs need
<u>two</u> completers.

In these sentences, the two completers are as much part of the basic structure as the third and fourth side of a square. The technical name for a sentence completer is **complement.** The basic pattern of an English sentence is determined by the answers to three questions: Is there a complement? Is there just one, or are there two? What *kind* are they?

For each of the seven basic patterns, the answers to these three questions are different. Most of the basic patterns you are likely to have studied before. But you may be studying several of them here for the first time.

PATTERN ONE: SUBJECT–VERB *(S–V)*

In the first pattern, there is no complement at all. This is the "bare-minimum" sentence in English. The predicate consists only of the verb and needs no "completer." All of the following headlines show the S–V pattern at work:

NURSES STRIKE

Founder Succumbs   Strike Ends

Feud Flares

Buses Collide

Giants lose   Killers Confess

Most sentences built on this model roughly fit one of the following formulas: "Somebody acts." "Something happens." "Something exists."

Somebody Acts: A stranger called.
                  The neighbor knocked.
                  Our visitors left.

Something Happens: The scaffold collapsed.
                      The music had stopped.
                      A letter has arrived.

Something Exists: The search continues.
                     Confusion reigned.

PATTERN TWO: SUBJECT–VERB–OBJECT (S–V–O)

In the second pattern, we encounter the first type of complement: the **object.** Objects typically appear after *action verbs.* The verb then carries the action of the subject across to the object. The object is often the *target* of the action. It may be the *product* of a performance. The object slot in a sentence is typically filled by a noun. (Sometimes it is filled by a word that can *take the place* of a noun.)

Subject	Verb	Object
Dogs	chase	cats.
The prisoners	were digging	a tunnel.
The mariner	shot	the albatross.
This factory	produces	appliances.
Englishmen	like	tea.
Our team	lost	the game.
My sister	is painting	a portrait.
Your rudeness	has embarrassed	your friends.

The verbs in this pattern carry the action *across* to the object the way a *trans*atlantic flight carries passengers *across* the Atlantic. These verbs are therefore often called **transitive** verbs. They are often labeled "trans." in a dictionary. Most of the sentences in this second pattern roughly fit one of the following formulas: "This affects that." "Something produces something else." "Somebody perceives (that is, hears, sees, feels) something."

In most actual sentences, the basic pattern merely provides the skeleton. This skeleton has been fleshed out by additional material that does *not* become part of the basic pattern. Look at the following sentences from John Steinbeck's short story "The Leader of the People." For each, what would be a stripped-down version of the basic pattern?

S–V   Jody ran to his chores.
              Carl turned fiercely on him.
              Outside, Jody whistled shrilly to the dogs.

S–V–O   His mother had finished the beans by now.
              He carried his black slouch hat in his hand.
              Mrs. Tiflin kissed Grandfather on the side of his beard.

YOUR TURN

WHAT'S MY LINE?

What does each of the following do for a living? For each of the two blank spaces in each sentence, fill in one single word. Make the first word state something the person *does*. Make the second word fill in a target, a product, a result, or the like. Make sure the completed sentence is a S–V–O sentence. Write on a separate sheet of paper.

Example: Photographers *take pictures*.

Optometrists _____ _____.
Projectionists _____ _____.
Morticians _____ _____.
Electricians _____ _____.
Dentists _____ _____.
Mechanics _____ _____.
Wardens _____ _____.
Veterinarians _____ _____.
Exterminators _____ _____.
Rangers _____ _____.
Comics _____ _____.
Registrars _____ _____.
Cashiers _____ _____.
Judges _____ _____.
Physicists _____ _____.

ACTIVITY 1

Read the following sentences. Decide whether each sentence is complete as it is, or whether it needs to be completed by an object. After the number for each sentence, write *C* if the sentence is complete. Write in a *possible object* if the sentence is incomplete. Include a noun marker with the object where needed.

Example: Bees sting.   (Answer) *C*
             Americans like   (Answer) *baseball*

1. My father expects.
2. Birds sing.
3. This lever controls.
4. My uncle is raising.
5. The neighbors complained.
6. The rain had stopped.
7. The writer requested.
8. The club will sponsor.
9. The ushers took.
10. The waiter had disappeared.
11. The session began.
12. The editorial condemned.
13. The salesman sold.
14. The bell rang.
15. The story described.
16. A fence surrounded.
17. The attempt has failed.
18. The car swayed.
19. His customers objected.
20. My parents are furnishing.

ACTIVITY 2

Here are some verbs that may either appear alone (Pattern One) or be completed by an object (Pattern Two): *write, leave, sing, lose, hunt, start, stop, return, answer, break.* "Jim left" is Pattern One; "Jim left the room" is Pattern Two. Use each of these words first in a Pattern One sentence (alone). Then use the same word in a Pattern Two sentence (with an object).

Example: Fred is leaving.
             Fred is leaving town.

(You need not use the same *subject* in both sentences.)

PATTERN THREE: SUBJECT–LINKING VERB–NOUN
(S–LV–N)

The third pattern looks very much like the second. There is typically a noun as the subject. Then there is the verb followed by a *second* noun. In the third pattern, however, the verb does not carry an action across to an object. Instead of an action verb, we have a different kind of verb here. This kind of verb *pins a label* on the subject. It links a description of the subject to the subject. Such verbs are called **linking verbs.**

Subject	*Linking Verb*	*Noun*
Linda	is	a sophomore.
Maria	became	a physician.
Mr. Burke	was	our minister.
Her father	remained	a citizen.
The production	seemed	a failure.
Our car	will be	a Ford.

The most common linking verb is *be* and its various forms: *is, are, was, were, has been, had been, will be,* and so on. When you use this verb between two nouns, the two nouns really point to the *same* person or thing. *Be* and the other linking verbs are like the "equals" sign in a mathematical equation. As a result, most of the sentences for Pattern Three roughly fit the formula "This equals that." The noun that is made equal to the subject is *not* the object of an action. We can call it the "predicate noun."

ACTIVITY

Write down the numbers of the following sentences on a sheet of paper. Then label them *(2)* for Pattern Two or *(3)* for Pattern Three. Does the verb carry an action across to the object? Or does the verb pin a label on the subject?

> Example: Loretta was a damsel.   (Answer) *(3)*
>   The knight fought the dragon.   (Answer) *(2)*

1. We were reading a romance.
2. The knights served their king.
3. His name was Arthur.
4. Guinevere became his queen.
5. Their knights performed feats.
6. Dragons roamed the countryside.
7. Magicians cast spells.
8. Merlin was a magician.
9. The knights defeated their enemies.
10. Lancelot had been their champion.
11. A lady loved Lancelot.
12. Lancelot rejected her love.
13. Lancelot remained a bachelor.
14. The lady became a nun.
15. Lancelot worshiped the queen.
16. His friend was Gawain.
17. These knights sought adventure.
18. The poet praised their courage.
19. These knights had become his ideals.
20. The poet lamented their deaths.

PATTERN FOUR: SUBJECT–LINKING VERB–ADJECTIVE (*S–LV–Adj*)

The fourth pattern starts exactly like the third and performs much the same function. Again the subject is followed by a linking verb that pins a label on the subject. This time, however, the label is not a noun but an **adjective.** This adjective points out *a quality of the subject.* Many of the linking verbs used in this pattern help us point out qualities that we can see, hear, taste, smell, or feel.

Subject	*Linking Verb*	*Adjective*
The house	is	green.
His car	looks	new.
Your mother	sounded	happy.
The food	tasted	delicious.
The air	smelled	fresh.
The paper	had felt	wet.
Leslie	seemed	pale.
The water	is turning	purple.

Here is a capsule review of adjectives:

ADJECTIVES: A CAPSULE REVIEW

(1) Adjectives typically point out qualities. Often they occur after words that show *degree*, like *very, fairly,* or *extremely:*

very pale	fairly pale	extremely pale
very ill	fairly ill	extremely ill
very happy	fairly happy	extremely happy

To tell an adjective from a noun, try putting *very* (used alone) in front of the word. *Very* does not fit in with nouns. We do not say "very house," "very bird," "very courage."

(2) Most adjectives have special forms for use in comparisons. Many adjectives add the endings –*er* and *est:*

Jean is *bright.* Laura is *brighter.* Joan is *brightest.*
Fred is *strong.* Jim is *stronger.* Tom is *strongest.*

Many other adjectives use *more* and *most* instead of these endings:

Fred is *muscular.* Jim is *more muscular.* Tom is *most muscular.*
Jean is *intelligent.* Laura is *more intelligent.* Joan is *most intelligent.*

(3) There are some typical suffixes that can tip you off to the fact that a word is an adjective. Such suffixes are –*able* (capable, adorable, favorable); –*ous* (nervous, delicious, courageous); –*ful* (wonderful, peaceful, hopeful); –*like* (warlike, childlike); –*some* (handsome, burdensome).

When an adjective replaces the noun after a linking verb, we can call it the "predicate adjective." The sentences that we get in this pattern roughly fit the formula "This appears so" or "This appears thus."

In the following sentences by John Steinbeck, the underlying pattern uses a linking verb. Can you recognize the underlying pattern, in spite of the additional material that has been used to flesh out the skeleton of the sentence? Note that in one or two of the sentences a *pronoun* has taken the place of a noun. Note that in one of the sentences one of the elements in the basic pattern has been *duplicated*. What would be a stripped-down version of each?

S–LV–N	My father was a government packer.
	That was the big thing in my father's life.
S–LV–Adj	The porch boards grew warm in the sunshine.
	Everyone but Jody remained silent.
	Her voice had become soft and explanatory.

ACTIVITY

Can you distinguish between Pattern Three and Pattern Four? Each of the following sentences uses a linking verb. Decide if the linking verb is followed by a noun or by an adjective. After the number of the sentence, write *N* for noun or *Adj* for adjective.

Example:	The attempt was *successful*.	(Answer) *Adj*
	The attempt was a *failure*.	(Answer) *N*

1. Fred has become a journalist.
2. His title sounds impressive.
3. His assignment will be sports.
4. His articles sound sincere.
5. Basketball is his hobby.
6. The action is fast.
7. The players look tense.
8. The crowd goes wild.
9. The spectators sound hoarse.
10. Suspense is the keynote.
11. Hairs turn gray.
12. Victory is sweet.
13. Defeat tastes bitter.
14. Friends become enemies.
15. The referee becomes a scapegoat.

WISE SAYINGS OF OLDEN TIMES

Can you find the underlying pattern in each of the following proverbs? After the number of the proverb, write *S–V, S–V–O, S–LV–N,* or *S–LV–Adj.*

1. Necessity breaks law.   (Welsh)
2. Poverty is a shirt of fire.   (Turkish)
3. A full belly makes a dull brain.   (American)
4. The flour tastes bitter to the fed mouse.   (German)
5. The rotten apple spoils his companion.   (American)
6. A good lawyer is a bad neighbor.   (Spanish)
7. The idler is the greatest thief.   (Estonian)
8. Habit strips sin of its enormity.   (Hebrew)
9. A young doctor requires a big cemetery.   (Dutch)
10. Death alone measures equally.   (Czech)
11. Like fish, guests are poisonous after three days.   (French)
12. An empty pocket goes quickly through the market. (Scotch)
13. A featherless arrow travels for a short distance.   (African)
14. Necessity never made a good bargain.   (American)

16. Faces turn red.
17. Fred remains calm.
18. The journalist is an observer.
19. His feelings remain neutral.
20. The truth is his goal.

PATTERN FIVE: SUBJECT–VERB–INDIRECT OBJECT–OBJECT (*S–V–IO–O*)

In building the fifth pattern, we start with the subject–verb–object pattern of Pattern Two. Again, we need an action verb that carries the action across to an object. This time we select verbs that describe a transaction between people. We make sure that the original object is something that can be *passed on* from one person to another: "The relatives gave money." "The owner sold the house." We then insert between the verb and the original object *the destination.* We put in the person or thing that the original object is *intended for:* "The relatives gave *Gertrude* money." The original object is called the **direct** object. The inserted object is called the **indirect** object.

Notice how the indirect object is inserted between the verb and the original object in each of the following pairs:

My father gave directions.
My father gave *the stranger* directions.

Frieda wrote a letter.
Frieda wrote *her mother* a letter.

Miss Crane taught Spanish.
Miss Crane taught *the freshmen* Spanish.

Some other verbs commonly used in this pattern are *ask, send, lend, offer, tell, show,* and *pass:*

Subject	Verb	Indirect Object	Object
Arvin	asked	*the principal*	a question.
Tourists	send	*their families*	postcards.
Jean	lent	*her neighbor*	her pen.
The clerk	offered	*the customer*	a sample.
Mr. Jones	will tell	*your family*	the news.
The agent	had shown	*the buyer*	the house.
Barbara	passed	*her guests*	the cookies.

In this pattern, the verb ties together three different nouns. These nouns all become part of the basic pattern of the sentence. Note that a pronoun may *take the place* of a noun in each of the three positions. In the following sentences by Ernest Hemingway, the indirect object is a personal pronoun:

Manuel offered *him* the cape again.
Fuentes handed *him* the sword.

Here are some additional verbs that can be used in Pattern Five: *pay, sell, throw, rent, owe.* Can you use each of these in a simple sentence that includes the "destination"?

ACTIVITY

In which of the following sentences could an *indirect object* be inserted between the verb and the original object? If there is no way of putting in an indirect object, write C after the number of the sentence—the sentence is complete as it is. If you *can* insert an indirect object, write it after the number of the sentence.

Example: Grandfather had left millions.   (Answer) *his children*
           Grandfather had locked the door.   (Answer) *C*

WHAT'S MY LINE?

Can you complete each of the following so that the result will be a *S–V–IO–O* pattern? Fill in a verb in the first blank in each statement. Fill in a noun in the second blank, and another noun in the third. (Use a noun marker with each noun if you wish.) Write on a separate sheet of paper. Compare your answers with those given by your classmates.

Make sure the first noun you fill in names those who can *receive* something or benefit from it. Make sure the second noun you fill in names *what* they receive.

Example: Lawyers *give people advice.*

Pharmacists ——————— ——————— ———————.
Teachers ——————— ——————— ———————.
Supervisors ——————— ——————— ———————.
Bankers ——————— ——————— ———————.
Nurses ——————— ——————— ———————.
Trainers ——————— ——————— ———————.
Advertisers ——————— ——————— ———————.
Pollsters ——————— ——————— ———————.
Realtors ——————— ——————— ———————.
Guides ——————— ——————— ———————.
Counselors ——————— ——————— ———————.
Witnesses ——————— ——————— ———————.
Pen pals ——————— ——————— ———————.
Missionaries ——————— ——————— ———————.

1. Fred helps his brother.
2. His brother sells encyclopedias.
3. The company distributes leaflets.
4. The leaflets give information.
5. The prospect sends a reply.
6. The salesperson visits the prospect.
7. People ask questions.
8. The salesperson shows the encyclopedia.
9. These volumes educate children.
10. Volume A teaches history.
11. Volume B covers geography.
12. The company pays a commission.
13. Customers must like the books.

14. The company guarantees satisfaction.
15. The parents may return their set.
16. The salesperson may lose his commission.
17. Guarantees can cause trouble.
18. The brother teaches sales techniques.
19. Fred carries the volumes.
20. A dozen make a set.

PATTERN SIX: SUBJECT–VERB–OBJECT–OBJECT COMPLEMENT (S–V–O–OC)

Pattern Six looks very much like Pattern Five. Again the verb is basically followed by two objects. This time, however, we do not start with a direct object and then *insert* an indirect one. Instead, we *add* a second object *after* the first. This second object *pins a label on the first object.* It gives us a title or a description for the first object. We call the second object in this pattern the "object complement." The first object and the object complement point to the *same* person or thing.

Subject	Verb	Object	Object Complement
The teacher	called	Einstein	*a genius.*
The students	elected	Miranda	*president.*
The hero	made	Fred	*his biographer.*
My friends	considered	the sale	*a success.*

In order to tell Pattern Five from Pattern Six, make sure you can see whether or not the two objects point to the same thing:

Indirect Object: The mother read *the children* a story.
Object Complement: The teacher called the story *a romance.*

Indirect Object: Fred lent *Tom* his bicycle.
Object Complement: Fred considered Tom *his friend.*

Indirect Object: Sue sent *Betty* a note.
Object Complement: The mother named the girl *Betty.*

Most of the sentences in this pattern fit roughly into the formula "Somebody calls this that" or "Somebody makes somebody something."

Many of the verbs for Pattern Six are used in connection with elections and appointments: *choose, nominate, elect, appoint, name.* Can you use each of these verbs in a simple sentence that includes first the person and then the person's new title, honor, or office?

SMILE WHEN YOU CALL ME THAT   YOUR TURN

In each statement, can you supply the label that would complete a *S–V–O–OC* sentence? For each statement, write down three or four *different* labels that would complete the blank. (Which labels are flattering? Which are unflattering? You may include some insults if you wish, but stay away from profanity.) Make sure each label is just one word—a noun.

1. A reporter may call a politician a ——————.
2. A king could make a commoner a ——————.
3. We can call a glum person a ——————.
4. The voters should elect our ex-governor ——————.
5. Criminals call police officers ——————.
6. The club could appoint you ——————.
7. His followers considered Abraham Lincoln a ——————.
8. His enemies considered Abraham Lincoln a ——————.
9. People call an unruly child a ——————.
10. We call unexpected money a ——————.
11. We can label a terrible mishap a ——————.
12. Their music made the Beatles a ——————.
13. People may call immigrants ——————.
14. A child can call its father ——————.

ACTIVITY 1

In each of the following pairs, one sentence follows Pattern Five, the other Pattern Six. If the two objects refer to different things, label the sentence 5. If the two objects refer to the same thing, label the sentence 6.

Examples: Fred called *the school a prison.*   (Answer) 6
            Fred paid *the teacher a compliment.*   (Answer) 5

1. My uncle sent Henry money.
2. Henry considered the money a loan.

3. The opposition called our candidate a coward.
4. The accusation did our candidate harm.

5. Fred offered the president his services.
6. The president appointed Fred treasurer.

7. Fred wrote Mary a letter.
8. Mary called his handwriting a disgrace.

9. A friend gave Bill a rabbit.
10. Bill named the rabbit Pete.

11. The club chose Ferdinand secretary.
12. This decision caused the club trouble.

13. The landlord rented Maurice a studio.
14. Maurice considers the landlord his benefactor.

15. The voters handed the incumbent a defeat.
16. The newspaper termed the election a fraud.

17. The class elected a girl chairman.
18. This result taught the boys a lesson.

19. Mr. Sims owes my father money.
20. My father calls Mr. Sims names.

ACTIVITY 2

Some verbs, like *make, leave,* and *call,* occur in both Pattern Five and Six. In each of the following pairs, label one sentence *5,* the other *6.*

1. Mr. Grant left his grandson a fortune.
2. The will left the grandson a millionaire.

3. The stranger made the boy a whistle.
4. The gift made the boy his friend.

5. The doorman called the lady a taxi.
6. The lady called the doorman a darling.

7. The Eskimos make the Arctic their home.
8. The Eskimo makes his children clothes.

9. The accident left Mrs. Brown a widow.
10. Mr. Brown left his daughter his business.

PATTERN SEVEN: SUBJECT–VERB–OBJECT–ADJECTIVE (S–V–O–Adj)

Pattern Seven can be easily derived from Pattern Six. Again we put an object after the verb and let the verb pin a label on the object. This time, however, the label is not a noun that *renames* the object. It is an adjective that *points out a quality* of the object.

THE LANGUAGE OF EVERY DAY

Many common expressions follow the pattern Subject–Verb–Object–Adjective. Write *Yes* after the number of a sentence if it fits the pattern. Write *No* if the sentence does not fit the pattern.

Example: Elizabeth got her feet wet.

(Answer)   *Yes*

1. His pleas left the audience cold.
2. The bystander gave the workers a hand.
3. This report will set the record straight.
4. The noise drove Ferdinand crazy.
5. Charles taught his dog tricks.
6. The neighbor cut my complaints short.
7. The boy set the bird free.
8. The disappointment had broken his heart.
9. The grandfather taught the boy manners.
10. These people should keep their powder dry.
11. Zorro gave his pursuers the slip.
12. The community wiped the slate clean.
13. His tales bored his listeners stiff.
14. The salesman offered his customer terms.
15. The news made my friends happy.

Subject	Verb	Object	Adjective
The supervisor	called	Bill	*lazy.*
Louise	found	the work	*difficult.*
Mr. Grant	painted	his house	*red.*
The committee	considered	the proposal	*foolish.*
Your help	has made	our task	*easy.*
Rover	had licked	the plate	*clean.*

The sentences in this pattern roughly fit the formula "Somebody made something different" or "Somebody left something unchanged." The way to make sure that you have Pattern Seven is to insert "is very" between the object and what follows it. If only "is" fits in, you have Pattern Six—an object followed by a second noun. If "is very" fits in, you have Pattern Seven—an object followed by an adjective.

Noun: Fred called the police officer *a spoilsport.*
        (Test: The police officer *is* a spoilsport.)
Adjective: The girl called Sam *handsome.*
        (Test: Sam *is very* handsome.)

Noun: The typhoon left the ship *a wreck.*
        (Test: The ship *is* a wreck.)
Adjective: The fire left my uncle *poor.*
        (Test: My uncle *is very* poor.)

Here are some actual sentences using Patterns Six and Seven. Can you tell which is which? Note that in one or two instances a pronoun has replaced a noun.

Grandfather considered him a boy. (John Steinbeck)
The servants swept the sand smooth. (Ernest Hemingway)
Scully practically made them prisoners. (Stephen Crane)

Your Turn: The following verbs are used in both Patterns Six and Seven: *call, consider, make.* Use each of these verbs in two sentences—one following Pattern Six (Object followed by another noun), the other following Pattern Seven (Object followed by an adjective).

ACTIVITY

Which of the following groups of words could be expanded so that they would fit Pattern Seven? If a group *can* be expanded, write a possible adjective after its number. If the group *cannot* be expanded, write C (for "complete").

Examples: Lois painted the kitchen.   (Answer) *pink*
        Herbert counted the money.   (Answer) *C*

 1. Simon rented the bus
 2. Fall turns the leaves
 3. Jimmy colored the elephant
 4. Columbus sighted land
 5. This powder turns water
 6. Vivian had lost her shoe
 7. This treatment renders snakes
 8. The question left the conductor
 9. My sister found his advice
10. The class studied wombats
11. The government freed the prisoners

12. The pizza made Luigi
13. The busboy wiped the table
14. The girl had dropped her baton
15. My friend kicked the door
16. The paper announced the news
17. Paula broke her promise
18. The judge had called the action
19. The customer considered the price
20. Roberta dried the dishes

REVIEW ACTIVITY

Identify the basic pattern in each of the following sentences. Write the appropriate abbreviation after the number of the sentence.

Examples: Father sent Albert money   (Answer) *S–V IO O*
            Tom is a mailman.   (Answer) *S–LV–N*

1. My family visited the beach.
2. Fred was driving the car.
3. Fred is my brother.
4. My father has been giving Fred lessons.
5. Fred loves cars.
6. The weather was perfect.
7. The sun was shining.
8. Sunshine makes people happy.
9. My mother smiled.
10. My father was humming a tune.
11. My sister was chewing gum.
12. Our dog barked.
13. The beach looked wonderful.
14. The water was lukewarm.
15. Lifeguards watched the swimmers.
16. The currents are dangerous.
17. Fred considers the lifeguards a nuisance.
18. His friends give the lifeguards trouble.
19. My sister calls Fred immature.
20. Fred ignores her remarks.
21. My mother had packed a lunch.
22. My family likes picnics.
23. My mother offered my sister a sandwich.
24. My sister watches her weight.
25. Dieters consider food dangerous.

S4
FOUR SIMPLE
TRANSFORMATIONS

Know the four most important simple transformations and put them to work.

Many of the sentences we encounter are simple statements. They often start with the subject. Then the verb makes a statement about the subject. However, many other sentences in a typical conversation are not statements but questions, warnings, or requests. In questions and requests, the material in the simple sentence is *reshuffled or rearranged*. The familiar basic patterns are changed, or "transformed." The changes we make in the basic patterns in order to adapt them to special purposes are called **transformations.**

Suppose you were showing a visitor from outer space the following samples of Earth language. Could you give him a rough general idea of how we tell apart statements, requests, and questions?

STATEMENTS

China buys chemicals from Japan

NO MULES ARE SOLD in Lynchburg anymore.

Nuclear power stages comeback

Baby Sleeps All Night Without Waking

REQUESTS

Take The Pledge

QUIT SMOKING   MAKE BIG MONEY

Start Walking.

QUESTIONS

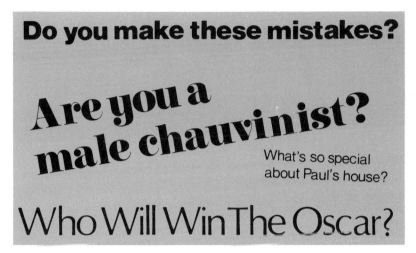

Do you make these mistakes?

Are you a male chauvinist?

What's so special about Paul's house?

Who Will Win The Oscar?

TRANSFORMATION ONE: REQUEST

When we shout a warning to someone, we need not identify the person first. We simply shout "Run!" or "Jump!" or "Watch out!" When we issue an order or make a request, we may simply say "Leave!" or "Stop!" or "Sit down." In all of these, we are using only the verb, *without a subject*. We can usually tell from the situation who is being shouted *at* or who is being ordered around. We say that in such cases the subject is "understood." The form of the verb that is used without a subject is called the request form.

Each of the seven basic sentence patterns can be turned into a request by two simple operations. First, we omit the subject. Then, we change the verb to the request form (or **imperative**). The material that *follows* the verb remains unchanged.

	Subject	Verb	Complements
S–V:	Jim	ran. Run!	
S–V–O:	The girl	closed Close	the door. the door!
S–LV–N:	Fred	was Be	my guest. my guest.
S–LV–Adj:	The students	were Be	quiet. quiet.

S–V–IO–O:	Jim	gave	Fred a pencil.
		Give	Fred a pencil.
S–V–O–OC:	The class	elected	Tom president.
		Elect	Tom president.
S–V–O–Adj:	Amanda	painted	the ceiling white.
		Paint	the ceiling white.

Even though requests do not need a subject, they are still complete sentences. Request sentences are the major exception to the rule that the typical English sentence has at least a subject and a predicate. Notice that some of the requests printed above are followed by an exclamation mark, some by a period. Can you explain the difference?

ACTIVITY

Rewrite each of the following sentences to turn it into a request. Omit the subject and change the verb to the request form.

Example: The carolers sang a song.
(Answer)   *Sing a song.*

1. The stranger lent Jim a dime.
2. The farmer locked the gate behind the cows.
3. Leonard is my friend.
4. Her husband did the dishes cheerfully.
5. The visitor was polite.
6. The judge set the prisoner free.
7. The Salvation Army helps the unfortunate.
8. His friends called him Louie.
9. The girls went back to the dormitory.
10. The farmer first caught the rabbit.
11. My parents were very patient with small children.
12. The boys acted unconcerned.
13. The committee reconsidered the decision.
14. The guests had fun.
15. Herbert became a member.
16. The firm gave the handicapped a break.
17. The class made Jim treasurer.
18. The mother read the children a story.
19. The customers were content.
20. The lecturer continued.

LEND ME YOUR EARS

The following lines from Shakespeare's *Julius Caesar* illustrate various uses of the request form. In each case, can you tell *which basic pattern* has been transformed? After the number of each passage, write the appropriate abbreviation for the sentence pattern to which the request transformation has been applied.

Example: *Have patience, gentle friends.*   *S–V–O*

1. *Go to the gate;* somebody knocks.
2. *Give me your hands all over,* one by one.
3.   O ye gods,
   Render me worthy of this noble wife!
4. *Be sudden,* for we fear prevention.
5. *Prepare the body then,* and follow us.
6. Friends, Romans, Countrymen, *lend me your ears.*
7. *Now be a freeman,* and with this good sword,
   That ran through Caesar's bowels, search my bosom.
8. Then *make a ring about the corpse of Caesar.*
9. *Give him a statue with his ancestors.*
10. *Run to your house,* fall upon your knees.

TRANSFORMATION TWO: THE PASSIVE

When we describe an action, we usually proceed from the "actor" to the action and from there to the target. We mention first the person who does something, then go on to *what* the person does, and finally point out the target of the action, or its result: "The batter hit the ball." "The lumberjack felled the tree." "The girl baked a cake." In all these sentences, the subject *does* something. We call the way such a sentence is put together an **active** construction. Sometimes, however, we start a sentence by mentioning first the target, or the victim, or the receiver: "*The town* was hit by an earthquake." "*The package* was damaged in transit." "*Jim* was promoted to corporal." Here, the subject has something *done to it.* We call the way such a sentence is put together a **passive** construction.

To produce a passive sentence, we have to start with a basic pattern that contains an object. We then perform three simple operations: First, we move the original object *in front of* the verb and make it the *subject* of the new sentence. Then we change the verb to a passive form, using the auxiliary *be (is, was, has been, will be)*. Third, we may omit the original subject altogether, or we may keep it *after* the verb and introduce it by the preposition *by*.

Active (*S–V–O*):　The officials canceled *the game*.
Passive:　*The game* was canceled by the officials.
Short Passive:　*The game* was canceled.

A rough general formula for the passive is "(Original object) is affected by (original subject)." Here are additional examples:

Active:　Her subjects adore the queen.
Passive:　*The queen* is adored by her subjects.

Active:　The players will repeat the performance.
Passive:　*The performance* will be repeated (by the players).

Active:　A mud slide had covered the house.
Passive:　*The house* had been covered by a mud slide.

Here is how the passive transformation works out in patterns with more than one completer:

(1) A second complement that *follows a direct object* stays in its original place in the sentence:

Active (*S–V–O–OC*):　The teacher called Einstein *a genius*.
Passive:　Einstein was called *a genius* (by the teacher).

Active (*S–V–O–Adj*):　Frieda called Jim *lazy*.
Passive:　Jim was called *lazy* (by Frieda).

(2) When a verb is followed by *two different objects*, two passives are possible. Either the indirect or the direct object may become the subject of the new sentence. Note, however, that the second passive is rarely used in current American English:

Active (*S–V–IO–O*):　A friend promised *Jim a job*.
First Passive:　*Jim* was promised a job (by a friend).
Second Passive:　*A job* was promised Jim (by a friend).

Active:　An admirer sent *Linda roses*.
First Passive:　*Linda* was sent roses (by an admirer).
Second Passive:　*Roses* were sent Linda (by an admirer).

ACTIVITY 1

Change the following sentences from active to passive. Make the original object the subject of the new sentence. Change the verb to the passive form. Put the original subject after the verb, introduced by the preposition *by*.

Example: The rain damaged the roof.
(Answer)   *The roof was damaged by the rain.*

1. A meteor struck the spaceship.
2. A truck had hit the pedestrian.
3. An auditor will examine the records.
4. An intern had performed the operation.
5. The voters have approved the stadium.
6. An avalanche surprised the skiers.
7. Burglars had ransacked the cabins.
8. The Beatles started the trend.
9. Bell invented the telephone.
10. Your peers will evaluate your performance.

ACTIVITY 2

For each of the following sentences, produce *two* passives.

Example: An uncle left Leonard a fortune.
(Answers)   (a) *A fortune was left Leonard by an uncle.*
            (b) *Leonard was left a fortune by an uncle.*

1. The clerk offered the customer a sample.
2. A friend had sent Jean a postcard.
3. A gossip had told my brother the story.
4. My aunt bought the children clothes.
5. Miss Crane will teach the children Spanish.

IN ACTION WITH STEPHEN CRANE

In the following sentences from a short story by Stephen Crane, a passive sentence has been expanded by additional material that was not part of the original basic pattern. Can you *reconstruct* the underlying basic pattern?

The combatants were actuated by a new caution.
The arrangements were swiftly made.
They were fairly blinded by the pelting of the snow.
The play of Johnny and the gray-beard was suddenly ended by another quarrel.

LANGUAGE AT WORK

TRANSFORMATION THREE: THE QUESTION

Sometimes we turn a statement into a question by simply raising our voice at the end to a higher pitch. In "He is ill" the tone of voice stays level. In "He is ill?" it goes up at the end. More often, however, we turn a statement into a question by rearranging some of the grammatical machinery.

Suppose you have punched out a simple statement on an imaginary future speech machine. If you were to push the "question" button in addition, the machine would have to perform *one* of the following three operations:

(1) *"He is ill"* is a statement. *"Is he ill"* is a question. Here we simply *put the verb in front of the subject.* This works with all forms of the verb *be* that consist of only one word: *"Are* the prints ready?" *"Was* the sale a success?" *"Were* the natives friendly?"

(2) If the verb includes *one or more auxiliaries, we switch the first auxiliary* so that it precedes the subject:

	Auxiliary	*Subject*	*Rest of Verb*
(The mail *has come.*)	*Has*	the mail	*come?*
(Fred *will graduate.*)	*Will*	Fred	*graduate?*
(The thief *was caught.*)	*Was*	the thief	*caught?*
(The date *has been set.*)	*Has*	the date	*been set?*
(The accident *could have been avoided.*)	*Could*	the accident	*have been avoided?*

(3) If there is *no auxiliary* that could be switched, we put a form of *do* in front of the subject:

(Fred *takes* Spanish.)	*Does*	Fred	*take* Spanish?
(Italians *love* music.)	*Do*	Italians	*love* music?
(Henry James *wrote* novels.)	*Did*	Henry James	*write* novels?

The same rules apply when questions begin with question words like *where, when, why,* and *how:*

Statement: The fair *will be held.*
Questions: Where *will* the fair *be held?*
             When *will* the fair *be held?*
             Why *will* the fair *be held?*

Statement: Gophers *damage* lawns.
Questions: Why *do* gophers *damage* lawns?
             How *do* gophers *damage* lawns?

Notice that *do* is also used in negative statements with *not.* Here, however, the subject does not change its position:

Affirmative: Teenagers *need* exercise.
  Negative: Teenagers *do* not *need* exercise.

Affirmative: Cereal *builds* muscles.
  Negative: Cereal *does* not *build* muscles.

Affirmative: The Indians *owned* horses.
  Negative: The Indians *did* not *own* horses.

In questions and negative statements, *do* and its various forms are used like an auxiliary. They *help* make up the complete verb. Can you see the question transformation at work in the following lines from Shakespeare's *Julius Caesar?* What were the original simple statements?

Do you know them?
Shall I do such a deed?
Good morrow, Brutus; do we trouble you?
Are we all ready?
But wherefore did you so much tempt the heavens?

Your Turn: Write *three* simple sentences in four versions each: (1) affirmative statement; (2) simple *Yes–or–No* question; (3) question with *when, where, why,* or *how;* (4) negative statement with *not.*

Examples: Fred had read Emerson.
            Had Fred read Emerson?
            When had Fred read Emerson?
            Fred had not read Emerson.

FOR LIMBERING UP

PUTTING A SENTENCE THROUGH ITS PACES

By applying the different simple transformations, we can put a sentence "through its paces." Turn each of the following statements first into a request, then into a passive sentence, then into a question.

Example: Jean prepared the food.
(Answers)   *Prepare the food!*
             The food was prepared by Jean.
             Did Jean prepare the food?

1. The riot squad has captured King Kong.
2. The monster crushed the giant insects.
3. The Klingons have prepared plans for invading the galaxy.
4. A scientist taught the chimp sign language.
5. The spacecraft will bypass Saturn.

Bonus Question: Can you apply *more than one* of the simple transformations to these sentences? Try turning each into a sentence that is passive and a question at the same time.

ACTIVITY

Change each of the following statements to a question. You may use both simple *Yes–or–No* questions ("Has he called?") and questions starting with *when, where, why,* or *how.* Use all parts of the original sentence; change only the verb or its position as necessary.

Example: Concord is a town in Massachusetts.
(Answer)   *Is Concord a town in Massachusetts?*

1. Emerson has been called our first American philosopher.
2. His father was a Unitarian minister.
3. The father died in 1811.
4. The mother educated five sons.
5. Young Emerson had been a teacher.
6. He followed his father into the ministry.
7. Emerson left the church in spite of his success as a preacher.
8. He had become a nonconformist.
9. Thoreau became his friend.
10. These men preached self-reliance.

11. Many Americans have read their essays.
12. Their individualism is part of our American tradition.
13. It forms part of the American creed.
14. Americans believe in the dignity of the individual.
15. They will always quote Emerson's words about independence.

TRANSFORMATION FOUR: "THERE-IS" SENTENCES

The fourth and final transformation from the basic sentence patterns is very simple. We often use the word *there* as a sentence opener, followed by a form of *be:* "There is . . ."; "There are . . ."; "There was . . ."; and the like. The word *there* is not the subject in such a sentence. The subject is *whatever it is* that is "there": "There was a *flood*"; "There is *a shortage.*" In these sentences, the verb follows *there;* the subject has been postponed.

	Verb	*Subject*
There	is	a surplus.
There	was	a surprise.
There	were	problems.
There	has been	an earthquake.
There	will be	exceptions.

Here are some examples of the *there* transformation from a fishing story by Ernest Hemingway:

There was a long tug.
There were birch trees in the green of the swamp on the other side of the river.
There were always trout in a place like that.

Your Turn: Make up five simple sentences on the "There is . . ." or "There are . . ." model. Use a different form of *be* each time.

REVIEW ACTIVITY 1

The four transformations of the simple sentence are brought about by changes in the form of the verb and by changes in the relationship between the verb and its subject. Make sure that you can identify *the complete verb and its subject* in each of the following sentences. Write down the subject and the verb of each sentence on a sheet of paper, putting *(S)* after the subject, *(V)* after the verb. If an auxiliary (including *do*) has been *split off* from the verb, put *(Aux)* after the auxiliary. If the subject has been omitted, put *(no S)* where the subject would normally appear.

Example: Where did your family spend the vacation?
(Answer)   *Did (Aux) your family (S) spend (V)*

Example: Send your cousins a letter.
(Answer)   *(no S) send (V)*

Example: The spectators were soaked by the rain.
(Answer)   *The spectators (S) were soaked (V)*

1. Visit the Navajos.
2. There are many Navajos in Arizona.
3. These people were assigned a reservation by the government.
4. Do Americans know their history?
5. How do these people live?
6. Have the Indians become voters?
7. Do the children have schools?
8. The tribe is governed by a council.
9. One member is elected chairperson by the tribe.
10. There are debates about the future of the tribe.
11. Tradition is upheld by the elders.

12. Change is considered inevitable by their children.
13. The reservation is visited by tourists.
14. The Indians are photographed by the visitors.
15. Has the nation forgotten these Americans?
16. Ask your friends this question.
17. Do your friends consider the Indian a citizen?
18. Does your state have reservations?
19. Plan a visit.
20. Bring your camera.

REVIEW ACTIVITY 2

For each of the above sentences, identify first the basic sentence pattern of the *original* sentence. Then indicate the transformation by which the *actual* sentence has been derived from the original. Use the following abbreviations. *Imp* for the request form, or imperative; *Ques* for questions; *Pass* for passive; *There* for "*there-is*" or "*there-are*" sentences.

Examples: Are the Navajos citizens? *(S–L–V–N) Ques*
Show your friends your pictures. *(S–V–IO–O) Imp*
There has been progress. *(S–V) There*
Change is considered dangerous by the elders.
    (S–V–O–Adj) Pass

Use modifiers to flesh out the skeleton of the bare-bones sentence.

S5
WHAT MODIFIERS
ADD

Few of the sentences we actually use consist only of the bare bones. To tell the whole story, to give the whole picture, we often need to fill in more information than is carried by the basic sentence parts. When we use the word *car* as the subject of a sentence, we often fill in other words that explain what kind of car it is and in what condition. Words that provide this kind of additional information are called **modifiers.** They change or *modify* the meaning of a word by giving us further details:

a *new* car
a *shiny new* car
a car *with a powerful engine*
a *foreign* car *with bucket seats*
a *black* car *in the center lane*

Each of the basic parts in a sentence may carry with it one or more such modifiers. Here are modifiers that might be used to flesh out the sentence "The girl read the letter":

Modifiers with the Subject:

The *tall* girl
The girl *in the red skirt*
The *dark-haired* girl *from Toledo*

Modifiers with the Verb:

slowly read
read *carefully*
read *with tears in her eyes*

Modifiers with the Object:

the *long* letter
the letter *from her mother*
the *brief* letter *with the sad news*

Look at the way different kinds of modifiers help us "tell the whole story."

S5a
Adjectives and Adverbs

Make full use of the two major kinds of single-word modifiers.

Single words used as modifiers are typically adjectives or adverbs. We use both of these types of modifiers constantly to fill in details. **Adjectives** modify nouns. They typically appear immediately in front of the noun they modify. They answer questions like "what kind?" or "which one?"

What Kind?	*blue* eyes	a *cold* wind
	hot water	a *portable* typewriter
	a *large* city	a *beautiful* hymn
	fresh flowers	*serious* mistakes

Which One?	the *tall* vase	the *German* plane
	my *blue* coat	the *American* car
	the *empty* tray	his *Japanese* camera
	the *yellow* envelope	our *new* set

Remember that typical adjectives can be recognized by three tests. First, they fit in after the linking verb in sentences like "The vase is _____." Second, they fit in after **intensifiers**—words like *very, fairly, extremely,* and *quite.* Third, they add *-er* or *-est* to

WHAT ADJECTIVES ADD

produce forms used in comparisons. (Longer adjectives are preceded by *more* and *most* instead.)

the *tall* vase	The vase is *tall.*
	The vase is very *tall.*
	This vase is *taller* than the other.
serious mistakes	This mistake is *serious.*
	This mistake is very *serious.*
	This mistake is more *serious* than the other.
a *beautiful* hymn	This hymn is *beautiful.*
	This hymn is very *beautiful.*
	This hymn is the most *beautiful* of all.

Adverbs typically modify verbs. They answer such questions as "When?" "Where?" or "How?" Many adverbs (but *not all*) consist of an adjective followed by the ending *–ly: fresh/freshly, new/newly, serious/seriously, beautiful/beautifully.*

	Subject	*Verb*	*Adverb.*
When?	The mail	came	*early.*
	The messenger	left	*immediately.*
	The train	is arriving	*now.*
	His reply	will come	*soon.*

Where?	The club	will meet	*here.*
	Her uncle	lived	*abroad.*
	The stars	twinkled	*above.*
	The men	went	*inside.*
How?	Fred	answered	*quickly.*
	The ship	veered	*sharply.*
	The hunter	moved	*cautiously.*
	The fire	spread	*rapidly.*

Adverbs also modify adjectives *and* other adverbs. They then answer such questions as "How well?" or "How much" or "To what extent?"

Adverb Modifies Adjective

The tray was *completely* empty.
The mail was *incredibly* slow.
Her parents had been *miserably* poor.

Adverb Modifies Adverb

The accident happened *unbelievably* fast.
He spoke English *moderately* well.

To help you recognize adjectives and adverbs, remember:

(1) When the *same* word is used as both adjective and adverb, the adverb is the form with *–ly:*

Adjective: The *silent* stranger nodded.
   Adverb: The stranger nodded *silently.*

Adjective: The *beautiful* bird sang.
   Adverb: The bird sang *beautifully.*

(2) Adjectives appear after *linking verbs;* they then say something about the condition of the subject. Adverbs appear after *action words;* they then say something about the manner of the action.

Adjective: The stranger was *generous.*
   Adverb: The stranger acted *generously.*

Adjective: The boy seemed *intelligent.*
   Adverb: The boy answered *intelligently.*

NOTE: The verb *be,* usually used as a linking verb, is followed by adverbs when it indicates *location:* "He is *here.*" "She was *there.*" "He had been *abroad.*"

A WORD FROM SCIENTISTS

Read the following passage about what air pollution might be doing to the atmosphere and to the worldwide climate. All the italicized words are adjectives. About each such word, ask: (1) "Am I sure what the word means?" (Explain the meaning in your own words.) (2) "How can I tell the word is used as an adjective?"

1. Apart from its *immediate* hazard to health, air pollution is a *potential* cause of *irreversible* changes in the *global* climate.
2. Some scientists say the *arctic* ice caps will grow; some offer *plausible* evidence that the ice caps will melt.
3. Some predict an *approximate* balance, so that the earth will remain *habitable*.
4. In this *excitable* era, *responsible* scientists voice *authentic* warnings.
5. But they also counter *irrational* fears with *scientific* facts.
6. The earth is like a *gigantic* heat machine fed by *solar* radiation.
7. The *climatic* balance is *delicate*, so that hardly *perceptible* changes could upset it.
8. But the effects of smog and exhaust fumes are very *diverse*.
9. Scientists are watching for the *earliest* signs of *harmful* effects on the world's weather.
10. In the *distant* future, a *uniform* layer of smog may reduce the *total* heat the earth receives from the sun.

(3) Adjectives are usually tied to one definite *position:* in front of a noun or after a linking verb. Most adverbs can *change* their position without changing the meaning of the sentence:

Fred answered *quickly.*
Fred *quickly* answered.
Quickly Fred answered.

The messenger left *immediately.*
The messenger *immediately* left.
Immediately, the messenger left.

FOR SENTENCE
PRACTICE

WATCHING THE WRITER AT WORK

Study the way adjectives modify nouns in the following sentences from Jack London's short story "To Build a Fire." Notice that *several adjectives* can modify the same noun:

He fed the *young* flame with wisps of *dry* grass and with the *tiniest dry* twigs.
Small pieces of *rotten* wood and *green* moss clung to the twigs.
The *brief* day drew to a close in a *long, slow* twilight.

Study the variety of adverb positions in the following sentences by Stephen Crane. Notice that *several adverbs* can modify the same verb:

The men around the stove stared *vacantly* at each other.
Upstairs the Swede was *swiftly* fastening the straps of his great valise.
He talked *arrogantly, profanely, angrily.*

Use the six sentences above as *model sentences.* For each, write a sentence of your own that follows the structure of the original as closely as possible. Use adjectives and adverbs at the same point in your sentence as the original author did. Here is an example:

Model Sentence: He talked arrogantly, profanely, angrily.
Imitation: She worked stubbornly, silently, joylessly.

Your Turn: Each of the following statements contains only the bare bones of a simple sentence. Rewrite each sentence, using modifiers to flesh it out. Use at least *one adjective* and *one adverb* in each sentence. Write on a separate sheet of paper.

Example: The whale attacked the ship.
(Answer)   The *gigantic* whale *suddenly* attacked the ship.

1. The creature approached the men.
2. The boy met a girl.
3. The mother called the child her darling.
4. The driver hit the brakes.
5. The students brought the teacher flowers.

ACTIVITY 1

Which of the nouns in the following sentences are modified by adjectives? Which sentences contain linking verbs that are followed by adjectives? Write *all adjectives* that a sentence contains after the number of that sentence. Write on a separate sheet of paper.

Example: Melville gave his native country a great novel.
(Answer)   *native, great*

1. Young Melville had been a seaman on an American whaler.
2. His famous book describes the dangerous voyage of the *Pequod*.
3. The mad captain had hired a strange crew.
4. One brawny harpooner was a superstitious heathen.
5. His companion was a gigantic Negro.
6. An additional harpooner was Indian.
7. The captain had lost a leg in the hunt for a mysterious white whale.
8. This moody man considered the white whale his mortal enemy.
9. The sailors saw immense herds of whales.
10. Numerous ships hunted the huge animals.
11. Often men were killed in their small boats.
12. An unlucky harpooner could be maimed by his rope.
13. Accidents were frequent.
14. These familiar mishaps did not deter the *Pequod* from her course.
15. Her fanatic captain was seeking revenge.

ACTIVITY 2

Which of the verbs in the following sentences are modified by adverbs? Which modifiers are *in turn* modified by adverbs? Write *all adverbs* that a sentence contains after the number of that sentence. Write on a separate sheet of paper.

Example: The sailors cheered wildly.
(Answer)   *wildly*

1. Now the *Pequod* was fast approaching its goal.
2. Various ships had recently sighted the great whale.
3. Again the sailors had paid dearly for their encounter with the white monster.
4. Captain Ahab waited impatiently for his chance.
5. Finally the lookout saw the huge hump below.
6. Soon the boats were giving chase.

7. The incredibly powerful whale easily destroyed the small boats.
8. He calmly ignored the harpoons.
9. One harpooner was caught in the badly tangled lines.
10. The ropes strapped his body firmly to the whale.
11. The wildly excited Ahab attacked the whale again in new boats.
12. Sharks hungrily circled the boats with their strangely silent crews.
13. The whale now seemed weak from his many wounds.
14. Ahab desperately exhorted his men.
15. The old enemies warily approached their final battle.

For Further Study: We often obtain an adverb by simply adding *–ly* to an adjective. But many adverbs do *not* have the *–ly* ending and some adjectives *do*. In a few cases, adjective and adverb are exactly alike. Which of the following sentences illustrate these possibilities? What other complications can you discover? For each of the italicized words, ask first *whether it is used as adjective or adverb.* Then explain why the word is an exception to the most common way of showing the difference between adjective and adverb.

1. The train was *fast.*
   The train stopped *fast.*
   We took a *fast* train.

2. The doctor recommended *daily* exercise.
   Fred exercised *daily.*

3. The man worked *hard.*
   The man *hardly* worked.

4. The neighbors had a *friendly* conversation.
   The man seemed *friendly.*
   His *friendly* smile surprised us.

5. The guests came *early.*
   Jim took an *early* train.

6. The food was *good.*
   His father cooked *well.*
   His father is *well.*

7. We paid our dues *monthly.*
   We paid our *monthly* dues.

8. We encountered a *lone* ranger.
   The ranger was *lonely.*
   Herbert was a *lonely* child.

9. The stranger had a *manly* appearance.
   His *manly* reply impressed us.

10. The club met *weekly*.
    The manager wanted a *weekly* report.

Use prepositions to link up details to the rest of the sentence.

Much of the modifying material that we work into a sentence comes in a package: It is part of a phrase. A **phrase** consists of several words that work together as a single unit. In a prepositional phrase, the first word is a **preposition,** a word like *at, in, by, of,* or *on.* The rest of the phrase is the noun that the preposition ties to the sentence: *at the door, in a hurry, by accident.* Here as elsewhere, the place of a noun may be taken by a noun substitute, such as a pronoun.

Many prepositions show a relationship *in space:*

Many
prepositions show
a relationship
in space.

above the clouds	*beyond* the hills
behind the barn	*under* the table
below the moon	*on* the chair
beside the door	*toward* the car
between his eyes	*within* reach

Many prepositions show a relationship *in time:*

about noon	*during* the intermission
after lunch	*since* the summer
before recess	*until* graduation

In the following examples, a prepositional phrase *modifies a noun.* It then does the work usually performed by an adjective:

WE CAN'T GO ON MEETING ABOVE THE CLOUDS.

the store *around the corner*	the girl *with the bun*
the sign *at the entrance*	the man *in the middle*
a walk *after lunch*	the boy *on the horse*

In the following examples, a prepositional phrase *modifies a verb.* It then does the work usually performed by an adverb:

stopped *at the entrance*	was seen *in the theater*
raced *around the corner*	will work *during the summer*
tried *without success*	had climbed *over the fence*

Several prepositional phrases may occur in the same sentence. They may be separated by other words from the word they modify. Also, more than one prepositional phrase may modify the same

Many prepositions show a relationship in time.

I'LL MEET YOU ABOUT NOON.

word. In the following sentences, can you tell which word each prepositional phrase modifies?

The boy *in the convertible* circled *around the block.*
A woman came *down the stairs in a hurry.*
Scouts *from our camp* had seen a lioness *with her cubs.*
The robbers had thrown the rest *of the loot into the river.*
The message *from the chief* filled the members *of our troop with fear.*

Your Turn: Each of the following statements contains only the bare bones of a simple sentence. Use prepositional phrases to flesh them out. Fill in a prepositional phrase (or several, if you wish) in each blank in a sentence. Write on a separate sheet of paper.

1. The girl —————— smiled ——————.
2. —————— a man —————— asked ——————.
3. Manuela sent her aunt —————— a box ——————.
4. People —————— call a politician —————— a man ——————.
5. —————— the car —————— went ——————.

ACTIVITY

Write *all prepositions* that a sentence contains after the number of that sentence. Write on a separate sheet of paper. Be prepared to explain in class *what* each prepositional phrase modifies.

Example: The sea eagles in Norway are cousins of the American eagle.
(Answer)   *in, of*

1. The eagles of Norway live along the coast.
2. The laws in that country do not protect these birds against hunters.
3. Dozens of birds are shot during the year.
4. Farmers consider the eagle a danger to their livestock.
5. Local authorities have in the past paid a premium for the bird.
6. Fortunately the eagle builds its nest on the rocks.
7. Sometimes the birds nest on islands.
8. These places cannot be reached from the villages without trouble.
9. The eggs are laid around Easter.
10. The fledglings stay in the nest until summer.
11. Soon the young birds soar over the countryside.
12. Visitors from America will not see eagles outside Norway.
13. The birds disappeared from England after 1908.
14. A few birds with their mates have been observed in Denmark.
15. The magnificent European eagle may not survive beyond this century.

WATCHING THE WRITER AT WORK

Study the role and position of the prepositional phrases in the following sentences from Ernest Hemingway's story "The Undefeated." Use each of these sentences as a model sentence. For each, write a sentence of your own that uses prepositional phrases at the same points the original author did.

It was quiet *in the café.*
At one table four men played cards.
Manuel went *through the long room to a small room in back.*
A man sat *at a table in the corner* asleep.

FOR SENTENCE PRACTICE

Use appositives to build up detail in a sentence.

The word *appositive* means "put next to" something else. An **appositive** is a second noun put immediately *after* a noun in order to tell us more about it. Most other modifiers blend with the rest of the sentence without any clear break. An appositive is usually set off by audible breaks in the flow of speech. In writing, the place of these breaks is taken by commas. Note that the appositive often carries along its own noun marker:

Jim, *a freshman,* was our secretary.
Mr. Smith, *an attorney,* presented the award.
Rip, *the watchdog,* had frightened the burglars.
She had lost the present, *a necklace.*

Using an appositive is a handy way of working in explanations that would otherwise have to be stated in a separate sentence. An appositive can help identify an unfamiliar person. It can help explain a difficult word:

S5c
Working in Appositives

Statement:	Jim discovered the fire.
Added Source:	Jim is my brother.
Result:	Jim, *my brother,* discovered the fire.
Statement:	We were dancing the Gopeck.
Added Source:	The Gopeck is a native dance.
Result:	We were dancing the Gopeck, *a native dance.*
Statement:	Rome was ruled by the patricians.
Added Source:	The patricians were descendants of its original citizens.
Result:	Rome was ruled by the patricians, *descendants of its original citizens.*

Notice that an appositive is often modified *in turn* by other modifiers. The noun used as an appositive may carry with it an adjective or a prepositional phrase:

The article described Houdini, a *famous* magician.
Jerry, a singer *from Pasadena*, was adored by my sisters.
Macky, a *tiny* monkey *from Brazil*, stole the show.

Your Turn: Each of the following statements contains only the bare bones of a simple sentence. Rewrite each sentence, using *appositives* to flesh it out. Use at least *one* appositive in each sentence. Write on a separate sheet of paper.

Example: His friend wore sandals.
(Answer)   His friend, *a sophomore from Duluth,* wore sandals.

1. The visitor had brought a present.
2. The ship approached its destination.
3. The stranger curiously eyed the group.
4. Her sister married a foreigner.
5. The boy needed more room for his pet.

ACTIVITY 1

Combine the two sentences in each of the following pairs into one sentence. Use the information in the second sentence as *an appositive* in the first.

Example: Noah Webster was born in Hartford. Hartford is a town in Connecticut.
(Answer)   *Noah Webster was born in Hartford*, a town in Connecticut.

1. Noah Webster was a famous lexicographer.
   A lexicographer is a maker of dictionaries.

2. Webster was educated at Yale University.
   He was a native of New England.

3. His profession was unprofitable.
   His profession was law.

4. Webster turned to a new occupation.
   The new occupation was teaching.

5. The textbooks were unsatisfactory.
   The textbooks were schoolbooks from England.

6. In 1783 Webster published a textbook.
   The textbook was a speller.

7. *The American Spelling Book* sold 80 million copies.
   It was an all-time best-seller.

8. In 1806 Webster published a different book.
   The book was a small dictionary.

9. This book prepared the way for his greatest work.
   His greatest work was his *American Dictionary*.

10. The dictionary included numerous Americanisms.
    Americanisms are new words from America.

ACTIVITY 2

Use appositives and other modifiers to flesh out the bare bones of the following simple sentences. Write *three* versions of each sentence. Use different modifiers each time.

Example: The cowboy rode.
(Answer)   *The* tired *cowboy rode* into town.
           The cowboy, a famous outlaw, *rode* slowly into the sunset.
           The cowboy from Wyoming *rode* away.

1. The singer sang a tune.
2. A girl answered the phone.
3. The man opened the letter.
4. Mary sent her friend an invitation.
5. The animal charged the hikers.

WATCHING THE WRITER AT WORK

FOR SENTENCE PRACTICE

Appositives can be very simple, giving us a brief label or identification. But they can also be more elaborate, giving us all kinds of details. Look at the way appositives are used in the following sentences by John Steinbeck. Use each of these as a *model sentence.* For each, write a sentence of your own that follows as closely as possible the structure of the original. Use your own words—keep the sentence structure of the original.

On Saturday afternoon Billy Buck, *the ranch-hand,* raked together the last of the old year's haystack.

Mama Tores, *a lean, dry woman with ancient eyes,* had ruled the farm for ten years.

And there was Pepé, *the tall smiling son of nineteen, a gentle, affectionate boy,* but very lazy.

REVIEW ACTIVITY

Each of the following sentences contains *one* modifier. What kind of modifier is it? After the number of the sentence, write the appropriate abbreviation: *Adj* for adjective; *Adv* for adverb; *Prep* for prepositional phrase; *App* for appositive. Write on a separate sheet of paper.

Example: The manager announced a new program.
(Answer)   *Adj*

1. The Smiths adopted a Korean orphan.
2. The prisoner escaped during the night.
3. Jim gradually raised his grades.
4. His father, an attorney, had read our proposal.
5. The news had spread rapidly.
6. Huge signs welcomed the visitor.
7. The widow left a fortune to the university.
8. A submarine had been sighted outside the harbor.
9. Athletes enjoyed special privileges.
10. Her cousin in Canada drove a truck.
11. Our schools welcome foreign students.
12. The fire completely destroyed the building.
13. Jim, our treasurer, read his report.
14. The boys had discovered a cave near the river.
15. The mayor, a Democrat, was reelected.
16. Her present was a book, a biography.
17. My aunt fed the stranger a hearty meal.
18. An unruly mob awaited the speaker.
19. His horse won the race easily.
20. Her mother had visited the country before the war.

S6
WRITING THE COMBINED SENTENCE

Combine simple sentences as part of a larger whole.

Even a simple sentence may contain several parts of the same kind. An action may be performed by two people instead of one. If a sentence names each of these people separately, it will have *two subjects:*

Fred and Michael left the building.
The owl and the pussycat went to sea.

Or a statement may mention two actions, and the sentence will have *two verbs:*

Fred *shortened and spliced* the wires.
The suspect *threatened and insulted* the officer.

Just as we can tie single words together by using an *and* or *or*, so we can combine several simple sentences into a larger unit. We start with two or more simple sentences, each with its own subject and predicate. We then weld them into a more complicated structure. The original subject-predicate groups are called **clauses.** A clause has its own subject and predicate. A single clause *may* stand by itself as a simple sentence. Or it may join with other clauses as part of a larger combined sentence.

Each of the following sentences *combines two clauses.* Can you point out the subject and the verb of each clause?

The wind whistled, and the waves roared.
The rope held, but the men were exhausted.
Fred barred the windows while Mike locked the doors.
The club canceled the trip because the roads were impassable.
The men were saved, though their equipment was lost.

Words like *and, but, while, because,* and *though* are called **connectives.** Connectives tie together whole clauses. (Some connectives also tie together words *within* a clause.) To tell different combinations of clauses apart, we have to distinguish *several major kinds of* connectives.

Coordinate independent clauses as part of a larger whole.

Some connectives simply join one clause to another. Such simple joining words are *and, or,* and *but.* We call them coordinating connectives, or **coordinators,** for short. When we coordinate the work of several people, we don't have to put one in charge over the others. We merely make them work *together.* When we coordinate two clauses, each remains *about equally important.* Each could still stand by itself as a separate sentence. It is still an **independent** clause.

In the following sentences, two clauses are about equally important. Can you point out the subject and the verb of each?

The girls made the posters, *and* the boys printed the tickets.
Often the group sang around the fire, *or* Fred played the guitar.
Sue likes dances, *but* her mother objects to them.

Some other words that are often used as coordinators are *for, yet,* and *so.* Can you chart the basic patterns linked in the follow-

S6a
How Coordination
Adds Up

ing examples, such as "S–V, yet S–V–O" or "S–LV–N, so S–V–IO–O"?

> Fred flipped the pages, *for* the story bored him.
> The buildings were old, *yet* the rents were high.
> The evening was warm, *so* we ate outside.

Look at the following sample sentences. In each sentence, two independent clauses are joined by a coordinator. In each case, can you explain the *connection* between the two clauses? For each, can you make up several sentences of your own in which the same coordinator signals a similar connection?

> Jody felt mean then, *so* he threw a rock at Mutt. (John Steinbeck)
> The Easterner's teeth were chattering, *and* he was hopping up and down like a mechanical toy. (Stephen Crane)
> He looked in the pool for his reflection, *but* his breathing troubled the mirror. (William Golding)
> The knife was with Pepé always, *for* it had been his father's knife. (John Steinbeck)

FOR SENTENCE PRACTICE

THAT'S A THOUGHT

In each of the following proverbs, two related thoughts are joined by a coordinator like *and* or *but*. Can you make up some "modern proverbs" that put together two related thoughts the same way? What "wise sayings" could you make up about modern times or the current scene? (Try using some of the proverbs below as *model sentences*—use your own ideas but follow the sentence structure of the original proverb as closely as you can.)

> Fools make feasts, and wise men eat them. (American)
> Man has the bow, but God has the arrows. (Russian)
> The world is your cow, but you have to do the milking. (American)
> God sends every bird its food, but he does not throw it into the nest. (American)
> Adam ate the apple, and our teeth ache from it. (Hungarian)
> Thirst is the end of drinking, and sorrow is the end of love. (Irish)
> The doctor dressed his wounds, but God healed him. (English)
> Poor people have poor ways, but rich ones have mean ones. (American)

And, but, and *so* are among the connectives most frequently used in everyday conversation. In writing a paper or making a speech, we often use heavier connectives with roughly the same meaning. Instead of starting an objection with *but,* we may use *however.* Instead of drawing a conclusion by saying *so,* we may use *therefore. However, therefore, furthermore,* and *besides* have several things in common with adverbs and may be called **adverbial connectives:**

Coordinating: Fred rushed to the station, *but* the train had left.

   Adverbial: Fred rushed to the station; *however,* the train had left.

Coordinating: Gerald had not paid his dues, *so* the club expelled him.

   Adverbial: Gerald had not paid his dues; *therefore* the club expelled him.

Coordinating: His lease had expired, *and* the building had been found unsafe.

   Adverbial: His lease had expired; *furthermore,* the building had been found unsafe.

Adverbials are more of a mouthful than the coordinators. They cause a more definite break in the flow of speech. In writing, coordinating connectives are usually preceded by a comma; adverbial connectives are usually preceded by a semicolon. (See the Mechanics chapter for more details.) Both types of connectives have one essential thing in common: The two clauses joined by the connective are merely *coordinated.* They remain grammatically *independent* and could still appear as separate sentences:

Fred rushed to the station. *But* the train had left.
Fred rushed to the station. *However,* the train had left.

Your Turn: Join the sentences in each pair three ways, using a different connective each time. Use only connectives listed in the preceding section. Make sure each combination makes good sense. Write on a separate sheet of paper.

   Example: The bell rang.
                Fred walked to the door.

(Answers)   *The bell rang, so Fred walked to the door*
                The bell rang, and Fred walked to the door.
                The bell rang; therefore Fred walked to the door.

1. The iceberg approached.
   The ship veered to the right.

2. The horse reared.
   The rider tightened his grip.

3. The girl smiled.
   The boy remained silent.

4. The audience applauded.
   The speaker continued.

5. Jim liked the work.
   He needed the money.

ACTIVITY

Connectives join single words and phrases as well as clauses. Which connectives in the following examples actually join clauses? If a connective joins two clauses, write down the subject and the verb of each clause. (Omit modifiers.) If a connective does *not* join two clauses, write *No*. Write on a separate sheet of paper.

Example: Martha played the flute, and Albert beat the drum.
(Answer)   *Martha played, Albert beat.*

1. The trees were blooming, and the farmers were afraid of late frosts.
2. The company was constructing a new factory and a huge warehouse.
3. The singer had caught cold; therefore the performance was canceled.
4. The police had arrested not the burglar but an innocent man.
5. The audience liked the play, but the critics considered it weak.
6. The men lost their way, for snow had covered the tracks.
7. My brother had applied for a scholarship; however, the application had arrived late.
8. Women in bright dresses and men in colorful costumes crowded the stage.
9. The contest has been postponed; besides, boys are ineligible.
10. The traffic had been heavy, so the guests were late.
11. Sometimes Father played ball with the boys, or Mother read the children a story.
12. The sign barred girls in shorts or boys without jackets.
13. Numerous contributions were pledged, yet only a fraction have been paid.

14. The old man had made a will; however, the courts declared it invalid.
15. Her grandfather had left his job and moved to Oregon.

KEEP A CIVIL TONGUE IN YOUR HEAD

Men have often been lectured about the way they talk about women. Some of what they say is flattering but insincere. Much of what they say is "condescending" or downright insulting. Study the following collection of popular sayings (by men) about women. Note that each has a dependent clause starting with a subordinator like *if* or *when* or *because*. How do you react to the sayings?

Make up a similar set of imaginary "popular sayings" about men, or boys, or husbands. Or your class may decide to choose some other worthy target. Make sure each saying includes a dependent clause introduced by a subordinator like *if*, *when*, or *because*.

When three women agree, the stars will come out in broad daylight. (India)
Where women are honored, the gods are pleased. (Arabia)
A woman is wrong until she cries.
Beware of beautiful women as you would beware of red pepper. (Japan)
If you are looking for love, take a wife. (India)
All women look the same after the sun goes down.
When you are taking a wife, shut your eyes tightly and commend yourself to God. (Italy)
You can't marry a widow because the widow marries you.

Use subordination to lock dependent clauses in place.

**S6b
What Subordination
Does**

Some connectives lock a clause in place. Such connectives are words like *if*, *when*, *as*, *while*, *where*, and *because*. We call them subordinating connectives, or **subordinators,** for short. They *sub*ordinate one clause to another. The clause they subordinate is like a two-wheel trailer attached to a car. The trailer can neither stand up by itself nor proceed under its own power. "If I were a millionaire" is a **dependent** clause; it does not normally stand by itself. We look for a main clause to attach it to. We ask, "If I were a millionaire, then what?"

In the following sentences from a bull-fighting story by Ernest Hemingway, the italicized parts are dependent clauses linked to the main clause by a subordinator:

Manuel pulled the door tight *until it clicked.*
Where they stood it was dark.
The crowd applauded Hernandez *as they marched across the arena.*
Manuel walked across the sand toward the barrera, *while Zurito rode out of the ring.*

Note the following points:

(1) Many subordinating connectives introduce a clause that tells *when* or *where* something takes place: *when, until, before, after, since, while, whenever, as, as soon as, where.*

Main Clause	Dependent Clause
Susan responded	*when* her name was called.
Irma left	*before* the mail came.
Years have passed	*since* the plans were approved.
The visitors talked	*while* we prepared the supper.

Other subordinating connectives introduce a clause that tells *why* or *under what condition: because, if, unless.*

Main Clause	Dependent Clause
The expedition failed	*because* supplies were lost.
The tournament will be held	*if* the weather improves.
The coach will resign	*unless* the players cooperate.

Like adverbs, the clauses introduced by subordinating connectives typically give information about time, circumstances, conditions. They are therefore traditionally called **adverbial clauses.**

(2) Sometimes you may not be sure whether a connective is a subordinator or a coordinator. You can be sure it is a subordinator if the clause it introduces can come *before* the main clause instead of after it.

Dependent Clause	Main Clause
When her name was called,	Susan responded.
If the weather improves,	the tournament will be held.
Unless we cooperate,	the coach will resign.

When you have a coordinator, switching the two clauses around produces nonsense, as in the following examples: "*But* the men were exhausted, the rope held." "*Or* Fred played the guitar, often the group sang."

(3) Several subordinating connectives are also used as prepositions: *until, before, after, since,* and *because* (in the combination *because of*). They are used as connectives when they are followed by a subject and a verb. They are used as prepositions when they are followed by a noun (and its various possible modifiers).

Connective: Our friends stayed until *the rain stopped.*
Preposition: Our friends stayed until *noon.*

Connective: The pool has been closed since *school started.*
Preposition: The pool has been closed since *the fall.*

Look at the following sentences from a famous short story by John Steinbeck. Each uses *more than one connective* to help combine several clauses as part of a larger sentence. Point out each coordinator and each subordinator that is used. (Can you find the subject and the verb of each clause?)

As he talked, Mama's face grew stern, and it seemed to grow more lean.

When he came to the canyon opening, he swung once in his saddle and looked back, but the houses were swallowed in the misty light.

The blade seemed to fly open in mid-air, and with a thump the point dug into the redwood post, and the black handle quivered.

Pepé had sharp Indian cheek bones and an eagle nose, but his mouth was as sweet and shapely as a girl's mouth, and his chin was fragile and chiseled.

Your Turn: Join the sentences in each pair in *three* different ways. Use only subordinating connectives listed in the preceding section. Make sure each combination makes good sense. Write on a separate sheet of paper.

Example: The stranger snored.
              The alarm rang.
(Answers)   *The stranger snored until the alarm rang.*
              The stranger snored before the alarm rang.
              While the alarm rang, the stranger snored.

1. People listen impatiently.
   Fred complains about everything.

2. Fred brings his own lunch.
   The cafeteria serves fish.

3. Fred makes a face.
   The teacher assigns homework.

4. Fred frowns.
   His friends praise his performance.

5. Fred gives the driver long lectures.
   He rides in a car.

ACTIVITY

In which of the following examples does a subordinator join a dependent clause to the main clause? If a subordinator joins two clauses, write down the subject and the verb of each clause. (Omit modifiers.) If there is only one clause, write *No*. Write on a separate sheet of paper.

Example: The crow dropped the cheese when the wily fox asked for a song.
The crow dropped, the fox asked.

1. People in many countries have enjoyed fables since Aesop wrote them in ancient Greece.
2. Aesop was a slave before his fascinating stories won him his freedom.
3. The reader remembers a fable easily because the story has a simple point.
4. The typical reader has known these stories intimately since childhood.
5. Children are fascinated when the animals in the fables act like human beings.
6. Grapes are sour if the fox cannot reach them.
7. The busy ant refuses help because the lazy grasshopper has been idle.
8. The greedy dog loses his meat when he grabs for its reflection in the water.
9. The mouse frees the trapped lion because of its gratitude for past kindness.
10. The mouse from the country rejects fine food in the city unless she can enjoy it in peace.
11. The fables about political topics have kept their meaning until modern times.
12. When the frogs asked the gods for a king, Jupiter sent them a heron.
13. This bird ate many frogs until the survivors complained to Jupiter.
14. The frogs longed in vain for their state before the arrival of the bird.
15. People should cherish their freedom while it lasts.

THE NEWS IN BRIEF

Reporters often try to cram all the essential facts of a news event into the first sentence of their story. Readers get the whole story "in a nutshell." They can then go on and get all the details in the rest of the news story.

Look at the following examples of "lead" sentences from news stories in the New York *Daily News*. How many clauses are there that help the writer pack the sentence with information? (What connectives or relative pronouns can you find?)

FOR BRANCHING OUT

Daily News

Japan Balks At Salvaging Sunken Sub

Tokyo

The Japanese government is opposed to efforts by an Australian salvage team to refloat a Japanese World War II submarine sunk off the coast of Australia, 70 miles northwest of Darwin.

Girls Play Baseball

The national Little League Baseball organization said yesterday that because of "the changing social climate" girls will be allowed to play on Little League teams.

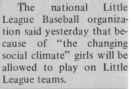

Fire Bomb Fizzles Out

An amateurish attempt to fire-bomb television station KQED failed early yesterday when the wind blew out the flame on the bomb.

Which Groups Grow the Fastest?

A report issued yesterday at City Hall disclosed that Koreans and Filipinos are the fastest-growing minority groups in San Francisco.

Wings Closed-So Jet Crashed

San Diego

The reason a carrier-based jet fighter crashed into a residential area here in March was that the pilot took off with the plane's wings folded, the Navy said Tuesday.

Write *three* similar "lead" sentences about recent news events. Use sentences with two or more clauses.

Use relative pronouns to tie dependent clauses into the main clause.

Most connectives merely hook up ready-made clauses. Words like *who, which,* and *that* provide a somewhat different kind of link. Like connectives, they can link a dependent clause to the main clause. But at the same time they produce *changes* in the dependent clause. They help us *adapt* it for use in the larger combined sentence. *Who* (with the two additional forms *whom* and *whose*), *which,* and *that* help us establish a close relationship between the parts of the larger sentence. We call these three words **relative pronouns.**

Look at the three major relative pronouns at work in the following sentences:

He was talking to a man *who was no longer listening.* (Hemingway)
The high door *that led into the bullring* was shut. (Hemingway)
The Swede moved toward the door *which opened upon the stairs.*
(Stephen Crane)

Relative pronouns do two different jobs at the same time. First, like a connective, they *relate* one clause to another. Second, like a pronoun, they *take the place of a noun* in the dependent clause. In the following pairs, look at what happens to the noun that occurs in *both* of the two separate statements:

Statement:	A band welcomed *the team.*
Added Source:	*The team* won the game.
Result:	A band welcomed the team *that* won the game.

Statement:	Fred looked for *the boy.*
Added Source:	*The boy* had borrowed his bicycle.
Result:	Fred looked for the boy *who* had borrowed his bicycle.

The kind of dependent clause that is introduced by a relative pronoun is called a **relative clause.** In the above examples, the relative clause *follows* the main clause. This happens only when the relative clause says something about the last noun in the main clause. Here, for instance, the relative clauses tell us "which team?" or "what boy?" When the relative clause tells us something about a noun *earlier* in the sentence, it has to be *inserted into* the main clause:

Statement:	*The boy* had disappeared.
Added Source:	*The boy* had borrowed my bicycle.
Result:	The boy *who had borrowed my bicycle* had disappeared.

Statement: *The directions* were wrong.
Added Source: *The directions* came with the machine.
Result: The directions *that came with the machine* were wrong.

Just as the relative clause may *relate to* one of several nouns in the main clause, so the relative pronoun may *replace* one of several different nouns in the dependent clause. The following pairs show some of the possibilities:

Statement: Bart owned *a plane.*
Added Source: *The plane* took mail to the islands.
Result: Bart owned a plane *which* took mail to the islands.

Statement: A steamer brought *mail.*
Added Source: The plane took *mail* to the islands.
Result: A steamer brought mail *which* the plane took to the islands.

Statement: Bart was going *to the islands.*
Added Source: The plane took mail *to the islands.*
Result: Bart was going to the islands, to *which* the plane took mail.

Like other dependent clauses, relative clauses are sometimes separated from the rest of the sentence by commas. These commas show that the relative clause is not part of the main point. It merely gives additional information. See Chapter Six, Mechanics, for details.

Your Turn: In each of the following groups, a possible main clause is followed by two statements giving further information about one of its nouns. *Write two different sentences for each group,* each time using the same main clause and turning one of the additional statements into a relative clause. Make sure each relative clause relates to the right noun. Write on a separate sheet of paper.

Example: The husband took the letter.
             The husband had waited impatiently.
             His wife had written the letter.
(Answer)   *The husband, who had waited impatiently, took the letter.*
             The husband took the letter that his wife had written.

1. The boys studied the rules.
   The boys were new on the team.
   The coach had written the rules on the board.

2. The girls criticized the remark.
   The girls had overheard the conversation.
   Linda had made the remark.

3. The book was about Jefferson Davis.
   The librarian had recommended the book.
   Jefferson Davis led the South during the Civil War.

4. The programs annoy my father.
   My brother watches the programs.
   My father prefers serious drama.

5. The secretary gave the man the information.
   The man had called.
   The staff had collected the information.

ACTIVITY

The words *who, which,* and *that* have various other uses besides their use as relative pronouns. In which of the following sentences are they actually used to relate one clause to another? For each sentence that has a main clause and a relative clause, *write down the whole relative clause.* If there is only one clause, write *No.* Write on a separate sheet of paper.

Example: The mother scolded the boy who had spilled the milk.
(Answer)   *who had spilled the milk.*

1. The movies that Americans see on television are sometimes very old.
2. The stars may be actors who were famous in the thirties.
3. "Adult" Westerns, which are now popular, were still unknown.
4. Romantic comedies were made for people who liked a happy ending.
5. There were no gangster movies in which justice did not triumph.
6. Which of these movies have you seen lately?
7. Today movies are made for people who have strong stomachs.
8. "Epics" that show extreme violence are often very successful.
9. Often young children see that kind of picture.
10. The ads that appear in our newspapers promise the spectator stark horror.
11. The typical movie shows a pagan empire that is overrun by savage hordes.
12. The hero is a bearded young man who has the strength of ten.
13. The people that the hero kills would fill a large theater.
14. The princess who rewards him with her love is stunningly beautiful.
15. Who can believe a word of such a story?

Use a noun clause to replace one of the nouns in the main clause.

S6d
Using Noun Clauses

Two statements may join up very loosely (like two people holding hands). But they may also merge permanently (like Siamese twins). A noun clause is special kind of dependent clause that has not just become *linked* to the main statement. It has become a part of it. It has *replaced* a part of the main clause.

In the combined sentence in each of the following sets, the noun clause is the part that fills in the "something" in the original:

Statement:	The manager said *something*.
Added Source:	The job was filled.
Result:	The manager said *that the job was filled*.

Statement:	Susan knew *something*.
Added Source:	Dr. Frankenstein was busy in the lab.
Result:	Susan knew *that Dr. Frankenstein was busy in the lab*.

A noun clause is so called because it fills a slot in the original sentence that would normally be filled by a noun. Many noun clauses start with *that*. Other noun clauses start with question words like *why, how, when,* and *where.*

The most common type of noun clause takes the place of the object after verbs like *say, tell, know, ask,* and *deny.* The noun clause then tells us *what* was said, or asked, or denied:

Noun:	Fred told *the story.*
Noun Clause:	Fred told *what he knew.*
Noun:	Mario knew *the address.*
Noun Clause:	Mario knew *where the family lived.*
Noun:	The principal asked *a question.*
Noun Clause:	The principal asked *why the door was locked.*

Notice that the word *that* has several uses. As a relative pronoun, it hooks a dependent clause *onto* a noun. As a special kind of connective, it puts a dependent clause *in the place of* a noun. Can you see this difference in each of the following pairs?

Relative Clause:	Fred knew the story *that the teacher mentioned.*
Noun Clause:	Fred knew *that the teacher had mentioned the story.*
Relative Clause:	He denied the charges *that the tenants had made.*
Noun Clause:	He denied *that he had made the charges.*

Here are some actual noun clauses in sentences written by Ernest Hemingway:

He realized *that the fire must have come the year before.*
He knew *where he was* from the position of the river.
Hopkins said very confidently *that none of them would make fun of his real girl.*

Your Turn: Fill in a noun clause in the blank space in each of the following sentences. Use some of the question words (*why, how, where, when*) as well as the special connective *that.* Write on a separate sheet of paper.

1. The police officer asked _____.
2. The astronauts reported _____.
3. The accused denied _____.
4. The sharp-eyed detective concluded _____.
5. Columbus wondered _____.
6. The bedraggled hikers heard _____.
7. The gnome explained _____.

8. The keeper announced ——————.
9. The nurse requested ——————.
10. Tina told her sister ——————.

ACTIVITY

Each of the following sentences contains a dependent clause. Which of these are *hooked onto* a noun? Mark these *R* for relative clause. Which *replace* a noun? Mark these *N* for noun clause. Write on a separate sheet of paper.

Example: The scientists knew that the attempt would be a failure.
(Answer)   *N*

1. Newspapers often headline the new discoveries that scientists have made.
2. The readers do not always know that years of hard work preceded the discovery.
3. They seldom ask when a new idea was first suggested.
4. Often the scientist who is praised in the newspapers is a member of a team.
5. Sometimes the original experiments were made by a scientist who has been forgotten.
6. The average person knows that Einstein made important discoveries.
7. The reader seldom remembers that a French woman discovered radiation.
8. Few newspaper readers remember the Danish physicist who studied the atom.
9. Do you know when vaccines were first developed?
10. Can you say how radio became possible?
11. Your library has many books about the people who created modern science.
12. Famous scientists have described how they made their discoveries.
13. Biographers have described the obstacles that scientists overcame.
14. These books show that success often comes after repeated failure.
15. Few readers would deny that books about science can be exciting.

REVIEW ACTIVITY

Each of the following sentences contains two clauses. What kind of word is used to tie the two clauses together? After the number of the sentence, write the right abbreviation: *Co* for coordinating connective; *Adv* for adverbial connective; *Sub* for subordinating connective; *Pro* for relative pronoun; *Spec* for special connective (connective used with a noun clause).

> Example: Our dog always barked when the neighbor worked in his yard.
>
> (Answer)   *Sub*

1. American cities bear names that come from many different languages.
2. English names were common where the early settlers came from Britain.
3. People in Boston know that a town in England has the same name.
4. The settlers used these names because they reminded them of home.
5. Numerous cities were called New London, and our biggest city is called New York.
6. Many people liked these familiar names, but other communities borrowed Indian words.
7. Chicago is an Indian word; however, the experts do not agree on its meaning.
8. Pontiac was a chief who fought for the liberty of his people.
9. Do you find names like Kalamazoo or Walla Walla when you study the map of your state?
10. The early settlers came from many nationalities; therefore, other languages are also represented.
11. Harlem has a Dutch name because Manhattan was settled by people from Holland.
12. Holland had occupied New York before the English conquered it in 1664.
13. Detroit has a French name, for it was part of the French colonies in America.
14. People who have lived in Louisiana remember other French names.
15. Did you realize that New Orleans is named after a French city?
16. Californians know why their place-names often come from Spanish.
17. Spanish missionaries named Los Angeles, which is "The City of the Angels."
18. San Francisco is the Spanish name of St. Francis, and San José is the Spanish name of St. Joseph.
19. Tourists encounter many similar names while they travel in California.
20. Place-names are fun to study; besides, they teach us something about American history.

CITY NAMES IN AMERICA

Several American city names appear in these photographs. What does each city name reveal about the people who settled and named the city?

Chimp Learns To Talk

Complains of Zoo Conditions

Use verbals to stretch your sentence resources.

Many of the building blocks that we use in the English sentence do double duty. The same kind of word, the same word forms or function words, often are capable of doing several different jobs in a sentence. Among the most versatile all-purpose sentence parts are the English verbals.

Verbals are forms like *writing*, *written*, and *to write*, or *eating*, *eaten*, and *to eat*. We first encounter these as *parts* of complete verbs. To make up a complete verb, they combine with auxiliaries like *be* (*am*, *was*) and *have:*

I *am writing*	we *were eating*
he *has written*	we *have eaten*
she *has been writing*	they *had been eating*
it *was written*	it *was eaten*
it *will be written*	it *had been eaten*

We can lift forms like *writing* and *eaten* out of their usual place in such combinations and put them to work in other parts of a sentence. They then give us an important added resource in building sentences. All of the italicized words in the following sentences are verbals. All are doing a variety of jobs *other* than serving as part of a complete verb.

Enterprising scientists try *to teach* chimpanzees *to talk.*
Apes usually fail *to master* the *spoken* word but can learn *written* and *printed* signals.
One chimp learned *to ask* for food by *signaling* with his hands.
Returning to his zoo, he found nobody *to talk* to.

Use participles to help build up detail in a sentence.

What is a "participle"? Participles are forms like *falling* and *fallen*, *driving* and *driven*, *bouncing* and *bounced*. They give us a way of getting "action" into a sentence in places other than in the complete verb. *Falling* and *driving* often refer to action now in progress. We call them "present" participles. *Fallen* and *driven* often refer to action completed in the past. We call them "past" participles. Do you see how the participle brings "action" into the final sentence in each of the following sets?

Statement:	Big Joe was killed by a tree.
Added Source:	The tree was *falling*.
Result:	Big Joe was killed by a *falling* tree.

WHILE ROME BURNS

Complete each of the following statements *in two ways,* using different kinds of independent and dependent clauses. Use a noun clause in at least one of your sentences. (Write on a separate sheet of paper.)

Example: The thunder rolled _____.
(Answers)   *The thunder rolled, but the rain had stopped.*
            The thunder rolled while the hikers ran for cover.

1. Nero fiddled _____.
2. Make hay _____.
3. Audiences love vampire movies _____.
4. With tears in her eyes Pauline remembered _____.
5. Little strokes fell great oaks _____.

Statement: We were filming a car.
Added Source: The car was *driven off a cliff by a stuntman.*
Result: We were filming a car *driven off a cliff by a stunt-man.*

In each final sentence, the participle is used as a modifier.

In the following sentences, notice how a participle replaces the adjective that would normally modify a noun. In the first group of sentences, only *present* participles are used:

Adjective: *Happy* children played in the garden.
Verbal: *Shouting* children played in the garden.

Adjective: The minister quieted the *noisy* mob.
Verbal: The minister quieted the *threatening* mob.

In the second group of sentences, only *past* participles are used:

Adjective: The people acclaimed their *new* leader.
Verbal: The people acclaimed their *chosen* leader.

Adjective: *Old* toys littered the attic.
Verbal: *Broken* toys littered the attic.

Present participles *all* have the *–ing* ending: *singing* birds, *barking* dogs, *galloping* horses, *roaring* lions. Past participles only *sometimes* have the *–en* or *–n* ending: *spoken* words, *known* criminals, *broken* glass, *fallen* leaves, *worn* clothes. Many other past participles end in *–d, –ed,* or *–t*: a *sealed* envelope, *bent* twigs, a *canceled* appointment, *painted* surfaces, *cooked* food. These forms with *–(e)d* or *–t* are the same that are used as complete verbs to show action in the past. In the following examples, the same word is first used as a complete verb after a subject, but then as a modifier in front of a noun.

Verb: Old Abe *cooked* the food.
Verbal: The men had gone without *cooked* food.

Verb: My friends *organized* a tour.
Verbal: My friend did not like *organized* tours.

Though participles are used as modifiers, they still have some features in common with verbs. Like verbs, they may carry an object or an adverb along with them. When a participle carries such material along with it, we call the whole combination a "participial phrase." Often such a phrase *follows* the word it modifies.

Statement: The mule collapsed.
Added Source: The mule was *carrying our supplies.*
Result: The mule *carrying our supplies* collapsed.

Statement: The crew members looked haggard.
Added Source: The crew members had been *rescued by the steamer.*
Result: The crew members *rescued by the steamer* looked haggard.

Your Turn: Combine the two sentences in each of the following pairs. *Work the information in the second sentence into the first* as a participle or participial phrase. Underline the participle or the whole phrase of which it is a part. Write on a separate sheet of paper.

Example: The sales representative opened the briefcase.
           The sales representative was talking rapidly.
(Answer)   The _rapidly talking_ sales representative opened the briefcase.

1. The receptionist flashed a quick smile.
   The receptionist was sitting behind the desk.

2. Mr. Brown welcomed us to his store.
   His store had been newly decorated.

3. Fred studied the booklet.
   The booklet was furnished by the company.

4. Marion alphabetized the cards.
   The cards were waiting for her on her desk.

5. The detective was looking for the documents.
   The documents were missing.

6. The money was kept in a safe.
   The safe was built into the wall.

7. The clerk took his time.
   The clerk was waiting on us.

8. The invitations did not mention a time.
   The invitations had been printed.

9. The man looked very young.
   The man had been chosen for the position.

10. The witness contradicted our testimony.
    The witness had been called by the defense.

ACTIVITY

In each of the following pairs, the same word is used two different ways. In one sentence, it is used as a complete verb or as *part* of a complete verb. In the other sentence, it is used as a participle that modifies a noun. Which is which? After the number of the pair, write the letter of the sentence in which a *participle is used as a modifier.*

Example: a. The defenders were *shouting* defiantly.
            b. The horsemen approached the defiantly *shouting* defenders.

(Answer)   *b*

1. a. Our ancestors *borrowed* words from the Indians.
   b. Our language contains words *borrowed* from the Indians.

2. a. The pioneers were *settling* a country with strange new plants.
   b. The pioneers *settling* the country found strange new plants.

3. a. The vegetables *eaten* by the Indians were unfamiliar to the settlers.
   b. The settlers had *eaten* different vegetables in Europe.

4. a. The Indians were *eating* squash.
   b. Americans *eating* squash call it by its Indian name.

5. a. The Indians *dried* meat for pemmican.
   b. Pemmican is made from *dried* meat.

6. a. Animals *hunted* by the Indians kept their Indian names.
    b. The Indians *hunted* strange animals like the moose.

7. a. An animal still *bearing* an Indian name is the raccoon.
    b. The raccoon is still *bearing* its original Indian name.

8. a. The skunk still carries a name *used* before the arrival of white settlers.
    b. The name of the skunk was *used* before the arrival of white settlers.

9. a. The *scurrying* chipmunk has kept its old name.
    b. The *chipmunk* is scurrying along the ground with its old name.

10. a. Many features of Indian culture are *disappearing*.
    b. Our language preserves some features of this *disappearing* culture.

11. a. The Indians *made* tepees from the skins of animals.
    b. Tepees were tents *made* from the skins of animals.

12. a. Indians *celebrating* a victory met for a powwow.
    b. The Indians were *celebrating* their victory at a powwow.

13. a. The settlers *dreaded* the Indian tomahawk.
    b. The tomahawk was the *dreaded* battle-ax of the Indian.

14. a. Some Indians *called* their money wampum.
    b. Some Indians used a kind of money *called* wampum.

15. a. Many Indian words came from tribes *living* along the Atlantic coast.
    b. The Indians using these words were *living* along the Atlantic coast.

S7b
Verbal Noun and
Infinitive

Experiment with the varied uses of verbal noun and infinitive.

Verbals have many varied uses, and we don't have special labels for them all. But two labels are worth remembering: When we use an *-ing* form to replace a noun, we call the result a **verbal noun.** When we put *to* in front of the plain form of a verb, the result is the *to* form, or **infinitive.**

Here are some typical uses of verbal nouns and infinitives in sentences from Ernest Hemingway's "Big Two-Hearted River":

He liked *to open cans.*
It was a good place *to camp.*
Hopkins spoke without *moving his lips.*
He had forgotten *to get water for the coffee.*

IN THE RING WITH EL TORO

Look at the following sentences from a bull-fighting story by Ernest Hemingway. In each, one or more participial phrases help the author pack the sentence with detail. Use each of the sentences as a *model sentence*. For each, write a sentence of your own that follows the structure of the original as closely as possible. Use participial phrases at the same points in each sentence as the original author did.

Over his head was a bull's head, *stuffed by a Madrid taxidermist*.

Zurito, *sitting on his horse, walking him toward the scene, not missing any detail*, scowled.

Manuel, *leaning against the barrera, watching the bull*, waved his hand and the gypsy ran out, *trailing his cape*.

FOR SENTENCE PRACTICE

In the following pairs, the place of a noun is taken by a verbal noun:

Noun:	*Speed* causes accidents.
Verbal Noun:	*Speeding* causes accidents.

Noun:	Carol enjoyed *the hike*.
Verbal Noun:	Carol enjoyed *hiking*.

Noun:	Mike saved the family from *starvation*.
Verbal Noun:	Mike saved the family from *starving*.

In the following pairs, the place of a noun is taken by an infinitive:

Noun:	*An escape* was impossible.
Infinitive:	*To escape* was impossible.

Noun:	Her answer was *a smile*.
Infinitive:	Her answer was *to smile*.

Stop eating

Astonishing variety

Enduring Loveliness

Like other verbals, verbal nouns and infinitives often combine with other material in a verbal phrase. They then carry along with them the same kinds of material that may accompany a verb:

Verb:	Fred *was learning a language*.
Verbal Phrase:	*Learning a language* takes time.

Verb:	Uncle Jim *was digging in the garden*.
Verbal Phrase:	Uncle Jim liked *digging in the garden*.

Verb:	Gerald *talked rapidly*.
Verbal Phrase:	Gerald started *to talk rapidly*.

Infinitives have other uses besides serving as noun substitutes. We frequently use them, not to replace, but to *modify* other parts of a sentence. In the following sentences, an infinitive modifies a noun:

He looked for a place *to park*.
The time *to act* has come.
We welcomed his decision *to resign*.

In the following sentences, an infinitive modifies a verb:

Fred paused *to think*.
His opponent played *to win*.
My uncle had come *to stay*.

Your Turn: In each of the following sentences, one noun is printed in italics. *Replace this noun in two different ways.* First, substitute a verbal noun. Then substitute an infinitive. You may use either the verbal alone or a verbal phrase. Write on a separate sheet of paper.

Example: The teacher started *the lesson.*
(Answer)   *The teacher started* typing the test.
            The teacher started to write on the board.

1. The farmer began *his chores.*
2. *The task* was impossible.
3. *Success* requires talent.
4. Fred caused his friend *grief.*
5. The boat started *its run.*
6. *This practice* is not allowed.
7. His solution was *a surprise.*
8. Jim hated *exercise.*
9. Frieda had learned *a lesson.*
10. *The idea* appeals to me.

ACTIVITY

Can you find the verbal nouns and infinitives in the following sentences? Remember that not every *–ing* form is a verbal noun. (*Writing* is part of a complete verb in "He *was writing.*") Remember that not every combination starting with *to* is an infinitive. (*To* is also used as a preposition, typically followed by a noun: *to* Paris, *to* Michael, *to* my mother.)

Write down every verbal noun or infinitive. If there is other material with it, include the whole verbal phrase. Write on a separate sheet of paper. If there is no verbal noun or infinitive, write *No.*

Example: Eliminating prejudice is not easy.
(Answer)   *Eliminating prejudice*

1. People must learn to tolerate differences.
2. Laughing at newcomers is immature.
3. Mature people do not feel superior to strangers.
4. We make bitter enemies by ridiculing other nationalities.
5. To insult other people is easy.
6. Making friends is difficult.
7. Differences in speech often cause people to snigger.

8. Perhaps you are living in New England.
9. Your speech may sound strange to a Californian.
10. You may have learned to recognize Southerners by their speech.
11. Imitating such differences does not require much wit.
12. Pronouncing New Jersey New *Joisey* does not make you a great comedian.
13. Students often enjoy studying different kinds of English.
14. Trained investigators are collecting information.
15. They try to distinguish the major American dialects.
16. Dialects vary from area to area.
17. Experts can tell your home state by listening carefully to your speech.
18. To identify dialects is easier in Europe.
19. Southern French sounds completely different to a student from Paris.
20. Understanding a Bavarian is difficult for a student from Berlin.

REVIEW ACTIVITY

Each of the following sentences contains a verbal. What kind is it? After the number of the sentence, write the right abbreviation: *Part* for participle; *Vn* for verbal noun; *Inf* for infinitive. Write on a separate sheet of paper. (Do not include any forms used as parts of a complete verb.)

Example: The time to decide is now.
(Answer)   *Inf*

1. Homer was a poet singing the glory of ancient Greece.
2. His heroes had left Greece to fight Troy.
3. Their aim was to punish Paris.
4. This Trojan prince became famous by stealing Helen.
5. The Greeks took various towns without winning the war.
6. They looted the captured cities.
7. Conquering Troy was not easy.
8. The Greeks began to quarrel.
9. The Greek commander had offended the dashing Achilles.
10. The discouraged Greeks were driven back to their ships.
11. Finally Achilles allowed his men to join their comrades.
12. His best friend led the brilliantly fighting troops.
13. In the end Achilles also decided to join in the battle.
14. He fought to avenge the death of his friend.

15. He found revenge by killing his chief enemy.
16. Hector had been the pride of the mourning city.
17. Losing Hector meant the loss of the war.
18. Homer wrote to commemorate great warriors.
19. Hearing about their exploits inspired his listeners.
20. Greek boys wanted to imitate the great Achilles.

IN THE WOODS WITH OLD BEN

William Faulkner is famous as a writer who makes the fullest possible use of the resources of the English sentence. The following sentences are from his story "The Bear," in which a young boy participates in the long drawn-out hunt for the bear called Old Ben. *How many different verbals can you find in these sentences?* Select three of these sentences as model sentences. For each, write a sentence of your own that follows the structure of the original as closely as possible. Use verbals in roughly the same places and the same ways the original author did.

NOTE: A "fyce" is a kind of small hunting dog.

Sam was waiting, wrapped in a quilt on the wagon seat behind the patient and steaming mules.

He ate his breakfast, hearing the dogs under the kitchen, wakened by the smell of frying meat or perhaps by the feet overhead.

Using the compass he ranged from that point; he was teaching himself to be better than a fair woodsman without even knowing he was doing it.

Even in his arms it continued to yap frantically, surging and straining toward the fading sound of the hounds like a collection of live-wire springs.

He knelt, holding the frantic fyce with both hands, hearing the abased wailing of the two hounds drawing further and further away, until Sam came up, carrying the gun.

It continued to fill with water until it was level full and the water began to overflow and the sides of the print began to dissolve away.

FOR SENTENCE PRACTICE

FOR FURTHER
STUDY

PUZZLES FOR THE AMATEUR LINGUIST

Linguists are people who study language the way botanists study plants or the way chemists study molecules. Much of the basic structure of the English sentence would be quite familiar even to the amateur linguist. But like botanists studying a new specimen, linguists will often find something new or different in an unusual sentence. They will next try to study various different examples of it, then draw their own conclusions about "how it works." The following assignments will give you a chance to investigate some of the more unusual things about the English sentence. How good are you at drawing your own conclusions when you watch language at work?

Assignment 1: The typical written sentence has at least a subject and a predicate. In conversation, however, we use many sentences from which the subject or a part of the predicate seems to be missing. The following list provides a sampling of such incomplete sentences. In each sentence, *fill in* the parts that seem to be missing. Put the parts you have added to the sentence in parentheses.

Can you draw any general conclusions about what parts of a sentence are often omitted in conversation? Is each example different, or do some of them illustrate the same kind of thing? Explain which examples seem to belong together. State the conclusions you have drawn.

1. Chilly today.
2. A nice mess!
3. Looking for a ride?
4. The bill collector again.
5. Good for you.
6. Good job.
7. Why be sad?
8. Roof leaking?
9. A letter for you.
10. Warm enough for you?
11. Better start now.
12. My locker key!
13. Delicious meal.
14. Beautiful day today.
15. Any news yet?
16. Missed again.
17. See you tomorrow.
18. Two dollars for a hamburger!
19. Forgot something?
20. Not working today?

Assignment 2: Some verbs appear both as action verbs and as linking verbs. Can you find these by studying the following sample sentences? In which of these sentences does the verb carry an action across to the object? In which of these sentences does the verb pin a label on the subject? Mark each sentence *AV* for action verb or *LV* for linking verb. If a verb can be used either way, explain the difference in meaning.

Example: a. Jean *smelled* the rose.
               b. The food *smelled* fresh.
               c. The animal *smelled* danger.
(Answers)   *a. AV b. LV c. AV*

1. a. Jim *tasted* the food.
   b. The food *tasted* good.
   c. Jim *tasted* garlic.

2. a. His face *seemed* familiar.
   b. His action *seemed* a mistake.
   c. The insult *seemed* deliberate.

3. a. The guard *sounded* the alarm.
   b. His voice *sounded* weak.
   c. The story *sounded* true.

4. a. The water *turned* purple.
   b. The car *turned* the corner.
   c. Fred *turned* the knob.

5. a. The traveler *felt* cold.
   b. The customer *felt* the cloth.
   c. The traveler *felt* the cold.

6. a. Mr. Brown *remained* single.
   b. Mr. Brown *remained* a citizen.
   c. The patient *remained* unconscious.

7. a. His father *became* an inspector.
   b. Her dress *became* her.
   c. Your conduct *becomes* an officer.

8. a. The farmer *grew* old.
   b. The farmer *grew* potatoes.
   c. The farmer *grew* a beard.

9. a. The patient *looked* fine.
   b. Linda *looked* a fright.
   c. The trees *looked* healthy.

10. a. The prisoner *got* thin.
    b. My uncle *got* rich.
    c. The customer *got* a receipt.

Assignment 3: Occasionally you will encounter a sentence that uses only the most basic grammatical machinery and yet does not seem to fit one of the seven basic patterns. Which of the following sentences can you fit into the familiar basic patterns? Which are different, and how? How many additional patterns would you need to make room for the sentences that are different? Explain which examples seem to belong together. State the conclusions you have drawn.

1. His uncle had died penniless.
2. He left the courtroom a free man.
3. The earthquake left the inhabitants homeless.
4. The prospector returned rich.
5. The guests arose hungry.
6. Gomez finished the game a champion.
7. Chris found his uncle an invalid.
8. The gunman shot the sheriff dead.
9. The producer left Hollywood a millionaire.
10. The sheriff left office rich.
11. The petitioners returned furious.
12. The police found the house empty.
13. Our leader rejoined the group optimistic.
14. The child had begun its life deaf.
15. Her aunt had died a Catholic.

Assignment 4: In questions, we normally put the first auxiliary in front of the subject: "*Have* the guests left?" "*Where can* we park the car?" If there is no auxiliary, we put a form of *do* in front of the subject: "*Do* your friends like books?" "How *does* this machine work?"

Do these rules apply to sentences that start with *who, whom,* or *what*? Study the following sample sentences carefully. State any special rules that they seem to follow. A hint on strategy: First check off any sentences that seem to follow the familiar rules. Then try to find out what is different in the rest.

1. What did the man say?
2. What changed your mind?
3. What has Jim bought?
4. Who took my paper?
5. Whom did your sister invite?
6. What can I give her?

 7. What had the speaker forgotten?
 8. What had upset his plans?
 9. What does an ornithologist study?
10. Who washed the windows?
11. Who wrote *Moby Dick?*
12. Who could the stranger have been?
13. Who could have warned these people?
14. Whom did the party nominate?
15. What will his title be?

Assignment 5: *Do* is used as an auxiliary in questions and in negative statements with *not*. What other uses of the word *do* and its various forms (*does, did*) can you discover? Two major additional uses of the word are illustrated in the following sentences. *Describe these two uses as accurately as you can.* Again, check off those sentences first that use the word in familiar ways. Then sort out the remaining sentences into the two major categories.

 1. Where did the host go?
 2. These decorations do look attractive.
 3. The boys did their work.
 4. Do remind your mother.
 5. This solution does not seem right.
 6. The soldiers did their duty.
 7. The liquid did leave a stain!
 8. Did the caller leave a message?
 9. My brother does the dishes.
10. Fred did neglect his assignments.
11. Do the group a favor.
12. His comments did seem ill-advised.
13. The reviewer did the book justice.
14. How does this gadget work?
15. Do teenagers admire artists?

Assignment 6: Typical adjectives have four major features in common: They appear as modifiers immediately preceding a noun (a *busy* day). They appear as complements following a linking verb (The line was *busy*). They fit in after *very* or *extremely* (He was very *busy*). They have forms with –*er* and –*est*, or *more* and *most*, for use in comparisons (*busier* than usual). One special subgroup of adjectives shares only *one* of these four features. Can you find these special adjectives in the following examples? Write down all the adjectives that you can use only in one of the four different ways. Is there anything they have in common—meaning, position, form?

1. The food was *delicious*.
2. Our *chief* objection concerned the food.
3. We followed our *talkative* guide.
4. The teacher drew a *straight* line.
5. The *main* course was fish.
6. Mr. Simson was the *principal* speaker.
7. Jim had forgotten the *unfortunate* incident.
8. Fred took the *only* copy.
9. His *sole* handicap was his height.
10. Your advice has been *helpful*.

Assignment 7: Normally, nouns and adjectives are two quite distinct classes of words. Nouns serve as subjects and objects; they are often preceded by noun markers like *the, a, this, my,* or *his;* they have special plural forms, often formed by adding *–s*. Adjectives serve as *modifiers* of nouns; they fit in after *very* or *extremely;* they have special forms for use in comparisons *(brighter–brightest; more beautiful–most beautiful)*. To some extent, nevertheless, the two classes overlap. A word that is typically used as a noun sometimes seems to be used as an adjective and vice versa. Can you find examples of such "crossing over" in the following sentences? Does the word that crosses over share all the features of the other class? Study the examples carefully. Describe the overlapping between these two categories—nouns and adjectives—as accurately as you can.

1. Uncle Tim hated the rich.
2. The wealthiest are not always the most charitable.
3. The city government had been reorganized.
4. Art teaches us love for the beautiful.
5. Herbert had been a child prodigy.
6. The nurses were tending the sick.
7. Newspaper readers like the unusual.
8. Her beauty treatments had cost a fortune.
9. His parents bought a brick house.
10. Books are printed in Braille for the blind.

11. Steel doors barred our way.
12. His doors were open to the most humble.
13. Only the very strong survived.
14. Grandfather wore a gold watch.
15. The stronger helped the weaker.

Assignment 8: There are several major ways of getting away from the most simple basic sentence patterns. You have studied the *major transformations*, like those used in questions and requests. You have studied several ways of *joining clauses* in a more complicated sentence. So far, you have usually looked at these possibilities separately, one at a time. The following sample sentences typically employ *several* such possibilities in the same sentence. Explain as fully as you can how each sentence is put together.

1. Look before you leap.
2. Where there is a will, there is a way.
3. Practice what you preach.
4. There are people who lock the barn after the horse has been stolen.
5. They that touch pitch will be defiled.
6. Speak softly and carry a big stick.
7. Who shall decide when doctors disagree?
8. The old days were great because the men who lived in them had mighty qualities.
9. He knew that men who have high hopes are often disappointed.
10. If we act now we may be called rash, but if we wait we may disappoint our friends.
11. Do not call a man happy until you have seen the end of his days.
12. Do you agree that a person who has not made any enemies cannot have made any friends?
13. Call my home if I am not there when you arrive.
14. If the motorists who noticed the stalled truck had called the police, the accident could have been prevented.
15. If there are questions, Mr. Brown will answer them before he leaves.

Assignment 9: Verbals are very versatile—they can perform many different functions. Can you describe the function performed by each of the verbals in the following sentences? Are any of these verbals used in ways not described in the section on verbals that you have studied? Sort out the examples for any such new or unfamiliar uses and describe them as fully as you can.

1. Mr. Brown taught his students to think.
2. Seeing is believing.
3. The family was eager to meet his new friend.
4. To be awake is to be alive.
5. To know how to do something well is to enjoy it.
6. I am happy to hear of your progress.
7. His friends did not know when to stop.
8. These incidents are impossible to forget.
9. The sudden turn caused the load to shift.
10. The mayor had asked the council to reconsider.

CHAPTER 3

Composition: Why, What, and How

Give your writing purpose, substance, and shape.

Children often use language for their own amusement. They chatter to themselves; they recite jingles for fun. As we get older, we more and more use language for a purpose: to get a message across to someone else. We use language to *communicate*. What does it take to make communication work?

Each example of communication in action is in some ways different from every other. But the same basic requirements for effective communication apply almost every time:

(1) *Know what you are trying to do.* Once you know what *task* you are trying to accomplish, you can think about how to use the resources and the tools at your disposal. Planning a talk or a paper is like planning a camping trip. *Where* you are going has a lot to do with what equipment you will need and what route you will follow.

(2) *Organize your material in a way that your audience can understand.* When speakers or writers want to get a message across, they cannot just ramble on. When they raise a question, they take their audience along to some sort of answer. When they describe a person, they bring together the necessary details so that

the audience "gets the picture." An effective speech, or a good article in a magazine, is laid out like a well-built house. A well-built house does not require a long walk between the dining area and the kitchen. It does not have stairs that lead nowhere. It has a *ground plan* that makes sense.

(3) *Think about the reactions of your listeners or readers.* When you say something startling, they want to see the facts or figures that show you are serious. When you ask for a change in a familiar pattern of doing things, they want you to show what good it will do. When you praise or blame someone, they want to see reasons. An effective speaker and writer has learned what it takes to get people's attention and to change their minds.

WRITING FOR FUN

BARE-MINIMUM POETRY

Sometimes, we write simply to have fun. We play with words; we try out a new way of putting words together. How do you like the following short-short poems? Write several minipoems on the subjects of your own choice.

The Shortest Poem in the World

I
Why?

—Eli Siegel

The Next Shortest Poem in the World

You,
Boo!

Fleas

Adam
Had 'em.

Summer Haiku
Pool
Peopl
e plop!
Cool.

—Edwin Morgan

Take a look at what writing can do for you as a person.

Much writing serves practical purposes. Customers write letters to order merchandise. Reporters write news stories to tell what is happening in the world. People who write cookbooks tell us how to cook a Japanese dinner or how to bake homemade bread. But people also write for more *personal* reasons. They feel: "There is something I want to say!" They write to tell us what they have seen. They write to tell us what they think and feel.

Do you ever feel: "I want to tell somebody about this"? Do you ever feel: "I've got to get this off my chest"? If you do, you are ready for the kind of writing that we do because we *want* to. Here are some of the kinds of writing that we do because they can give us a personal satisfaction:

(1) *Writing to tell about yourself.* We want people to know and respect us as individuals. How many people know your name? How many people know something about how you feel and what you think? How many people know about what kind of home you come from or what part of town? If you had twenty-five words or less to tell other people one single important thing about yourself, what would you say?

Read the following student paper. What does it tell you about the person who wrote it? Could you give a "capsule portrait" of the writer? Have you, or has someone you know, had similar experiences or feelings?

Growing Up (or Just Growing)

In grade school I was behind the other kids because of my speech and reading problems. All the kids at recess would yell, "You are a dummy, you are a dummy," and so on. I thought they were right because all my grades showed it, except math. I had no self-confidence.

Through the first five years of grade school I was very clumsy. I would drop books and drop trays in the cafeteria, and trip myself when I walked. In sixth grade, I became interested in sports. The class had its annual field day, a type of track meet. Each classroom would make its own team compete against each other. The classes also had basketball teams in the winter and softball teams in the spring. I went out for all of the teams. I was not the best, but I was

not bad. The thing that I could do was run and
run fast. This shocked the other kids because
I was so clumsy. Then came a lot more name-
calling from the kids. I did not know why
they were doing this, and it hurt me. When
somebody won a race, the kids told how good
he was. When I won, they called me names. I
think that I broke the pecking order.

In the seventh grade, I did not go out for
football because my parents were afraid that I
would lose my temper when I played. I went out
for basketball and track and made the first team.
Between the seventh and eighth grades, I started
to grow. In three months, I grew seven inches.
At the start of eighth grade I began to play
football. I was much bigger than everybody; I
was six feet tall. I was faster than most of
the backs that we played against. The other
team would not run the ball towards me, so I
just ran them down. It was the first time in my
life that I was really good at something and
knew it. It was a new feeling of pride.

Your Turn: Write about something that helps show what kind of
person you are. Write about something you do, or something that
has happened to you, or some problem that you have encountered.

(2) *Writing about other people.* Much of what we read (or
see on the screen) gives us a chance to learn about other people.
We try to understand why they do what they do. We try to imagine
how they feel. A good time to learn something about other people
is when something unusual happens to them or when they have
to make an important decision. We learn something about other
people when something unusual puts them to the test.

How, in your own words, would you sum up what the author
of the following paper learned about her little brother?

Shooting Essay

When my little brother was about nine years
old he received a BB gun for Christmas and was
trembling all over with excitement in anticipa-
tion of his first kill. He kept jabbering on
about how he wanted to kill a squirrel or shoot a

bunch of sparrows. "After all, sparrows aren't
worth anything," he said.

I remember him leaving the house when my dad
finally agreed to take him out for his first
killing. When they returned, my brother and dad
went straight to the basement. My brother had an
anxiety about him, but was not excited or nervous
as when he left. This was a businesslike concen-
trated anxiety. He had no time to stop and talk
and tell me what happened. I went to the basement and saw my dad had something in a box and my
brother was standing beside him.

My brother told me he had shot a bird but
hadn't killed it, just wounded it. My dad said
it would be better just to kill it, but my
brother insisted he'd take care of it. It would
be all right. His eyes had a very hurt, yet
pleading, expression in them like when something
you've been planning to do for a long time has
just been refused by your parents.

My brother claimed at that time he'd never
shoot another thing. I think the poor bird
flopping around like a captured butterfly, peep-
ing with fear, and the blood on the wing was
just too much for him to handle at his age.

Your Turn: A. Can you pretend you are the brother or the father
described in the above paper? How do you think the one or the
other would have told the same story?

B. Describe one single scene or event that made you understand something about another person.

(3) *Writing to register a grievance.* People take pen in hand
to tell us what is *wrong.* They feel they have been mistreated, and
they complain. They see something that is unfair, and they protest.
Usually, the person who complains wants us to take some action—
to do something about what is wrong. Do you sympathize with
whoever wrote the following paragraph? How do *you* feel about
the subject?

Vandalism

Vandalism can be described as destruction or
defacing of public or private property. Vandals,

I think, are cowards, because the only time they
will deface property is when there is nobody to
stop them. The vandals think they are having fun,
but all they are doing is making their parents pay
more taxes. So if you see someone destroying
public or private property, stop them--before they
wreck your property.

Your Turn: A. Pretend you are an undercover agent for the
sheriff's office, and you have infiltrated a local gang of youthful
vandals. Prepare a report on what kind of people commit acts of
vandalism and why.

B. Write about something that has bothered *you*. Tell the
reader what you think is wrong.

(4) *Writing to express your feelings.* Writing gives us a chance
to express how we feel. We write down how we react to the things
around us. We look at something, and we tell the reader what ideas
and feelings it brings to mind. We know that the reader might
feel *differently.* What ideas and feelings come to your mind when
you think of the human hand? Are they similar to or different
from the ideas and feelings in the following student-written poem?

The Hand

The hand is the downfall of man.
This measly piece of flesh that gives
The signal of life or death,
This pointing extremity that thrusts
War, poverty, and pollution,
The instrument of hate, lust, envy, and war--
                Stop!
Lower your filthy fist!
Lower the pointer of destruction!
                Stop!
Resume your natural form, hand.
Be what you are--
The human tool of love and peace,
The extremity that shows friendship and affection,
The instrument of fortune, beauty,
And Resurrection.

Your Turn: Write a poem, or a short piece of prose, about the eye, or the ear, or the head, or the body.

(5) *Letting your imagination run free.* At times we get tired of the same humdrum routine. We imagine ourselves in a different time, in a different place. We say to ourselves: "What if . . . ?" Have you ever imagined yourself at some point in the distant future? How would your glimpse of the future be different from the scene described in the following paper?

Last Man on Earth

A lone figure emerges from a crude shelter constructed of wooden crates and broken boards. He staggers to a filthy, debris-ridden stream flowing across the barren land. After thirstily gulping the filth, he turns and is wracked by convulsive vomiting. His strength ebbs and he painfully and slowly crawls back to his hut. Once inside he pulls himself to his feet, searching for some solid sustanance. Finding a moldy crust of bread, he stuffs it between his cracked and bleeding lips, forcing himself to swallow the unpleasant food. Upon falling to the dirt floor, the exhausted man just lies in the filth. The forsaken man painfully raises himself to his feet. He tumbles heavily against the wall of his shack, causing the shabby construction to collapse about him. Stunned, he lies under the debris moaning softly. Gritting his teeth against the pain, he forces himself to his knees and crawls away from the mound. Once clear, he rolls to his back and squints through blood-shot eyes at the particle-clustered sky. After a moment he turns his head to the side, looking at the scene of destruction in the distance. Slowly he rises to his feet. He stumbles. He gasps for a moment. He rises again, first to his knees, then to his feet. With his arms outstretched

and his face uplifted to the heavens, he
cries this plea in a voice of anguish,
"Never let it happen again, God. Not
to anyone. Ever!" With this he falls
outstretched upon the barren, lifeless
ground, never to rise again. The time-
the near future. The place- Earth.

—from *Cumflaging Together*

Your Turn: Do you ever imagine yourself in an imaginary role as
Tarzan, Superwoman, or a scientist of the future? Write about an
imaginary adventure or encounter with yourself as the hero or
heroine.

Learn to write a paragraph that does one limited job.

Paragraphs are to writing what rungs are to a ladder. If paragraph breaks are placed at the right intervals, readers can feel that
they are getting somewhere and that they are going there one step
at a time. If you start a new paragraph after every second or third
sentence, your writing will get too choppy. Readers will feel that
they are asked to take too many short steps that do not really get
them anywhere. If you go on for a page or two without a paragraph break, readers will feel lost. They will grope for something
that will give them a sense of direction.

Each of the following student-written paragraphs does one
limited job. It concentrates on doing one thing well—doing enough
with it so that readers can say: "Yes, you have done what you set
out to do. You have filled in *one* major part of a larger picture."
Can you sum up in your own words what each paragraph concentrates on? In a sentence or two, try to pinpoint the limited job
that each writer set out to do.

C2
WRITING A
PARAGRAPH

On the Old Westward Trail

An old log cabin stands abandoned along the old westward trail,
inviting the curiosity of many tired hikers. The attic offers much to
those who wander up there. In the middle of the floor the boards
creak and feel as if they are falling through. Old antiques and furniture lie in boxes in the corners, worth a lot to the owner but nothing
on the market. Grey dust covers everything, giving it an eery effect.
Spiders crawl silently down their silken webs which are hanging
from the ceiling and walls. Old pictures and other interesting objects

from the late 1800s lie buried in the thick dust. Big black rats, giving off a shrill squeak, quietly run behind the boxes. The walls creak with the blowing wind and then all of a sudden it becomes silent once again.

Goalie Without a Mask

It was our big game of the season against one of the better teams in our town. We were 15–0 for the season, having a great year. We were shorthanded at the start of the game, having only six players: no line changes, no rest for anyone. We had our regular starting offensive line of three players—a center, right wing, left wing—and two defensemen, left and right, but no goalie. I had played goalie before, but only fooling around. I volunteered and they suited me up. But, since I can't see without my glasses, I couldn't wear a goalie's mask. I would have to be ultra careful and extra quick or else lose my head. I was scared, but I had to play. The game went smoothly for the first two periods with the usual 10 to 20 shots on net, roughing up with checks, some illegal hitting, and broken plays. But the game was dominated by defensive plays on both sides. I made easy saves, for most of the shots were soft. The score was 0–0 after two periods. Then the roof came down. The other team skated and skated, shot and shot; finally I couldn't stop everything. I was out of gas, and they scored 5. They came down on a 3-on-2 and their point man took this blast, like a cannon, which I never saw. It was deflected—into my net? No! My Face! I was out, seeing stars. My cheek swelled up, and I quit goalie forever. I saved a goal but almost lost my face.

Grandma Was a Lady

When Grandmother got in the car to leave early that morning, she had on white cotton gloves, a navy-blue straw sailor hat with white violets on the brim, and a navy-blue dress with small white dots in the print. The collar and cuffs were white organdy trimmed in lace. At the neckline was a purple spray of cloth violets containing a sachet. She wanted to make sure that if they found her dead on the highway because of a car wreck, they would know she was a lady.

To Be Free

It would be wonderful to be free, to decide for yourself what you are going to do. But it is kind of funny: during your life you are never really free. When you are born, you stay with your parents till you are old enough to get married, and when you're married, you're not free. You are always with your wife, and if you have children, you spend a lot of time with them. Even if you're not married and living on your own, you must have some kind of job. So you're not really free, because every day you have to get up and go to work. It is as if someone else is running your life.

The Eager Beaver

Then, in the fading light, from a shielded area at the edge of a deep pool, could be heard a muffled slapping, like the stamping of bare feet on a wet surface. As we approached, the sound became more distinct, stopped only for a second, and resumed at a more determined rate. We cut the small outboard motor and drifted closer. There, atop one of his damaged works of art, was an infuriated beaver, a natural engineer with a natural talent for stopping water. He was repairing and adding onto his home. It had been the packing and pounding of his hard flat tail on the mud packed surface that we had heard. What forced this constructor of seemingly natural bridgeworks to rebuild doggedly in this wasted area so soon after its recent desolation? All other creatures of the marshland seemed to have given up. But he continued to build, stacking his freshly cut limbs with the pride and dexterity of a brick mason.

Write a paragraph that groups related details around a major point.

C2a
Developing the
Paragraph

The difference between a skimpy paragraph and a meaty one is the difference between a casual remark and the kind of talking-to that makes a point sink in. To write a well-developed paragraph, you have to be able to *follow through*. Think of writing a paragraph as a process that goes through three major stages:

(1) *Group together related details*. For instance, in writing about a car, stick to information about *one* thing. List all the safety features. Or, collect all the data that show why the car is cheap to operate. Or, write down all the styling features that make it look different from an earlier model. The following lists collect related details for several different paragraphs about the same person:

DETAILS ABOUT LOOKS

tall for a boy his age
dark hair, combed back but fairly short and not too wavy
tends to walk with his shoulders back and chin stuck out in front
his eyes have a sort of half-twinkling, half-questioning look
likes to wear dark shirts

Composition

lets other people start the conversation
likes to hum or whistle as he walks
looks politely bored in class
likes to laugh at other people's jokes but seldom tells any himself
is friendly to newcomers but does not go out of his way to make new friends

DETAILS ABOUT INTERESTS

does not go in much for sports
plays trumpet in the band
spends hours at home playing records
hates math
is good at making posters
collects stamps

(2) *Write a topic sentence.* The **topic sentence** says what the details in a paragraph add up to. It states the conclusion that you reach by looking at several related pieces of information. It pulls the various sentences in a paragraph together by stating what they have in common. Topic sentences for the lists of details that you have just read might look like this:

TOPIC SENTENCE ABOUT LOOKS

Tom's unusual appearance makes me recognize him from a hundred yards away.

TOPIC SENTENCE ABOUT CHARACTER

Tom is friendly but not particularly outgoing or aggressive.

TOPIC SENTENCE ABOUT INTERESTS

Tom is artistic rather than the athletic or intellectual type.

Look at the related pieces of information in each of the following sets. Could you funnel the details in each set into a topic sentence that "sums up"?

SET A

—The City of Pullman, Washington, is named after George D. Pullman, the man who invented the sleeping car.
—Denver, Colorado, is named for James Denver, a soldier and administrator of the western frontier.

—Mississippi's capital of Jackson is named for the seventh President of the United States.

—Cleveland, Ohio's largest city, gets its name from Moses Cleveland, a man who invested a lot of money in the area.

—Trenton, New Jersey, gets its name from William Trent, who first laid out the town in 1714.

—Kit Carson, the adventurous scout of the western frontier, has given his name to Nevada's capital city.

TOPIC SENTENCE A: _____

_____

SET B

—In every wolf pack, there is a top-ranking male who takes on the most important decision-making responsibilities.

—He is the strongest, fastest, wisest, and most experienced wolf in the pack.

—A second-ranking male serves as a strong assistant who directs most of the routine activities of the pack.

—He keeps a close eye on the newborn pack members and leads them on the hunt.

—The top-ranking female is another key individual in the pack.

—She looks after her pups, but she also plays an active role in helping to detect and capture prey.

TOPIC SENTENCE B: _____

_____

(3) *Develop your topic sentence by filling in all relevant details.* An observation or a piece of information is **relevant** when it actually illustrates the point made in the topic sentence. If the topic sentence is about the new *look* in cars, only those features of a car are relevant that we can actually *see*. The fact that the cars use a new type of fuel pump would be *irrelevant*, since the pump is under the hood.

To get a satisfactory paragraph, you must have enough relevant detail to make your topic sentence clear and convincing. Readers must say to themselves: "Yes, there *is* something to what you said" or "There *is* some truth in what you claimed." Here is a sample of a well-developed paragraph, with the topic sentence in italics:

> *Tom is friendly but not particularly outgoing or aggressive.* He likes to listen to other people but does not say much himself. He usually

expects someone else to start the conversation. Tom has a good sense of humor, but he shows it mostly by laughing at other people's jokes. He is friendly to newcomers, but he does not go out of his way to meet them. If you want to make friends with Tom, you have to take the initiative yourself.

Here is a well-developed paragraph about safety features in cars:

> *There are many tested safety features that the average motorist is not likely to have in his car.* Did you know that passengers riding in a car are much safer if their seats face backward rather than forward? If a passenger *has* to face forward, he should wear a safety belt with shoulder straps. More solid structural steel supporting the roof would keep cars from being crushed when they turn over. This means the end of the hardtop convertible, which has a roof held up by practically nothing at all. Dashboards should be free of protruding knobs and similar lethal devices.

For beginners, it is good practice to put the topic sentence *at the beginning* of the paragraph. They thus state their main point first and then fill in the details that support it. Later they can experiment with other possible patterns. They can present their details first and then, *at the end*, draw the conclusion that the details support. (Once in a while, they may merely state the facts and let the readers draw the conclusion *for themselves*.)

ACTIVITY 1

Select one of the following topics: this year's cars; this year's fashions; this year's most drawn-out news story; this year's best (or worst) movie. For the topic you have chosen, make *two* different lists of details that seem to "go together." Write a topic sentence that sums up your details for each list.

ACTIVITY 2

Choose one of the following paragraphs as a model. Write a paragraph of your own in which you *start* the same way as the original writer and then follow up in your own way.

MODEL 1

> *Few people realize that trail bikes and snowmobiles can have a devastating effect on nature and wildlife as well as on people.* First, they all burn gas, polluting the air somewhat at least. Second, they are

THE LONG AND SHORT OF IT

To write a well-developed paragraph, we have to be able to do two things. First, we have to be able to state a point. Then, we have to be able to *follow up:* We have to be able to explain, to support, to fill in. Often a writer uses a *short* sentence to make his point. Then he uses one (or more) *longer* sentences to follow up. Look at this "one-two" effect in the following model pair of sentences by Mark Twain. Do one or more similar pairs of your own: Use the same overall pattern, but write on a subject of your own choice.

Model: *Noise proves nothing.* Often a hen who has merely laid an egg cackles as if she had laid an asteroid.

Examples: Laughter proves nothing. Often a grouch who has certainly caused misery smiles as if he had originated the funny.

Laughter proves nothing. Often a hyena who is merely looking for a meal laughs as if he had already eaten "the whole thing."

FOR LIMBERING UP

very loud and not only hurt people's ears but at times scare an animal into literally running itself to death, especially in winter, when animals are experiencing natural difficulties anyway. Trail bikes can cause gulleys and ravines just by making a trail on a steep side of a mountain. They remove the watershed protection mechanism that nature has designed.

Your Turn: Few people realize that _____

MODEL 2

The more I am exposed to studies of the environment, the more discouraged I get. It seems that everything people do damages the environment in some way. I recently learned that, by trying to protect the Sequoia National Park from fires, man has endangered the big redwood trees. Sequoia groves are a fire climax community and are kept going in part by ground fires. Man's protection of the community has halted all ground fires. Now the litter on the ground is so deep that a ground fire is impossible. A fire now would develop into a crown fire that would destroy the groves completely.

Your Turn: The more I am exposed _____

Study the basic paragraph unit in three major kinds of writing.

Regardless of the kind of writing you do, the basic features of the good paragraph stay the same: It deals with *one* key point, *one* stage in a process, *one* important step in an argument. It does justice to what it takes up. It fills in the necessary details, reasons, operations. Nevertheless, different kinds of writing require somewhat different procedures. The same basic principles are applied in somewhat different ways. In this section, you will take a look at the basic paragraph unit in three kinds of writing:

—*Narration:* writing about events, actions, incidents;

—*Description:* writing about scenes, objects, people;

—*Exposition:* presenting information, ideas, opinions.

(1) In narrative writing, a paragraph often tells about one major **incident.** In telling the story of a hike or of a hunting trip, you don't simply mention one thing after the other. The reader gets tired of a story that goes "and then . . . and then . . . and then. . . ." The successful writer tries to concentrate on *one important or interesting happening at a time.*

Here are two paragraphs focused on one incident each. What is the major point or impression that each paragraph is trying to bring out?

On the third night the sea went down a bit, although it was still blowing hard. About four o'clock an unexpected deluge came foaming through the darkness and knocked the raft right round before the steersmen realized what was happening. The sail thrashed against the bamboo cabin and threatened to tear both the cabin and itself to pieces. All hands had to go on deck to secure the cargo and haul on sheets and stays in the hope of getting the raft on her right course again, so that the sail might fill and curve forward peacefully. But the raft would not right herself. She would go stern foremost, and that was all. The only result of all our hauling and pushing and rowing was that two men nearly went overboard in a sea when the sail caught them in the dark.

—Thor Heyerdahl, *Kon-Tiki*

The dreaded moment had arrived: It was Ann's turn to present her paper to the class. Though she had worked on her paper for several days, she knew she sounded uncertain and confused. The sheets of paper seemed to rustle noisily every time she made the slightest movement. Her eyes never wandered to the other students in the room but remained fixed on what she was reading. Even so, she was so nervous that she had trouble trying to keep her place in reading. Small specks of perspiration appeared on her forehead, and she wished she were a thousand miles away. When she finally sat down, she let out a long shaky sigh of relief.

REMEMBER: Successful writers do not merely tell *what* happened. They *show how it happened*. They give enough detail so that readers can imagine they are actually watching the scene being described.

What details would you use to fill in the following skeleton outlines and turn them into well-developed paragraphs?

Weak: The driver could not back the truck out of the narrow driveway.

Better: The driver could not back the truck out of the narrow driveway. *First*, he _____ . *Then* _____ . When this did not work either, he *finally* _____ .

Weak: Despite our desperate efforts, our packs kept sliding down the icy slope.

Better: Despite our desperate efforts, our packs kept sliding down the icy slope. When they *first* started to move, we thought _____ . But we *soon* realized _____ . *At this point* we tried _____ . *When all this was in vain* _____ .

I KNOW THE FEELING

When people tell us the story of an incident or event, they often do more than just tell us what happened. They often tell us what they *felt*. How would you sum up in one word the feeling expressed in each of the following paragraphs? Write a paragraph of your own about an occasion when you strongly felt resentment, sadness, hope, or some other powerful emotion.

```
    I remember being terribly scared one night.
My friends and I were out throwing apples at
cars. It was hot out. We were hiding behind
my grandparents' fence, which runs along the
road. We hit a lot of cars. One time, two men
stopped and jumped out. They ran after us. I
took off running across my grandparents' yard.
I ran into a birdbath and knocked it down. I
```

FOR BRANCHING OUT

Composition

felt as if I had broken my knee against it. I
climbed up on my grandparents' garage roof.
The sweat was rolling down my face. My stomach
felt empty as if it was going to cramp up on
me. I tried to lie still and not make a sound.
I could see four men walking below me. I could
hear them mumbling to themselves. I lay there
for at least an hour.

     The weather today was wonderful.
It was warm outside and the sky was
clear, the sun shining. It seemed to
make the whole day feel great. So I
took a look outside my window and
noticed a Blue Jay singing just below
my window. He was sitting on a branch
and I think he was trying to call for
his mate. I could hear the sound he
was making. And the way he gave the
sound was not like an average whistle
but a short burst of sound. And the
sound was something like having a
tennis shoe on and rubbing it against
the floor, not a high sound or
dragging your feet across the floor,
but a sound like a normal walk, with a
little pressure applied forward. While
I was watching, I gave the Blue Jay a
short whistle and he seemed to have
heard my whistle cause he turned his
head and looked to both sides. But
he still kept on giving a short burst
of sound.

     I miss Daddy so much. I cried
the other night. It seems as if it just
happened yesterday. I never knew I
could bear so much pain and still live.
I'm going back in time to the moment my
brother ran in screaming "Daddy was

shot in the head". He cried and I
almost went crazy--at that very moment
it seemed as if the world was coming
to an end. All I wanted was to go back
in time and I jumped out of bed without putting on my bra and ran to the
car. All I did was scream, cry, and
pray. I prayed all the way and I felt
I was losing my mind. I finally came
to the hospital where I saw the doctor
and my first cousin (the one who was
there when he was killed). All they
did was shake their heads. I wanted
to die. I couldn't stand it. I
screamed and they tried to give me
something to put me to sleep. All I
cried was "God please bring him back,
please, please." It was too late. He's
gone and he'll never be back. The
hardest thing to do was to tell my
mother and the rest of the family I
loved so much that Daddy was gone. I
remember the hatred I felt. I was mad
at the world. All I pray now is that
we meet him some day.

Your Turn: Write a paragraph that contains plenty of *external action*. Limit it to one major incident. Use vivid detail—make sure the reader can imagine he is actually watching what happens.

(2) In descriptive writing, a paragraph often covers one major **aspect** of a larger subject. For instance, it may describe *one* major part of a mechanism, *one* outstanding factor in a person's appearance, *one* striking feature of a landscape. A description cannot take up everything all at once. It must cover one major ingredient in the total picture at a time.

Explain how the following paragraphs focus the reader's attention on one limited aspect of a larger subject:

Occasionally we would pass a village, a straggle of huts along the side of the road, surrounded by small fields of feathery cassava bushes and forlorn plantain trees with tattered leaves hanging listlessly in the sun. A band of hysterically barking curs would chase the lorry, and the pot-bellied children would stand in the ditch, white teeth gleaming, pink palms waving madly. At one such village we stopped and bought a huge bunch of bananas for sixpence and gorged ourselves on the delicately scented fruit until we felt sick.

—Gerald M. Durrell, *The Overloaded Ark*

One of the most striking things about Chief Jim was his impoverished appearance. His dark wiry hair was usually in bad need of a haircut. His broad-rimmed cowboy hat had lost its original color and shape many years ago. He usually wore a pair of patched and dirty jeans, apparently the only pair he had. With it went a rust leather shirt with tattered fringes at the bottom. His boots were badly worn and coated with dust. Only the gleaming silver and gold rings he wore on several fingers reminded the townspeople that he was one of the richest men in this part of Nevada.

In writing such a paragraph, observe a basic rule of descriptive writing: Never be content with just a general label. Never just call a mountain "majestic," or someone's dress "too loud." Use your paragraph to show *what* makes the mountain majestic. What details could you suggest to help fill in the following skeleton outlines?

Weak: Lately, my sister Eileen has started to take an interest in stylish clothes.

Better: Lately, my sister Eileen has started to take an interest in stylish clothes. The dresses she wears to school ———— ————————. Her skirts and blouses ————————. The other day she went shopping for a ————————. The accessories she wears with it ————————.

Weak: This part of the park contains some spectacular scenery.

Better: This part of the park contains some spectacular scenery. Following the main path from the campground, we see ————————. Immediately above it we notice ————————. The whole is set against a background of ————————.

Your Turn: Write a paragraph describing *a typical street* in your hometown. Use plenty of detail, but try to make all of it support one major impression. Try to bring out one typical quality.

Or, write a paragraph about something (or somebody) *very unusual* that you have observed. Concentrate on one major feature or quality. Try to make your description as real as possible for someone who is unfamiliar with what you describe.

(3) Many paragraphs first *state a general conclusion* and then give several **examples**:

Main Point:	*Many big cities have large-scale programs for urban renewal.*
First Example:	In St. Louis, a huge downtown area was razed.
Second Example:	In Detroit, modern apartments have replaced several slum areas.
Third Example:	In San Francisco, many decaying city blocks are being redeveloped.

Can you do a similar outline for each of the following paragraphs? (In the third paragraph, which sentence is the topic sentence?)

Some high school students show their immaturity by noisy behavior at football games. At one game last year, I sat behind a group of students who embarrassed everyone by their actions. Instead of joining in the school yells, they would make up their own, mostly insults. This year there seem to be two or three in every football crowd that heckle the announcers. They consider it a brilliant stroke of humor if they boo when the announcer asks for applause for a favorite player. They applaud loudly when someone is asked to move a car that was parked illegally. At one game recently, a small group of geniuses started singing—badly off key—every time the band tried to play.

Every two or three years, the toy manufacturers seem to go overboard on military toys. During the last Christmas season, every second television commercial advertised guns and tanks. For years, the country has been flooded with toy rockets, from the little ones that come with your cereal to the large economy size that cost a proud parent $19.99. This year, combat toys will be more realistic than ever, with authentic battle noises. Santa Claus is going to deliver life-sized plastic guns, with authentic recoil and the whistling sound of real bullets. If there are any small boys in your household, it will be hard to fight this trend. You might try sealing off your chimney.

The ancient Greeks had gods that seemed in some ways human. These gods were something new in the history of man. Before then, the gods and goddesses that man worshiped were as unlike him as possible. Ancient Egypt had gods that were half man and half animal. Everyone had seen pictures of the Sphinx, a huge creature the size of a Pyramid, with a lion's body and a human face. Egyptian sculptors showed other gods with the shape of a man and the beak of a bird or the shape of a woman with the head of a cat. Farther east, in the countries that are now Persia and Iraq, the gods of ancient times assumed even more weird and fantastic shapes. Monstrous shapes, such as winged lions with the heads of bulls, expressed the fears of man in these early civilizations.

This type of paragraph illustrates one of the most basic rules of good writing: *Give an example.* Never state a general point in a sentence all by itself. Always try to follow it up. Anyone can make a general statement. Only someone who knows what he is talking about can provide the necessary examples.

Unconvincing: Science teachers expect too much of their students.

Convincing: Science teachers expect too much of their students. *For example* _____. *Another example I remember is* _____. *But the most striking instance of this occurred when* _____.

Unconvincing: High school athletes are often among the top students academically.

Convincing: High school athletes are often among the top students academically. My brother Fergus, *for instance,* _____. On the same team were two of his friends who *can serve as examples* _____. *If any further examples were needed,* I could mention _____.

Your Turn: On the basis of your own observation, state a general conclusion about *typical current behavior of high school students.* For example, you may want to say something about their interest or lack of interest in schoolwork, in various kinds of school activities, or the like. You may want to say something about their attitude toward adults, toward their parents, or toward each other. Use your general statement as a topic sentence in a well-developed paragraph. Provide several detailed examples to make the statement convincing.

C2c
Comparison and Contrast

Write a paragraph that carries through a comparison or contrast.

Some paragraphs do a special job. The writer takes time out to clear up a difficult point or to distinguish clearly two things that are often confused.

(1) Many paragraphs *explain something that is new or un-familiar* by comparing it to something that the reader knows. When such a comparison is carried through in detail, we call it an **analogy.** We make use of analogy when we call electricity a "current." We know that it does not really flow through a wire in the same way water flows through a pipe. But there is enough similarity for us to use the familiar flow of water to help explain what happens when we turn on the light or the electric stove.

Explain in your own words how the following paragraph traces an analogy:

> Sometimes the whale is killed outright, but more often it either races away on the surface or dives deep, as if to ponder its distressing predicament. This one was a "sounder," and rope whirred out of a locker in the bow of our ship as the whale plunged down. Then began a battle between whale and man that can best be appreciated by those who have played a fighting fish on rod and line—except that this fish was no salmon to be measured in pounds but a beast the size of a large Coast Guard cutter. The hook is as heavy as a plowshare, and twice its size. The leader is not a thin strand of gut but twenty fathoms of three-inch nylon cord, and the line is an even stouter hemp rope. The rod is the heavy steel mast of the catcher, up which the line runs and which bends to the strain of the whale as the angler's rod does to that of the salmon. And the reel at the butt of the rod—now taking in line, now letting it run—is the watcher's winch. On this winch, our fat cheerful Scottish engineer played the whale, as in his youth he had played salmon in his native Highland rivers.
>
> —R. B. Robertson, *Of Whales and Men*

The important thing in such a paragraph is to *carry the comparison through.* If you can go through it step by step, you can be sure that your analogy really fits, that it will really explain something to your reader.

The following skeleton outline maps out a paragraph developing the analogy between a current of electricity and the flow of water. What details would you fill in at each point?

Weak: The flow of electricity is similar to the flow of water.

Better: The flow of electricity is similar to the flow of water. Where water is carried by pipes, ——————————. Just as a faucet is used to ——————————. Just as water pressure varies, so ——————————. Just as water may be used to provide energy for machines, so ——————————.

Your Turn: Write a paragraph that develops a detailed comparison to follow up one of the following topic sentences:

A camera is like the human eye.
A football game is like a battle.
————————— is like a —————————. (Fill in a pair of your own choice.)

(2) Many paragraphs develop a **contrast** between two or more things. Often the best way to describe or explain something is to show how it is *different* from something else. We explain what a jet plane is by contrasting it with a plane powered by an ordinary piston engine. We show the essential features of an independent school by contrasting it with a public school.

Show how a contrast is followed up in each of the following paragraphs:

The genuine team sports are more likely to teach someone sportsmanship than sports that are basically designed for individual competition. The football player does not play for his own glory. He can win only if the whole team wins. He wants his teammates to do as well as they can. The track star is thinking first of all of himself. He gets personal publicity. When he is a member of a school team, he may be jealous of his teammates. True sportsmanship means that a player will take a back seat to someone else if necessary.

It seems to me that the professional athlete is basically more honest in his attitude toward sports than the amateur. The professional loves sports just like the amateur, and he may have high standards of sportsmanship. But to him sports is also a business. He tries hard, and he is paid in proportion to his effort. If he is a famous baseball player, the public may even know his exact salary. The amateur has more of a problem. Often he needs some kind of support so that he can train regularly. Traveling to competitions costs money. Someone has to pay the bill. Colleges offer scholarships or find part-time jobs for their outstanding athletes. The amateur does not always know whether he is getting his expenses back or whether he is actually being paid for his services.

Your Turn: Write a paragraph modeled on one of the paragraphs in the preceding exercise. Choose one raising a point on which you have a definite opinion of your own. Use your own paragraph to state your own opinion. Make use of *contrast* to help organize the paragraph.

Learn to write paragraphs that can become steps in an argument.

An argument in the popular sense results when we merely *contradict* someone. An argument in the technical sense results when we do some of the things that are needed to *convince* someone. A well-developed paragraph may be devoted to one essential step in an argument designed to produce conviction.

(1) Often a paragraph *explains a new word* or an important idea. Such a paragraph often starts with a **definition** of the word—an attempt to sum up in a sentence or two exactly what the word means. Usually examples follow so that the reader can see what the word means *in practice*. The following paragraph follows this general scheme. Read it carefully and explain how it is put together.

> One-upmanship is the art of impressing other people. You are "one up" on someone if you have said something impressive, something that makes the other person feel inferior. At the beginning of this year, I met three new students who all knew the art of one-upmanship. One said that his brother was a lieutenant in the Marine Corps. The other told me that he had been at a school that had its own fully equipped television studio. The third had just come from an exclusive prep school in New England. To play the game, I should have thought of an answer that would put me "one up" in turn. To the first, I should have replied that my uncle is the adjutant to the Commanding General of the Corps. To the second, I should have said that our school has an electronically operated language lab. To the third, I should have said that my father is a professor at Harvard. Unfortunately, none of these things is true.

Filling in the examples is especially important when we define words like *mature* or *fair*. Some people will label something immature or unfair just because they don't like it. If we want our readers to agree with such a label, we have to explain what our standards of maturity or fairness are.

Do you see how the paragraph sketched out in the following skeleton outline would fill in the examples needed to give meaning to the idea of fairness? What examples would *you* fill in?

Weak: Being fair means giving all people their due.

Better: Being fair means giving all people their due. *For instance, ——————————. To give a somewhat different example, ——————————. The same thing is true when ——————————.*

Your Turn: Write a paragraph that defines a term for some type of behavior or for a *character trait*. Choose a word that your reader might not be familiar with, like *hypochondria* or *snobbery*. Explain the word and give several examples.

(2) Often a paragraph gives the **reasons** for a statement that the writer has just made. The writer may state a proposal and then give the arguments in its favor. Or the writer may present a personal decision and then *explain why* the decision makes sense. Such a paragraph is effective when the reasons given clearly support the point made in the topic sentence.

How, and how well, do the following paragraphs present the "reasons why"?

> A space station would be an ideal site for television and radio transmitters. The short waves used in television will not go round the curve of the earth, which is why our present stations have such a limited range and we have to use enormously expensive coaxial cables or relays if we want to send television over great distances. But a station up in space, looking down on an entire hemisphere, could broadcast its programs to half the planet at one time. Of course, programs from the earth's surface would be beamed up to the space stations and relayed from there. Two or three such stations could provide complete coverage for the whole earth.
>
> —Arthur C. Clarke, *Going into Space*

> After my freshman year in high school, I decided not to take any more part in student government. Going to meetings, and planning for them, took too much of my time. Often I did not have enough time to study. At first I thought it was great to be excused from class because of some important errand. Later I found out it was I who missed out. I also found out that participating in student government may cost a person some friends. A candidate for office runs *against* someone. If he is elected, he may make some unpopular decisions.

REMEMBER: It is not enough that the reasons you give for your position sound good to you. The reasons you give must sound good to your reader.

The following skeleton outline maps out the kind of paragraph that turns a mere "unreasonable" opinion into a "reasoned" argument. What reasons do you think might fill the blanks?

Weak: I have never joined any of the clubs in high school. I just don't like them.

Better: I have never joined any of the clubs in high school. *In the first place,* ——————. *Also,* ——————.

Furthermore, _____. From all this it must
be obvious that _____.

Your Turn: Write a paragraph presenting your attitude toward
some part of the extracurricular activities in your high school. Give
the reasons for your attitude. If possible, pick an area where you
happen to have strong feelings of approval or disapproval, prefer-
ence or dislike.

REVIEW ACTIVITY

Study the following paragraphs and answer the following
questions about each:

(1) What is the *purpose* of the paragraph? Is it designed to
tell about an incident, to explore one part of a larger picture, to
give examples for a general point, or what?

(2) What is the *structure* of the paragraph? Does it have a
topic sentence? What connecting links are used? Does it make use
of repetition?

(3) Are any of these paragraphs *different from the model paragraphs* you have studied? In what ways?

1. "Fence" was a dirty word in the American West of the last
    century, as every loyal television fan knows. The cattleman was
    king, and he needed the open range to operate. His cattle had
    to have free access to grass and water. There could be no fences
    cutting across the long dusty trails to the railroad stations from
    which the cattle would be shipped. There was trouble ahead for
    the farmer who would fence in his land to keep the longhorns
    out of his corn. He was lucky if he merely had his fences cut and
    torn down. If we can believe the television scriptwriters, many a
    sodbuster trying to fence in his land bit the dust.

2. I was always a child who touched things and I have always
    had a tremendous curiosity with regard to sensation. If I knew
    what playing a game felt like, particularly against or in the com-
    pany of experts, I was better equipped to write about the playing
    of it and the problems of the men and women who took part in
    it. And so, at one time or another, I have tried them all, football,
    baseball, boxing, riding, shooting, swimming, squash, handball,
    fencing, driving, flying, both land and sea planes, rowing,
    canoeing, skiing, riding a bicycle, ice-skating, roller-skating,
    tennis, golf, archery, basketball, running, both the hundred-yard
    dash and the mile, the high jump and shot put, badminton,

angling, deep-sea-, stream-, and surf-casting, billiards and bowl-
ing, motorboating, and wrestling, besides riding as a passenger
with the fastest men on land and water and in the air, to see
what it felt like. Most of them I dabbled in as a youngster going
through school and college; and others, like piloting a plane,
squash, fencing, and skiing, I took up after I was old enough to
know better, purely to get the feeling of what they were like.

—Paul Gallico, *Farewell to Sport*

3.   Midget racing is a wonderful way of keeping growing boys out
of trouble. It is true that most parents are not happy about the
idea at first. They think that midget racing will make a boy a
showoff. They are afraid that he will play the daredevil driver
when he later drives the family car. However, they can soon see
the benefits a boy derives from this fast-growing sport. Everyone
working with midget racing cars learns something about mechanics. Races are run according to very definite rules, and the
participants soon learn that in order to participate they must
behave responsibly. Above all, keeping the tiny racers in running
condition and attending to the rest of their equipment gives the
boys something to do.

4.   Everyone has heard the word "self-reliance." Emerson wrote
a famous essay about it. He felt that people should trust in their
own ability. They should think and act for themselves. Like many
such terms, this one had no real meaning for me until it was
demonstrated to me in real life. Last year I met a blind girl named
Gail. She was extremely slender and fragile-looking, but she
always insisted on finding her way around the school by herself.
When she sat in a room with several of us, there was sometimes
an uneasy silence, because we thought she might resent our
acting too cheerful and thoughtless in her presence. On such
occasions, she would say something casual or show us how fast
she could write in Braille. She never asked for anyone's pity.
She was truly self-reliant.

C3
WRITING A PAPER

Write a paper that takes the reader along from point to point.

Some people write the way they speak. They ramble. Once in
a while they present an interesting idea, but they don't *do it justice*.
The frustrated readers keep saying to themselves: "What is the
point?" "Where are we?" "Where are we headed?"

To take their readers along, writers have to give a definite
shape to their material. They have to plan and organize. They do

HELPING THE READER FOLLOW

FOCUS
Focus steers the reader's attention.

STRUCTURE
Structure helps the reader find the way.

TRANSITION
Transition helps the reader get from A to B.

not simply put down ideas as they come to mind. They bring in ideas where they *fit*, where the ideas will contribute their share to the piece of writing taken as a whole.

As you put a paper together, keep in mind three key qualities found in first-rate writing:

—Good writing has **focus.** It singles something out and brings it into focus the way a camera does. Effective writers do not scatter their fire. They know that, if an idea is worth stating, it is worth supporting. They may spend all their time hammering home *one* major point.

—Good writing has **structure.** In a building, each part of the structure is in its place for a reason. Like architects, effective writers put the parts of their composition where they are needed and where they will do the most good. Effective writers will present, in order, three or four good reasons for their position, so that one will reinforce the other. They will use their most interesting examples at the beginning, to arouse interest. They will save their strongest argument till the end, to clinch the point.

—Good writing provides **transitions.** It helps readers get from *A* to *B*. It provides the directional signals that tell readers "now the main question," "now the third major point," "now several more examples."

C3a
Focusing on a Subject

Deal with a limited subject, concentrating on one point at a time.

Most inexperienced writers take on more than they can handle. They try to describe the scenic wonders of America in 500 words. They try to answer in one short theme all the questions that historians have raised about the strengths and weaknesses of democracy. As a result, the beginner's writing is often too thin. Readers already know that Niagara Falls and Yosemite Park are among "the scenic wonders of the world." They will not really be interested until a paper zeroes in on *one* such scenic wonder and begins to take a *close, detailed look* at it.

To say something worthwhile, writers must bring one particular subject or issue *into focus.* Remember the following guidelines:

(1) *Limit your subject.* Narrow down a large possible topic till you arrive at something you can discuss in detail:

Very Large:	City Life in the United States
Still Large:	Urban Architecture in the Middle West
Limited:	A House of Old St. Louis

Very Large:	America—the Melting Pot
Still Large:	Italian Immigrants in New York
Limited:	An Italian Boy in a Brooklyn School
Very Large:	Our Heritage of Freedom
Still Large:	Freedom and Discipline in High School
Limited:	I Want to Dress as I Please

(2) *Unify your paper around a central idea.* The most effective short paper is one that concentrates on one major impression or on one major point. Try to formulate in one key sentence what the material in your paper adds up to. What was the main impression you carried away after looking at the Victorian mansions in an old section of town? What is the main point you are trying to make about the way a high school can reconcile "discipline" and "freedom"?

Topic:	Victorian Mansions in San Francisco
Central Idea:	The gingerbread façades of Victorian houses make us homesick for an age when buildings did not have to be coldly efficient and functional.
Topic:	Why I Prefer Baseball to Football
Central Idea:	In baseball, all depends on the player's skill; in football, much depends on sheer physical strength.
Topic:	Freedom to Dress and High School Discipline
Central Idea:	Students should be allowed to dress in a way that expresses their individuality.

(3) *Develop one point at a time.* Weak writing is often the result of too much hurry. One point carefully explained, with three or four solid examples, is worth more than three or four brilliant ideas casually tossed off and soon forgotten. After mentioning an idea, stay with it: provide examples, evidence, background, clarification.

Underdeveloped:	I had been a lonely child, and when I went to kindergarten I was afraid of the other children.
More Solid:	Being alone most of the time made me so timid that when I had to start to school I was petrified of the other children.
	—In the kindergarten I cried for my mother until I must have driven the teacher insane.
	—I made my mother stand outside the classroom and tearfully watched her through the glass portion of the door. Finally, when the teacher got my attention, Mother would leave.

LANGUAGE SERVES OUR PURPOSE

For what purpose is language
used in each of these examples?

Underdeveloped: I have a special dislike for people who do not appreciate and respect beautiful things.

More Solid: I have a special dislike for people who mistreat fine things. Nothing angers me more than people who

—ruin the engine of a car by not keeping enough oil and water in it

—break the backs, and turn down the corners of pages of books

—scratch the surface of fine wood with rings or buttons

—erect signboards along a road winding up a beautiful hill

—break into a lovely scene on the stage with some harsh and inappropriate comment

Your Turn: Each of the following topics appears in three versions: "very large," "intermediate," and "limited." After the number of the topic, arrange the letters labeling each version in the proper order going *from the broadest possible version to the one that is most clearly limited.* Be prepared to explain in class why you arranged them the way you did.

Example: a. The Secret of Business Success
          b. How to Sell a White Elephant
          c. Qualities of a Successful Salesperson

(Answer) *a, c, b*

1. a. Skydiving as a Hobby
  b. The Love of Adventure
  c. Dangerous Sports

2. a. Getting Along with People
  b. Good Manners Pay Off
  c. How I Learned to Listen to People

3. a. A Pack Trip into the Sierra
  b. The First Ten Miles Are the Hardest
  c. Vacationing in the Great Outdoors

4. a. Freedom of Speech
  b. Newscasters and Editorial Opinion
  c. Topics a Newscaster Must Not Touch

5. a. The Secret of Safe Driving
  b. Three Sure Ways to Dent Your Car
  c. Things a Motorist Should Know

Composition

6. a. A Good Athlete Is a Good Loser
   b. The Spirit of Fair Play in Sports
   c. Sports and Character

7. a. The American Heritage
   b. How to Be a "Democratic" Committee Head
   c. Democracy in Our Everyday Lives

8. a. Teachers and Schools in *David Copperfield*
   b. An Unforgettable Book
   c. The Love of Literature

9. a. The World of Entertainment
   b. How Adult Are "Adult Westerns?"
   c. Popular Television Shows

10. a. The Free Enterprise System
    b. What I Learned on the Paper Route
    c. Effective Sales Techniques

ACTIVITY 1

For each of the following topics, write down *two different central ideas* that you could concentrate on in writing a paper on the subject.

Example: New Modern Office Buildings Downtown
(Answer)   *(a) The towering new buildings of glass and steel make people feel small and insignificant. (b) The streamlined new buildings are the appropriate symbol for an industrial civilization.*

1. High School Classmates with a Foreign Language Background
2. Being the Only Child (Boy) (Girl) in a Family
3. Advertising at Christmas (Thanksgiving) (Easter)
4. How to Criticize Someone Diplomatically
5. Why Baseball Is Such a Popular Game

ACTIVITY 2

In each of the following pairs, one passage gives *superficial* treatment to several underdeveloped ideas; the other passage *develops a more limited idea in more solid fashion*. Which is which? Be prepared to show in detail the difference between the two versions.

1.   a. A student seriously interested in her high school studies finds her path blocked by serious obstacles. Her friends are often more interested in extracurricular activities than in serious learning. At home, the main source of entertainment is the television set, and few parents set an example by a serious interest in books, lectures, or plays. When one considers the need of our society for highly trained leaders, one can see that the lack of respect for learning can be very harmful to the future of our country.

b. A student seriously interested in her high school studies is often discouraged from hard work by the attitude of her peers. If she passes up parties and other get-togethers in favor of studying, she is often ridiculed and sometimes ignored at subsequent activities. Her friends admire film stars rather than scientists and scholars; they know movie scenes by heart but care little who discovered uranium. At school, conversation turns around who stirred up trouble last week and who dated the campus football hero rather than what a famous writer said in a new book.

2.   a. As a child I was lucky enough to be taught the value of money. I remember working in the tomato harvest on my uncle's farm, counting the long hours in the sun that it took me to earn a single dollar. Somehow a dollar means something different when you stand in line for it, sweaty and with an aching back, at the end of a long day in the fields. When I had my paper route in junior high school, I learned to value my share of what I took in—and to protect it against losses through papers miscounted or lost, or through customers who always promised to pay the next time.

b. Today's children are ill prepared for the responsibilities they will encounter as adults. Few of them learn to accept "I should" instead of "I want." Most of them learn to spend money, but few learn to earn it. Few of them learn that a promise should be a firm commitment, something they should not be able to get out of with a vague excuse. Will these future voters give their votes only to the candidate who promises something for nothing? Will they follow political leaders who in every difficult situation promise an easy way out? What we need is a return to more demanding schoolwork, stricter discipline, and respect for authority.

Work out a pattern of organization that fits your material.

After we have limited ourselves to a manageable subject, we start collecting the raw material. We gather facts, we collect examples, we remember a relevant incident. But even while we are

C3b
Organizing the Material

still collecting the material, we start *sorting it out*. We cannot just present it all helter-skelter to our readers, asking them to make sense of it as best they can.

Organizing a paper means arranging the material so that it will *make sense*. Examples that illustrate the same point must be put together so that the reader can see what they add up to. It must be clear what happened first, what happened later, and what was the final result. The effective writer keeps shifting things around until everything falls into place.

Employ the following methods to organize the raw material for a theme:

(1) *Sort facts and examples into major categories.* Often you can organize the material for a short theme by grouping the details under three or four major headings. Try not to set up *too many* major headings, each covering only a skimpy selection of material. Even a paper covering seven or eight major categories easily begins to sound *miscellaneous*, making the reader lose interest.

Suppose you have collected a long list of things drivers do that make them a menace on the highways:

—drive fast to show off
—signal for a left turn and then go straight ahead
—watch people walking down the street
—make pedestrians scramble to safety
—refuse to let others pass
—always take a dare
—do window-shopping from the car
—move over to the turning lane at the last minute
—boast of the car's power
—believe they can stop on a dime
  etc.

As you look over your list, you realize that some of these belong together. For instance, the window-shopper and the people-watcher seem to illustrate the same basic problem: failure to concentrate on driving the car. One way of organizing the material in this list would be to put together all the things that might be done by the same *kind of person:*

I. The Speed Devil
    —drives fast to show off
    —boasts of the car's power
    —claims ability to stop on a dime
    —always takes a dare

FOR LIMBERING UP

BE A SMASHING SUCCESS ON YOUR FIRST DATE

Americans like to buy "how-to" books teaching them how to be a success in every imaginable social situation. One "Guide to Dating" covered the following types of dates: first dates, double dates, dutch dates, meet-the-family dates, church dates, study dates, prom dates, car dates, blind dates, dinner dates, stay-at-home dates, spectator-sports dates, active-sports dates, concert dates, and museum dates. If *you* were writing a guide, how would you sort these out into *major categories?* Omit items that do not fit your scheme, and substitute items of your own choice if you wish.

Write a table of contents for your projected book. Make sure your various headings are grouped under several major categories.

II. The Big Shot
    —makes pedestrians scramble to safety
    —refuses to let others pass
    —honks horn to intimidate other drivers
    —talks big to traffic officers

III. The Looker
    —does window-shopping from the car
    —cranes neck to watch other people
    —slows to a crawl to watch other driver being tagged

IV. The Daydreamer
    —signals for a left turn and goes straight ahead
    —moves over to turning lane at the last minute

(2) *Arrange your major headings in a logical order.* Here are some of the most basic ways of moving the reader along from one logical step to the next:

Chronology: stresses the order of events *in time:* "What happened first? Then what happened? What was the exact sequence of events?"

Cause and Effect: stresses the way one thing *led* to another: "What set the chain of events in motion? What was the first result? In turn, what effects did *it* cause?"

Pro and Con: plays conflicting ideas off against each other to produce a balanced result: "What are the main arguments on the one side? What are the main arguments on the other side? What common ground, if any, is there?"

Here is how the writer of a history textbook might organize a chapter on the Great Depression. Note how the major headings prepare the reader for a chain of causes and effects:

    I. Weaknesses of the "Boom"
    II. First Danger Signals
    III. The Great Crash
    IV. Effects on the American Economy
    V. Worldwide Repercussions

Here is how a student writer might organize a paper on whether or not a school newspaper should be subject to censorship. Note how the third section reaches middle ground between the two extremes:

    I. The Case for Censorship
    II. The Case for Complete Editorial Freedom
    III. A Plea for Voluntary Self-control

(3) *Consider different strategies for presenting your material to the reader.* When there are different possible ways of handling the logical relationships in a paper, choose the order that is best for reaching the readers. Are they likely to be more familiar with one part of your topic than with another? Are they likely to react negatively to any part of your argument? Consider one of the following strategies:

Familiar to Unfamiliar: in comparing different kinds of gasoline engines, start with the kind of piston engine familiar to most readers; take the readers along from what they already know to what is new.

Simple to Difficult: in explaining a new approach to mathematics or to English grammar, always start with a *simple* example; build up to the more complicated illustrations gradually.

Safe to Controversial: in defending an unpopular point of view, show first that you agree with the majority view *up to a point;* most readers will consider a new or differ-

ent opinion if you first convince them that you
are a reasonable person.

Study the following student theme to see how the writer has
organized the material. The central idea of the paper is that Homer's
Odysseus has traits of character that make him a true epic hero.
The writer has collected various examples of the hero's behavior
and sorted them out into three major categories: courage, cunning,
and eloquence. The strategy employed is "familiar to unfamiliar":
We all expect the hero to have courage, but we do not always as-
sociate cunning with the hero (many of us expect cunning in the
villain). Perhaps what we are least used to is to have the hero be a
"talker"—a man who loves to make speeches.

The Crafty Odysseus

Central Idea:

As we follow Homer's account of the adventures
of Odysseus, we see that the hero's survival
against formidable odds is no accident. Odysseus
had several outstanding personal qualities that
made him a fit hero of Homer's epic.

First Quality:

example 1

example 2

example 3

The first quality that we expect in the epic hero
is courage. Odysseus displayed courage when he
and his men had to pass Scylla, knowing that some
of his men and maybe he himself would be devoured by the monster. He also showed his courage when he blinded the Cyclops in the Cyclops'
cave. His final test of courage came when he con-
fronted and destroyed the offending suitors who
had made themselves at home in his palace at
Ithaca during the years his travels kept him away
from his faithful wife and his son.

Second Quality:

example 1

example 2

The second major quality of Odysseus is perhaps not one we would expect in a modern hero,
but it is shared by many legendary heroes of the
past. Odysseus was famous for his craftiness, his
cunning. He used his craftiness to advantage when
he told the Cyclops that his name was "No Man."
When the Cyclops told his friends that "No Man"
was trying to kill him, they called him a fool and
refused to help. Again the wily Odysseus showed
his cunning when he told his men how to escape
from the blinded Cyclops' cave. Since the giant

felt the backs of the sheep as he let them pass out of the cave, Odysseus and his men rode to freedom clinging to the bellies of the bleating sheep.

Third Quality: The third major asset of Odysseus was a quality seldom associated with the strong, silent, modern hero: eloquence. Odysseus was always confident of his ability to talk convincingly in time of need.

example 1   He talked to the father and mother of Princess Nausicaa in such a pitiful way about his plight, explaining how they could help him, that they did

example 2   so. Also, he complimented them with such lavishness that he found favor in their eyes.

The reason that we are well aware of Odysseus' outstanding qualities is that he is proud of them and ready to prove them when challenged. When someone challenged his ability to throw the discus, he threw it so far that the crowd gazed in awe. The epic hero of Homer's time did not believe in selling himself short.

Your Turn: How good are you at tracing the organization of a piece of writing? Assume that each of the following excerpted pieces represents the high points of a short paper or article. How would you describe the structure and strategy of each piece?

A Look at the Territory

A ride out the Stevenson Expressway to the Harlem Avenue exit and then to Sixty-third Street takes about twenty minutes. If the driver watches the scenery, he realizes he is driving through the territory of the working American, the truck driver or mechanic—the "middle American." . . .

The houses are crowded closely together but neat, enclosed by wire fences to keep the intruder at bay. . . .

The residential areas reveal poor planning: one residential area has a trucking firm, a school, an apartment complex, and a trailer park. . . .

In many homes, both parents work as blue collar or semiskilled workers. Kids see their fathers come home dirty, hot, and often angry, happy to watch television and smoke a cigar. . . .

Children know that their parents are in debt and that both parents work to keep the family together. . . .

Day and Night

When my sister and I were younger, a lamp that was given to my mother by her mother somehow got broken. Mother found out later that my sister had broken the lamp, but she had already falsely accused me without taking time to think that my sister might have been at fault. My mother thought of her as good while I supposedly was bad. . . .

My sister would always volunteer to do things around the house. Every time someone dirtied a dish she would wash it. I would have to be told before I did anything. . . .

When a holiday came, my sister would always be the one to buy a present for my mother. I always spent my money on myself. . . .

My sister never wears makeup or wigs or loud clothes. . . .

My sister gets serious about every boy that she dates and always seems to get hurt. . . .

ACTIVITY 1

A. Here is a list of instructions often given to students on how to write essay answers to test questions. Assume that you are preparing a booklet on how to do well on essay examinations. Group the instructions under *no more than three or four major headings.* Write down your major headings, using Roman numerals to number them. After each heading, simply write the numbers of those of the following instructions that you think fall under that heading.

1. Find out exactly what the question asks you to do—for instance, to explain, to compare, or to summarize.
2. Don't spend a great deal of time on the first one or two questions.
3. If you are asked to list "three reasons" or "three qualities," don't give more than is asked for.
4. Use specific details and examples to support general points.
5. Save some time for rereading and revising your answers.
6. Do not pad your answers by bringing in material not related to the question.
7. Break up long answers into paragraphs.
8. Never merely skim over a test question to "get the general idea."
9. If different questions count differently in an overall point score, try to give each question no more time than it rates in the total score.

10. Outline long answers in your mind before you start writing—decide on three or four major points and the order in which you are going to cover them.
11. In writing about ideas or books, try to use direct quotations wherever possible.
12. Check the instructions to see whether you are supposed to answer "in *one* sentence" or "in one well-developed paragraph," whether you are expected to "list" reasons or to "discuss" them.

B. What would be the most *logical* order in which to present your major headings? Why?

ACTIVITY 2

In the following outline, *one* item under each major heading does not seem to fit as well as the others. After the numeral for the heading, write down the letter of the *item that does not seem to fit*.

Accident-Prone Teenage Drivers

    I. The Speed Demons
       A. The hot-rod enthusiast
       B. The sports-car fan
       C. The antique-car fancier

    II. The Boors
       A. The road hog
       B. The pedestrian hunter
       C. The people watcher
       D. The horn honker

    III. The Show-offs
       A. The fast starter
       B. The slowpoke
       C. The "hair-raising-turn" specialist

    IV. The Beginners
       A. The "on-ramp" blocker
       B. The engine staller
       C. The brake slammer
       D. The daydreamer

Provide the links that help your reader follow from point to point.

When you write a paper, you chart your course from one major point to the next. Make sure your readers can see the route you are traveling—help them follow along. Provide the map and set up the signposts that will help your readers find their way.

In writing, and especially in *revising* your papers, help your readers follow by giving them three kinds of assistance:

(1) *Provide a "program" statement early in your paper.* Especially in a short paper, do not make this statement too formal or elaborate: "In discussing this subject, I shall proceed through the three following steps. . . ." Instead, try to word your central idea or your key question in such a way that it provides the clue to how the paper is going to be put together.

What hints does each of the following give the reader about the organization of what is to come later?

Central Idea: Anyone who wants to change the structure of city government must do battle with at least three major groups, one firmly entrenched, another almost equally old, and the third a relative newcomer to the scene.

Central Idea: After weighing the arguments of both the conservationists and the highway engineers, the interested citizen must conclude that at least some parkland will have to be sacrificed for road-building purposes.

Key Question: What conclusions can we form by studying the case histories of several low-income families displaced by urban development?

(2) *Make use of the "echo" effect of words and phrases referring to the same main topic or key idea.* In a well-focused passage, we often find a network of words and phrases referring in different ways to the same major point. These help us keep our attention focused on the subject being discussed.

Here is the network of key words and phrases from a page about courtship in modern America:

. . . the traditional formal rules governing *courtship* . . . every step of *courtship* . . . the formal mores of *courtship* . . . young woman *entertaining* a young man in her home . . . "rating" *dating* . . . *true courtship* . . . prestige *dating* . . . modern *courtship practices* . . . *courting habits* of society

(3) *Use words and phrases that link one part of your paper clearly to the next.* Such **transitional phrases** spell out the connection between one group of sentences and another. They help the reader follow the sequence of events in time or the order of steps in an argument. (Note that a writer will sometimes use a whole *sentence,* or even a short paragraph, to help the reader make the transition from one major point to the next.)

Here are typical transitional phrases and the patterns of organization that they fit:

Chronology:	at first . . . then . . . after a short interval . . . years later . . . soon . . . now . . . at an early stage
Enumeration:	in the first place . . . also . . . furthermore . . . secondly . . . the third major point . . . finally . . . in conclusion
Logical Argument:	on the one hand . . . on the other hand . . . therefore . . . but . . . nevertheless . . . it is true that . . . however . . . as a result

Point out all transitional phrases in the following rough outline of an article on the industrial society of the future:

We can now draw a skeleton outline of industrial society in the year 2000. It may live in settled peace or still under the threat of war. It may be democratic or totalitarian. But life in it will have certain predictable features. . . .

First, it is plain that everyone will have at his elbow several times more mechanical energy than he has today. The greater part of the world's electrical energy will be generated from nuclear fuels. . . . Therefore, it will be possible to carry the fuel, and to generate the energy, wherever it is wanted. . . .

Second, there will be advances in biological knowledge as far-reaching as those that have been made in physics. . . . As a result, starvation will be headed off by the control of the diseases and the heredity of plants and animals. . . .

Third, the structure of our society will be profoundly changed by automation. The man who works or tends a simple machine will be extinct. One machine will do the work of ten typesetters; another will displace a hundred auto workers. . . .

In a profound sense, therefore, the choice ahead of us is this: Can we, step by step, turn the men who do our repetitive work into men with individual skills? . . .

ACTIVITY 1

In the following passage, one key idea is echoed by various words and phrases that refer basically to the same thing. After the number of each sentence, write down the word that echoes this key idea in that particular sentence.

The Song of the Universe

(1) Anyone tuning in a radio hears static in between stations. (2) The same noise may drown out a distant station altogether. (3) In the same way, the physicist training a radio telescope on space hears a steady drone.

(4) The noisiness of space was first discovered by a physicist working for the Bell Telephone Company. (5) The company had found that its radiotelephone transmission across the Atlantic was subject to interference. (6) Its investigation found several types of radio frequency disturbance. (7) One of these was space static coming from various points in our galaxy.

(8) Out of the hissing, spluttering noise of the universe a single radio frequency has been found. (9) It is the frequency of the chirping of the hydrogen atom. (10) The hydrogen atom is the source of the "song" of the universe that echoes through the vastness of space.

ACTIVITY 2

After the number of each sentence, write the transitional phrase that links it to what went before.

A Champion Remembered

Joe Louis, probably the best boxer who ever lived, had known poverty and despair. (1) In the first place, he was born on a sharecropper's cotton patch in Alabama. (2) It is true that the place had been rented as a cotton and vegetable farm. (3) The vegetables did not feed a family with seven children, however. (4) Soon his father became seriously sick. (5) But the family had no money to send him to a hospital. (6) He therefore died in a state institution.

(7) Later, a widower married Joe's mother. (8) Joe got a little more food as a result. (9) Then the family went to Detroit, where the stepfather worked in an automobile factory. (10) The Depression, however, threw him out of work. (11) As a result, the family went on relief. (12) Years later, Joe wrote a check to return the relief money to the government.

(13) Joe Louis finally became rich and famous. (14) Money brought him no peace of mind, however. (15) On the one hand, he earned more than most of the great names of American sports. (16) On the other hand, his good-natured naïveté made him spend freely on his friends and "investments." (17) He at last found himself unable to pay the huge tax share he owed the government. (18) The former champion therefore had to raise money by fighting bouts he was bound to lose. (19) In the end, he signed up as a wrestler. (20) He will always be remembered as one of the great ones nevertheless.

C3d
Beginnings and Endings

Know how to make a good first impression and how to conclude on a strong note.

A good beginning can help a paper get the attention it deserves. A good conclusion can help it make a strong impression on the reader's mind. Keep the following in mind in working out an effective beginning and ending for your theme:

(1) *A good* **title** *is honestly informative, mercifully brief, and freshly or imaginatively worded.* Some titles merely sketch out the territory:

How Successful Candidates Talk
The High Cost of Divorce

Other titles state the major point:

The Safe Car You CAN'T Buy
Beware of Diet Fads

Often the title sets the **tone**—formal or informal, humorous or bitter:

How Soft Words Sell Soap
A Pollution Solution
I Hate Subways

(2) *A good* **introduction** *puts readers in a receptive frame of mind and takes them into the heart of the subject.* An effective introduction may

—link the subject to the *reader's own problems* or interests:

The Horror of Exams

Do exams frighten you? Do you score poorly on tests just

because of your nervousness? Do you feel that on an exam you never perform at your best? . . .

—tie a specific story to a familiar *general situation:*

Game's End

Children have changed a good deal, and it is understandable that they should have. Everything else has changed right along with them. When I was a child on a California ranch. . . .

—start with a typical or outstanding *example:*

My Worst Enemy

Ever since, at the age of four, I tried to ride my tricycle up too steep a hill and almost split my skull open, I have proven to be my own worst enemy. . . .

—use a striking or revealing *quotation:*

Monseigneur

"Of his pleasures, general and particular, Monseigneur had the . . . noble idea that the world was made for him." This quotation from *Tale of Two Cities* is a good description of the philosophy of Monseigneur, the Marquis d'Evremonde. . . .

—set out to correct a common mistake or *misunderstanding:*

Survival of the Fittest

Too often the babysitter is pictured as a happy-go-lucky teenager who throws the children into bed, raids the icebox, and becomes glued to the television set almost before the parents are out of the door. To judge from my own unfortunate experiences, this picture has little to do with reality. . . .

(3) *A good* **conclusion** *leaves the reader with a strong and unified impression.* It may

—restate the key question or *central idea:*

. . . Can we afford to substitute the excitement of athletic entertainment for a concern with physical fitness for all? Can we afford the luxury of so much disdirected effort?

FOR THE MEDIA
WATCHER

WHAT'S NEW IN MAGAZINES

You cannot tell a book by its cover. Can you tell an article by its title? Look at the following titles of magazine articles. What do you think each article would be about? What kind of article do you think it would be? Would you want to read it? (Why, or why not?)

Man-endangered species?

SuperGUIDE To A
SuperCOOL Summer

A Trip To The Celluloid Archives

a guide to ethnic happenings

IN DEFENSE OF MACHO

boom times on the PSYCHIC FRONTIER

the NONHYPHENATED AMERICANS

Jobs... AT YOUR OWN RISK

THE PULITZER FLAP

DAREDEVIL SPORTS: what it takes besides bravado

Pastor for the POOR

Bonus: Write three imaginary titles for magazine articles you would like to read.

—draw a *logical conclusion* that the rest of the paper has led up to:

. . . So, in the end, it all comes to this: our friends abroad are disappointed in our leadership because they expect us to live up to our own high ideals. In the turmoil of world politics, this is not always easy to do.

—use a *key quotation* to sum up a major point or the prevailing mood:

> . . . Many of the men who contributed to the progress of modern science were at first dismissed as cranks or impractical dreamers by their neighbors. As Mark Twain once said, "The man with a new idea is a crank until the new idea succeeds."

—show how the specific point of the paper fits into a *larger picture:*

> . . . The overemphasis on test scores in our schools reflects a general tendency in American society. Americans admire "facts and figures"—ratings, averages, and statistics of all kinds. In and out of school, they will have to learn that some of the most important facts about human beings cannot be measured in statistical figures.

ACTIVITY

After the number of each of the following introductions, write down one sentence that explains how the writer *leads the reader into the subject* of the paper.

1.   Spare the Rod . . .

I was born as the first and last child of perfectly average parents. It infuriates me to hear people talk about spoiled "only child" children. I can top most only children by the fact that I am really the only young person in my family, since I do not even have any cousins. Yet I do not consider myself spoiled. . . .

2.   Conform, Conform

Volumes have been written about the tendency of the American teenager to do more or less exactly what "the others" do. I did not really experience the full force of teenage conformity until I entered high school. . . .

3.   I Want to Know Why

A famous American educator once said, "Education is the deliberate attempt to form men in terms of an ideal." What is the ideal guiding those that set up courses to be taken by the average American high school freshman or sophomore? . . .

4.   In Praise of Diligence

When he was an apprentice in his brother's printing house, Benjamin Franklin would spend a few minutes at lunch time to "despatch" a light (vegetarian) snack. The rest of his lunch period he spent studying his books—on arithmetic, or navigation. This habit is only one striking illustration of Franklin's obsession with the *useful* employment of one's time. . . .

5.   The Plight of Local Government

If you are an average future citizen, you are likely to take only a very mild interest in the affairs of local government. And yet the streets you will use driving to work, the schools that will educate your children, the policemen and firemen that will protect your property, the very water you drink—all these have to be attended to and provided by competent and responsible local authorities. . . .

C3e
Outline and Summary

Use outlines and summaries as helps in grasping and strengthening organization.

To help themselves follow and remember a lengthy argument, good readers outline and summarize it in their minds as they read. To make sure that their papers are well organized, good writers outline the major steps. Every so often, they stop to sum up for themselves what they have covered. Remember the following points when making use of *written* outlines and summaries:

(1) *A rough* **working outline,** *revised as the paper takes shape, helps a writer marshal ideas.* Few experienced writers ever write a page without first jotting down a few major ideas in a tentative order. Such outlines are not written to be rigidly *followed.* Rather, they help the writer visualize what can stay in its tentatively assigned place and what needs to be *shifted around.*

Here is a working outline for a paper on how to encourage academic excellence in the typical high school:

I. recognition of academic work
    honor roll
    honor society

II. extracurricular activities
    debating society
    drama club
    science club

III. intellectual environment
    lecture series
    paperback sale

(2) *A formal* **topic outline** *is a convenient means of showing the organization of a paper or article.* When such an outline is submitted with a long paper or research report, readers can see its overall plan at a glance. They can form an estimate of how adequately the writer has covered the subject, of how logically the material has been subdivided.

Note the use of numerals and letters to label the topics, subtopics, and sub-subtopics in the following typical outline:

Ceramics as a Hobby

CENTRAL IDEA: The person making ceramics as a hobby must learn to pay careful attention to each major step.

I. Preparing materials
  A. Preparing the clay
    1. Digging your own clay
    2. Making the clay workable
  B. Mixing the glaze

II. Shaping the clay
  A. Free-form earthenware
  B. Using the potter's wheel

III. Firing in a kiln
  A. The first firing
    1. The firing
    2. The cooling process
  B. The second firing
    1. Applying the glaze
    2. Firing for glaze effect

In writing an outline, remember to:

—Subdivide a main topic only if there are *several* examples, or steps, or categories to be listed as subtopics. If you have "A.

Honor roll," you need somethiing like "B. Honor society." If "A."
is the *only* example you give under "recognition for academic
work," do *not* list it in the outline, since you are not *subdividing*
your major point.

—Use grammatically *parallel wording* for related topics to
show that they go together. For instance, "Preparing the clay" and
"Mixing the glaze," or "Tabulation of the figures" and "Evaluation
of results."

—Make sure that each major *paragraph,* and each major *part
of a paragraph* that covers several related points, is represented
by a topic or subtopic.

(3) *A* **summary** *makes possible an instructive overall view of
an argument or a process.* Often we find it hard to grasp a logical
argument until we see its major steps together in a summary. We
find it hard to remember important information until it has been
boiled down to its essentials. Practice in summarizing both their
own work and that of others makes writers look for major points
and the way they follow each other in well-organized writing.

To prepare a summary of about one-third or one-fourth the
length of the original, you should:

—Choose *key sentences* and strip them down to the main
point they convey.

—Omit everything that is merely introduction, or casual *inci-
dental comment,* or *repetition* for clarity or emphasis.

—Reduce *examples,* illustrations, and facts and figures to the
absolute minimum, perhaps one for each major point.

Compare the two following passages in detail, to see what
exactly has been kept and what has been omitted in the summary:

ORIGINAL: The invention of the process of printing from movable
type, which occurred in Germany about the middle of
the fifteenth century, was destined to exercise a far-
reaching influence on all the vernacular languages of
Europe. Introduced into England about 1476 by William
Caxton, who had learned the art on the Continent,
printing made such rapid progress that a scant century
later it was observed that manuscript books were seldom to be met with and almost never used. Some idea

of the rapidity with which the new process swept forward may be had from the fact that in Europe the number of books printed before the year 1500 reaches the surprising figure of 35,000. The majority of these, it is true, were in Latin, whereas it is in the modern languages that the effect of the printing press was chiefly to be felt. But in England over 20,000 titles in English had appeared by 1640, ranging all the way from mere pamphlets to massive folios. The result was to bring books, which had formerly been the expensive luxury of the few, within the reach of all. More important, however, was the fact, so obvious today, that it was possible to reproduce a book in a thousand copies or a hundred thousand, every one exactly like the other. A powerful force thus existed for promoting a standard, uniform language, and the means were now available for spreading that language throughout the territory in which it was understood.

—Albert C. Baugh, *A History of the English Language*

SUMMARY: Printing from movable type, invented in Germany about 1450 and brought to England about 1476, had a far-reaching influence on all European languages. Within a hundred years, manuscript books had become rare. Though at first most printed books were in Latin, over 20,000 titles in English had appeared by 1640. Books were now within the reach of everyone and could exert a powerful standardizing influence upon language.

REVIEW ACTIVITY

Study the following passage by a *well-known professional writer*. What basic features of good writing does it illustrate? Write a one- or two-sentence answer to each of the following questions:

1. What is the writer's general subject and how has she narrowed it down?
2. Quote the sentence or part of a sentence that best sums up the writer's central idea.
3. Most of the specific examples in this passage are found in the third and fourth paragraphs. How would you label the two major categories into which these examples have been sorted out?
4. What logical order or general strategy accounts for the overall order in which the different parts follow each other?
5. Is there a key idea that is repeated in different words pointing to roughly the same thing? Select the word that best sums up this key idea, and list several *other* words that point to the same idea in other ways.
6. List half a dozen transitional expressions that provide a bridge at important points in this passage. Include the two or three words that *follow* the transitional expressions; omit the rest of the sentence.

7. What makes the title effective?
8. What makes the first sentence an effective introduction?
9. What makes the last sentence an effective conclusion?
10. When you have finished answering these questions, write a summary in which you reduce the passage to about one-fourth its original length.

PHYLLIS McGINLEY

Keeping Up with the Joneses, Jr.

Youth is a perfectly wonderful commodity and far too valuable, as Shaw has pointed out, to be wasted on the young. Yet like all human benefactions, it has its penalties, which in today's urgent society have frighteningly increased. I don't think I am merely nostalgic when I contend that being a child nowadays is a tougher proposition than it was when my generation and I compared arithmetic answers between classes or devoured bread-and-pickle sandwiches on the front porch after school. For one thing, it isn't as much fun.

On the surface this assertion may sound like gibbering nonsense. Never before in history has childhood had so much attention paid to its welfare and its amusement. It is cosseted, pampered, immunized against unhappiness as against polio or whooping cough.

Also on the surface, its pattern of traditional play seems not to have changed very much since my time—or since Tom Sawyer's or Alexander's. Little boys still scuffle on pavements with friends as truculently as if they were enemies. Little girls, curls or pigtails bobbing, still swing ropes to identical chants I remember, leaping like dervishes at the climactic command of "Salt, Vinegar, Mustard—PEPPER!" Baseballs thud into gloves too large for hands they encase. Kites fly, forts get built out of snow, summer waters divide where frolicking bodies flash through them like dolphins. But there is a difference in the way the games are played.

That nimble child with the skip rope may not be bounding merely for the pleasure of physical activity. Perhaps she practices leaps so that at ballet class on Saturday morning she can improve her *tour jeté* and be able to star in the spring show. There is a contest arranged for kite flyers, wtih cash awards donated for the winners by the chamber of commerce—so reeling a paper toy in and out of the sky is serious business. The champion builder of snowmen has his picture in the paper. That ballplayer exercises his arm apprehensively.

Will he or will he not be included in a Little League, where he and the rest of his team can own uniforms and a coach and listen to parents cheering from genuine grandstands? The swimmer vies for medals. Those vague dreams and rewards of "When I grow up" have suddenly become concrete goals, scaled to child's size. The play has turned professional. And the ordinary competitive instinct of the young is being channeled into a frenzy of keeping up with, or learning to surpass, all the little Joneses in the neighborhood.

There is nothing wrong with healthy competition. But there is, it seems to me, something both wrong and unwholesome about harassing those below their teens into too early insistence on success. A success, that is, imposed from above. In the same society which has made so much recent outcry about the perils of conformity in the adult world, a kind of terrible conformity of effort is being forced upon youth.

—from *Sixpence in Her Shoe*

For Writing Practice: Write a practice paper on one of the following topics. Write about 300 words—no more than five or six paragraphs. (Your teacher may ask you to hand in a topic outline with your finished paper.) *Narrow your topic down your own way* and give your paper a title of your own.

Competition Among Teenagers
Little League Baseball for Girls
What I Have Learned About
    Contests
Diets and Dieters
Comic Strips Popular with
    Teenagers
Troublemakers
What Parents Don't Understand
Every Teacher Is Different
Teachers Are All the Same

C4
WRITING AND
OBSERVATION

Learn to trust your own eyes.

Good writers do not have to lead exceptionally exciting lives. They do not have to be surrounded by brilliant people. Their experiences may be similar to those of people who are very ordinary. The difference is that they take in more of their experiences. Good writers are trained *observers*. They notice the shapes and colors and sounds of things. They notice the smiles and frowns and gestures that make one person different from another. When they put down in words the things they have observed in the world around them, we say: "How true to life!"

Learn to make use of your own firsthand observation. Look with your own eyes. Study and practice what it takes to make your reader say: "You are very observant" or "You have a good eye for detail" or "That is how it is!"

Pack your writing with authentic firsthand detail.

C4a
Going into Detail

When we are standing in front of a mountain, we can point to it and say: "How beautiful!" When we are standing on the rim of the Grand Canyon, we can spread our arms and say: "This is great!" But when we are writing about the experience, it is not enough to keep using words like *beautiful* and *wonderful* and *magnificent* and *picturesque*. Something will be missing: the mountain. To make the reader see what we saw (and feel what we felt), we have to bring in convincing *detail*. We have to give the reader sights to see, sounds to hear, and textures to touch and feel.

Try the following to give your writing the "authentic touch":

(1) *Distrust the general label.* The trouble with a general label like *beautiful* is that it fits so many different beautiful things. The function of detail is to show what makes *one* beautiful thing different from every other. Ask yourself: "What was actually there?"

Can you see the difference between the general picture and actual detail in both of the following pairs?

General: My room isn't very neat. My dresser is cluttered with all kinds of personal belongings—little things that mean nothing to a stranger and yet mean a lot to me. My closets are packed with all kinds of things that have accumulated over the years.

Detail: My room isn't very neat, but the clutter on my dresser is made up of parts of me—*letters, perfumes, a stray handkerchief, a picture of "The Man," a necklace, a silk scarf.* When I open one of my closets, I have to scramble back as *a stiff crinoline jumps out at me and old discarded gloves and purses tumble down from the top shelf.*

—student theme

General: Spring is the wonderful time of the year when the birds return and the trees come back to life. After the dead of winter, the wild animals in field and forest bask in the first warm rays of the sun.

Detail: I can tell spring has come back when the birds are back— *the modest little wrens, the brilliant cardinals, the cheerful robins, the quiet bluebirds, and the ostentatious blue jays. The industrious "measuring worm" methodically and patiently measures the slender new blades of grass. The chattering squirrel supplements its diminishing supply of nuts by nibbling at the soft new leaf buds of a tree.*

—student theme

(2) *Try to select details that add up.* Try to pick out the details that go together, that will help the reader see "the whole thing." Study the following passage by one of the great reporters of all time. How, in your own words, would you state the one basic point that he was trying to make? How many details can you point out that all tell the same story?

On the beach itself, high and dry, were all kinds of wrecked vehicles. There were tanks that had only just made the beach before being knocked out. There were jeeps that had burned to a dull gray. There were big derricks on caterpillar treads that didn't quite make it. There were half-tracks carrying office equipment that had been made into a shambles by a single shell hit, their interiors still holding the useless equipage of smashed typewriters, telephones, office files.

There were LCT's turned completely upside down, and lying on their backs, and how they got that way I don't know. There were boats stacked on top of each other, their sides caved in, their suspension doors knocked off.

In this shore-line museum of carnage there were abandoned rolls of barbed wire and smashed bulldozers and big stacks of thrown-away life belts and piles of shells still waiting to be moved. In the water floated empty life rafts and soldiers' packs and ration boxes, and mysterious oranges. On the beach lay snarled rolls of telephone wire and big rolls of steel matting and stacks of broken, rusting rifles.

On the beach lay, expended, sufficient man and mechanism for a small war.

—Ernie Pyle, *Brave Men*

(3) *Use words that refer accurately to specific sights, sounds, smells, and tastes.* Notice how many different accurate and specific words the writer of the following passage had at his command for various *sounds:*

> From morning until night, the recreation building resounds to the *blare* of the jukebox, the *clink* of coffee cups, the *clatter* of bowling pins, the *click* of billiard balls, the gentle *creak* of lounge chairs, and the *splash* of languid bodies in the swimming pool.
>
> —student theme

In the following passage, can you pick out a dozen words that help the writer conjure up the actual sights and sounds he encountered? For each word, can you spell out what it makes you see or hear?

> Then, suddenly, out of a mass of leaves along a great black branch, trouped a delightful procession. The first monkey was an old male, his tail crooked over his back, peering from side to side as he walked out along the branch. He was coal-black, with the tips of the fur on his back tinged with green, so that he had a speckled appearance. His chest was white, and of his little black face the area on and around his nose was white also, a large heart-shaped patch as glistening white as a snowball. The hair on his head was long and stood up straight, so that he looked not unlike a golliwog stalking disdainfully through the branches. Close on his heels came his two wives, both smaller than he, and both very timid, for they had young. The first carried a minute replica of herself slung at her breast. It was as small as a newly born kitten, and it hung under its mother's body, its long arms wrapped around her and its small hands clasping tight to the fur on her back. The other baby was older and walked cautiously behind its mother, peering fearfully down at the great drop below him, and uttering a plaintive cheeping cry.
>
> —Gerald M. Durrell, *The Overloaded Ark*

(4) *Help your reader with comparisons and analogies.* One writer compared the houses in a new part of town to "low little *boxes* with picture windows and a *dab* of wrought-iron ornament." Rachel Carson, famous for her vivid description of natural objects, used the following comparisons in *The Edge of the Sea:*

In the surge at the rim of the ledge the dark fronds of oarweeds swayed, *smooth and gleaming as leather.*

There had been sudden ominous showers in the night, with rain *like handfuls of gravel flung on the roof.*

The mud flats were strewn with the shells of that small exquisitely colored mollusk, the rose tellin, *looking like scattered petals of pink roses.*

For Reading and Writing: The following passage is by an American writer admired for his vivid account of the objects of nature. Study it carefully as a model for the effective use of authentic detail. Write down your answers on a separate sheet of paper to the questions that follow the passage, and be prepared to discuss your answers in class.

FOR LIMBERING UP

LIFE FORMS ON PLANET EARTH

How would you make someone who was born on a tree-less planet imagine what a tree looks like? How would you explain to someone living in a world without birds what birds are like? How would you show someone from a waterless planet what it feels like to live by the water? Look at the following passages about trees and birds and water by writers who "know how." In each passage, point out the details that are most likely to make a reader say: "I can see it now!" Try your hand at a passage of your own (or a brief talk) in which you make your audience see one of the following: your favorite tree; your favorite birds; an unusual setting that you know well (farmland; desert; a waterfront; a river bank; mountain country).

The solid and well-defined fir-tops, like sharp and regular spearheads, black against the sky, gave a peculiar, dark, and sombre look to the forest. The spruce-tops have a similar but more ragged outline—their shafts also merely feathered below. The firs were somewhat oftener regular and dense pyramids. I was struck by this universal spiring upward of the forest evergreens. The tendency is to slender, spiring tops, while they are narrower below. Not only the spruce and fir, but even the arbor-vitae and white-pine, unlike the soft, spreading, second-growth, of which I saw none; all spire upwards, lifting a dense spearhead of cones to the light and air, at any rate, while their branches straggle after as they may.

—Henry Thoreau

Crossing the Delaware, I noticed unusual numbers of swallows in flight, circling, darting, graceful beyond description, close to the water. Thick, around the bows of the ferryboat as she lay tied in her slip, they flew; and as we went out I watch'd beyond the pier-heads, and across the broad stream, their swift-winding loop-ribands of motion, down close to it, cutting and intersecting.

—Walt Whitman

Now I hear the sea sounds about me; the night high tide is rising, swirling with a confused rush of waters against the rocks below my study window. Fog has come into the bay from the open sea, and it lies over water and over the land's edge, seeping back into the spruces and stealing softly among the juniper and bayberry. The restive waters, the cold wet breath of the fog, are of a world in which man is an uneasy trespasser; he punctuates the night with the complaining groan and grunt of a foghorn, sensing the power and menace of the sea.

—Rachel Carson

ALAN DEVOE   PROSE MODEL 1

The Kitten

A kitten is not a pretty thing at birth. For many days it is a wriggling mite of lumpy flesh and sinew, blind and unaware, making soft sucking noises with its wet, toothless mouth, and smelling of milk. Daily, hourly, the rough tongue of the tabby ministers to it in its helplessness, glossing the baby-fur with viscid spittle, licking away the uncontrolled dung, cleaning away the crumbly pellet of dried blood from its pointed ears. By that tenth or fourteenth day when its eyes wholly unseal, blue and weak in their newness, the infant cat is clean to immaculateness, and an inalienable fastidiousness is deep-lodged in its spirit.

It is now—when the kitten makes its first rushes and sallies from its birthplace, and, with extraordinary gymnastics of its chubby body, encounters chair-legs and human feet and other curious phenomena— that it elicits from man those particular expressions of gurgling delight which we reserve for very tiny fluffy creatures who act very comically. But the infant cat has no coy intent to be amusing. If he is comic, it is only because of the incongruity of so demure a look and so wild a heart. For in that furry head of his, grim and ancient urges are already dictating.

Hardly larger than a powder-puff, he crouches on the rug and watches a fleck of lint. His little blue eyes are bright, and presently his haunches tense and tremble. The tiny body shivers in an ague of excitement. He pounces, a little clumsily perhaps, and pinions the fleeting lint-fleck with his paws. In the fractional second of that lunge, the ten small needles of his claws have shot from their sheaths of flesh and muscle. It is a good game; but it is not an idle one. It is the kitten's introduction into the ancient ritual of the kill. Those queer little stiff-legged rushes and prancings are the heritage of an old death-dance, and those jerkings of his hind legs, as he rolls on his back, are the preparation for that day when—in desperate conflict with a bigger beast than himself—he will win the fight by the time-old feline technique of disembowelment. Even now, in his early infancy, he is wholly and inalienably a cat.

—from "Our Enemy, the Cat," *The American Mercury Reader*

1. In one sentence each, define or explain: *immaculate, inalienable, fastidious, elicit, incongruity, demure, ague, pinion, fractional, feline.*
2. List *ten* different specific words that the author uses to describe different movements of the cat.
3. List *three* striking details that a superficial observer might have missed.
4. List *three* comparisons or analogies that the author uses to help his readers visualize what he describes.
5. Using your own words, sum up in one sentence the central idea or unifying overall impression that this passage conveys.

Your Turn: Most papers about dogs describe a friendly affectionate dog, yipping enthusiastically while his youthful owner roams the fields or streets. Usually, it is hard to tell one of these creatures from another. Describe a *real* dog the way Alan Devoe described a real kitten. (300 to 400 words)

ACTIVITY 1

How many specific words do you know to describe different *sounds?* Choose a situation that gives a listener a chance to sort out many different noises—for instance, lunchtime in the cafeteria, a symphony orchestra tuning up, feeding time in a bird sanctuary, animal noises on a farm. Write a paragraph in which you show your ability to use accurate and specific words for different sounds.

ACTIVITY 2

Write about a place where many different details seem to tell "the same story." You might write about an automobile graveyard, a used-car lot, a city district that is going downhill, a train station, or the like. Concentrate on details that go *together*. Make sure your reader will not be able to say at the end: "What is the point?"

ACTIVITY 3

Does your home community still have a typical nineteenth-century American courthouse, city hall, railroad station, or state capitol? One writer described the typical county courthouse as a "commanding, almost invariably square symmetrical structure with cupolas on its four corners, columns by its four entrances, and some sort of center tower on top. . . . The one in Hillsboro, about halfway between Dallas and Austin, built of golden stone, with elaborate Corinthian columns starting at the second story, is a gem of its kind. . . . Courthouses are ideal buildings for the lazy sightseer. If you've seen one side, you've seen all four sides, though you might miss the inevitable Civil War monument unless you drive around the square."

Relying on firsthand observations, describe a major public building that has a distinctive style. (300 to 400 words)

Make your writing come to life by vivid accounts of actions and events.

Some people complain that nothing ever happens to them. But alert observers are aware of the little dramas that go on every day. They see the signs of effort or tension or suspense. They see the people around them act out their resentments, and triumphs, and frustrations. They have a sense of the *dramatic*—of whatever brings on hope, fear, disappointment, suspense, or surprise. Try your hand at writing about the little dramas of every day. Then you will be ready to do justice to the big exciting events if and when they happen.

When you are trying to give your writing a dramatic touch, remember the following guidelines:

(1) *Use circumstantial detail to make your story seem real.* Fill in the authentic touches that make your readers feel they are eyewitnesses to the scene. In the following passage, note how a new cage for a captured animal is described in such concrete detail that readers can see the cage taking shape in front of them:

> The next day the carriers returned from Mamfe, staggering under the weight of a huge petrol drum. This had to *be cut in half, lengthways, all the rust scraped out,* and *any trace of petrol removed by boiling water in it for twenty-four hours.* Then the shrew was removed from his cage while *a sliding door was fitted in the bottom.* The *whole cage was then placed on top of one half of the drum;* thus, by opening and closing the sliding door, I could let the shrew in and out of his private bathing pool.
>
> —Gerald M. Durrell, *The Overloaded Ark*

(2) *Use words that graphically project action, movement, effort, struggle, or conflict.* Newspaper editors tell their reporters to use words that make the story *go.* Words like *walk, fall,* and *laugh* are routine; words like *stagger, hurtle,* and *guffaw* are more dramatic. Notice in the following passage all the words and details used to make an account of everyday events more dramatic:

Dull: Last night a boy spilled a cup of punch on me and ruined my beautiful new organdy dress.

Dramatic: The punch cup *skidded* across the saucer and *splashed* into my lap, *patterning* my lovely blue organdy dress with pink.

Dull: Finally, when I had almost given up, a boy came across the room and asked me to dance.

Dramatic: He *bowed* before me. My moment had come! I *fluttered my eyelashes* experimentally and rose in what I considered my most feminine and gracious manner. "I'd love to!" I *cooed*.

Dull: She spent all afternoon sitting in a rocking chair and talking about the days when she was a young girl.

Dramatic: Sitting erect in her rocking chair that *moved unhurriedly back and forth like the pendulum of a clock,* she talked of her long-gone family and the gay days of her girlhood spent in that very room and at that very piano.

(3) *Use dialogue and gestures to mirror feelings.* Make your characters *act out* their reactions the way the participants do in the following scene:

A teacher I had long ago, Mrs. Lynde, was a stooped little woman who wore glasses and always tiptoed round the room hunting for trouble. One day she was gliding about from desk to desk grading workbooks. I watched her for a time, but after a while, I glanced around the room and she was nowhere to be seen. Supposing she had quit grading books and stepped into the hall, I arose and in a voice loud enough for all those about me to hear, said "Where's Granny?" Just as I uttered the words I turned my head and saw her standing at my right ready to grade my workbook. My face turned crimson and great drops of perspiration stood upon my forehead, but she only smiled down over me and said, "Is it too warm in the room for you, my dear?"

(4) *Make your story add up.* Do not give your readers a chance to ask: "What is the point?" Do not let your story ramble on forever, each new installment starting with "and then. . . ."

Focus your story to bring out a major point or to leave your readers with a unifying overall impression. For instance, a hunting story may focus on:

—effort and suspense, leading to success or disappointment;
—fear, and the triumph over fear;
—the thrill, but at the same time the vague sense of guilt, after the kill.

FOR THE MEDIA
WATCHER

SPORTSWRITER FOR A DAY

A good sportswriter must know how to convey dramatic action. What could a future sportswriter learn about dramatic detail from the following passage?

An inning begins; the pitcher takes his warm-up tosses, now as in the days half a century ago, and after three, four, or five of these he steps aside and the catcher whips the ball down to second base. The second baseman tosses it to the shortstop, two yards away, and the shortstop throws it to the third baseman, who is standing halfway between his own base and the pitcher's box; the third baseman, in turn, tosses it over to the pitcher, and the inning can get started. To vary from this formula is unthinkable; from the little leaguers up to Yankee Stadium, it is as one with the laws of the Medes and the Persians.

Then action: players shifting about, pounding their gloves, uttering cries of encouragement (which, like all the rest, are verbatim out of the script of 1900); and the batter approaches the plate, swinging two bats (another ironclad requirement), tossing one aside, planting his feet in the batter's box, and then swinging his single bat in determined menace. The fielders slowly freeze into fixed positions; for a moment no one anywhere moves, except that the pitcher goes into his stretch, takes a last look around, and then delivers—and then the frozen pattern breaks, the ball streaks off, men move deftly from here to there, and the quick moments of action are on.

—Bruce Catton, "The Great American Game," *American Heritage*

Your Turn: What was the most exciting game or other *sports event* that you have witnessed? Write an account of it, using enough realistic detail so that readers can imagine they are among the spectators. Make your account dramatic enough for readers to share in the excitement. (300 to 400 words)

For Reading and Writing: Study the following action-packed account by a master storyteller. How does the author make his account of action and events vivid and unforgettable? Write down your answers to the questions that follow the passage, and be prepared to discuss your answers in class.

JACK LONDON   PROSE MODEL 2

The Dominion of Man

Four men gingerly carried the crate from the wagon into a small, high-walled back yard. A stout man, with a red sweater that sagged generously at the neck, came out and signed the book for the driver. That was the man, Buck divined, the next tormentor, and he hurled himself savagely against the bars. The man smiled grimly, and brought a hatchet and a club.

"You ain't going to take him out now?" the driver asked.

"Sure," the man replied, driving the hatchet into the crate for a pry.

There was an instantaneous scattering of the four men who had carried it in, and from safe perches on top of the wall they prepared to watch the performance.

Buck rushed at the splintering wood, sinking his teeth into it, surging and wrestling with it. Wherever the hatchet fell on the outside, he was there on the inside, snarling and growling, as furiously anxious to get out as the man in the red sweater was calmly intent on getting him out.

"Now, you red-eyed devil," he said, when he had made an opening sufficient for the passage of Buck's body. At the same time he dropped the hatchet and shifted the club to his right hand.

And Buck was truly a red-eyed devil, as he drew himself together for the spring, hair bristling, mouth foaming, a mad glitter in his bloodshot eyes. Straight at the man he launched his one hundred and forty pounds of fury, surcharged with the pent passion of two days and nights. In midair, just as his jaws were about to close on the man, he received a shock that checked his body and brought his teeth together with an agonizing clip. He whirled over, fetching the ground on his back and side. He had never been struck by a club in his life, and did not understand. With a snarl that was part bark and more scream he was again on his feet and launched into the air. And again the shock came and he was brought crushingly to the ground. This time he was aware that it was the club, but his madness knew no caution. A dozen times he charged, and as often the club broke the charge and smashed him down.

After a particularly fierce blow, he crawled to his feet, too dazed to rush. He staggered limply about, the blood flowing from nose and mouth and ears, his beautiful coat sprayed and flecked with bloody slaver. Then the man advanced and deliberately dealt him a frightful blow on the nose. All the pain he had endured was as nothing compared with the exquisite agony of this. With a roar that was almost lionlike in its ferocity, he again hurled himself at the man. But the man, shifting the club from right to left, coolly caught him by the under jaw, at the same time wrenching downward and backward. Buck described a complete circle in the air, and half of another, then crashed to the ground on his head and chest.

For the last time he rushed. The man struck the shrewd blow he had purposely withheld for so long, and Buck crumpled up and went down, knocked utterly senseless.

"He's no slouch at dog-breakin', that's wot I say," one of the men on the wall cried enthusiastically.

"Druther break cayuses any day, and twice on Sunday," was the reply of the driver, as he climbed on the wagon and started the horses.

Buck's senses came back to him, but not his strength. He lay where he had fallen, and from there he watched the man in the red sweater.

" 'Answers to the name of Buck,' " the man soliloquized, quoting from the saloonkeeper's letter, which had announced the consignment of the crate and contents. "Well, Buck, my boy," he went on in a genial voice, "we've had our little ruction, and the best thing we can do is to let it go at that. You've learned your place, and I know mine. Be a good dog and all'll go well and the goose hang high. Be a bad dog, and I'll whale the stuffin' outa you. Understand?"

As he spoke he fearlessly patted the head he had so mercilessly pounded, and though Buck's hair involuntarily bristled at touch of the hand, he endured it without protest. When the man brought him water he drank eagerly, and later bolted a generous meal of raw meat, chunk by chunk, from the man's hand.

—from *Call of the Wild*

1. In one sentence each, define or explain: *instantaneous, surcharge, pent, exquisite, ferocity, cayuse, soliloquize, consignment, genial, ruction.*
2. List *ten* specific words that project vigorous or dramatic action.
3. List *three* details that help make the reader feel like an eyewitness.
4. List *three* details that effectively mirror emotions, feelings, or reactions.
5. Using your own words, sum up in one sentence the unifying overall impression that this passage conveys.

Your Turn: Have you ever had a chance to witness a real struggle or contest—between two people, or between man and animal, or between man and nature? If you cannot think of a real-life struggle, do you remember an especially vivid struggle or contest that you have watched on the television or movie screen? Recreate the contest for your reader.

ACTIVITY 1

What was the greatest surprise you have ever had? When were you most deeply disappointed? Have you ever deeply resented something that happened to you? When were you most deeply upset? What would you say if you were asked to talk or write about the experience that brought on one or the other of these feelings? Could you help your audience relive the experience? Could you make them share the feelings you felt?

ACTIVITY 2

Billy Graham once said, "The child learns more about the law of gravity when he falls out of a tree than he does from the lips of his elders." Did you ever have an experience that taught you *something people are often told* but don't believe until they find out the hard way, on their own? Tell the story of what happened. (300 to 400 words)

ACTIVITY 3

An old Mexican proverb says, "When you keep your mouth shut, the flies cannot get in." From your experience or observation, can you tell a story that would show how true (or false) this proverb is? Have you or someone you know well ever gotten into trouble by not keeping "your mouth shut"? Or, have you ever observed how trouble can result if someone *keeps quiet* at the wrong time?

Give your writing human interest by convincing accounts of other people.

C4c
Writing About People

There are many interesting subjects to write about. But the most interesting subject to most of us is other people. We are curious about what other people say, do, and think. To satisfy this curiosity, we do everything from listening to the latest gossip to reading the kind of character study that we find in a great novel.

When we study the people described in a good novel or play, we find that the writer knows how to show us a true *individual*. In everyday life, we do not always pay attention to the *person*. We type someone as a member of a group or class: Polish, Mexican, Jewish, Catholic, Oriental. We've all heard comments like "Don't take a class from Miss Ettlinger. She is German." Or "Don't try to argue with Jack. He's Catholic." If we always put a big stamp on people that says "Catholic" or "Irish" or "black," we are not likely to get to know them as individual human beings.

Do the following when you are trying to get your readers to know someone as an individual:

(1) *Pick out the details of physical appearance that will help your readers visualize the person.* Include details that show not only how the person looks but also how the person thinks or feels. Does the person make use of sweeping gestures when talking? Do the person's fingers drum nervously on the surface of a desk or table? Does the person brush the hair out of his or her eyes with a particular absentminded motion?

Notice how the following passage is packed with details that help us *see* a person and, at the same time, make us imagine what she is like. If you were asked to sum up your impression of this person in one sentence, what kind of "capsule portrait" would you provide?

(2) *Use revealing incidents to show a person's character.* To make us see what kind of person he or she is, show us how the person *acted.* Describe the kind of situation that puts a person's character to the test. Here is how an English writer found out something about the feelings and attitudes of a friend from India:

> Once upon a time I went for a week's holiday on the Continent with an Indian friend. We both enjoyed ourselves and were sorry when the week was over, but on parting our behavior was absolutely different. *He was plunged in despair. He felt that because the holiday was over all happiness was over until the world ended. He could not express his sorrow too much.* But in me the Englishman came out strong. I reflected that we should meet again in a month or two, and could write in the interval if we had anything to say; and under these circumstances I could not see what there was to make a fuss about. It wasn't as if we were parting forever or dying. "Buck up," I said, "do buck up." *He refused to buck up, and I left him plunged in gloom.*
>
> —E. M. Forster, *Abinger Harvest*

(3) *Quote typical sayings, favorite expressions, revealing remarks.* Before your readers can feel that they "know" a person, they will want to hear the person *talk.* Notice how the use of dialogue helps us get a feeling for what someone is like—even when that someone is not at all a talkative person:

> Poppa, a good quiet man, spent the last hours before our parting moving aimlessly about the yard, keeping to himself and avoiding me. A sigh now and then belied his outer calm. Several times I wanted to

GUESS WHO?

Write a "Guess Who" paragraph about a public figure much in the news, or about an entertainer (television or movie star, or musician) popular with people in your age group. Describe the person's appearance, typical behavior, gestures, or ways of talking. *Leave out* any obvious clues like name, address, or the like. Read your paragraph to the class and have them guess the person you had in mind.

Grandma Moses loves to receive visitors. When standing on her feet she is stooped—she is arthritic and has a curvature of the spine—but sitting down *she is straight and diminutively regal*, all ninety-five pounds (at a guess) of her. Her *white hair is carefully arranged*, and she wears a black ribbon around her neck, a pink sweater and a pinker print dress, brown cotton stockings and black low-heeled shoes. She smooths her hair now and then; *her fingers are gnarled and arthritic but her grip is secure; she shakes hands firmly and her hands have not the least tremor.* One speaks to her in a normal voice and she does not have to cup her ear.

—Harold C. Schonberg, "Grandma Moses," *New York Times Magazine*

say that I was sorry to be going, and that I would miss him very much. But the silence that had always lain between us prevented this. Now I realized that probably he hadn't spoken more than a few thousand words to me during my entire childhood. It was always: "Mornin', boy"; "Git your chores done, boy"; "Goodnight, boy." If I asked for a dime or nickel, he would look beyond me for a moment, grunt, then dig through the nuts and bolts in his blue jeans and hand me the money. I loved him in spite of his silence.

For his own reasons, Poppa didn't go to the depot, but as my sister and I were leaving, he came up, a cob pipe *jutting* from his mouth, and stood sideways, looking over the misty Kansas countryside. I stood *awkwardly* waiting for him to say something. He just grunted—three short grunts. "Well," Maggie Lee said nervously, "won't you be kissin' your Poppa goodbye?" I picked up my cardboard suitcase, turned and kissed his stubby cheek and started climbing into the taxicab. I was halfway in when his hand touched my shoulder. "Boy, remember your momma's teachin' . . . You'll be all right. Just you remember her teachin'. . . ." I promised, then sat back in the Model T taxi. As we rounded the corner, Poppa was already headed for the hog pens. It was feeding time.

—Gordon Parks, *A Choice of Weapons*

What would you put in a one-sentence "capsule portrait" of this author's father?

For Reading and Writing: In *A Walker in the City*, Alfred Kazin writes about his childhood. Study the following passage from the book. Can you sum up in one sentence what his mother came to mean to him during his period of growing up? Can you point to one or two details that best symbolize what he is trying to say about his mother? Read the passage, and answer the questions that follow it.

PROSE MODEL 3   **ALFRED KAZIN**

My Mother's Kitchen

The kitchen held our lives together. My mother worked in it all day long, we ate in it almost all meals except the Passover *seder*, I did my homework and first writing at the kitchen table, and in winter I often had a bed made up for me on three kitchen chairs near the stove. On the wall just over the table hung a long horizontal mirror that sloped to a ship's prow at each end and was lined in cherry wood. It took up the whole wall, and drew every object in the kitchen to itself. The walls were a fiercely stippled whitewash, so often rewhitened by my father in slack seasons that the paint looked as if it had been squeezed and cracked into the walls. A large electric bulb hung down the center of the kitchen at the end of a chain that had been hooked into the ceiling; the old gas ring and key still jutted out of the wall like antlers. In the corner next to the toilet was the sink at which we washed, and the square tub in which my mother did our clothes. Above it, tacked to the shelf on which were pleasantly ranged square, blue-bordered white sugar and spice jars, hung calendars from the Public National Bank on Pitkin Avenue and the Minsker Progressive Branch of the Workman's Circle; receipts for the payment of insurance premiums, and household bills on a spindle; two little boxes engraved with Hebrew letters. One of these was for the poor, the other to buy back the Land of Israel. Each spring a bearded little man would suddenly appear in our kitchen, salute us with a hurried Hebrew blessing, empty the boxes (sometimes with a sidelong look of disdain if they were not full), hurriedly bless us again for remembering our less fortunate Jewish brothers and sisters, and so take his departure until the next spring, after vainly trying to persuade my mother to take still another box. We did occasionally remember to drop coins in the boxes, but this was usually only on the dreaded morning of "midterms" and final examinations, because my mother thought it would bring me luck. She was extremely superstitious, but embarrassed about it, and always laughed at herself whenever, on the morning of an examination, she counseled me to leave the house on my right foot. "I know it's silly," her smile seemed to say, "but what harm can it do? It may calm God down."

The kitchen gave a special character to our lives; my mother's character. All my memories of that kitchen are dominated by the nearness of my mother sitting all day long at her sewing machine, by the clacking of the treadle against the linoleum floor, by the patient twist of her right shoulder as she automatically pushed at the wheel with one hand or lifted the foot to free the needle where it had got stuck in a thick piece of material. The kitchen was her life. Year by year, as I began to take in her fantastic capacity for labor and her anxious zeal, I realized it was ourselves she kept stitched together. I can never remember a time when she was not working. She worked because the law of her life was work, work and anxiety; she worked because she would have found life meaningless without work. She read almost no English; she could read the Yiddish paper, but never felt she had time to. We were always talking of a time when I would teach her how to read, but somehow there was never time. When I awoke in the morning she was already at her machine, or in the great morning crowd of housewives at the grocery getting fresh rolls for breakfast. When I returned from school she was at her machine, or conferring over *McCall's* with some neighborhood woman who had come in pointing hopefully to an illustration—"Mrs. Kazin! Mrs. Kazin! Make me a dress like it shows here in the picture!"

The kitchen was the great machine that set our lives running; it whirred down a little only on Saturdays and holy days. From my mother's kitchen I gained my first picture of life as a white, overheated, starkly lit workshop redolent with Jewish cooking, crowded with women in housedresses, strewn with fashion magazines, patterns, dress material, spools of thread—and at whose center, so lashed to her machine that bolts of energy seemed to dance out of her hands and feet as she worked, my mother stamped the treadle hard against the floor, hard, hard, and silently, grimly at war beat out the first rhythm of the world for me.

—*A Walker in the City*

1. Pretend you are a sharp-eyed observer who has a chance to look around this kitchen. You don't know the people living here. Point out all *telltale details* that tell you something about them.

2. The words *Jewish, Hebrew, Yiddish,* and *Israel* all help show the ethnic (or religious) background of these people. Can you give a quick explanation of each word? (How are they different?) What is Passover?

3. Some of the words in this selection are very *specific.* They concretely identify objects, actions, noises—things we can see and hear. Other words in this selection are very *general*—they stand for "abstract" qualities of people or of their lives. Make two columns: In one, fill in some unusually specific words from this passage. In the other, fill in some very general words that the author uses as labels for the experiences and feelings of these people.

4. Write a one-paragraph portrait of the author's mother. Compare your portrait with others written by your classmates.

5. Have you known people like the mother described in this passage? Compare or contrast her with one of the people closest to you when you were a child.

Your Turn: Write a candid portrait of a person you know well who is associated in your mind with a definite *place*—workshop, home, farm, office, or the like. Write about someone whose personality is closely tied in your mind to the setting where you have usually observed the person.

ACTIVITY 1

Write about someone of whom you could truly say: "Clothes make the man (or woman)." Choose someone whose costume and mannerisms seem to you to go well with the kind of person she or he is. You might write about a rodeo performer, a rock and roll star, a minister, a doctor, a scoutmaster, a tennis player. Or write about someone of whom you could say: "Appearances deceive." Write about someone whose appearance is at odds with the kind of person he or she really is.

ACTIVITY 2

Describe someone *different* from the people you meet every day. For instance, write about an "old-timer" in a small community, an exchange teacher from abroad, or someone with an unusual occupation. Make your description as lifelike as you can.

WHAT'S IN A FACE?

The pictures on these pages are photographs of three famous people by a famous photographer. Pretend you have never heard of these people and never read about their careers and personalities. Ask yourself: "What kind of person do I see? How would this person talk, act, feel, or think?"

ACTIVITY 3

Have you ever disliked someone who later turned out to be only half as bad or quite different from what you thought? Write a paper on someone that you *changed your mind about* in this fashion.

ACTIVITY 4

Americans are often said to worship youth and to neglect or ignore older people. Have you known any *old people* well enough to write about their character, their outlook, their attitude toward life? Write a paper about an older person (or couple) that you had a chance to know well.

C5
WRITING AND
THINKING

Learn to sort out your ideas and present them in logical order.

The human mind is not a computer, where every operation is performed systematically and with no nonsense. When we think about an important issue, many different ideas may be jumbled together in our minds. Many of these ideas may be vague and half finished—suspicions that we have never really checked on, hints that we have never followed up. Besides, we are easily distracted. We start thinking about lunch, or last night's party, or the arithmetic homework for the next day.

Obviously, our readers will find it hard to follow our thinking if it thus proceeds by fits and starts. We must help them find their way. In the finished paper we do not just present the muddled ideas we had at the beginning. We present the *end result* of our thinking —ideas we have thought through, presented in the most intelligible order.

In defending their views on a serious issue, writers must be able to perform different kinds of logical operations. They must be able to sort things they have observed into major categories. They must look at evidence and reach a logical conclusion. They must be able to compare and contrast things, to show in what ways the things are similar and in what ways different. The following sections will provide you with the finger exercises and practice runs that will help you improve your skill in performing these operations.

Learn how to make a reader follow the major steps in a process.

Clear description of a process is required in *directions* or instructions: How do you make old-fashioned apple pie? How do you build a model airplane? Clear description of a process helps us understand *how something works:* How does a tape recorder imprint sound on a magnetic recording tape? How does a refrigerating unit lower the temperature? Much of what we study in science classes is concerned with the processes at work *in nature:* How does sediment build up on the ocean floors? What leads to the eruption of a volcano?

Tracing a process can help teach us how to write accurately and objectively. An **objective** description requires faithful attention to what is *there.* In an objective account, the question is not: "How do I *think* a tape recorder ought to operate?" or "How would I *like* volcanoes to act?" The attitude is "Here are the facts." Notice the factual tone in the following account of the first stage in the woodchuck's getting ready for hibernation:

> The woodchuck moves with *slower gait,* and emerges less and less frequently for feeding-trips. *Layers of fat have accumulated* around his chest and shoulders, and there is *thick fat in the axils of his legs.* He has extended his summer burrow to a *length of nearly thirty feet,* and has fashioned a *deep nest-chamber at the end* of it, far below the level of the frost. He has carried in, usually, a little hay. He is ready for the Long Sleep.

Remember the following guidelines:

(1) *Concentrate on essentials.* Knowing that your favorite mixing bowl is a pretty blue does not help a reader bake a perfect cake. The question is: "What do the readers *need* to know if they are to understand what is going on or if they are to perform this operation successfully on their own?" Notice how strictly relevant everything in the following passage is to the stage of the process that is being described:

> When the temperature of the September days falls below 50 degrees or so, the woodchuck *becomes too drowsy* to come forth from his burrow in the chilly dusk to forage. He remains in the deep nest-chamber, *lethargic, hardly moving.* Gradually, with the passing of hours or days, his coarse-furred body *curls into a semi-circle,* like a foetus, nose-tip touching tail. The small *legs are tucked in,* the hand-like *clawed forefeet folded.* The woodchuck *has become a compact ball.* Presently the *temperature of his body begins to fall.*
>
> —Alan Devoe, *Lives Around Us*

FOR LIMBERING UP

FIRST, YOU PUT YOUR TWO KNEES CLOSE UP TIGHT; THEN, YOU SWING THEM TO THE LEFT AND YOU SWING THEM TO THE RIGHT...

ROBOT DANCE INSTRUCTION

THE ROBOT THAT FOLLOWS INSTRUCTIONS

Assume that science has finally perfected a robot that looks like a human being and can do everything human beings can do. There is one hitch: The robot has to be told *exactly* what to do. It knows literally *nothing* about the little tasks we perform half automatically every day. Tell the robot *exactly* what to do when performing the following simple tasks:

—combing its hair;
—washing its face;
—putting on socks and shoes;
—eating a simple meal;
—brushing teeth;
—putting on a jacket.

You may want to team up with a classmate. See if your instructions are detailed enough so that your classmate can be a robot doing *only* what he or she is told.

(2) *Break a process up into major stages.* When you merely give your readers the many details that make up a process, they lose interest. They cannot get a clear overall picture. When you tell your readers to perform in order twenty-five different operations, they will give up hope that they can ever master that many steps. If you group the first five together as a first major stage, they will feel that at least *something* has been accomplished. Then, after they draw a deep breath, they will be ready to go on to the next installment. Here are two processes broken up into major stages:

Hibernation: I. Preparation for the winter
                II. Cessation of activity
               III. Sleep
                IV. Awakening

Baking Pie: I. Making the dough
                II. Making the filling
               III. Baking the pie.

(3) *Use economical technical terms.* In describing a process, you need simple and efficient labels for materials, tools, ingredients, or parts. You cannot always call a trowel "that triangle-shaped thing that you put on the mortar with." On the other hand, difficult or new technical terms need to be *explained* to readers unfamiliar with them. Too *many* new terms will confuse such readers.

Notice how clearly the necessary technical terms are explained in the following passage:

> Your heart is about the size of your fist and is snugly enclosed in a *tough protective covering called the pericardium.* Attached to the body only by the great blood vessels stemming from its base, it hangs within your chest, pointing diagonally downward toward the left. It is divided into two parts, right and left, by a bloodtight wall. Each part forms a separate pump. Each of these two pumps, in turn, has *two interacting chambers: the auricle*, which receives blood into the heart from the veins, and *the ventricle*, which forces it out again into the body through the arteries.

(4) *Make imaginative use of comparison and analogy.* Technical writers must know how to relate unfamiliar details to familiar everyday sights, shapes, and events. They always ask: "What does this look like that the reader knows? How does this resemble a familiar everyday procedure?" Here are some imaginative comparisons used in descriptions of natural processes:

> By midsummer the large red jellyfish have grown from the *size of a thimble to that of an umbrella.*
>
> Deep-sea fish that are blind compensate for their lack of eyes with marvelously developed feelers and long, slender fins with which they grope their way, *like so many blind men with canes.*
>
> The sediments on the floor of the deep sea are the result of *the most stupendous snowfall* the earth has ever seen—the steady downward drift of materials from above, *flake upon flake,* layer upon layer —a draft that has continued for hundreds of millions of years.

For Reading and Writing: In the following passage, a famous American writer describes a natural process as it happened according to one scientific theory. Study the way she makes the process clear and intelligible to her readers. Write down your answers to the questions that follow the passage, and be prepared to discuss your answers in class.

RACHEL CARSON   PROSE MODEL 4

The Birth of the Moon

The new earth, freshly torn from its parent sun, was a ball of whirling gases, intensely hot, rushing through the black spaces of the universe on a path and at a speed controlled by immense forces. Gradually the ball of flaming gases cooled. The gases began to liquefy, and Earth became a molten mass. The materials of this mass eventually became sorted out in a definite pattern: the heaviest in the center, the less heavy surrounding them, and the least heavy forming the outer rim. This is the pattern which persists today—a central sphere of molten iron, very nearly as hot as it was 2 billion years ago, an intermediate sphere of semi-plastic basalt, and a hard outer shell, relatively quite thin and composed of solid basalt and granite.

The outer shell of the young earth must have been a good many millions of years changing from the liquid to the solid state, and it is believed that, before this change was completed, an event of the greatest importance took place—the formation of the moon. The next time you stand on a beach at night, watching the moon's bright path across the water, and conscious of the moon-drawn tides, remember that the moon itself may have been born of a great tidal wave of earthly substance, torn off into space. And remember that if the moon was formed in this fashion, the event may have had much to do with shaping the ocean basins and the continents as we know them.

There were tides in the new earth, long before there was an ocean. In response to the pull of the sun the molten liquids of the earth's whole surface rose in tides that rolled unhindered around the globe and only gradually slackened and diminished as the earthly shell cooled, congealed and hardened. Those who believe that the moon is a child of earth say that during an early stage of the earth's development something happened that caused this rolling, viscid tide to gather speed and momentum and to rise to unimaginable heights. Apparently the force that created these greatest tides the earth has ever known was the force of resonance, for at this time the period of the solar tides had come to approach, then equal, the period of the free oscillation of the liquid earth. And so every sun tide was given increased momentum by the push of the earth's oscillation, and each of the twice-daily tides was larger than the one before it. Physicists have calculated that, after 500 years of such monstrous, steadily increasing tides, those on the side toward the sun became too high for stability, and a great wave was torn away and hurled into space. But immediately, of course, the newly created satellite became subject to physical laws that sent it spinning in an orbit of its own about the earth. This is what we call the moon.

There are reasons for believing that this event took place after the earth's crust had become slightly hardened, instead of during its partly liquid state. There is to this day a great scar on the surface of the globe. This scar or depression holds the Pacific Ocean. According to some geophysicists, the floor of the Pacific is composed of basalt, the substance of the earth's middle layer, while all other oceans are floored with a thin layer of granite, which makes up most of the earth's outer layer. We immediately wonder what became of the Pacific's granite covering and the most convenient assumption is that it was torn away when the moon was formed. There is supporting evidence. The mean density of the moon is much less than that of the earth (3.3 compared wtih 5.5), suggesting that the moon took away none of the earth's heavy core, but that it is composed only of the granite and some of the basalt of the outer layers.

—from *The Sea Around Us*

1. Among the details the author mentions, point out *three* that in your opinion do most to help give an objective, factual tone to the passage. What are some of the things that help make the reader feel that this is not science fiction?
2. Write a short paragraph to show how the *omission* of one of the details mentioned in the first half or so of the passage would make the rest harder to understand or to believe. Can you show that in the description of a process the reader could easily be tripped up if one or two essential facts are left out?
3. Write an outline in which you break up the process described into three or four major steps.
4. In one sentence each, explain or define *six* technical or everyday terms used by the author in a more specific technical sense.
5. Point out *three* ways in which the events described are related to more familiar everyday events by comparison and analogy.

Your Turn: Drawing on material from science textbooks or science encyclopedias, write *your own* description of an important *natural process:* the circulation of the blood, the stages of development of a moth or butterfly, or the like. Do not simply copy material from a book—present the material in such a way that your reader will understand the details and at the same time get a clear overall picture.

ACTIVITY 1

Prepare one solid paragraph (100 to 150 words) for a directions-writing contest. Give directions on how to do *something that looks simple and easy* but is really difficult: easing a big car into a small parking space; threading a fine needle; tying a bowtie. Have a jury of your classmates choose, from among the entries, the one most likely to give real help to a person trying to follow the instructions.

ACTIVITY 2

Give clear and workable instructions to your reader on how to make something that he or she could produce on a *"do-it-your-self"* basis. How should the reader proceed to build a coffee table? Or knit a sweater? Remember that much of what you take for granted (or have learned the hard way) will have to be explained to your reader.

ACTIVITY 3

For the benefit of the interested layperson, describe the basic process that explains the operation of a car engine, tape recorder, television set, smog-control unit, sewing machine, or similar *piece of equipment*. Explain necessary technical terms.

C5b
Sorting Things Out

Sort people, things, and ideas into appropriate categories.

No one could find his way around a library if librarians did not use some system of **classification**. When librarians receive a new book, they examine it to see whether to put it under "fiction" or "nonfiction"; whether to put it on the shelf marked "American Literature," the one marked "English Literature," or the one marked "World Literature."

Much confusion would result if we did not have ways of putting things into convenient bins or pigeonholes, putting things that belong together into one major group or class. Many such groupings are *conventional*. They are well-established, ready-made: "Catholic-Protestant-Jew"; "curricular-extracurricular." The writer has a job to do when either *there are no* ready-made classifications or when the ready-made classifications seem superficial or unfair.

Classification helps us see a *pattern*. It helps us make sense of confusing data. Here are three examples of how a writer might classify people:

STUDENTS IN LIBRARY

I. "Intellects"—finish one book and go on to the next; browse through books on the shelves; check out piles of books to take home
II. "Plodders"—go to the library only for specific assignments; get them over with as quickly as possible and leave
III. "Pranksters"—use library as a place to while away the time; whisper, pass notes, play practical jokes

CHURCHGOERS

    I. "Sunday Christians"—participate in the ceremonies of the church but are very little concerned with spiritual matters the rest of the week

    II. "Moralists"—very strict in their judgments of other people; watch and criticize their neighbors

    III. "Dedicated Christians"—try to bring their religious outlook to bear on their own lives

AMERICAN PRESIDENTS

    I. "Idealists"—know American history; believe in the unique role of America in the larger world; work toward the realization of American ideals

    II. "Party Workers"—work their way up through party politics; owe their first loyalty to the party; work closely with old-time party associates and friends

    III. "Outsiders"—popular figures who became famous in a field other than politics; newcomers to the problems of government

Often we set up classifications for immediate *practical application*. A grocer might sort apples out of a barrel as follows: *big* ones—to be sold at a premium price; *small* ones—to be sold at a bargain price; *spoiled* ones—to be thrown out. (There is no need to sort the spoiled ones out into big and small, since this sorting would not serve any *purpose*.) Similarly, a writer might sort crimes out into "crimes of passion," "crimes from necessity," "crimes reflecting mental illness," and "professional crime." The writer's purpose may be to suggest different ways of *dealing with* the different types.

In working on a paper devoted to classification, ask yourself the following questions:

(1) *Are there enough basic categories?* Students who divide governments into democracies and dictatorships will soon realize that they need a third category in between, such as government by an élite. Students who sort out political candidates into Republicans and Democrats may find that they need *sub*categories, such as "liberal Republicans" and "conservative Republicans."

(2) *Is the principle of selection clear?* If we classify cars by *price*, we may come up with "high, medium, and low." If we classify cars by *use*, we may come up with "prestige cars, family cars, and sports cars." Often a scheme of classification breaks down because the writer shifts from one principle of selection to another.

(3) *Is the classification appropriate to your purpose?* In classifying meat, a weight watcher may want to distinguish between "fatty" and "nonfatty"; a budget watcher between cheap and expensive; a member of certain religious groups between "forbidden" and "allowed." For the purpose of determining citizenship we may have to classify people according to where they were born. For the purpose of studying the way they talk we may classify them according to where they grew up. For the purpose of studying their social background we may classify them according to what section of a city they now live in.

For Reading and Writing: The following passage by a famous American writer of novels and short stories raises some of the questions that we have to consider when we classify people. What do you learn from this passage about the problems we encounter when we try to sort people into simple types? Write down your answers to the questions at the end of the passage, and be prepared to discuss your answers in class.

PROSE MODEL 5   **JOHN STEINBECK**

Good Guys and Bad Guys

One afternoon, hearing gunfire from the room where our television set is installed, I went in with that losing intention of fraternizing with my son for a little while. There sat Catbird with the cretinous expression I have learned to recognize. A Western was in progress.

"What's going on?" I asked.

He looked at me in wonder. "What do you mean, what's going on? Don't you know?"

"Well, no. Tell me!"

He was kind to me. Explained as though I were the child.

"Well, the Bad Guy is trying to steal Her father's ranch. But the Good Guy won't let him. Bullet figured out the plot."

"Who is Bullet?"

"Why, the Good Guy's horse." He didn't add "You dope," but his tone implied it.

"Now wait," I said, "which one is the Good Guy?"

"The one with the white hat."

"Then the one with the black hat is the Bad Guy?"

"Anybody knows that," said Catbird.

For a time I watched the picture, and I realized that I had been ignoring a part of our life that everybody knows. I was interested in the characterizations. The girl, known as Her or She, was a blonde, very pretty but completely unvoluptuous because these are Family Pictures. Sometimes she wore a simple gingham dress and sometimes a leather skirt and boots, but always she had a bit of a bow in her hair and her face was untroubled with emotion or, one might almost say, intelligence. This also is part of the convention. She is a symbol, and any acting would get her thrown out of the picture by popular acclaim.

The Good Guy not only wore a white hat but light-colored clothes, shining boots, tight riding pants, and a shirt embroidered with scrolls and flowers. In my young days I used to work with cattle, and our costume was blue jeans, a leather jacket, and boots with run-over heels. The cleaning bill alone of this gorgeous screen cowboy would have been four times what our pay was in a year.

The Good Guy had very little change of facial expression. He went through his fantastic set of adventures with no show of emotion. This is another convention and proves that he is very brave and very pure. He is also scrubbed and has an immaculate shave.

I turned my attention to the Bad Guy. He wore a black hat and dark clothing, but his clothing was definitely not only unclean but unpressed. He had a stubble of beard but the greatest contrast was in his face. His was not an immobile face. He leered, he sneered, he had a nasty laugh. He bullied and shouted. He looked evil. While he did not swear, because this is a Family Picture, he said things like "Wall dog it" and "You rat" and "I'll cut off your ears and eat 'em," which would indicate that his language was not only coarse but might, off screen, be vulgar. He was, in a word, a Bad Guy. I found a certain interest in the Bad Guy which was lacking in the Good Guy.

"Which one do you like best?" I asked.

Catbird removed his anesthetized eyes from the screen. "What do you mean?"

"Do you like the Good Guy or the Bad Guy?"

He sighed at my ignorance and looked back at the screen. "Are you kidding?" he asked. "The Good Guy, of course."

Now a new character began to emerge. He puzzled me because he wore a gray hat. I felt a little embarrassed about asking my son, the expert, but I gathered my courage. "Catbird," I asked shyly, "what kind of a guy is that, the one in the gray hat?"

He was sweet to me then. I think until that moment he had not understood the abysmal extent of my ignorance. "He's the In-Between Guy," Catbird explained kindly. "If he starts bad he ends good and if he starts good he ends bad."

"What's this one going to do?"

"See how he's sneering and needs a shave?" my son asked.
"Yes."

"Well, the picture's just started, so that guy is going to end good and help the Good Guy get Her father's ranch back."

"How can you be sure?" I asked.

Catbird gave me a cold look. "He's got a gray hat, hasn't he? Now don't talk. It's about time for the chase."

—from "How to Tell Good Guys from Bad Guys," *The Reporter*

1. In one sentence each, define or explain: *fraternize, cretinous, voluptuous, convention, acclaim, gorgeous, immaculate, immobile, anesthetize, abysmal.*

2. List the *three* details that in your opinion show most clearly that the author is *making fun* of television Westerns.

3. Write one paragraph to explain why someone like Mr. Steinbeck would consider the categories of "Good Guy," "Bad Guy," and "In-between Guy" inadequate or insufficient.

4. Write one paragraph in which you describe a scheme of classification that you yourself have found to be inadequate or unfair.

5. Have Westerns changed since this passage was written? Write an outline listing four or five basic character types in current Westerns. Fill in a few characteristic details after each heading.

Your Turn: Write a paper in which you sort *one* of the following into a few major categories: the *sports* in which you are most interested; *careers* opening to women; *songs* currently popular with teenagers. Use detailed examples to illustrate each major type.

ACTIVITY 1

Sometimes we find people classified according to major *character types.* (For instance, can you explain the difference between an "extrovert" and an "introvert"?) Pretend you are a psychologist hired by the school board to describe four or five major character types found among the students of your high school. Describe the major features of each type. Use authentic detail from your own observation.

ACTIVITY 2

Classify the *movies* you have seen in the last few years, or the *movie stars* that seem to have proved most popular since you became a movie fan. Are there clear-cut major categories? Limit yourself to a few major types; use detailed examples.

ACTIVITY 3

Teachers and librarians often compile lists of recommended "books for young people" or "books for adolescents." Usually, such lists are designed to encourage an interest in books other than Westerns and detective fiction. Can you classify *recommended books* of this type that you yourself have read? For each major type you set up, use detailed examples—mention actual characters, incidents, and the like from the books.

Back up your opinions with convincing evidence.

One major reason people talk or write is to express an opinion. They want to tell us what they think. They want us to know how they feel about a given problem or a given issue. Writing that expresses an opinion does two things at the same time. It tells us something about the subject at hand—the facts, the event, the issue, the situation—whatever it is that the writer cares about. But the writing also tells us something about *the writer:* his or her attitudes, standards, judgments. We can see what conclusions the writer has drawn. We can see what the writer expected and if or why the writer was disappointed.

Look at the following passages. Which stays closest to the facts? (Which tells you most about its subject?) Which is colored most strongly by the writer's opinions? (Which tells you most about the author?) In each passage, show where and how the author's opinion enters into the writing. Explain what each passage tells us about the person who wrote it.

> It happened at the West Fourth Street station. Between stops a man came to our section of the train. He said that he had a gun and that no one had better move. But "Mr. Tweed" didn't hear him. He was too caught up in his own world to wonder about the rest of us. When the train stopped, he got up to leave the car. It was probably his stop. I doubt if the move involved any heroics. But who knows whose life he may have inadvertently saved? He's dead and his murderer is held by the police. Some man grabbed the gunman as soon as he turned toward "Mr. Tweed" and fired. The rest of us are alive and unharmed.

> *Let's Make a Deal* comes to life on weekday afternoons, appropriately following the soap operas for contrast, for though on most soap operas we are shown the human drama writhing and dragging itself from crisis to crisis, we all know that John will get Martha or Jane, but whether he does or not, it really isn't important because all of that nonsense is just a game anyway (except to those overripe house-

C5c
Stating an Opinion

wives who fortify themselves with screwdrivers and Kleenex in between the vacuuming and shopping). But *Let's Make a Deal* is something else altogether. It is real. It is the truth. It is the all-powerful
magnet, pulling and straining from all corners of this great land of
ours, the masses of poor, hungry people to the contrived paradise of
TV's big giveaway.

The day has almost come when the sky will never be seen again.
Tall buildings are blocking our vision of the sky, the sun, and the
stars. The bright neon signs have replaced the starry specks we see
each night. Large cities have replaced the open land. It looks as if the
Earth will never be the same again.

On the surface, *Star Trek* is nothing more provocative than an
adventure in time and space. One week the Klingons invade; the next
week, the starship *Enterprise* is helplessly locked in a time zone.
Although we have all seen these plots a dozen times before, they are
not important. The point is whether or not the network can maneuver
your thoughts into the web of the great American Dream. The name,
as you can see, the *Enterprise*, does not fail to suggest one of America's
most sacred foundations—the system of free enterprise and equal
opportunity. Captain Kirk is the clean-cut athletic Midwestern Joe
College type. He is America's paragon of virtue. However, those who
have watched *Star Trek* regularly cannot help but see the decided
fanaticism and militancy of his character. The 400-member crew is
the army, or, in the case of society, the general masses. The captain
and the officers of the bridge comprise the élite. They never die. They
never sin. The crew of course is expendable. The bridge alone can
make the decisions and alone is capable of solving the problems, for
they are the great ones—up there.

We often say: "I'm entitled to my own opinion." But that does
not mean that anybody else has to *listen* to your opinions and take
them seriously. What is necessary to make an audience take your
opinions seriously? How do you make people listen to what you
think and feel?

To make readers take your opinions seriously, you have to
back them up. Their question is not just: "What do you think?"
They will also ask: "What *makes* you think so?" Much writing
about issues and ideas follows a simple pattern: First, a statement
of the author's opinion; then, the facts, figures, and observations on
which the opinion is based. The author's opinion, stated perhaps
at the end of an introductory paragraph, becomes the unifying
thesis, or central idea, that holds the rest of the paper or article
together.

AMERICAN STYLES: Chapels

Look at this photograph of the Pearson Point Baptist Church on Puget Sound in the state of Washington. Does it remind you of other chapels you have seen? Describe the typical, small American church to a pen pal who has never seen a small American town.

AMERICAN STYLES: State House

FOR WRITING
AND DISCUSSION Look at this photograph of the Massachusetts State House built in 1793. Have you seen the state house in your own state? Does it look similar or different? Describe the old-style American state house to a pen pal abroad who is interested in American institutions.

AMERICAN STYLES: Mission Church

Look at these photographs of mission churches in California and Arizona. Pretend you are an eighteenth-century Spanish priest. Write a letter home to Spain about the new church you have just seen built in the New World.

FOR WRITING
AND DISCUSSION

FOR BRANCHING
OUT

COLUMNIST FOR A DAY

Columnists are often people with strong opinions who react to the passing events of the day. Some tell us what they think about the large-scale political events of our time. But others comment on events happening on a smaller stage. Pretend you are a columnist and you have chosen one or more of the following "minor league" events on which to comment. Do you think your readers should care one way or the other? Do you think you can *get* them to care?

Cemetery Removal Opposed

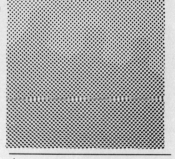

Washington, D.C. — Some 350 Yavapai people stand to lose their land, if a controversial Dam is built, flooding their homes and their venerated cemetery. The federal government, in the process of negotiating the removal of the Yavapais from their homeland, replied to the Indians' plea that the Dam would flood their sacred cemetery, giving them the following options:

To remove the dead before the dam floods the area.

To erect a statue to memorialize the dead after the area is flooded.

Or, to build a dike around the cemetery. This would be in opposition to the Yavapai belief that the morning sunrise must always shine on the graves.

All three alternatives have been rejected by the Yavapais. "I do not know how our people will sleep when the dead are covered up," said one Yavapai elder, speaking in his own language. "To the white man this means nothing. But to us, it is deep in our souls," he said.

TV DINNERS TUNED OUT

Crewmen from 6 U. S. Steel Corp. ore carriers in the Great Lakes went on strike last weekend after learning the company planned to serve them TV dinners, not cooked meals, on ships this year. The wildcat walkout is by members of a United Steel Workers Local.

Doors N' Windows Go

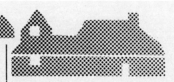

For a year now, Mark has been living in a historical monument, an old Victorian house built in 1876. The house was intended to be restored as part of a new Historical Park, but a new freeway made it impossible to move the house, since the entire second floor would have to be disassembled to pass under the freeway. Mark paid a low rent, but the landlord refused to make even the smallest repairs. When Mark fell behind in his rent, the landlord threatened eviction. Over a month ago the city con- demned the house because of in- adequate wiring. When the city called a hearing about the condemna- tion, the landlord did not even ap- pear. Instead, he came by the house in a truck, took a crowbar and tore out most of the doors and two windows. Mark made a tactical re- treat to the back of the house and boarded it up. This is where things stand at present.

(1) *State your opinions as concretely as possible.* Do not say what you think in such a very general way that the reader must ask: "What exactly do you have in mind? What, concretely, are you talking about?" Can you see how concretely the author of the following passage states his opinion of the "men from other planets" to be found in science fiction?

> In the modern literature on space travel I have read about *cabbage men and bird men;* I have investigated the loves *of the lizard men and the tree men,* but in each case I have labored under no illusion. I have been reading about a man, *Homo sapiens,* that common earth- ling, *clapped into an ill-fitting coat of feathers* and retaining all his basic human attributes *including an eye for the pretty girl who has just emerged from the spaceship.*
>
> —Loren Eiseley, *The Immense Journey*

(2) *Provide enough supporting material* to make your readers say: "Yes, you have made your point. I can see that there is some- thing to what you say." Support your opinions with the following kinds of material:

FACTS AND FIGURES

> *No one can any longer call this town a cultural desert.* Attendance at the annual concert series was *up 40 percent* over last year. There are now at least *three amateur theater companies* regularly producing plays. The two record shops on Main Street that used to sell mainly popular songs now have *extensive collections* of classical music and opera. The classical music station is *in the black for the first time* in its ten-year history.

Primarily a team game, baseball is also the game for the individualist. The team play is essential, and when you watch closely you can see it, but the focus is usually on one man. *A base runner* streaks for second with the pitch, falls away while in full stride, and slides in in a cloud of dust, baseman stabbing at him with gloved hand, umpire bending to peer through the murk and call the play; *an outfielder* runs deep and far, arching ball coming down—apparently—just out of his reach, trajectories of fielder and baseball coming miraculously together at the last, gloved hand going out incredibly to pick the ball out of the air; *a pitcher* who has been getting his lumps looks about at filled bases, glowers at the batter, and then sends one in that is struck at and missed . . . always, some individual is trying for an astounding feat of athletic prowess and, now and then, actually accomplishing it.

—Bruce Catton, ''The Great American Game,'' *American Heritage*

Mexican children still have an old-fashioned respect for adults. The typical Mexican child would rather bite off his tongue than openly make fun of his elders. This respect was demonstrated one day when I approached three small boys in Cuernavaca to ask the way to a restaurant. There is nothing on earth so funny to the Mexican as a *gringo* trying to speak Spanish. I tried to ask my question, but the more I tried, the worse I got. I could tell that the mirth was swelling up inside of them until they were about to burst; yet they kept their faces straight until I finally gave up and was walking away. Then I heard them explode in laughter and I turned to look back at them. Instantly they composed their features and pretended they were no longer interested in me, and made as if they were talking about something else.

(3) *Limit your claims to what you can support.* The more sweeping you make your statements, the harder you will have to work to make them stick. Ask yourself: Am I exaggerating for effect? Do I claim to know more than I really do? Will the reader accuse me of jumping to conclusions? If what you say is only partly true, or is not the whole story, tell the reader so. Notice how cautiously the author of the following passage states his opinion about the causes of juvenile delinquency:

Judges of juvenile courts say that there is *no single cause* of delinquency. Certainly *one cause* is a feeling of insecurity on the part of the young offenders. *Among the factors* contributing to insecurity are

poverty, liquor in the home, father coming home drunk, strained relationships between parents, often accompanied by harsh language
and quarrels in the presence of the children—all these things generate
fear and help to lay the foundations for later crime. *Many children
are insecure because they are not loved,* A recent study of juvenile
offenders shows that *in many homes* there are signs of insecurity and
delinquency before the youngster reaches eight years of age.

—Billy Graham, "Juvenile Delinquency and its Cure," *American Mercury*

For Reading and Writing: The following passage was written by
a television critic known for her strong opinions. How would you
sum up her main point in your own words? What does she do to
back up her main point? Do you agree with her? (Why, or why
not?)

MARYA MANNES   PROSE MODEL 6

Television: The Splitting Image

In the guise of what they consider comedy, the producers of television commercials have created a loathsome gallery of men and women patterned, presumably, on Mr. and Mrs. America. Women liberationists have a major target in the commercial image of woman flashed hourly and daily to the vast majority. There are, indeed, only four kinds of females in this relentless sales procession: the gorgeous teen-age swinger with bouncing locks; the young mother teaching her baby girl the right soap for skin care; the middle-aged housewife with a voice like a power saw; and the old lady with dentures and irregularity. All these women, to be sure, exist. But between the swinging sex object and the constipated granny there are millions of females never shown in commercials. These are—married or single—intelligent, sensitive women who bring charm to their homes, who work at jobs as well as lend grace to their marriage, who support themselves, who have talents or hobbies or commitments, or who are skilled at their professions.

To my knowledge, as a frequent if reluctant observer, I know of only one woman on a commercial who has a job; a comic plumber pushing Comet. Funny, heh? Think of a dame with a plunger.

With this one representative of our labor force, which is well over thirty million women, we are left with nothing but the full-time housewife in all her whining glory: obsessed with whiter wash, moister cakes, shinier floors, cleaner children, softer diapers, and greaseless fried chicken. In the rare instances when these ladies are not in the kitchen, at the washing machine, or waiting on hubby, they are buying beauty shops (fantasy, see?) to take home so that their hair will have more body. Or out at the supermarket being choosy.

If they were attractive in their obsessions, they might be bearable. But they are not. They are pushy, loud-mouthed, stupid, and—of all things now—bereft of sexuality. Presumably, the argument in the tenets of advertising is that once a woman marries she changes overnight from plaything to floor-waxer.

To be fair, men make an equivalent transition in commercials. The swinging male with the mod hair and the beautiful chick turns inevitably into the paunchy slob who chokes on his wife's cake. You will notice, however, that the voice urging the viewer to buy the product is nearly always male: gentle, wise, helpful, seductive. And the visible presence telling the housewife how to get shinier floors and whiter wash and lovelier hair is almost invariably a man: the Svengali in modern dress, the Trilby (if only she were!), his willing object.

Woman, in short, is consumer first and human being fourth. A wife and mother who stays home all day buys a lot more than a woman who lives alone or who—married or single—has a job. The young girl bent on marriage is the next most susceptible consumer. It is entirely understandable, then, that the potential buyers of detergents, foods, polishes, toothpastes, pills, and housewares are the housewives, and that the sex object spends most of her money on cosmetics, hair lotions, soaps, mouthwashes, and soft drinks.

Here we come, of course, to the youngest class of consumers, the swinging teen-agers so beloved by advertisers keen on telling them (and us) that they've "got a lot to live, and Pepsi's

got a lot to give." This affords a chance to show a squirming, leaping, jiggling group of beautiful kids having a very loud high on rock and—of all things—soda pop. One of commercial TV's most dubious achievements, in fact, is the reinforcement of the self-adulation characteristic of the young as a group.

As for the aging female citizen, the less shown of her the better. She is useful for ailments, but since she buys very little of anything, not having a husband or any children to feed or house to keep, nor—of course—sex appeal to burnish, society and commercials have little place for her. The same is true, to be sure, of older men, who are handy for Bosses with Bad Breath or Doctors with Remedies. Yet, on the whole, men hold up better than women at any age—in life or on television. Lines on their faces are marks of distinction, while on women they are signatures of decay.

—*Saturday Review*

1. In one sentence each, define or explain: *guise, liberationist, relentless, commitment, bereft, tenet, transition, presence, invariably, susceptible, dubious, self-adulation, ailment, burnish, distinction.* (Can you find out what a "Svengali" is—or was?)

2. The author often uses language that clearly shows that she *disapproves* of something. List a dozen words that show "This I dislike" or "This I have a poor opinion of." (Can you make a similar list for words she uses that show *approval* instead?)

3. Make a collection of slogans or catchy phrases from *current* television commercials. What do you think of them? How do you react to them?

4. Pretend you are a vice-president of a television network. Write a letter to Marya Mannes to tell her what *changes* have occurred in TV commercials to improve the "feminine image." Or, write a letter *to* a network vice-president to tell him your opinion of the way women currently appear in television commercials.

5. Study the way women currently appear in popular television shows. What roles do they play? What seems to be the attitude of producers and writers toward the female characters? How is the audience supposed to react to them? You may want to limit your study to one *type* of show: comedies, Westerns, crime shows.

Your Turn: Choose one of the following:

A. Is there a group or class of people who, in your opinion, do not always get the credit they deserve? Write a *"letter of ap-*

preciation" about one such group. For instance, you might write about doctors, police officers, custodians, musicians, secretaries, older sisters, or high school principals. Use examples from your own observation and experience.

B. Is there a group or class of people whose behavior or attitudes, in your opinion, leave much to be desired? Write a "*complaint*" about one such group. For instance, you might write about grandparents, blind dates, campus big shots, big-name entertainers, or star athletes. Use concrete examples.

ACTIVITY 1

Even before the invention of television, the British philosopher Bertrand Russell said that modern parents "provide their children with far too many passive amusements, such as shows and good things to eat. . . . The pleasures of childhood should in the main be such as the child extracts himself from his environment by means of some effort and inventiveness." In your opinion, does today's teenager have a similar problem? Is he or she too much of a passive consumer of entertainment with not enough opportunity for exertion and "inventiveness"?

ACTIVITY 2

Young people are often undecided about whether they want to be "different" or "just like everybody else." In your opinion, is it better to express your own individuality or to conform to the customs and practices of the group? (300 to 400 words)

Use comparison and contrast to bring out characteristic traits and important distinctions.

C5d
Comparison and
Contrast

Every day we encounter newspaper reports or magazine articles that compare and contrast related things: football in the United States and in Canada; railroads in the last century and railroads now; commercial and educational television. Comparison and contrast serves several major purposes:

—It makes us *notice* things. When we compare folk tales from different countries, we may discover an important common feature, such as a belief in magic. When we study democracy in ancient Greece, we may discover an important difference from our own type of democratic rule: In Greece, the "free" citizens who enjoyed the vote were a small upper class in a small city-state.

—It helps us proceed from the *familiar to the unfamiliar*. We help the reader visualize a new car design by saying that the fenders are something like car X, the hood like car Y, the windshield like car Z.

—It helps us *choose*. We use comparison and contrast to make a reader fully aware of the alternatives. We use comparison and contrast to show why we consider one thing superior or inferior to another. Here is how one sportswriter tried to explain why he preferred baseball to football:

> Take a baseball crowd. It is good tempered, yet anything but meek. The crowds are best when the teams are not really in contention. They're smaller but friendlier. . . . Football and other contact sports are another thing. They bring out another strain in us, the streak of meanness and bullying that we share with everyone else. A football crowd is impressive, but in a scary kind of way. It is a show of strength. . . .

When we compare and contrast, we have to *line up* things so that the reader can see important similarities or differences. We can organize a comparison in two major ways:

(1) *Try a* **point-by-point** *comparison*. Suppose you are writing a paper on whether young men or young women are better drivers. Perhaps you have three major qualities of a motorist that you want to take into account: mechanical aptitude; decisiveness (ability to make the right decision quickly in a crisis); and personal attitude toward driving (unlike girls, many boys use their driving to show how grown-up and masculine they are, taking many unnecessary risks to prove that they have courage, manliness, and what not).

Your reader would probably get the whole picture best if you lined up your material like this:

I. Mechanical aptitude (discussion of *both* boys and girls, with boys coming out ahead)
II. Decisiveness (discussion of *both* boys and girls, with boys coming out ahead on this one, too)
III. Mature personal attitude (discussion of *both* boys and girls, with girls coming out ahead on this one)

WESTERNS HAVE GROWN UP

In the two following paragraphs, a student compares the "children's Westerns" that he remembers from his earlier days with the more recent "adult Westerns" that people see on the screen today. Which does he seem to prefer? Why? Can you do a similar two-paragraph paper on a kind of movie or television program that has *changed* since you first started watching it? (Your class may want to do this "study-in-contrast" as a *group writing* project, with different members of the class contributing details to the two contrasting descriptions.)

In the old Westerns, the hero rode a big white horse and was in love with the rich farmer's pretty daughter. The villain, who rode a big black ugly horse, was a foreman of the farmer's ranch but was rustling cattle on the side and changing the brands. He also had his eye on the rancher's daughter, but only because he wanted the old man's ranch and money. After a wild chase toward the end of the plot, the hero catches the rustlers and delivers them to the sheriff, who throws them in jail where they belong. In the end, the hero and the rancher's pretty daughter are together at a big outdoor celebration cookout—square dancing and singing happy cowboy songs with a cast of sixty or seventy handclapping friends and well-wishers in the background.

In the current "adult Western," the same basic plot may be found, but there have been a number of changes made. The hero is no longer a handsome, clean-looking young fellow but usually a saddle tramp, a scroungey-looking thing. Though he falls in love with the girl, her father hates him and causes no end of trouble. The cattle rustler is no longer satisfied with stealing cattle but kidnaps the girl and is just getting ready to torture her when justice starts to catch up with him. The climactic fight is a brutal contest, with the hero getting shot but staggering to his feet to shoot the horse out from under the villain, who then falls over a cliff and dashes his head on some rocks (the camera flashes over this scene to give the audience a good look at the results). For entertainment, the townspeople no longer square dance but are more likely to stage a ghastly lynching scene. Fun and games for all!

TWO FACES OF THE CITY

FOR DISCUSSION
AND WRITING Pretend you have just arrived in the big city from Puerto Rico.
Write a letter to your friends back home in which you try to make
them feel the contrast between the two faces of the city.

WANTED BY THE TROJANS

ODYSSEUS

IDENTIFYING TRAITS:
Excellent Public Speaker
Cool Under Fire
Loves Good Food and Wine

WANTED BY THE TROJANS

ACHILLES

IDENTIFYING TRAITS:
Poor Public Speaker
Impulsive and Moody
Indifferent to Food
and Wine

(2) *Try a* **parallel-order** *comparison.* You will finish your whole discussion of the first group at one time. But then, in discussing the second group, you will take up the major qualities in exactly *the same order* as in discussing the second group. Here is the parallel-order scheme applied to a comparison of two characters from literature:

Odysseus and Achilles as Epic Heroes

I. Odysseus as epic hero
    A. Great warrior—(unsurpassed in archery, etc.)
    B. Accomplished orator—(successful in pleading his own cause)
    C. Shrewd counselor—(carefully weighing facts and situations)
    D. Very human character—(loves good food and wine)

II. Achilles as epic hero
    A. Great warrior—(triumphs over Hector)
    B. No great speaker—(tends to be haughty and insolent)
    C. Impulsive person—(quick to yield to resentment)
    D. Half divine—(indifferent to food)

For Reading and Writing: In the following passage, Maya Angelou writes about her childhood in Arkansas. Can you sum up in your own words the contrast between the morning scene and the evening scene? Were you surprised by her description of the early morning mood? Did you expect the change in the evening? Why did she put these two scenes together for contrast?

PROSE MODEL 7   **MAYA ANGELOU**

In Cotton-Picking Time

Each year I watched the field across from the Store turn caterpillar green, then gradually frosty white. I knew exactly how long it would be before the big wagons would pull into the front yard and load on the cotton pickers at daybreak to carry them to the remains of slavery's plantations.

During the picking season my grandmother would get out of bed at four o'clock (she never used an alarm clock) and creak down to her knees and chant in a sleep-filled voice, "Our Father, thank you for letting me see this New Day. Thank you that you didn't allow the bed I lay on last night to be my cooling board, nor my blanket my winding sheet. Guide my feet this day along the straight and narrow, and help me to put a bridle on my tongue. Bless this house, and everybody in it. Thank you, in the name of your Son, Jesus Christ, Amen."

Before she had quite arisen, she called our names and issued orders, and pushed her large feet into homemade slippers, and across the bare lye-washed wooden floor to light the coal-oil lamp.

The lamplight in the Store gave a soft make-believe feeling to our world which made me want to whisper and walk about on tiptoe. The odors of onions and oranges and kerosene had been mixing all night and wouldn't be disturbed until the wooded slat was removed from the door and the early morning air forced its way in with the bodies of people who had walked miles to reach the pickup place.

"Sister, I'll have two cans of sardines."

"I'm gonna work so fast today I'm gonna make you look like you standing still."

"Lemme have a hunk uh cheese and some sody crackers."

"Just gimme a coupla them fat peanut paddies." That would be from a picker who was taking his lunch. The greasy brown paper sack was stuck behind the bib of his overalls. He'd use the candy as a snack before the noon sun called the workers to rest.

In those tender mornings the Store was full of laughing, joking, boasting and bragging. One man was going to pick two hundred pounds of cotton, and another three hundred. Even the children were promising to bring home fo' bits and six bits.

The champion picker of the day before was the hero of the dawn. If he prophesied that the cotton in today's field was going to be sparse and stick to the bolls like glue, every listener would grunt a hearty agreement.

The sound of the empty cotton sacks dragging over the floor and the murmurs of waking people were sliced by the cash register as we rang up the five-cent sales.

If the morning sounds and smells were touched with the supernatural, the late afternoon had all the features of the normal Arkansas life. In the dying sunlight the people dragged, rather than their empty cotton sacks.

Brought back to the Store, the pickers would step out of the backs of trucks and fold down, dirt-disappointed, to the ground. No matter how much they had picked, it wasn't enough. Their wages wouldn't even get them out of debt to my grandmother, not to mention the staggering bill that waited on them at the white commissary downtown.

The sounds of the new morning had been replaced with grumbles about cheating houses, weighted scales, snakes, skimpy cotton and dusty rows. In later years I was to confront the stereotyped picture of gay song-singing cotton pickers with such inordinate rage that I was told even by fellow Blacks that my paranoia was embarrassing.

But I had seen the fingers cut by the mean little cotton bolls, and I had witnessed the backs and shoulders and arms and legs resisting any further demands.

Some of the workers would leave their sacks at the Store to be picked up the following morning, but a few had to take them home for repairs. I winced to picture them sewing the coarse material under a coal-oil lamp with fingers stiffening from the day's work. In too few hours they would have to walk back to Sister Henderson's Store, get vittles and load, again, onto the trucks. Then they would face another day of trying to earn enough for the whole year with the heavy knowledge that they were going to end the season as they started it —without the money or credit necessary to sustain a family for three months. In cotton-picking time the late afternoons revealed the harshness of Black Southern life, which in the early morning had been softened by nature's blessing of grogginess, forgetfulness and the soft lamplight.

—from *I Know Why the Caged Bird Sings*

1. Explain the italicized words: "the white *commissary*," "*weighted* scales," "*stereotyped* picture," "*inordinate* rage," "my *paranoia*."

2. How far removed is the average person in city or suburb from these "rural" Americans? Describe them and their life-style in your own words.

3. From each of the two contrasting parts, can you pick *one* sentence that best sums up the contrast between the morning mood and the evening mood?

4. Arrange with your classmates to have the same pair or group of people *act out* two different conversations. Make the two conversations show the difference in mood "before" and "after" a contest, a meeting, or other important event. (Or, you and your classmates may want to act out the morning scene and the evening scene at the grandmother's store.)

Your Turn: Write two different paragraphs about the same scene at different times. For instance, you might write about your school —crowded and deserted. Or you might write about your home on an ordinary day and on a very special occasion.

ACTIVITY 1

How important are the differences, if any, in interests, attitudes, and behavior of *boys and girls*? Compare and contrast the boys and girls you have observed on major points: how they talk; or what they expect of other people; or what their attitude is toward school. Where possible bring in authentic incidents from your experience.

ACTIVITY 2

Many major spectator sports compete for the sports fan's interest: baseball, football, tennis, basketball (and many others). Pretend you have been hired as a consultant to help a stadium owner or a television network project the future popularity of these sports. Compare and contrast major features of *two* of the four sports listed above. Concentrate on what the sports fan likes or is interested in.

Study and practice what makes writing lively and imaginative.

C6
WRITING AND
IMAGINATION

Much poor writing reads as if it had been put together by a machine. It delivers facts and statistics the way a scale we step on delivers a card with our weight. It gives instructions with the impersonality of a telephone directory. Such writing is depressing to read: It has no personal meaning for the reader. The reader must feel that the message means something to him or her as a person. This is possible only if the message was *sent* by a person—by a genuine human being.

There are several basic qualities that give good writing a human touch:

(1) *A sense of humor.* Among the English-speaking writers most widely read and translated are Charles Dickens and Mark Twain. They have one thing in common: They refuse to be always deadly serious and businesslike and dull. They write with a twinkle in the eye. They have a lively sense for whatever it is about people that makes them amusing, ridiculous, or hilarious.

(2) *An interest in people.* No one can be a good writer who never cares how other people think or feel. A good writer knows what readers will find exciting and what depressing. A good writer knows what they care about or what they can be *made* to care about if approached the right way.

(3) *A sense of wonder.* A good writer cannot afford to act blasé, to pretend to have seen it all. On the contrary, a good writer knows how to bring out what is interesting or fascinating about

things that we have all observed. He or she takes familiar things and looks at them from a new angle, or puts them together in new combinations.

Know when and how to employ the lighter touch.

A good writer is not always dead serious. She or he knows how to use the lighter touch when dealing with things that are trivial or amusing. We distrust the judgment of a writer who is fanatically serious about things that really do not matter. In fact, even deadly serious matters often have another, lighter side.

Mark Twain has often been considered the greatest of all humorous writers—and also the most American of American humorists. Suppose you were talking to a little green man who has just stepped out of a space capsule. He asks you: "What on Earth are they laughing about?" Give him some tentative answers based on your study of the following samples of American humor as written by Mark Twain:

The station buildings were long, low huts, made of sun-dried, mud-colored bricks, laid up without mortar (*adobes*, the Spaniards call these bricks, and Americans shorten it to '*dobies*). The roofs, which had no slant to them worth speaking of, were thatched and then sodded or covered with a thick layer of earth, and from this sprung a pretty rank growth of weeds and grass. It was the first time we had ever seen a man's front yard on top of his house.

We asked a passenger who belonged there what sort of a place it was. "Well," said he, after considering, and with the air of one who wishes to take time and be accurate, "it's a h--l of a place."

If you pick up a starving dog and make him prosperous, he will not bite you. This is the principal difference between a dog and a man.

I thought of the anecdote (a very, very old one, even at that day) of the traveler who sat down to a table which had nothing on it but a mackerel and a pot of mustard. He asked the landlord if this was all. The landlord said:

"*All!* Why, thunder and lightning, I should think there was mackerel enough there for six."

"But I don't like mackerel."

"Oh—then help yourself to the mustard."

THAT'S A LIKELY STORY

Do you ever read a news item that makes you say: "They made this one up"? Look at the following samples of the kind of news story that newspapers sometimes use to fill space. Assemble (or make up) a similar collection of unlikely news stories for a "zany" newspaper.

A motorist in Ontario was arrested after he turned his head to yell "sucker" at a wedding party and crashed into a parked car.

A magician in Zambia told a group of people they could bury him for two and a half hours and he would emerge alive. He charged one kwacha for performing the trick but he was dead when the group dug him up.

A farmer in England yawned so wide that it took doctors seven hours to close his mouth.

A motorist had stopped his car on the Golden Gate Bridge in San Francisco to inspect a flat tire. As he got out of the car, a woman pulled over behind him and shouted: "Don't jump! Don't jump!"

A missing railroad car with mail was found on an obscure, seldom-used siding in Perryville, Maryland, after a two-year search, postal officials said. The railroad had no explanation of how the car got on the siding from the 90-mile an hour passenger train that was pulling it.

To do good is noble; to teach others to do good is nobler, and no trouble.

There's a new remedy on the market for baldness. It's made of alum and persimmon juice. It doesn't grow hair, but it shrinks your head to fit what hair you have.

Here are some familiar techniques employed by humorous writers:

(1) *Stressing the unexpected or inappropriate.* A fly alighting on the nose of someone making a solemn speech is funny because it is contrary to what we expect. One of the most common ways of achieving a humorous effect is to look at the funny side of something that went wrong:

> Some black morning every cook will come into her domain to find her slaves suddenly become foes. *Knives bite the hand that wields them, cups stick to saucers, plates shatter, sinks stop up, stoves burn the pudding, toasters scorch the bread, spoons leap from the fingers, corkscrews crumble the cork in the bottle.* On such a day there is no use trying to deal with such malevolence. Despite your best diplomacy, cakes will refuse to rise, meat to turn tender, vegetables to remain green or savory. The sensible policy is either to warm up yesterday's macaroni and cheese or else take the family out to dinner until the storm blows over.
>
> —Phyllis McGinley, *Sixpence in Her Shoe*

(2) *Exaggerating for comic effect.* Often something that is extreme or unreasonable needs just a little exaggeration to make it appear ridiculous. Here is how one English observer made fun of all the time spent during an American college football game on things *other than* playing the game:

> The enormous clock ran off seconds when the ball was actually in play. It stopped when the game stopped. And the game *was always stopping.* Referees threw down little colored flags; linesmen ran on, *like half-crazed surveyors,* with measuring equipment; trainers and first-aid men trotted up with *water, sponges, liniment, perhaps disinfectant, brandy, antibiotics, blood transfusions, oxygen tents,* God knows what; players came off, other players went on; three men in white occasionally *turned somersaults;* the cheerleaders *leapt and wildly gesticulated,* the obedient fans noisily responded.
>
> —J. B. Priestley, *Journey Down a Rainbow*

(3) *Using the wrong style for the subject.* We chuckle when someone discusses a trivial subject in very high-flown language, and vice versa. How, for instance, does the following passage contrast with what we would expect in a zoology textbook?

The rhinoceros is dying out. It's best to come right out with these things no matter how much it hurts. Some *goody-goodies* would probably *stall around for a while* and try to break it to you by starting gently with something like, "Say, the Rhino is certainly a charmer." But we're all adults around here, right? *Pow! Right between the eyes!* The rhinoceros is dying out.

—Henry Morgan, "The Rhinoceros," *Saturday Review*

(4) *Playing on the meanings and associations of words.* When we use a **pun,** for instance, we use the same word at the same time with two different meanings:

I enjoyed the riding school thoroughly, and *got on—and off—*as well as most.

—Winston Churchill

Remember that, in any discussion of a serious subject, a little humor goes a long way. Even when the main purpose of a paper is to amuse the reader, not every reader will see every joke. Some readers may be offended by some of the jokes they do see:

—*Avoid humor that is thoughtless or cruel.* Stuttering, to someone who cares about people and their problems, is no joke. Foreigners are funny mostly to people too ignorant to realize that they themselves are foreigners when they travel abroad. A joke is in bad taste if it is aimed at something a person cannot help: looks, race, accent, physical handicaps, age, and the like.

—*Avoid overuse of a humorous pseudoformal style.* One way of having fun with language is to use big words for little things: "Then came the *sacred ritual* of punch *imbibing.* The *lad* on my left was supposed to furnish my partner and me with the *invigorating liquid.*" This kind of thing is easily overdone.

—*Avoid overuse of slangy informality.* Used imaginatively and one at a time, slang words can give writing a welcome humorous touch. When they are used too routinely, they merely sound disrespectful.

For Reading and Writing: Study the following passage by one of America's master humorists. Can you tell why this writer enjoyed a tremendous success? Write down your answers to the questions that follow the passage, and be prepared to discuss your answers in class.

WHAT'S FUNNY?

People say that adolescents have a special liking for "sick humor."
Do you? Using this cartoon as a sample, could you make up a short
definition of "sick humor?"

"Oh, no, Ma'm — I can assure you the spray is perfectly harmless!"

S. J. PERELMAN

To Sleep, Perchance to Steam

To anybody around here who is suffering from a touch of insomnia these days (surely no more than a hundred-to-one shot), the sequence of events in my bedroom last night may have a certain clinical interest. About nine o'clock, after a brisk session with the newscasters, I shuddered for approximately half an hour to relax my nerves, plugged a pair of Flents into my ears, and tied on a sleep mask. I probably should have waited until I got into bed before doing so, as I took a rather nasty fall over a waste-basket, but in a few moments I was stretched out, busily reviewing the war news and adding up the family bank account, with my pulse furnishing a rich musical background. When this palled, I read several chapters of Durfee's "Monasteries of the Rhône" with no success whatever until I discovered I had forgotten to remove my mask. As soon as I did, I was amply rewarded, for I found that with a little practice I was able to handle the strategy of the war and add up my bank account while vagabonding down the Rhône.

At this point, I regret to say, I tarnished an otherwise perfect record by falling into a slight doze. I must have been asleep almost fifteen minutes when I awoke suddenly and realized I had neglected to take a sedative before retiring. I promptly went out into the kitchen for a cup of hot milk with which to dissolve the nepenthe tablet and found Delia, our buxom cook, seated on the knee of her policeman friend. Actually, we have no cook called Delia, but we do have an impassive Englishman named Crichton and he was seated on the knee of a policewoman. The general effect was the same: a scene of coarse, steamy intimacy rivalling Hogarth's "Gin Lane." Muttering "This rivals Hogarth's 'Gin Lane'," I stalked back to bed just in time to discover that the annual outing of the Clan-na-Gael was beginning directly beneath my window. Egged on by shrill cries of approval from the ladies' auxiliary, strapping bosthoons executed nimble jigs and reels, sang come-all-ye's, and vied with each other in hurling refuse cans the length of the street. The gaiety was so spontaneous and impulsive that I could not refrain from distributing several bags of water as favors. The gesture moved the crowd deeply, a few of its members even offering to come and include me in their horseplay. Unfortunately, my good-natured refusal caused considerable pique and the revellers disbanded shortly. The sky and I were turning gray when, without any preamble, a woman in the apartment directly overhead began beating her husband mercilessly. Unable to withstand his screams, I finally gathered up all the available bedding, wrapped my head in it, and lay in a cedar chest in the foyer until routed out by the odor of coffee.

—from *The Best of S. J. Perelman*

1. In one brief sentence, define or explain: *insomnia, clinical, pall, vagabond, tarnish, sedative, nepenthe, buxom, impassive, bosthoon, vie, refrain, pique, preamble, foyer.*
2. What is the main source of humor in this passage? Explain it briefly and give at least two examples.
3. What is a second major feature that seems to be typical of Mr. Perelman's humor? Can you choose one that makes him *different* from other humorous writers you have read? Explain your choice briefly and give an example.
4. In the last third of the passage, read the three sentences that start "The gaiety was so spontaneous. . . ." Does he mean what he says? Can you recognize the way language is used here? Do you have a label for it? Explain briefly what makes these sentences different from ordinary straightforward statements.
5. Is there anything about Mr. Perelman's humor that some of his readers might consider as being not really funny or as being in bad taste? Explain.

Your Turn: Part of growing up is to develop a sense of humor about one's *own* problems. Describe an experience or situation where "the joke was on *you*." Make the reader see the funny side of the experience, but if possible also show him what you learned from it.

ACTIVITY 1

Fashions in humor change. What kind of humor is currently most fashionable with high school students? Bring together authentic examples and try to work out some general conclusions.

ACTIVITY 2

Sometimes the most effective humorous incidents are *unintentional*—slips of the tongue, advertisements that were meant to be serious but are funny, and the like. Collect and discuss several examples of such unintentional humor.

ACTIVITY 3

Write a humorous treatment of problems faced by *one* of the following: coach, police officer, principal, waitress, lifeguard, paper boy, school nurse, janitor. Try to make your paper *add up* by describing problems that are in some way related—that show something about the nature of the job or the person.

Know how to give your writing a fresh, imaginative quality.

C6b
The Writer and Fantasy

Effective writers must learn to look at familiar subjects from their own personal points of view. They must convince the reader that they have taken a *fresh look*. As you read the work of first-rate writers, look for the features that give their writing a fresh, imaginative twist. Follow their example in some of the following ways:

(1) *Look for the little dramas that are often acted out around us in everyday life.* Here is an episode from family life reported by one alert observer:

> We stayed for a while at a resort hotel near Veracruz. There was a Mexican family occupying the table next to ours in the dining room— Papa, Mama, and six children. Papa, a tall, handsome man, was one of the most important lawyers in Mexico City. . . . One morning he arrived a few minutes later than the others for breakfast. His bacon and eggs and fried beans were placed in front of him and he was ready to fall to when his wife spoke to him. Their youngest, a boy of about two, was not eating his food. The noted lawyer quietly put down his napkin, left his breakfast, took a chair beside the baby, and began the job of feeding him with a spoon. The little boy had a toy telephone alongside his dish of cereal. It is the custom among Mexicans to answer the telephone by saying "Bueno!" The father would feed the child a spoonful of breakfast, then pick up the tiny receiver and say into it, "Bueno!" Then another spoonful of cereal, and another "Bueno!" and so on until the dish was empty. By that time, of course, Papa's breakfast was as cold as the snow on the summit of Mt. Orizaba.
>
> —H. Allen Smith, "Mexico's Model Children," *Americas*

(2) *Explore unusual associations and analogies.* Notice how unexpected the comparison is in the following passage and yet how well it fits the situation. Here is what the writer said about one of his first days on a farm:

Wednesday. My cow turned out to be a very large one. The first time I led her out I felt the way I did the first time I ever took a girl to the theater—embarrassed but elated. In both instances the female walked with a firmer step than mine, seemed rather in charge of the affair, and excited me with her sweet scent.

—E. B. White, *One Man's Meat*

(3) *Take a fresh look at proverbs and familiar phrases.* The person who sagely repeats "Where there's smoke there's fire" is not likely to be a great original thinker. Here is what happened to one familiar proverb when an imaginative writer began to examine it:

Take as a first sample the proverb that is perhaps the best known in our language: *Birds of a feather flock together.* But they don't. Ask any first-class naturalist. If the wise old men had taken another look they would have seen that the last thing birds ever want to do is to flock together. In ninety-nine cases out of a hundred they keep away from their own species, and only flock when it is absolutely necessary. So much for the birds. But the proverb is really supposed to refer to people and then it is wrong again. People "of a feather" do not flock together. Tall men fall in love with little women. A girl with a beautiful fair skin and red hair marries a man who looks like a reformed orang-outang.

—Stephen Leacock, *Winnowed Wisdom*

(4) *Look at familiar things from a new perspective.* Jonathan Swift, in *Gulliver's Travels,* made such everyday articles as a handkerchief and a pocket watch puzzling and fascinating simply by making us look at them through the eyes of the six-inch-high inhabitants of Lilliput. American sports look new and weird when we look at them through the eyes of a newly-arrived foreign student. Earth customs look strange and amusing when we look at them through the eyes of a visitor from another planet.

When we let our imagination run free, it becomes **fantasy.** It takes us to faraway places, makes us share fantastic adventures, lets us see weird and wonderful sights. But often even the most freely imaginative writing is more than a mere escape to never-never land. A science fiction writer may take us to the planet Mars so that we may look back with new understanding to the civilization we left behind.

THE LANGUAGE OF SYMBOLS

Symbols carry a message. (Can you state in your own words the message carried by each of the symbols on this page?) But symbols also appeal powerfully to our emotions and our imaginations. (Choose one of the symbols on this page—talk or write about some imaginary scene or situation it brings to your mind.)

For Reading and Writing: The following passage was written by one of the most imaginative of modern writers of science fiction. It describes events taking place half a century away. Does it also say something about here and today? Write down your answers to the questions that follow the passage, and be prepared to discuss your answers in class.

PROSE MODEL 9   **RAY BRADBURY**

August 2026

In the living room the voice-clock sang, *Tick-tock, seven o'clock, time to get up, time to get up, seven o'clock!* as if it were afraid that nobody would. The morning house lay empty. The clock ticked on, repeating and repeating its sounds into the emptiness. *Seven-nine, breakfast time, seven-nine!*

In the kitchen the breakfast stove gave a hissing sigh and ejected from its warm interior eight pieces of perfectly browned toast, eight eggs sunnyside up, sixteen slices of bacon, two coffees, and two cool glasses of milk.

"Today is August 4, 2026," said a second voice from the kitchen ceiling, "in the city of Allendale, California." It repeated the date three times for memory's sake. "Today is Mr. Featherstone's birthday. Today is the anniversary of Tilita's marriage. Insurance is payable, as are the water, gas, and light bills."

Somewhere in the walls, relays clicked, memory tapes glided under electric eyes.

Eight-one, tick-tock, eight-one o'clock, off to school, off to work, run, run, eight-one! But no doors slammed, no carpets took the soft tread of rubber heels. It was raining outside. The weather box on the front door sang quietly: "Rain, rain, go away; rubbers, raincoats for today. . . ." And the rain tapped on the empty house, echoing.

Outside, the garage chimed and lifted its door to reveal a waiting car. After a long wait the door swung down again.

At eight-thirty the eggs were shriveled and the toast was like stone. An aluminum wedge scraped them into the sink, where hot water whirled them down a metal throat which digested and flushed them away to the distant sea. The dirty dishes were dropped into a hot washer and emerged twinkling dry.

Nine-fifteen, sang the clock, *time to clean.*

Out of warrens in the wall, tiny robot mice darted. The rooms were acrawl with the small cleaning animals, all rubber and metal. They thudded against chairs, whirling their mustached runners, kneading the rug nap, sucking gently at hidden dust. Then, like mysterious invaders, they popped into their burrows. Their pink electric eyes faded. The house was clean.

Ten o'clock. The sun came out from behind the rain. The house stood alone in a city of rubble and ashes. This was the one house left standing. At night the ruined city gave off a radioactive glow which could be seen for miles.

Ten-fifteen. The garden sprinklers whirled up in golden founts, filling the soft morning air with scatterings of brightness. The water pelted windowpanes, running down the charred west side where the house had been burned evenly free of its white paint. The entire west face of the house was black, save for five places. Here the silhouette in paint of a man mowing a lawn. Here, as in a photograph, a woman bent to pick flowers. Still farther over, their images burned on wood in one titanic instant, a small boy, hands flung into the air; higher up, the image of a thrown ball, and opposite him a girl, hands raised to catch a ball which never came down.

—from *The Martian Chronicles*

1. The author of this passage is a master of concrete description. List half a dozen words that are especially effective in making the reader visualize shape, appearance, or movement. Be prepared to discuss in class the picture they call up before the reader's eyes.
2. Point out one detail in the description of the house that makes the house and what goes on there seem real or convincing.
3. Among the details given about the equipment of the house, point out the one that seems to you the most unexpected or imaginative. Explain your choice in a sentence or two.
4. Dozens of writers and movie makers have tried to imagine what the results of nuclear war would be like. Write one paragraph explaining what makes this passage an unusual or fresh treatment of this familiar subject.
5. Does this passage have a specific message for the reader to remember? Sum up in one sentence what you think might be its major point.

Your Turn: A writer once imagined how, as a survivor of nuclear war, he would be writing a *manual of instructions* for future generations who had lost all the accumulated knowledge and skills of our civilization. Among other things, he tried to include instructions for making safety matches and a wheelbarrow. He also included whatever parts of Shakespeare he knew by heart. Imagine that you have been given the chance to write a memo for survivors of nuclear war. Include only the most essential information or advice, but try to make it detailed enough so that it will be useful.

ACTIVITY 1

Imagine that you suddenly found yourself living in an ancient and advanced civilization that nevertheless lacked *one basic invention* that we take for granted: writing, or the wheel. What would life be like in such a place?

ACTIVITY 2

Most new business products have to be "practical." What kind of *new product* would you like to see invented if the inventor could be given a free hand to be as extravagant and imaginative as he pleased? One writer's choice was an "irresistible alarm clock" that would flood the room with sunshine and the scent of wild roses and "evoke a zest to grab life by a leg." Describe *your* choice in detail, and try to make it attractive to your reader.

ACTIVITY 3

Do you ever make up imaginary stories to go with faces you see in a crowd or with pictures you see in a newspaper or magazine? From a newspaper or magazine, clip a *picture that you find interesting or unusual*. Ignore the original caption—make up your own story to go with the picture. Your teacher may provide a picture for the whole class to write about.

For Branching Out: Suppose you have just been hired as an assistant *scriptwriter* for a variety of fantasy movies. Here are brief capsule descriptions for several of them. Write a scene for one of these. (You may want to collaborate with some of your classmates.)

1. The hero (or heroine) lives in our time but awakens from suspended animation to find himself (or herself) in a drastically altered future society. Our time traveler becomes involved in a power struggle between two factions trying to dominate the future society.
2. After their ship sinks off the coast of Africa, members of a Hollywood team find themselves unwilling guests of a mad scientist. They gradually discover, to their horror, that their host uses his laboratory to operate on captured jungle animals to turn them into

near-human monsters: the gorilla-man; the panther-man; the hyena-man; and so forth.

3. In a strange faraway country, vampires have become an organized force to reckon with and have taken over most of the society. They round up human captives and take them to their vampire castles. A guerrilla force of freedom-loving humans is planning to infiltrate the castle of the chief vampire.

FOR DISCUSSION
AND WRITING

MAN AND THE MACHINE

Here is how someone retold a story that he read in a science fiction comic book many years ago:

A man stumbled into Doctor X's office and noticed a machine by an open window. He fiddled with the dials and put in his name and the year and day. The dials lit up, and the machine sent out a card that said, "You will be struck by lightning and killed at 6:00 tomorrow morning." The man was fascinated. He pressed a button labeled "Death Averted" and jumped five years in time. He saw that he would be rich and successful—but that he was going to be in an airplane accident. Then he pressed "Death Averted" and went ten years ahead. This time he had a lovely wife and happy children—but there was going to be a business disaster and he would commit suicide. Again he pressed "Death Averted" and went ahead fifteen years. The man was so busy seeing what a wonderful, successful, happy life he would have that he didn't see that dawn was coming. He paid no attention to the open window and the rising wind. And then, suddenly, the man was struck dead by lightning. At 6:00 a.m.

1. How did you think the story was going to end? Could it have ended in any other way?
2. What would you say is the point of this story?
3. Could you write a brief science fiction story about a machine of the future?

C7
WRITING AND
READING

Use the results of your reading in your own writing.

Good writers put the results of their reading to work in their own writing. Here are some of the ground rules you should follow in discussing the work of other writers or in drawing material from what they have written:

(1) *Try to understand what a writer is doing.* As you read a book or an article, your attitude should be: "Let me see what this writer is trying to do." Many readers are too impatient. Let them encounter a strange new idea and they will exclaim: "How ridiculous! I must expose this writer as a quack." A fair-minded reader would say instead: "What a strange new idea! I wonder how this writer arrived at it? Let me see how the writer backs it up."

(2) *Try to look at a book or article as a whole.* Any writer can make a factual mistake or say something snide in a moment of irritation. That does not make the book as a whole unreliable or ill-natured. Do not imitate book reviewers who pick away at minor faults and miss the larger picture. Try to keep in mind the questions that matter: "What is the plan of the book as a whole? How well does the book as a whole do its job?"

(3) *Quote only what fairly represents the intention of an author.* Make sure that any authors you quote *said* what you claim they said. Make sure that they *meant* what you claim they meant. Do not quote a phrase or a sentence out of context. Pay attention to what led up to it or what followed.

Make your book report a fair and informative account of a book considered as a whole.

C7a
The Book Report

A book report shows that the person doing the report has read the book. But a good book report does more. It shows that the person doing the report has read the book *well*, has formed a fair estimate of what the book as a whole is trying to accomplish, and can point out major features that make the book what it is.

Though there are many different kinds of books, the kind that you are most likely to do a report on is a novel; or a biography; or an account of travel, discovery, or adventure. A good report on this kind of book typically includes at least one solid paragraph each on *several* of the following major features. Select those features that seem most important for an understanding of your particular book:

PLOT

What *happens* in the book? Can you summarize the events that make for excitement or suspense? Can you point out the high points or major stages in a person's life that are treated in a biography? Can you summarize the causes and effects stressed by an author writing about a period in history? Make sure that your summary of actions and events does not *take over the whole report*. Different authors may describe the same events in quite different ways. Telling your readers about the plot is not the same as telling them all about the book.

SETTING

How important is the *place* or the region where the events happen? Often, our major interest in a book is in what we learn about life in a certain place at a certain time: Virginia when it was still a British colony, or an island in the Pacific during World War II.

CHARACTER

What do we learn about the *people* that get most of the attention? What kind of person is the central character of a novel or the person treated in a biography? What is the person after? What makes the person act the way he or she does? What is the person's attitude toward others—faith in them or suspicion toward them? What is the person's most important motive, or problem, or goal?

THEME

What major *idea* remains strongest in the reader's mind? Does one thing just happen after another, or does the book as a whole change the reader's attitude or opinions in some important respect? Did the author have a specific purpose? Perhaps it was to clear the reputation of an important historical figure; or to show us something about the true nature of patriotism, or of loyalty, or of love.

MOOD

Often *what* the book deals with is less important than the *spirit* in which people and events are described. What is the prevailing tone—grim, cheerful, discouraging? Does the book make the reader laugh or cry? What kind of person does the author seem to be—easygoing or serious, calm and fair or always ready to quarrel and find fault?

In writing a book report, your major concern should be with the book itself. Often, however, your reader can form a better estimate of the book if you provide additional information about its background and intended purpose. For instance, how important is it for the reader to know something about the *author*? Or, is the appeal of the book limited to a particular *audience*?

As you prepare your own book reports, remember the following advice:

—*Use well-chosen short quotations.* Sparing use of short quotations is the best way to make your account of the book seem authentic, and to convey to your reader some of the characteristic flavor of the book.

—*Concentrate on essentials.* Limit yourself to a few important points and explain and illustrate those well.

—*Remember that your reader may not have read the book.* When you mention people and places, remember to explain to your reader who and what they are.

Study the following sample book report. Be prepared to discuss your answers to two major questions: *Which* major features of the book does the report cover? *How,* and how well, is each major point developed? See whether you can find in this sample some of the qualities of a good book report that have just been described.

Seven Years in Tibet by Heinrich Harrer

Heinrich Harrer's book, *Seven Years in Tibet,* is an action-packed story of seven thrilling but trying years in Tibet, five of those in Lhasa. It relates the struggle of Heinrich Harrer and his companion, Aufschnaiter, against nature and the Tibetan people.

The author's trek was from a British internment camp in India through the Himalayan Mountains to find sanctuary in the "Forbidden City of Lhasa." The Himalayan Mountains, 20,000 feet above sea level, with rarefied air and raging blizzards, reaching 50 degrees below zero centigrade, afforded Harrer few days of pleasure climbing and were a constant challenge to him. However, like a true mountaineer, Harrer momentarily forgot the physical hardships when he beheld the Himalayas . . . "looming ahead like a white capped God."

The second challenge in *Seven Years in Tibet* was the Tibetan fear of what Harrer and Aufschnaiter might do to their country. "Posing as Indians, with hair and beard dyed black, and skin stained," they tricked the superstitious people and the wary officials in every town along the way. The closer they traveled to Lhasa, however, the easier it became because the people felt that since the strangers had been allowed this far perhaps there was not much to fear from them.

After gaining entrance to Lhasa, an accomplishment practically unheard of, they were cordially welcomed and entertained hospitably by the people. The Lhasa officials tried in vain to send them away but finally let them stay after realizing they would do no harm. Their second year in Lhasa, which was their fourth year in Tibet, Heinrich Harrer became . . . "the confidant of the youthful Dalai Lama . . . loaded with constant gifts . . . and granted complete freedom." They built, while there, a fountain and an irrigation canal. They introduced volleyball, ice skating, and tennis.

The author of this story does an excellent job of portraying the Tibetan people as they are, simple and happy. Describing his personal feelings about the land itself, Harrer writes, "Wherever I live, I shall feel homesick for Tibet. I often think I can still hear the wild cries of geese and cranes and the beating of their wings as they fly over Lhasa in the clear cold moonlight."

FOR DISCUSSION AND WRITING

NOVELIST FOR A DAY

Read the following summary of a book about two high school students. If you had never heard of this book before, would this summary make you want to read it? Why or why not? *Choose a scene* from this summary—and then write your own version of it. Pretend you are the novelist and you are writing part of a chapter for your novel.

In *The Pigman*, John Conlan and Lorraine Jensen are fifteen-year-old sophomores who live in New York. While playing the telephone game of calling random listings to see how long they can engage the party in conversation, they happen to call a Mr. Pignati, later called the Pigman. . . . Keeping their "find" from two other friends, Dennis and Norton, Lorraine and John visit Mr. Pignati, who gives them a check for ten dollars for their supposed charity organization, the pretext of the phone call. When they arrive at his home, he tells them his wife is away and he enjoys zoo visiting. He asks them to go with him sometime. Conversation about animals brings them to see his collection of figurine pigs from all over the world, a hobby begun years ago, when he gave his wife the gift of one as a joke about his name.

Gradually, they become fond of this nearly-sixty-year-old man who offers them wine when they visit him. Together they visit Beekman's where he used to go with his wife, Conchetta. He buys some favorite foods first, then hosiery for Lorraine, and finally skates for all of them.

Daily visits after school lead John and Lorraine to tell Mr. Pignati the truth about themselves, to which he responds by admitting the death of his wife. After these two declarations John begins to skate up and down the hallway. The Pigman joins him, John then goes up the stairs calling after the older man who, in his attempt to follow John, suffers a heart attack.

While recuperating in the hospital, he tells John and Lorraine to use his house and to visit Bobo, the baboon he visited daily in the zoo. John decides to throw a party one evening and with the large crowd of teenagers there, pandemonium breaks out in skating, trying on Conchetta's old clothes, drinking, and some fighting. At the height of the celebrating, Mr. Pignati returns home, and the police, who have been called because of the noise, escort Lorraine and John to their homes.

Trying later to patch things up, Lorraine and John invite the Pigman to go to the zoo to feed Bobo. The old man, still saddened by the wild party he returned to, agrees to meet them there. Too late, they discover Bobo's cage is empty; the old man gives out a wail at his realization of the animal's death and collapses in death himself.

ACTIVITY 1

Read the following "capsule reviews" of books written for or about adolescents. Pretend you were answering a letter from a publisher trying to find out what kinds of books young people like to read. Which of these books would you want to read most? Why? Which of these books would you want to read least? Why?

1. John Donovan's I'LL GET THERE: IT BETTER BE WORTH THE TRIP tells of Davy who lives with his grandmother following his parents' divorce. He experiences great love in his life with his grandmother and his dachshund Fred. But then his grandmother dies and that warm world shatters. Davy must live with his career-centered, self-centered mother in a large city apartment building. She has no understanding of boys or dogs, so life becomes grim for Davy. Although he experiences better communication with his father and his father's second wife, Davy's mother feels it is her "duty" to raise him.

2.   UP A ROAD SLOWLY by Irene Hunt is the story of Julia, whose mother dies when she is still young and whose older sister, a kind of "second mother" and idol to Julia, marries and leaves home. Julia's father sends her to live just outside of town with an unmarried aunt. When her father remarries, Julia chooses to remain with her aunt. Julia, who might be labeled a "spoiled brat" at the novel's opening, experiences many "growing pains," but she eventually emerges as a mature and independent young woman. This is a book that treats candidly a young girl's problems of finding her identity in a broken home.

3.   HIS ENEMY, HIS FRIEND, by John Tunis. Hans von Kleinschrodt is a German officer assigned to a small French village lying on the coast of the English Channel. The story is set in the last days of the Second World War. The German is a decent man, well-educated, and from an aristocratic family. Before the war he had been a champion soccer player. He wants to treat the French villagers as fellow human beings and even organizes the youngsters into a team. The young boys worship him much to the disgust of the officer in charge. When the officer in charge is assassinated, Hans is ordered to kill five hostages from the village. Years later, Germany and France set up a championship soccer game between the best team of each nation. Hans and a young French boy whom he had trained are the stars of the two teams.

4.   A TEACUP OF ROSES, by Sharon Mathis. This short novel [is] about a family that is both black and impoverished. The story is told from the point of view of Joey who has dropped out of school to go to work in the hope that his brilliant and athletic younger brother can complete high school and go to college. The older brother, Paul, has just been released from a drug clinic but is a worry to family members who wonder if he will return to his old habit. The mother can see nothing but good in Paul and is willing to sacrifice the other boys' futures to help this son.

5.   SOUL CATCHERS, by Frank Herbert. A book that builds with spellbinding intensity is this story of a young Indian graduate student in anthropology who works summers as a counselor in a boys camp. Slowly he becomes convinced that his mission is to expiate the sins of the white man toward his people by taking the life of an "innocent." Led by the voices of the crows who are his totem, he kidnaps a thirteen-year-old in his charge and takes off into remote regions of the Olympic Mountains. During their terrifying journey, a strange and deep affection develops between the boy and the Indian. The boy has a chance to escape when the Indian becomes ill, but he stays to nurse his captor back to health.

The Indian comes to feel that he can kill the boy only if the boy asks him to do so.

ACTIVITY 2

Here is a list of books that are often recommended to high school students. Your teacher may ask you to choose one or more of these for a book report.

R. L. Stevenson, *Treasure Island*
Walter Van Tilburg Clark, *The Ox-Bow Incident*
Stephen Crane, *The Red Badge of Courage*
Mark Twain, *The Adventures of Huckleberry Finn*
Charles Kingsley, *Westward Ho!*
James Hilton, *Lost Horizon*
Charles Dickens, *A Tale of Two Cities*
Antoine de Saint-Exupéry, *Wind, Sand and Stars*
Ernest Pyle, *Brave Men*
Joseph Conrad, *Typhoon and Other Stories*
Rudyard Kipling, *Captains Courageous*
Richard Henry Dana, *Two Years Before the Mast*
Thor Heyerdahl, *Kon Tiki: Across the Pacific by Raft*
Eve Curie, *Madame Curie*

Use the research report to bring together information and ideas from different sources.

C7b
The Research Report

On many subjects, we accept the opinion of a single expert. We don't argue with the plumber, and we usually trust our doctor to prescribe what is necessary. On other subjects, however, we cannot simply accept an opinion ready-made. Information about the early history of our community, for instance, may be *scattered* in a variety of sources: old newspapers, diaries kept by old-timers, a history of the county or the state. On some subjects we have to sort out *conflicting* testimony. A Northern and a Southern historian, for instance, may disagree about important events during what the one calls the "American Civil War" and the other calls the "War between the States."

A good writer must learn to bring together and to sift and evaluate material from a variety of sources. A solid paper or article often requires preliminary **research:** hunting for missing information, comparing conflicting accounts, checking of sources that seem superficial or unreliable. By writing short research reports, you can prepare yourself for the kind of research often expected of a writer.

In a research report, you try to show that you have become somewhat of an *authority* on the subject you have investigated. Remember the following guidelines:

(1) *Narrow down your area of investigation.* The whole point of a research report is to cover a limited problem more *thoroughly* than you could in an ordinary theme. "What kind of a person was Benjamin Franklin?" is a very broad question. "How did he develop an interest in science?" is more limited.

(2) *Show that you have studied several sources.* Never simply copy a page from an encyclopedia article. Instead, bring together *in the same paragraph* what two or three people have said about the same point. What do they agree on? Where do they differ? Who seems to be more nearly right? (See Chapter Seven on how to find source material in the library.)

(3) *Wherever possible, provide accurate and exact information.* Refuse to be satisfied with such vague expressions as "a fairly large number." Try to give exact dates, figures, locations:

> With more bathrooms, dishwashers, washing machines and sprinklers we are using some 60 gallons more per day per person than our grandparents did in 1900. But industry uses 11 times more than it employed in 1900—some 110 billion gallons of water a day. Why? It takes 200,000 gallons to make a ton of viscose rayon; 65,000 gallons to make a ton of steel. A large paper mill needs 22 million gallons a day; a gallon of gasoline requires 7 to 10 gallons of water for processing.

(4) *Use efficient ways of reproducing material directly from your sources.* Never simply quote big chunks of material from an article or book. Limit direct quotation to key statements and important phrases. Learn to use three important tools:

The Paraphrase:	When you paraphrase a statement, you are simply putting it into *your own words*. This way, you can leave out unimportant and irrelevant material, and you can make sure that the reader gets the gist of a passage.
The Excerpted Quote:	Preserve the *highlights* of a longer quotation and use spaced periods to indicate your omissions (see M 6a).

LET'S TRY TO BE FAIR

Prominent athletes, like other prominent figures, some-times complain about their treatment at the hands of news-papers and newsmagazines. Find *three* different newspaper or magazine articles about an athlete who, in recent months (or in recent years) has been much in the news and who may have been the subject of controversy or criticism. You might choose a prizefighter, tennis star, football or baseball player, or swimming champion. From your different sources, can you piece together a *fair* picture of what he or she is like as a person? Present your findings as a brief oral or written report. Try to include some short revealing quotations from the person who is the subject of your report.

The Partial Quote: Work quoted phrases and parts of sentences closely into *sentences of your own.* This technique makes possible smooth reading without the stop-and-go effect of long complete quotations.

Can you see how the following passage makes use of all three of these tools?

Tradition and written records tell us that primitive navigators often carried with them birds which they would release and follow to land. The frigate bird or man-of-war bird was the shore-sighting bird of the Polynesians (even in recent times it has been used to carry messages between islands), and in the Norse Sagas we have an account of the use of "ravens" by Floki Vilgerdarson to show him the way to Iceland, "since seafaring men had no loadstone at that time in the north. . . . Thence he sailed out to sea with the three ravens. . . . And when he let loose the first it flew back astern. The second flew up into the air and back to the ship. The third flew forward over the prow, where they found land."

In thick and foggy weather, according to repeated statements in the Sagas, the Norsemen drifted for days without knowing where they were. Then they often had to rely on observing the flight of birds to judge the direction of land. The *Landnamabok* says that on the course from Norway to Greenland the voyager should keep far enough to the south of Iceland to have birds and whales from there. In shallow waters it appears that the Norsemen took some sort of soundings, for the *Historia Norwegiae* records that Ingolf and Hjorleif found Iceland "by probing the waves with the lead."

—Rachel Carson, *The Sea Around Us*

(5) *Make sure the reader can see who said what.* When you quote several different sources, make sure each quotation is clearly *attributed* to the right author and the right book or article. When you write *"She* also said . . ."* leave no doubt in the reader's mind about who is meant by *she.*

For Reading and Writing: One way of training a writer to bring together material from different sources is to have the writer compare, on one major point, several books by the *same author.* The following passage deals with the typical hero in the books of Horatio Alger, which were at one time read by young people in millions of American homes. How well has the author of this passage solved the problem of talking about several different books more or less at the same time? Write down your answers to the questions that follow the passage, and be prepared to discuss your answers in class.

PROSE MODEL 10   **FREDERICK LEWIS ALLEN**

Our Hero

The standard Horatio Alger hero was a fatherless boy of fifteen or thereabouts who had to earn his way, usually in New York City. Sometimes he had to help support a widowed mother with his bootblacking or peddling; sometimes his parentage was unknown and he lived with an aged and eccentric miser, or with a strange hermit who claimed to be his uncle. It might even be that his father was living, but was having trouble with the mortgage on the old farm. Always, however, the boy had to stand on his own feet and face the practical problem of getting on.

This problem was set before the reader in exact financial detail. On the very first page of *Do and Dare,* for example, it was disclosed that the young hero's mother, as postmistress at Wayneboro, had made during the preceding year just $398.50. Whenever "our hero" had to deal with a mortgage, the reader was told the precise amount, the rate of interest, and all other deails. When our hero took a job, the reader could figure for himself exactly how much progress he was making by getting $5 a week in wages at the jewelry store and another $5 a week tutoring Mrs. Mason's son in Latin. Our hero was always a good boy, honest, abstemious (in fact, sometimes unduly disposed to preach to drinkers and smokers), prudent, well-mannered (except perhaps for the preaching), and frugal. The excitement of each book lay in his progress toward wealth.

Always there were villains who stood in his way—crooks who would rob him of his earnings, sharpers who would prey upon his supposed innocence. His battles with these villains furnished plenty of melo-drama. They tried to sell him worthless gold watches on railroad trains, held him up as he was buggy-driving home with his employer's funds, kidnapped him and held him prisoner in a New York hide out, chloroformed him in a Philadelphia hotel room, slugged him in a Chicago alley-tenement. But always he overcame them—with the aid of their invariable cowardice. (There must be many men now living who remember the shock of outraged surprise with which they discovered that the village bully did not, as in Alger books, invariably run whimpering away at the first show of manly opposition, but some-times packed a nasty right.) The end of the book—or series of books, for often several volumes were devoted to the varied adventures of a single boy—found our hero well on his way toward wealth: a fortune which might reach to more than a hundred thousand dollars, which, to the average boy reader of the seventies and eighties, was an astronomical sum.

—from "Horatio Alger, Jr.," Saturday Review

1. In one brief sentence each, define or explain: *parentage, eccentric, hermit, abstemious, prudent, frugal, melodrama, tenement, invariable, astronomical.*
2. Make a brief outline listing no more than four or five major points that the author takes up in describing the typical Horatio Alger hero.
3. Quote *three* phrases from different parts of the passage that all point to the central point or major theme on which this account is focused.
4. There is only *one* example of direct quotation in this passage. What is it? Can you explain in a sentence or two *why* those particular words were quoted directly?
5. What feature of this passage is most likely to convince the reader that Mr. Allen has actually *read* (and studied) the books he is discussing? Explain and illustrate in a sentence or two.

Your Turn: Write a paragraph in which you quote *three different authors* on the same major point or problem. Include a sentence or two of your own in which you explain how the information or opinions in the three quotations add up. On what do the authors agree? Where do they disagree? For instance, you might check an encyclopedia and two history books or biographies on one of the following: Is the cherry tree episode told about George Washington fact or legend? How well did Abraham Lincoln get along with his wife? Was Benjamin Franklin successful as a businessman? What was Thomas Jefferson's attitude toward slavery?

ACTIVITY 1

Draw on three or four sources—newspaper articles, editorials, or pamphlets—for a research report on what your local area is doing about a *current community problem*. For instance, does your community have traffic congestion, a smog problem, crowded schools, inadequate public transportation, unsafe public parks? Limit your general subject to a topic that you can discuss in detail. Use statistics and other factual material where appropriate; make use of paraphrase and direct quotation in drawing on your sources.

ACTIVITY 2

Read at least three articles or books about a well-known person who *made his way against great odds*. Then write a biographical paper presenting the most important part of what you have learned about the person. Choose someone like Booker T. Washington, Malcolm X, Frederick Douglass, Helen Keller, or Madame Curie. Select material that will help your reader understand the person's background, character, and achievement. Try to include some revealing firsthand quotation. Use material from at least *three* different sources.

FURTHER STUDY

WRITING FOR THE MEDIA

Some writing is person-to-person. A boy or a girl in camp writes a letter home. A sales representative writes a memo to a supervisor. A student leaves a note for a teacher. But other kinds of writing are done for an audience of thousands (or millions) of people. Daily, the modern mass media of communication pour out words, words, words. These words reach people of all ages, from all parts of the country, from all walks of life. What common needs, what common interests are served by media that reach millions of people?

The following assignments give you a chance to get an inside view of how the media use language. These assignments give you a chance to become acquainted with the legwork and the "penwork" of people who write for newspapers, magazines, radio, television, and the movies.

Assignment 1: Sometimes we read a news report that is a true classic. It describes an event that will be long remembered by literally millions of people. How much do you remember of the event described in the following newspaper report?

AMERICAN FLAG PLANTED

The two men walked easily, talked easily, even ran and jumped happily so it seemed. They picked up rocks, talked at length of what they saw, planted an American flag, saluted it, and talked by radiophone with the President in the White House, and then faced the camera and saluted Mr. Nixon.

"For every American, this has to be the proudest day of our lives," the President told the astronauts. "For one priceless moment in the whole history of man, all the people on this earth are truly one."

Seven hours earlier, at 4:17 P.M., the Eagle and its two pilots thrilled the world as they zoomed in over a rock-covered field, hovered and then slowly let down on the moon. "Houston, Tranquillity base here," Armstrong radioed. "The Eagle has landed."

At 1:10 A.M. Monday—2 hours and 14 minutes after Armstrong first stepped upon the lunar surface—the astronauts were back in their moon craft and the hatch was closed.

In describing the moon, Armstrong told Houston that it was "fine and powdery. I can kick it up loosely with my toe.

"It adheres like powdered charcoal to the boot," he went on, "but I only go in a small fraction of an inch. I can see my footprint in the moon like fine grainy particles."

Armstrong found he had such little trouble walking on the moon that he began talking almost as if he didn't want to leave it.

"It has a stark beauty all its own," Armstrong said. "It's like the desert in the Southwestern United States. It's very pretty out here."

THE EAGLE HAS LANDED

TWO MEN WALK ON THE MOON

HOUSTON, July 20—Man stepped out onto the moon tonight for the first time in his two-million-year history.

"That's one small step for man," declared pioneer astronaut Neil Armstrong at 10:56 P.M. EDT, "one giant leap for mankind."

Just after that historic moment in man's quest for his origins, Armstrong walked on the dead satellite and found the surface very powdery, littered with fine grains of black dust.

A few minutes later, Edwin (Buzz) Aldrin joined Armstrong on the lunar surface and in less than an hour they put on a show that will long be remembered by the worldwide television audience.

Your Turn:

1. Pretend you are one of the team that landed. With your teamates, *act out* the events. Improvise: Make up your own dialogue. Or pretend that you are a radio reporter who accompanied the mission. Improvise your own live coverage of the event.

2. Pretend you are a *commentator* for a local radio or TV station. You have two or three minutes to express your thoughts and feelings about the "giant leap for mankind."

3. Write a news report of an imaginary *future event* of similar importance—a truly historic "first." For example, you might write about the first landing on a planet outside the solar system. Or you might write about some momentous development or discovery that will change the course of human history.

Assignment 2: Some famous news stories deal with a tragic event, a great collective disaster. What would your feelings be if you had just opened your morning newspaper and were reading the following news report?

KENNEDY IS KILLED BY SNIPER AS HE RIDES IN CAR IN DALLAS; JOHNSON SWORN IN ON PLANE

DALLAS, Nov. 22—President John Fitzgerald Kennedy was shot and killed by an assassin today.

He died of a wound in the brain caused by a rifle bullet that was fired at him as he was riding through downtown Dallas in a motorcade.

Vice President Lyndon Baines Johnson, who was riding in the third car behind Mr. Kennedy's, was sworn in as the 36th President of the United States 99 minutes after Mr. Kennedy's death.

Mr. Johnson is 55 years old; Mr. Kennedy was 46.

Shortly after the assassination, Lee H. Oswald, who once defected to the Soviet Union and who has been active in the Fair Play for Cuba Committee, was arrested by the Dallas police. Tonight he was accused of the killing.

SUSPECT CAPTURED AFTER SCUFFLE

Oswald, 24 years old, was also accused of slaying a policeman who had approached him in the street. Oswald was subdued after a scuffle with a second policeman in a nearby theater.

President Kennedy was shot at 12.30 P.M., Central Standard Time (1:30 P.M., New York time). He was pronounced dead at 1 P.M. and Mr. Johnson was sworn in at 2:39 P.M.

Mr. Johnson, who was uninjured in the shooting, took his oath in the Presidential jet plane as it stood on the runway at Love Field. The body of Mr. Kennedy was aboard. Immediately after the oath-taking, the plane took off for Washington.

Standing beside the new President as Mr. Johnson took the oath of office was Mrs. John F. Kennedy. Her stockings were spattered with her husband's blood.

Gov. John B. Connally, Jr., of Texas, who was riding in the same car with Mr. Kennedy, was severely wounded in the chest, ribs and arm. His condition was serious, but not critical.

The killer fired the rifle from a building just off the motorcade route. Mr. Kennedy, Governor Connally and Mr. Johnson had just received an enthusiastic welcome from a large crowd in downtown Dallas.

Mr. Kennedy apparently was hit by the first of what witnesses believe were three shots. He was driven at high speed to Dallas Parkland Hospital. There, in an emergency operating room, with only physicians and nurses in attendance, he died without regaining consciousness.

Mrs. Kennedy, Mrs. Connally and a Secret Service agent were in the car with Mr. Kennedy and Governor Connally. Two Secret Service agents flanked the car. Other than Mr. Connally, none of this group was injured in the shooting. Mrs. Kennedy cried, "Oh no!" immediately after her husband was struck.

Mrs. Kennedy was in the hospital near her husband when he died, but not in the operating room. When the body was taken from the hospital in a bronze coffin about 2 P.M., Mrs. Kennedy walked beside it.

Her face was sorrowful. She looked steadily at the floor. She still wore the raspberry-colored suit in which she had greeted welcoming crowds in Fort Worth and Dallas. But she had taken off the matching pillbox hat she wore earlier in the day, and her dark hair was windblown and tangled. Her hand rested lightly on her husband's coffin as it was taken to a waiting hearse.

Mrs. Kennedy climbed in beside the coffin. Then the ambulance drove to Love Field, and Mr. Kennedy's body was placed aboard the Presidential jet. Mrs. Kennedy then attended the swearing-in ceremony for Mr. Johnson.

—*New York Times*, Nov. 23, 1963

Your Turn:

1. Pretend you are a radio reporter doing a *live coverage* of the President's motorcade in Dallas. Improvise: Make up your own running coverage of the events.
2. Team up with your classmates: Pretend you are a radio or TV reporter conducting an *interview* with one or more of the people mentioned in the report.
3. Oswald, the man accused of killing President Kennedy, was shot down and killed and thus never brought to trial. Have you ever read or heard anything about this man? You may want to prepare an imaginary courtroom speech that he might have made if he had been brought to trial.
4. Write an imaginary news report of some other *historic event* that you have read about. Some possible events are the French revolution, the American revolution, Lincoln's assassination, the attempted assassination of Hitler in 1944, the fall of Rome, a famous battle.

Assignment 3: Much mass media coverage is devoted to the doings of *people* in the news. The mass audience is always eager to hear about celebrities, to read about people who for one reason or another have caught the public eye. Who are some people that *you* are interested in reading or hearing about? Would you be one of the people likely to be interested in reading the following interview from a national magazine? (Why or why not?)

Your Turn:

1. Restage the interview. Or, with your classmates, stage some *imaginary interviews* with other celebrities that you have been reading about.
2. Write an imaginary interview with a historical personage, now dead.

Assignment 4: Much mass media coverage is "human interest" material. We read and hear about unknowns. We become interested in some of the strange or unusual things they do.

just a girl from *Laurel, Mississippi*

Leontyne Price took to music like lint to navy blue. "My mother was a soloist in the local Methodist choir, my papa played the tuba in the church band and I wore out the Victrola needle when I was four.

"In high school, I joined the glee club and sang in the church choir. In college (Central State in Ohio), I joined the glee club and sang in the church choir. I was getting as predictable as the Victrola. But mama, who was the most liberated woman there ever was, wasn't satisfied. She had fire like no one I've known and she took me to hear Marian Anderson in Jackson, Mississippi. It accomplished exactly what she wanted it to accomplish. I woke up! I was excited! I was thrilled with this woman's manner, her carriage, her pride, her voice. This was something else again.

"Shortly after that, I won a scholarship to Juilliard and while there, I sang Mistress Ford in *Falstaff* and, lo and behold, Virgil Thomson was in the audience (so don't ever think that you're not being watched) and he offered me a part in *Four Saints in Three Acts*. Someone heard me *there* and offered me Bess in Gershwin's *Porgy and Bess*. And again, something happened that moved me to a new plateau. I heard Callas sing *Butterfly* and that day, I vowed it was going to be opera or nothing. Some of mama's fire had finally caught flame."

Today, Leontyne Price is the first Black diva in history. She is called the "prima donna assoluta" and a 42 minute ovation at *Butterfly* last September was the longest recorded ovation in the Met history.

—from *Ebony*, March, 1974.

Composition

Why do you think people like to hear about a character like the one described in the following excerpt from a magazine article?

They buried Joe Dorgan last July 3, two days after a stroke killed him at the age of 79. There was a short service in a wood-frame Catholic Church in Cumming, Ia., the population of which wouldn't fill a good block in Chicago. Father John Ryan, two altar boys, six casket bearers, eight official mourners and 26 other people were there.

"Joseph was a good man," and Father Ryan, "—a bit of a character, as we all know, but a lovable one."

Sitting in a back pew, William Wimer, a Des Moines attorney who had handled Dorgan's legal work, listened as the priest continued. "He was a recluse of the first water," Wimer says. "He liked solitude." Wimer says that, in recent years. Dorgan's company on the farm was 25 cats. Other friends described him in a variety of terms: "a challenge," "difficult," "unpredictable," "a queer person," "an 'aginner'," "a man of hatreds," "a shrewd businessman," "no dummy," articulate." His closest chums say he was "warm and friendly," belying the "crank" image he cultivated with those not so close.

Joe was one of five children of Richard and Bridget Dorgan. The eldest, Mame, died as a child, Frank (who died in 1916). Alice (who died in 1960) and Joe all remained single and stayed on the family farm. One sister, Mrs. Harkin's mother, married, and the marriage was against the wishes of Richard Dorgan, one friend says. "Joe's dad was bitter against that," the friends says, "and he never had any use for that family again. It was a grudge that was picked up by Joe and Alice."

Dorgan, who had only an eighth grade education, built his estate by aggressively farming in his younger years. "He was a tough, wiry fellow," says Emmett Hartz, 68, a neighbor who knew Joe for more than 60 years. "He'd amaze you how he could shovel so much corn on the hottest of days. In his time, he was quite a farmer, but in later years, he let everything go to pieces. He wouldn't spend any money on fertilizer or anything like that, and production fell off. He didn't seem to care."

Joe Dorgan nurtured seething hate for government. "He got mad about having to pay so much income tax," Hartz recalls. "He had a fine herd of Angus cattle—maybe 60 to 70 head He decided he was not going to sell those cattle and let the government get its hands on any more of his money. He let those cattle live as long as they could. He kept them penned in the winter and would feed them the corn he grew, and then in the spring he'd chase them out to the fields for the summer." Many of the cattle lived to be 15 years old and reached weights of over a ton. "I saw one of them," Wimer recalls, "big as an elephant, with a rear end six axe handles wide."

Wimer recalls that Dorgan wouldn't sign up for Social Security payments during the first 10 years he was eligible. "I finally conned him into signing up by telling him that if he didn't take what was rightfully his, it would go to someone else," the attorney said. "After that, he drew about $120 a month. He had the check mailed to my office in Des Moines, so he could come into the city once a month and pick it up. Coming to Des Moines was the only real event in the guy's life."

—from Chuck Offenburger, "Joe Dorgan's Strange Last Will," *Ebony*

Your Turn:

1. With your classmates, restage some of the interviews that led up to this article. (You may want to include an imaginary interview with Joe Dorgan when he was still alive.)

2. Do a series of similar interviews to put together a portrait of an actual person as seen through the eyes of people who know him or her. You might do a portrait of the mayor of your town, the chief of police, a sportscaster or disc jockey for a local station, the publisher of a local newspaper, the richest (or the poorest) person in your town.

Assignment 5: Many free-lance writers make a living writing for *special-interest* magazines. They turn out hunting stories, sports profiles, car ratings, travel tips, or science fiction adventures. Read the following excerpt from a story in a science fiction magazine. How many different features or ingredients can you identify that would seem familiar or predictable to science fiction fans?

THE DISCOVERY OF PLANET EARTH

At a time approximately two thousand years earlier, when Jesus was a boy in Nazareth and Caesar Augustus was counting up his statues and his gold, a race of creatures resembling soft-shelled crabs on a planet of a star some two hundred light-years away became belatedly aware of the existence of the Great Wall of China.

Although it alone among the then existing works of Man was quite detectable in their telescopes, it was not surprising they had not noticed it before. It had been completed less than 250 years before and most of that time had been lost in the creeping traverse of light from Earth to their planet. Also they had many, many planets to observe and not a great deal of time to waste on any one. But they expected more of their minions than that, and 10,000 members of a subject race died in great pain as a warning to the others to be more diligent.

The Arrogating Ones, as they called themselves and were called by their subjects, at once took up in their collective councils the question of whether or not to conquer Earth and add humanity to their vassals, now that they had discovered that humanity did exist. This was their eon-long custom. It had made them extremely unpopular over a large volume of the galaxy.

Your Turn:

1. Pretend you are the editor of a science fiction magazine. You have just received the above sample of a story that a free-lance writer is trying to sell you for your magazine. What would you tell the author?
2. What do you think is going to happen in the rest of the story? Write a continuation of the story.
3. Write an account of the best (or the worst) science fiction plot you have ever encountered in print or on the screen.

CHAPTER 4

Oral Language: Making Yourself Heard

Speak fluently and coherently to an audience that you understand and respect.

When we first meet strangers, we wonder, (1) will they say anything? and (2) what will they say, and in what tone? A personnel manager, when there is a position to fill, wants to *interview* the applicant—wants to hear what the applicant says and how she or he says it. When a police officer stops us for a possible traffic violation, what we say and how we say it may mean the difference between a ticket and no ticket. More basically, how we express our thoughts and feelings has much to do with what relationships we form with other people.

As you try to improve the effectiveness of your own speech, remember three major areas that need attention:

(1) **Articulateness:** *Tell people clearly and directly what you know, think, and feel.* Unless you are exceptionally glib, you are likely to worry too much, to be distracted too easily and discouraged too soon. Each of us must learn simply to plow ahead, to say what is on our minds. Articulate people have learned to express themselves easily and fluently, without strain.

(2) **Coherence:** *Make your presentation add up.* Listeners must remember the point of your story, or the name of your product, or the gist of what you want them to do. Some people raise interesting questions, bring in all kinds of side issues, and finally leave the listener confused. Like a good writer, an effective speaker must learn to marshal ideas and to concentrate on what is important.

(3) **Strategy:** *Take into account the background and the feelings of your audience.* When you want a friend to correct a bad blunder, you mention the matter tactfully instead of gloating over the mistake. When you want your audience to change their opinions on an important point, you make little headway by implying that they are all fools. You try to show that you agree with them up to a point. Then you bring in evidence that perhaps they have overlooked.

In speech, as in writing, confidence comes with practice. As a student, you have a unique opportunity to practice on a captive audience: your classmates, and your teachers. Make use of every opportunity to recite, to present an oral report, to sit on a panel, to make a speech, to moderate and discuss and debate.

Practice the "acting-out" activities that will help you build up your experience and confidence as a speaker.

O1
ACTING OUT

Some people who talk naturally in private freeze when their turn comes to speak up in a group. They have trouble trying to live up to the first rule for successful speaking in public: *Act human.* A speaker has to learn not to look like a wooden Indian. He or she has to learn to get into the spirit of the thing. The face has to express the speaker's emotions; gestures have to underline the speaker's meaning. The message has to come not just from the voicebox but from the speaker as a person.

The following are the kinds of loosening-up and branching-out activities that will help you become a more effective speaker:

—PLAYING THE ROLE. In heroic times, a leader did not only lead his warriors in battle. He knew how to speak in council with dignity and pride. How would you recite one of the following speeches, made by Indian chiefs acknowledging defeat in their uneven struggle with the conquering whites?

I appeal to any white man to say, if ever he entered Logan's cabin hungry, and he gave him not meat; if ever he came cold and naked, and he clothed him not. During the course of the last long and bloody war, Logan remained idle in his cabin, an advocate for peace. Such was my love for the whites, that my countrymen pointed as they passed, and said, "Logan is the friend of the white men." I had even thought to have lived with you, but for the injuries of one man. Col. Cresap, the last spring, in cold blood, and unprovoked, murdered all the relations of Logan, not sparing even my woman and children. There runs not a drop of my blood in the veins of any living creature. This called on me for revenge. I have sought it: I have killed many: I have fully glutted my vengeance. For my country, I rejoice at the beams of peace. But do not harbour a thought that mine is the joy of fear. Logan never felt fear. He will not turn on his heel to save his life. Who is there to mourn Logan?—Not one.

I am tired of fighting. Our chiefs are killed. Looking Glass is dead. Toohulhulsote is dead. The old men are all dead. It is the young men who say no and yes. He who led the young men is dead. It is cold and we have no blankets. The little children are freezing to death. My people, some of them, have run away to the hills and have no blankets, no food. No one knows where they are—perhaps they are freezing to death. I want to have time to look for my children and see how many of them I can find. Maybe I shall find them among the dead. Hear me, my chiefs, I am tired. My heart is sad and sick. From where the sun now stands I will fight no more forever.

Your Turn: Prepare to give a short speech in which you speak the imaginary "last words" of a leader of a defeated tribe, nation, or army that you have read about.

—JOINING IN THE DIALOGUE. Much language is **dialogue**—two or more people speaking to each other, often in a very ordinary situation. Study the give and take of dialogue in the following excerpt from a "boy-meets-girl" story. Have three people in your class team up to read the parts of the narrator, the boy, and the girl. Do they sound the way you think they should? Are they getting the people and the tone of the conversation right? Team up with your classmates to do one of the following: (1) Write and act out what you think would be the *next* conversation between the two people on the train; (2) Write and act out a different "boy-meets-girl" conversation.

At last the young man said, "Are you from New York?"

He didn't know what he was saying. He felt foolish and unlike young men in movies who do such things on trains.

"Yes, I am," the girl said.

"What?" the young man said.

"Didn't you ask if I was from New York?" the girl said.

"Oh," the young man said. "Yes, I did."

"Well," the girl said, "I am."

"I didn't know you were from New York," the young man said.

"I know you didn't," the girl said.

The young man tried very hard to smile the way they smiled in pictures.

"How did you know?" he said.

"Oh, I don't know," the girl said. "Are you going to Sacramento?"

"Yes, I am," the young man said. "Are you?"

"Yes, I am," the girl said.

"What are you doing so far from home?" the young man said.

"New York isn't my home," the girl said. "I was born there, but I've been living in San Francisco most of my life."

"So have I most of mine," the young man said. "In fact all of it."

"I've lived in San Francisco practically all of my life too," the girl said, "with the possible exception of them few months in New York."

"Is that all the time you lived in New York?" the young man said.

"Yes," the girl said, "only them first five months right after I was born in New York."

"I was born in San Francisco," the young man said. "There's lots of room on these two seats," he said with great effort. "Wouldn't you like to sit over here and get the sun?"

"All right," the girl said.

She stepped across the aisle and sat across from the young man.

"I just thought I'd go down to Sacramento on the special Sunday rate," the young man said.

"I've been to Sacramento three times," the girl said.

The young man began to feel very happy. The sun was strong and warm and the girl was wonderful. Unless he was badly mistaken, or unless he got fired Monday morning, or unless America got into a war and he had to become a soldier and go away and get himself killed, he had a hunch some day he would go to work and get acquainted with the girl and marry her and settle down.

He sat back in the sunlight while the train rattled along and smiled romantically at the girl, getting ready for the romance.

—William Saroyan, "Romance"

—The Language of Gestures. An effective speaker does not just "stand there." The *whole person* talks. Look at the following drawings. For each drawing, write a brief caption to show what you think the person is saying. Compare your captions with those written by your classmates. How do you know what each person is saying?

Your Turn: **Pantomime** is the art of conveying your message by using gestures *only*. Team up with your classmates for an experiment in pantomime. Act out *silently* several of the following:

1. A neighbor drops in for a friendly visit and is offered a cup of coffee and a piece of cake. At first, he (she) politely refuses but then accepts, complimenting the host (hostess) on the delicious cake and excellent coffee.

2. A job applicant tries to make a good impression on a very cool, unfriendly interviewer. The applicant is extremely friendly and keeps praising his (her) qualifications. The interviewer is very standoffish and doubtful.

3. A boxing champion is interviewed before a fight. He boasts of his past victories and brags about what he is going to do to his opponent. The interviewer acts as "straight man," very seriously feeding the athlete questions.

4. An impatient customer in a restaurant tries to get better service from an unfriendly and hurried waiter (waitress). The customer makes various requests, but has a hard time trying to make the waiter (waitress) pay attention.

5. A small boy resists his first haircut. The parent tries to coax and scold him into letting the barber begin. The barber tries to do his best under very trying circumstances.

6. A police officer comes to the house to try to arrest somebody. The person he is trying to arrest keeps protesting that the officer made a mistake and has the wrong person. The officer is determined to do his duty. (You may want to bring a relative of the person to be arrested into the act.)

7. Write a similar scene of your own. Let your audience interpret what is happening.

—THE LANGUAGE OF EMOTIONS. People and whole societies differ in how much emotion they show when they talk. In the early epics and sagas, strong men weep when they lose their comrades in battle. American movies and books for years had strong silent heroes who kept their poker face in the face of appalling tragedies. If you *wanted* to show emotion, could you do it? Try the following "acting-out" activities:

1. You are meeting a person in the street. Your reaction is
   —recognition;
   —surprise;
   —embarrassment;
   —failure to recognize;
   —annoyance.

2. Prepare to perform the "emotional symphony." Each person in the class will act out, in *sounds and gestures,* one of the following: fear, despair, grief, joy, anger, happiness, fatigue, doubt, meanness, guilt, silliness, relief, friendliness. A "conductor" will call on each person to act out, both individually and together. Start when the conductor gives you the signal; stop when the conductor shuts you off. (Like a real symphony, your performance may have solos, duets, trios, etc., as well as the full orchestra for the grand finale.)

—INTERACTING WITH THE AUDIENCE. Every teacher, preacher, and public speaker has known audiences whose middle name could have been "Apathy." What does it take to get the attention of an audience? What does it take to make them laugh or applaud? What does it take to make them stand up and cheer?

The following experiment will help make you and your classmates more aware of what goes on in a listener's mind. Usually, much of what the audience feels remains below the surface. People think to themselves: "That's very true!" or else: "Don't you believe it!" For this experiment, instruct your audience to express feelings more clearly and openly. Make them use signs of approval and disapproval from the whole scale of possible audience reactions:

Very Positive: Shouts of "Beautiful!" "Yes, Sir!" "That's telling them!"; choruses of "Ohs" and "Ahs"; etc.

A GOOD AUDIENCE IS HARD TO FIND

THE ART OF PANTOMIME

Tell your listeners that you want them to think of English words made on the model of *tip-top, knickknack,* and *riffraff.* Help them find the following words by acting them out. (Which are *hard* to act out?)

Pong-Pong	singsong
zigzag	mishmash
seesaw	chitchat
crisscross	dingdong
flip-flap	pitter-patter

Clearly Positive: Vigorous nodding, polite clapping, mumbled comments like "That's right," etc.

In Between   Coughing, yawning, shifting in chairs, looking at watches, etc.

Negative: Mumbles of dissent; soft hissing or booing; impatient gestures

Very Negative: Loud hissing or booing; stamping of feet; shouts of "The nerve!" "Lies!" "Throw the bum out!" etc.

To "activate" audience response, let each of several speakers present ten to fifteen statements designed to get audience reaction. Use statements beginning

"Girls are ——————."
"Teenagers are ——————."
"Teenage boys should be ——————."
"Teachers are ——————." etc.

Bonus Question: Do people in the audience always react the way you expect? What makes them react differently from what you would have predicted?

FOR FURTHER PRACTICE: Sounding Things Out

ACTIVITY 1

Look at the following poems for "talking softly and crying out loud." Choose two or three to read. Can you make them sound just the way the poet would have wanted them to sound?

Out Loud   OUT LOUD   **OUT LOUD**
BY EVE MERRIAM

     Try saying the words in a poem not silently
to yourself, but aloud.
     How will it sound if you're allowed
to speak as loud as you want?

    Out Loud.

    OUT LOUD.

    Now,
how will it sound?
    OUT LOUD.
    Ow,
wow, LOWOWOWOWOWOWOWOWOWOWOWOWOWD!

                —Eve Merriam, *Out Loud*, 1973

Alarm Clock

in the deep forest
there were ferns
there were feathers
there was fur
and a soft ripe peach
on a branch within my

    r-r-r-r-r-r-r-r-r-r-r-r-r-r-r-r-r-r-r-r-r-r-r-r-r-r-r-r-r

Umbilical

You can take away my mother,
You can take away my sister,
but don't take away
my little transistor.

I can do without sunshine,
I can do without Spring,
but I can't do without
my ear to that thing.

I can live without water,
in a hole in the ground,
but I can't live without
that sound that sound that sound that sOWnd.

Markings: The Exclamation

!

The racing flag whips out:
no second place,
no third-in-show.
Winner take all.
GO!

!

Markings: The Semicolon

;

Diver on the board
lunges toward the edge;
hedges;
takes a deep breath;
hesitates;

plunges.

—Eve Merriam, *Finding a Poem*

Your Turn: Write and read out loud, a poem that says what one of the following would say if it could talk:

—a leaking faucet;
—a subway train;
—a strong wind;
—a heavy rain;
—the surf;
—a windshield wiper;
—a musical instrument;
—you name it!

ACTIVITY 2

Read one of the following student-written poems. Or find a poem you like in a collection of student poetry that you have encountered. Can you read the poem so that it sounds just right for the mood the author intended?

```
The sand is slowly blown into dunes
    which build higher and higher
Beyond, palm trees slowly sway

A bird, its wing hurt, tries desperately to fly
finally comes to land on the hot sand
and is engulfed in the sand
    and finally covered

The sand is slowly blown into dunes
    which build higher and higher.
```

Loneliness

```
A woman old and grey
sits rocking to a tune in her mind.
She remembers her old friends
Who are dead now.
She remembers when she was a child.
Her mind flashes to a funeral.
She cries within herself.
Her memories of the past
Are her only future.
```

HIROSHIMA

```
Like a flying
fish
Bringing its silver head
out of the white capping
clouds
Its white belly bursting with
eggs of destruction
```

```
Hiroshima lay resting quiet
in the august morning
thunder lit the sky
it was raining morning
skin pealed from the corner
of hollowed eyes
breath lay hidden in
sunken chests
a star exploded into the arms
of night and the white shadow
fish was seen gliding behind
the SUN.
```

ACTIVITY 3

Stage a choral reading of the following poem by Carl Sandburg. Can you assign people with just the right voices to the different parts?

"Wilderness" by Carl Sandburg

First Voice:

There is a wolf in me . . . fangs pointed for tearing gashes . . . a
red tongue for raw meat . . . and the hot lapping of blood—I
keep this wolf because the wilderness gave it to me and the
wilderness will not let it go.

Second Voice:

There is a fox in me . . . a silver-gray fox . . . I sniff and guess.
I pick things out of the wind and air . . . I nose in the dark
night and take sleepers and eat them and hide the feathers
I circle and loop and double-cross.

Third Voice:

There is a hog in me . . . a snout and a belly . . . a machinery for
eating and grunting . . . a machinery for sleeping satisfied
in the sun—I got this too from the wilderness and the
wilderness will not let it go.

Fourth Voice:

There is a fish in me . . . I know I came from salt-blue water-
gates . . . I scurried with shoals of herring . . . I blew water-

spouts with porpoises . . . before land was . . . before the water
went down . . . before Noah . . . before the first chapter of Genesis.

Fifth Voice:

There is a baboon in me . . . clambering-clawed . . . dog-faced . . .
yawping a galoot's hunger . . . hairy under the armpits . . .
here are the hawk-eyed hankering men . . . here are the
blonde and blue-eyed women . . . here they hide curled asleep
waiting . . . ready to snarl and kill . . . ready to sing and give
mild . . . waiting—I keep the baboon because the wilderness
says so.

Sixth and Seventh Voices:

There is an eagle in me and a mockingbird . . . and the eagle flies
among the Rocky Mountains of my dreams and fights among the
Sierra crags of what I want . . . and the mockingbird warbles in
the early forenoon before the dew is gone, warbles in the
underbrush of my Chattanoogas of hope, gushes over the blue
Ozark foothills of my wishes—And I got the eagle and the
mockingbird from the wilderness.

All:

O, I got a zoo, I got a menagerie, inside my ribs, under my bony
head, under my red-valve heart—

Boy and Girl Alternate:

And I got something else: it is a man-child heart, a woman-child
heart: it is a father and mother and lover: it came from
God-Knows-Where; it is going to God-Knows-Where—for I am
the keeper of the zoo: I say yes and no: I sing and kill and work:
I am a pal of the world:

All:

I came from the wilderness.

O2
SPEAKING TO THE
PURPOSE

Prepare a short talk that serves a definite purpose.

Speech is less finished, less carefully polished than writing.
It is more *improvised.* Speakers must be able to think on their feet.
They must keep going even if they cannot remember an important
quotation they were going to use or an example that was going to
be an important part of their evidence.

To help you stay on your feet when you give a short talk, remember the following guidelines:

(1) *Immerse yourself in the material.* Always collect more material than you will be able to use. This way you can select the most telling points. Good speakers always sound as if they know more about their subject than they tell. Observe how in a question-and-answer session a good speaker brings in additional examples, explores interesting sidelines, amplifies points previously made.

(2) *Fix the main outline of your speech firmly in your mind.* Even if you temporarily lose the thread of your talk, you should be able to return to the main outline by saying: "The second major point is . . ." or "A third major advantage of the new policy turns out to be. . . ."

(3) *Speak from notes.* Memorizing a whole speech puts a tremendous nervous strain on the speaker. At the opposite extreme, a speech that is read word for word from a prepared text is likely to have a "canned" quality. The best compromise is to have detailed notes. These should clearly reflect the outline of the talk. They should contain all important terms, examples, figures, quotations, and the like. The speaker can follow the notes closely and yet make up the actual words and sentences fresh in front of the audience. The speaker is free to expand or cut as needed.

(4) *Remember the echo effect.* Before the echo can come back to you from the canyon walls, you have to raise your voice and shout. Before you can expect your audience to be interested in you, you have to act as if you are interested in them. Many successful entertainers manage to convey the impression that they like, respect, or even admire their audience. The audience then in return likes, respects, and admires *them.* Don't frown at the audience, *smile* at them. Most of them will smile back.

Try your hand at preparing a short speech that serves a definite purpose. Many talks serve one of three major purposes:

—to *report,* to inform, to demonstrate;
—to *explain,* to analyze, to interpret;
—to *persuade,* to influence, to inspire.

The following three sections discuss one major kind of talk from each of these three areas: the factual demonstration; the interpretative talk or analysis; the promotional or "sales" talk, designed to persuade the listener of the merits of a product or a policy.

O2a

The Demonstration

Demonstrate the major stages of a process or operation.

Everyone at one time or another is called upon to demonstrate the proper operation of a tape recorder, a sewing machine, or a projector. A supervisor must show a new worker the right way to perform a job. A sales representative must demonstrate to a possible customer the operation of a new camera or a new type of transmission. If the operation is complicated, the listener is likely to be confused by the many new terms and minor details. An effective speaker knows how to sort things out so that the listener can grasp the major principles and see the details as part of the whole.

There are two ways of clarifying a complicated process:

(1) *Find the basic principle of operation* that ties all the different steps together. In explaining the operation of a tape recorder, focus on the fact that sound waves must be changed into a magnetic field that can be imprinted on a tape. In explaining American football to a British friend, make sure to get at the basic features: How does a team get *possession* of the ball? How does it *move* the ball? How does a team *score?*

(2) *Divide a complicated operation into its major stages.* No one can remember the steps in operating a sewing machine or in baking a cake if you merely present them as a dozen different things to do. Most listeners will give up the fourth or fifth time you say "And then you do this . . ." and "And then you do that." Group the different steps clearly under several major headings:

I. Getting Things Ready
II. Mixing the Dough
III. Baking the Cake
IV. Frosting the Cake

In demonstrating the operation of a projector or a recorder, you will usually have the machine with you. You will point to its various parts and actually perform the various operations you describe. In doing so, always try to make your description *clear* rather than *exhaustive:* Do not confuse your audience by giving the technical name for every button, lever, switch, and other parts of the machine.

In explaining the operation of a new type of engine or the principles of a game, you will often rely on the help of a diagram or chart. If you prepare such a visual aid yourself, remember that the whole point of a diagram is to bring out *essentials*—not to give a complete realistic picture of every minor detail.

ACTIVITY 1

Prepare to demonstrate the operation of a movie projector, sewing machine, or other piece of equipment. Choose a machine that requires of the operator more than simply the ability to push a few buttons. Explain the operation in such a way that your audience will be able to make the thing work.

ACTIVITY 2

Describe a production process, such as the making of a car, airplane, or missile. Break the process up into important major stages that will remain clearly fixed in the listener's mind.

ACTIVITY 3

Assume that the rest of the class is a group of visiting students from England. Explain to them the major principles of American football or baseball. Make sure not to confuse them with miscellaneous details.

ACTIVITY 4

Choose a job or service in which you consider yourself somewhat of an expert. Make sure it is something that requires skill or experience—for instance, bathing a baby or keeping up a lawn. Give a presentation that will teach someone else how to do the job.

Clarify a complicated situation.

**O2b
The Analysis**

Good speakers know how to make sense out of a confusing mass of details. Effective news commentators know how to bring out the major trends in the confusing events of a week or month. We say that they **analyze** the news—they examine it in order to sort it out into major categories, in order to find the underlying pattern. Lecturers do a very similar job when they talk about political trends in Latin America or about the economic future of India. They identify major causes or isolate important factors. They sort out facts and details to help us *understand* what is going on.

The most basic pattern of organization for this kind of analysis simply presents three major causes, or four major categories, or five important factors. A typical scheme of organization would look like this:

Why U.N.?

Introduction: Today, serious doubts are often raised about the membership of the United States in the United Nations.

Body of the Talk: There were three main reasons why this country originally joined the United Nations.

    A. The first of these reasons was . . .

    B. The second major reason was . . .

    C. The third reason, often forgotten, was . . .

Conclusion: Our original reasons for joining the world organization are still valid today.

A well-known educator once made a speech explaining what makes someone a good student. The educator sorted the qualities of the good student out into three major categories:

    I. The power of *attention*—the ability to take in exact details instead of just getting a vague picture

    II. An *open mind*—the ability to consider seriously things that seem at first shocking or absurd

    III. *Independence*—the ability to make up one's mind instead of just repeating what somebody else has said

Could you fill in each one of these categories with several examples from your own reading and experience? Is there an important category that has been forgotten here? After changing the categories as needed and after collecting good convincing examples for each, you would be ready to give your own talk on "How to Become a Good Student."

The obvious question about this kind of organization is: What should be the order in which the major points are presented? Often it pays to start with the most familiar or the most easily understood. The speech about the good student might well start with the "power of attention" because most listeners will accept this idea without much of a struggle. They all know that the student who cannot pay attention is likely to be handicapped in academic work. Once the listeners feel that the speaker is reasonable and talking sense, they may listen with interest to ideas that are unfamiliar or difficult to grasp.

SPEECH TO THE INTERPLANETARY COUNCIL ON MARTIAN AFFAIRS

Here is how one student started an imaginary speech about a make-believe event:

It is with deep regret that I begin my report this evening, for as Social Director of the Interplanetary Council on Martian Affairs it is my unpleasant duty to inform you that our elaborate plans for the "Welcome Earthlings Week" celebration have been abandoned. Only long and serious consideration of all aspects of the situation has prompted me to cancel the preparations for the gala festivities. However, I feel this step is being taken in the best interests of all parties concerned. This conclusion was reached shortly after my visit to Earth. So that you may understand the factors influencing my decision, I will recount the major events of my journey.

What happened to the distinguished Martian traveler during his visit to Earth? What made him change his mind about welcoming earthlings to his planet? Prepare to give a speech in which you complete the Director's story.

FOR BRANCHING OUT

ACTIVITY 1

Prepare a talk in which you analyze *what accounts for a student's success* socially or academically. For instance, what are three major factors that help make a student popular with classmates? What are three major habits that make for fruitful study? What major causes account for a student's interest in a subject like science, or history, or foreign language? Limit yourself to three or four major categories and make sure you can provide evidence or examples for each.

ACTIVITY 2

Looking back over the last year or so, can you discover any *major trends in the behavior of your classmates*—in dress, manners, language, attitude toward authority? Prepare a talk in which you examine three or four major trends of this kind and show whether they are in any way related.

ACTIVITY 3

Read the *letters to the editor* published in your local newspaper during the last several weeks. Can you classify these letters in any way? Are there perhaps several major types of people who can be relied on to write a letter on a given subject? Prepare a talk in which you discuss three or four major types of typical letter-to-the-editor writers. Use excerpts from the actual letters in your talk.

ACTIVITY 4

Select *an issue currently being debated* in your community or state. Study newspaper articles, editorials, letters to the editors, campaign literature, or the like that deal with it. Prepare a talk in which you sort out the arguments presented or the views expressed. Can you identify three or four major arguments pro and con? Use excerpts from the materials you have read.

O2c
The "Sales Talk"

Promote a product or an idea.

Often we are not content merely to explain something to an audience. We want the audience to take some kind of action: to buy a product, to adopt a policy. We are not merely trying to inform; we are trying to *persuade*. The promotional talk, or "sales talk," must do what an informative talk would do *and more*. Sales people must demonstrate the operation or uses of a product. But they must also show how the product fits the customer's needs. Political candidates must not only explain what their programs *are*. They must also show how their programs would meet the needs or satisfy the aspirations of the voter.

Since speakers must do justice to *both the product and the customer*, they may try a basic two-step organization. In presenting a new automatic camera, for instance, sales people might first describe basic features of the camera and then show how these would satisfy the needs of the customer:

    I. Features of the Camera
        A. Rapid cartridge loading
        B. Check on correct distance built into viewfiender
        C. Fully automatic adjustment of lens opening
        D. Fully automatic adjustment of shutter speed

    II. Advantages to Customer
        A. No fumbling with film while outdoors
        B. No "forgetting" to set right distance
        C. No delay in taking action shots of children or sports

When speakers turn from the promotion of a product to the promotion of an idea or policy, a somewhat more complicated scheme of organization may be required. For instance, political candidates may describe a *situation*, then analyze its *causes*, then suggest the necessary *remedies*. The more directly their proposed solutions follow from their analyses, the more persuasive their talks will be. The following is a simplified outline of a famous speech illustrating this pattern. The speech is the first inauguraal address of Franklin Roosevelt, elected to the Presidency at the height of the Great Depression:

1. *Plea for support*
   "In every dark hour of our national life a leadership of frankness and vigor has met with that understanding and support of the people themselves which is essential to victory. I am convinced that you will again give that support to leadership in these critical days. . . ."

2. *Description of the situation*
   "In such a spirit on my part and on yours we face our common difficulties: the withered leaves of industrial enterprise lie on every side; farmers find no markets for their produce; the savings of many years in thousands of families are gone. More important, a host of unemployed citizens face the grim problem of existence. . . ."

3. *Analysis of the causes*
   "Yet our distress comes from no failure of substance. Plenty is at our doorstep, but a generous use of it languishes in the very sight of the supply. Primarily, this is because the rulers of the exchange of mankind's goods have failed through their own stubbornness and their own incompetence. . . ."

4. *Change in attitude required for recovery*
   "The measure of the restoration lies in the extent to which we apply social values more noble than mere monetary profit. . . ."

5. *Program for specific action*
   "Restoration calls, however, not for changes in ethics alone. This nation asks for action, and action now. Our greatest primary task is to put people to work. . . ."

Persuasive speakers are always tempted to skimp on description and analysis. Some commercials say nothing specific about the product; they merely try to make us feel how wonderful it would be to own one. The more intelligent your listeners are, the more impatient they are likely to be with this approach. Before they buy a product or vote for a candidate, they want *to be informed.* They want to make up their own minds. In preparing a promotional talk for an intelligent audience, remember that there is such a thing as trying too hard.

ACTIVITY 1

Prepare a "sales talk" for *a new product* that you have found interesting or useful. Take into account the needs, habits, or possible objections of your audience.

ACTIVITY 2

Prepare a talk in which you advocate *a change in a familiar procedure* or type of behavior. For instance, you might recommend a change in school activities or regulations—parking or driving privileges for students, procedures for assigning students to classes, requirements for graduation, patterns of interschool athletic competition. Try to spell out the proposed change in adequate detail, and try to make it attractive to your audience.

ACTIVITY 3

Prepare a talk in which you ask your audience to *reconsider a law, policy, or bond issue recently turned down by the voters.* Avoid name-calling; stress arguments that you think a reasonable, intelligent listener should be willing to accept.

ACTIVITY 4

Prepare a talk in which you *nominate a person* known to your audience for a real or imaginary office, honor, or reward. Possible topics could range from "Jim Thorpe for Best-Dressed Man on Campus" to "Ms. Greene for Principal of the Year." (If you can make your talk humorous rather than insulting, you may want to nominate someone for a booby prize of some sort.)

O3
PARTICIPATING IN
DISCUSSION

Participate constructively and responsibly in discussion.

Constructive discussion is an important feature of any society where people are not simply content to do as they are told. In the classroom, at committee meetings, and at hearings of all kinds we exchange information, compare points of view, and try to agree on a course of action. Often such exchanges take the form of an **informal discussion,** a give-and-take without rigid ground rules and agenda. Sometimes the exchange has a more definite format, as in a **panel discussion.** Here a number of specially qualified people pool their expert information or present different viewpoints for the audience to evaluate.

When discussion is fruitful, the participants feel satisfied because no one has simply forced her or his own views on everybody else. Instead, they have come to understand better the contribution of each member. They have reached some sort of agreement that is approved by the majority and at least respected by the minority that remains unconvinced.

To help make discussion fruitful, follow these guidelines:

(1) *Participate.* Make sure to contribute something, it only to show that you are interested, that you are listening, that you believe in the right of individuals to make their voices heard. If you do not have a statement to make, ask a question. Ask somebody to clear up something that you failed to understand. There is a good chance that something that confused you confused other people too.

(2) *Give the other person a chance.* The whole purpose of discussion is lost when one or two people dominate an exchange of opinion. After you have had your say, let other people have theirs —even if they disagree with you, even if you think you have something much more important to say next. When someone replies to you, do not always feel that you must defend your position yourself. Let a third person join in.

(3) *Stick to the point.* No discussion can be fruitful if everyone merely waits a turn to raise a completely new issue. To give the discussion coherence, everyone must be willing to listen as well as to talk. When your turn comes, *respond* to what has been said before and *then* try to steer the discussion closer to the points that interest you most. If you want to change the subject, explain why and see whether the majority is ready to move on.

(4) *Work toward a meeting of minds.* Half an hour of discussion will not make anyone change his or her mind completely on any important issue. People change their opinions gradually, if at all. Be prepared to settle for partial agreement. After some ex-

ploratory talk by various people, try to steer toward what you think people of goodwill could reasonably accept. Do your share to help formulate the "sense of the meeting." Sometimes there is a **moderator** for the discussion. The moderator's job is more than simply to introduce the participants and to say something pleasant when tempers begin to flare. In fact, the moderator's main job is to *keep the discussion moving forward,* to try to build on what has been covered. Moderators try to find common ground: "Perhaps we could agree on this. . . ." "Would you settle for the following? . . ." They will ask people to clarify points that were left vague; they will raise questions that seem implied in what has been said. Though they should never simply cut someone off, they may well move in to suggest that a point taken up at the wrong time may be postponed until later.

In the typical discussion, *much that is simply good manners is at the same time good sense.* When someone else starts speaking at the same time as you do, be sure to say, "Pardon me. Go ahead." Four out of five times, persons who have found you considerate of their right to speak will in turn be considerate of your point of view. When someone points out an error in facts or figures you have presented, admit that the person may be right. Above all, do not take every disagreement personally. Differences of opinion are inevitable when people with different backgrounds and interests share their views.

ACTIVITY 1

Prepare to participate in an *informal class discussion* of one of the topics listed below. After the discusion, ask yourself how well you have done on each of the following points: Have you contributed some specific examples, facts, incidents, illustrations, and the like as well as your bare opinion? Have you made an effort to understand the reasoning behind opinions different from your own? Have you helped steer the discussion toward possible areas of agreement? (In a large class, the teacher may divide students into two or three groups.)

1. Are today's teenagers too disrespectful toward authority, or are they merely independent?
2. What if anything can be done to encourage teenagers who have lost interest in school to continue their education?

3. Is it true that today's teenager is given too few chances to assume real responsibility?

ACTIVITY 2

Prepare to participate in a *panel discussion* on a topic that (1) has recently been (or still is) a source of discussion or controversy in your community, and (2) requires you to work up relevant background material from newspaper or magazine articles or other sources. For instance, your panel may discuss a topic like a zero-growth ordinance, a bond issue for schools or parks, a program for urban redevelopment, an important revision of city government. You may want to ask your listeners to evaluate the members of the panel as follows:

Which of the members did most to *explain* the issues?
Which member was most effective in presenting his or her *own point of view?*
Which member seemed most capable of *learning something personally* from the discussion, adjusting an opinion or changing a personal viewpoint when warranted?

ACTIVITY 3

Prepare to serve as *moderator* of a small group discussion dealing with a topic like student government, student discipline, relations between students and teachers, or the like. After the discussion, chart and evaluate your contribution to the performance of the group.

BEING A GOOD LISTENER

FURTHER STUDY

One way of improving your skill as a speaker is to listen to accomplished speakers and to study the secret of their success. When we are bored by a talk or lecture, we often say that we are not interested in that particular subject. But one of the tests of good speakers is exactly that they *make* the subject interesting. After hearing an exceptionally good speaker, can you point out some of the ways in which he or she made the talk come to life?

THE POWER OF THE SPOKEN WORD

SUSAN B. ANTHONY

"The only question left to be settled now is: Are women persons? And I hardly believe any of our opponents will have the heartihood to say they are not. Being persons, then, women are citizens; and no state has a right to make any law, or to enforce any old law, that shall abridge their privileges or immunities. Hence, every discrimination against women in the constitution and laws of the several states is today null and void. . . ."

MARTIN LUTHER KING

"I have a dream that my four little children will one day live in a nation where they will not be judged by the color of their skin, but by the content of their character."

FRANKLIN D. ROOSEVELT

"In every dark hour of our national life, a leadership of frankness and vigor has met with that understanding and support of the people themselves which is essential to victory. I am convinced that you will again give that support to the leadership in these critical days."

Assignment 1: Which *television news commentator* do you consider most popular or most successful? Study the commentator's *manner* of speaking. Note characteristic postures, gestures, and facial expressions. What about the commentator's typical style of delivery—speed, emphasis, humor? Do you notice any personal mannerisms? Prepare a brief commentary in which you *imitate* the commentator's style.

Assignment 2: Have you had a chance to listen to speeches or oral presentations by *candidates for local or state office?* Evaluate the performance of one of them as a speaker. If possible, pay attention to both *what* the candidate says and *how* she or he says it. If the presentation was effective, what made it so? If it was weak, what were the reasons? Present your findings in an oral report.

Assignment 3: Listen to records of *speeches by a famous twentieth-century speaker,* such as Franklin D. Roosevelt, Sir Winston Churchill, or John F. Kennedy. As fully as you can, describe characteristic features. Try to pay attention to both substance or content and style or delivery. Choose a passage to read to the class, imitating the style of the original speaker.

Assignment 4: Watch an *interview or discusion program* on television. Describe and evaluate the performance of the major participants. Did the program as a whole add up? Or did it seem aimless? If it was succesful, who deserved the major share of the credit? If it seemed a failure, who was to blame? Present your findings in an oral report. (Your teacher may ask you to team up with classmates to *restage* a shortened version of a recent program.)

Assignment 5: The makers of television commercials know that the audience is not always eager to listen to their message. Consequently, they have developed various devices designed to make the viewer more apt to listen to their sales pitch. Make a study of at least *five* different television commercials. Describe some of the techniques used to get the audience to hear the message. Can you discover some strategies that might also be of use to a public speaker? Be prepared to present your findings in an oral report to your class.

Guide to Manuscript Revision

ab . . . . Spell out abbreviation (M7b)

adv . . . . . . Use adverb form (U2c)

agr . . . . . . Make verb agree with subject
          (or pronoun with antecedent) (U3a, U3b)

ap . . . . . . Use apostrophe (M2b)

cap . . . . . . Capitalize (M2a)

coll . . . . . . Use less colloquial word (U2a)

cs . . . . . . Revise comma splice (M4a)

d . . . . . . Improve diction (W4)

dev . . . . . . Develop your point (C2a)

div . . . . . . Revise word division (M7a)

DM . . . . . . Revise dangling modifier (U3c)

frag . . . . . . Revise sentence fragment (M3b)

FP . . . . . . Revise faulty parallelism (U4d)

gr . . . . . . Revise grammatical form or construction (U4b)

awk . . . . . . Rewrite awkward sentence (U4)

lc . . . . . . Use lower case (M2a)

MM . . . . . . Shift misplaced modifier (U3c)

P . . . . . . Improve punctuation (M3, M4, M5)

¶ . . . . . . New paragraph (C2)

no ¶ . . . . . . Take out paragraph break (M7a)

ref . . . . . . Improve pronoun reference (U3b)

rep . . . . . . Avoid repetition (U4a)

shift . . . . . . Avoid shift in perspective (U4c)

sl . . . . . . Use less slangy word (U2a)

sp . . . . . . Revise misspelled word (M1)

st . . . . . . Improve sentence structure (U4)

t . . . . . . Change tense of verb (U1a)

trans . . . . . . Provide better transition (C3c)

w . . . . . . Reduce wordiness (U4a)

CHAPTER
5

Usage: Making the Right Choice

Use the right kind of language at the right time.

During an ordinary day, we hear English used in various ways. We hear changes in the language as we listen to members of *different groups*. We are likely to hear one kind of English from the person in overalls and working boots and a different kind from the person dressed for the business office. A radio announcer talks differently from a factory supervisor. The way a person talks has a great deal to do with what kind of job she or he holds, what kind of people she or he works with.

In addition, each member of a group will vary language somewhat depending *on the situation*. Some occasions call for a sport shirt, some for a tie. Some call for fashionable shoes, some for casual. Similarly, some situations call for fairly *informal* language; others for a more formal variety. Someone discussing a subject casually with a few friends might say at the end: "I guess that just about winds it up." But, if giving a formal talk to a larger group, the person might say: "This brings me to the conclusion of my remarks."

Everyone must learn to use the kind of language that is just about right for the time and place. The differences that set various kinds of English apart are called differences in **usage.** Differences in usage are of three major kinds:

—differences in the way we *pronounce* words;
—differences in the *words we choose* to describe the same thing;
—differences in the way we *combine words* in a phrase or sentence.

There are three important reasons for studying usage:

(1) *The right kind of language counts on the job.* Many jobs are open only to people who can use *standard* English.

(2) *Writing is more formal than speech.* Writers do not simply write the way they talk. The language we find in articles and books is less chatty than natural conversation. When we write, we *shift gears* to the more formal kind of English we use in serious writing.

(3) *An effective speaker and writer must have a good ear.* No one to whom all gravies taste the same can be a good cook. Learn to listen for the way different people use our common language. By studying the colorful **variety of** English usage, you can learn to *vary* your own style of speaking and writing to achieve different effects.

Your Turn: How good is your ear for differences in usage? Look at the following examples of language in action. What makes the examples in each group different from those in the other two? In each case, for what purpose is language being used? What effect would the language used have on its audience?

THE WAY PEOPLE
TALK

I AM NEW HERE MYSELF

Pretend you grew up in a small town in Wyoming, and you have just moved to New York City. Every so often you hear people use an expression that seems familiar to everybody but you. How quickly would you catch on to what these expressions mean? Look at the italicized words in the following sets. From looking at the way they are used, could you tell what they mean? Write a brief explanation of each word for the *next* newcomer to the city. Write on a separate sheet of paper.

1. When a *shlimazl* buys an umbrella, the sun comes out. A *shlimazl* buys a suit with two pairs of pants and promptly burns a hole in the jacket. If a *shlimazl* made coffins, people

would stop dying. If it rains gold, it is the fate of a *shlimazl* to be under a roof.

A shlimazl is —————.

2. Come on—lay out some *shekels*. His father has more *shekels* than you have hairs. Moses taxed the Israelites half a *shekel*.

A shekel is —————.

3. To a *landsman*, I offer special bargain prices. A new immigrant could turn to a *landsman* for a job. A successful immigrant would help find a job for a *landsman*. Her uncle was a *landsman* he had known even in the old country.

A landsman is —————.

4. You shouldn't take a *klutz* like that to a high-class restaurant. She was the brightest girl in the class, but she married a real *klutz*. Mary liked to dance, but the *klutz* she was with kept stepping on her toes.

A klutz is —————.

5. I didn't ask your advice—what are you, a *kibitzer*? At Harvey's poker game, there were always more *kitbitzers* than players. When our house was remodeled, Father drove the workers crazy with his *kibitzing*.

A kibitzer is —————.

6. It takes *chutzpa* to drive up to the unemployment office in a fancy late-model car. With his usual *chutzpa,* the accused denied everything. It takes *chutzpa* to ask a dollar twenty for a hot dog.

Chutzpa is —————.

Be able to speak and write standard English.

When people speak of "good English," they usually mean **standard** English. Standard English is the language of our institutions—of school and church and government. It is the language of mass media—of radio and television. We find it in almost everything that appears in print—newspapers, books, magazines, and circulars. Anyone who works in an office must be able to speak and write standard English. Anyone who wants to be a teacher, minister, lawyer, doctor, or engineer must be able to use it easily and well. Making allowance for differences in pronunciation, standard English is basically the same in all parts of the country.

STANDARD AND NONSTANDARD
A BIRD'S-EYE VIEW

Nonstandard English is spoken by many people at home or on the job. When they go to school, write a letter to the editor, or transact official business, they have to be able to shift to standard English. *Standard* English is the language of prestige occupations and most white-collar jobs.

Here are the most clear-cut features of *nonstandard speech:*

Verb Forms:	he don't, you was, I says; knowed, growed; have wrote, had went; I seen, she done
Pronoun Forms:	them cars, this here book, that there truck; hisself, theirself; ourself, yourself
Connectives:	without you give it back; on account of it rained; being as she was sick
Double Negatives:	never hurt nobody; didn't have no time

In their homes and on the job, many people speak a kind of English that differs from the standard variety. They speak **nonstandard** English. Much of the vocabulary and much of the working machinery of standard and nonstandard is exactly the same. The difference lies in forms and expressions that are common in everyday speech and, therefore, noticeable. In the following sentences, some of the most familiar features of nonstandard English appear in italics:

I didn't know you *was* waiting.
The motor *don't* sound too good.
What happened to *them* forms?
I *ain't* seen her.
Fred did it all by *hisself.*

The forms of nonstandard English are not errors or mistakes. They are merely different. They are used by people the way they have learned them, in accordance with the rules of their kind of English. But in many situations, nonstandard English is *out of place.* When we see a nonstandard form on a written page, it seems to stick out. When someone is applying for a white-collar job, nonstandard English is a handicap. Many people look down on someone who says "ain't." Whether you approve of their attitude or not, you have to take it into account.

The student who speaks nonstandard English at home or with friends must learn to shift to standard English when speaking in public or when writing something down. To be able to do so, the student has to recognize the most common nonstandard forms.

Shift from nonstandard to standard verb forms.

U1a
Standard Verb Forms

Verbs are words like *ask, bring, shorten, accelerate,* and *organize.* Verbs change to show changes in *time.* Almost all English verbs change from present to past. Such "time changes" are called changes in **tense.**

Today we *work.*	Yesterday we *worked.*
Today I *bring* the food.	Yesterday he *brought* the food.

Verbs also change to show changes in *number.* When we talk about the present, verbs change to show the change from "one single third party" to "several." The change from "one" to "several" is the change from **singular** to **plural.**

One train *stops.*	Several trains *stop.*
One girl *works* there.	Several girls *work* there.

Sometimes the verb even changes when the subject changes from *I* to *you:* "I *was* late" but "You *were* late." *I* and *we* are "first person"—we are talking about "Number One." *You* is "second person"—we are talking *to* a second party. *He, she, it,* and *they* are "third person"—we are talking about one or more third parties.

Some of the verb forms of nonstandard English are *different* from those of standard English. Look at the following inventory of nonstandard verb forms. Do you use any of these in ordinary conversation? If so, study and practice the forms that replace them in standard English.

he don't	*Do not* or *don't* is standard after all plural subjects (the locks *don't* work; the doors *don't* close). *Do not* and *don't* are also standard after *I* and *you* (I *don't* believe you; you *don't* have to come). After all other single subjects the standard form is *does not* or *doesn't.* Be sure to use *doesn't* (or *does not*) for "one single third party."

Standard: He *doesn't* understand. She *doesn't* live here. The lock *doesn't* work. The door *doesn't* close. My father *doesn't* see well. It *doesn't* bother me. That *doesn't* mean anything. Money *doesn't* impress him. *Doesn't* he like you? Why *doesn't* she answer? Crime *doesn't* pay.

we was, you was, they was

Was is standard after all singular subjects except *you* (he *was* absent; I *was* there; time *was* up). After *you* and *all plural subjects* the standard form is *were*. Be sure to change *we was, you was, they was* to *we were, you were, they were.*

Standard: You *were* right. *Were* you there? We *were* talking. They *were* tired. The men *were* leaving. The *wheels were* turning. When *were* you living there? They *were* carefully selected. We *were* told to leave. Why *weren't* we invited? *Weren't* you one of his friends?

knowed, growed, throwed

Flowed and *showed* are standard. But for *know* the past form is *knew*, for *grow* it is *grew*, for *throw* it is *threw*, for *blow* it is *blew*.

Standard: No one *knew* the answers. His father *threw* us out. The trees *grew* very slowly. Every afternoon the wind *blew*. The men *knew* Lincoln. What *grew* in the garden? Jim *threw* a perfect pass.

have wrote, had went

Many verbs have one form for the simple past. They have another *different* form for use after the auxiliaries *have* and *be*. Change *have wrote* to *have written*. Change *has went* to *has gone*.

Standard: The boy *wrote* a letter. He *had written* a letter before. The letter *was written*. They all *went* home. They *have gone* home. They *should have gone* earlier. We *ate* breakfast. *Have* they *eaten* yet? All the food

ENGLISH VERBS
A CHECKLIST OF STANDARD FORMS

Present	Past	Perfect
begin	began	have begun
bend	bent	have bent
blow	blew	have blown
break	broke	have broken
bring	brought	have brought
burst	burst	have burst
catch	caught	have caught
choose	chose	have chosen
come	came	have come
dig	dug	have dug
do	did	have done
drag	dragged	have dragged
draw	drew	have drawn
drink	drank	have drunk
drive	drove	have driven
drown	drowned	have drowned
eat	ate	have eaten
fall	fell	have fallen
fly	flew	have flown
freeze	froze	have frozen
go	went	have gone
grow	grew	have grown
know	knew	have known
ride	rode	have ridden
run	ran	have run
see	saw	have seen
sing	sang	have sung
speak	spoke	have spoken
swim	swam	have swum
take	took	have taken
throw	threw	have thrown
wear	wore	have worn
write	wrote	have written

Verbs with two *past* forms: *dived* or *dove; dreamed* or *dreamt; lighted* or *lit; sank* or *sunk*

Verbs with two *perfect* forms: *have proved* or *have proven*

was eaten. He *broke* the glass. Someone *had broken* it. It *was* already *broken*. She *rode* the bus. He had never *ridden* a horse. Someone *stole* his wallet. His wallet *had been stolen*. She *wore* a new coat. She had never *worn* it before.

I seen, he done

In standard English, forms like *seen* and *done* cannot by themselves serve as complete verbs. Insert auxiliaries, or "helping verbs," like *have* and *be*.

Standard: I *saw* your friend. I *have seen* her paintings. He *did* us a favor. He *has done* it before. We *ran* to the door. He *had run* the whole distance. She *swam* to the shore. We had *swum* in the lake.

drownded, busted, drug, brung

The standard forms are *drowned, burst, dragged, brought*. Other standard forms to remember are *bent* (for *bended*), *caught* (for *catched*), *dug* (for *digged*).

Standard: Several swimmers *have drowned* there. The pipe *burst*. He *dragged* the garden hose across the lawn. Carl *had brought* the paper in. He *had bent* the wire. Three of them *were caught*. The men *dug* a trench.

For Oral Practice: Read the following sentences over several times, paying special attention to the italicized words. ALL THE FORMS USED ARE STANDARD ENGLISH.

Her friends *don't* care. Her sister *doesn't* know. The tree just *grew*. Jean *had written* a letter. We *were* glad to get your note. I *had seen* his picture in the paper. I *saw* him lock the door. Wait until she *has done* her homework. He always *did* his work. Someone *stole* her purse. That *doesn't* impress me. Baseball *doesn't* interest me. You *were* lucky. They *were* right. We *were* last. We *went* back. He *had gone* home. We *should have gone* to the meeting. The boys had *brought* a salad. The girls *had caught* a snake. Someone *had drowned*. We *knew* the truth. He *threw* the letter into the fire. *Have* you *eaten*? No one *ate* the dessert. Someone *had broken* the glass. The bell doesn't work. *Were* you in the house? I *have seen* this movie. I *saw* it last year. She *has done* much for the school. I *have done* nothing wrong. I *did* everything you told me.

ACTIVITY 1

In each of the following sentences, a verb has been omitted. Supply the appropriate *standard form* of the verb listed in parentheses at the end of the sentence. Fill in only one single word. Write on a separate sheet of paper.

Example: Simon had ——————— a huge fish.   (catch)
(Answer)   *caught*

1. Last Saturday I ——————— her wash her car.   (see)
2. Actually we could have ——————— by train.   (go)
3. We ——————— several weeks ago that our mission was a failure. (know)
4. The reduced rate ——————— not apply now.   (do)
5. At the beginning they ——————— sure their team would win.   (be)
6. Most of the students had ——————— their books and notes. (bring)
7. Everyone squirmed when Robert ——————— a high note.   (blow)
8. When the light suddenly turned, you ——————— the right thing. (do)
9. Last winter the water froze and several pipes ———————.   (burst)
10. When the room got cold, he ——————— another log onto the fire. (throw)
11. We could have ——————— lunch before we left.   (eat)
12. Some voters ——————— not fully understand today's issues.   (do)
13. Paul copied over the last page he had ———————.   (write)
14. The last time I saw you, you ——————— planning a trip.   (be)
15. Alfred had ——————— all the way home from school.   (run)

ACTIVITY 2

Use this activity first for oral practice. Then write down the forms called for by the instructions. USE ONLY STANDARD FORMS. Write on a separate sheet of paper.

1. Fill in a form of *do:*
   Money ——————— not solve all problems. He has ———————
   a great service. He ——————— what he could. Your figures
   ——————— not seem correct today. Jack ——————— not work
   right now.

THE WAY PEOPLE TALK

TO BE OR NOT TO BE

The verb *to be* is everywhere in the English language. It has more forms than any other English verb: *be, am, are, is, was, were, has been, will be,* and so forth. It has many different uses in the English sentence. But some dialects of English make sentences work without many of the uses of *be* that people expect in "mainstream" English. Look at the following examples of black English as written down by black American writers. How many different places can you find where mainstream English would insert a form of *be*? Where would mainstream English use a *different* form of *be*?

Who was there?—Now who you asking!
There is some good white people and some bad ones.
Things bound to get better 'cause they can't get no worse.
It's your world—you the man I pay rent to.
I'm the man but you the main man.
Why, you always in good form. You got more foam than Alka Seltzer.
I'm living on the welfare and things is stormy.
They Communist, girl! Don't you know that?
All the folks from four plantations was invited.
We just plain working folks.
The mailman going to ring that bell this morning.
You aiming to iron all them things?
You right on time today—right on time.

2. Use each of these verbs in turn: *catch, steal, eat, bring, see.*
   The natives had ——————— a pig.

3. Use each of these verbs in turn: *go, ride, swim, run, write.*
   The boy should have ——————— home.

4. Fill in *was* or *were:*
   I ——————— exhausted. The leaves ——————— dry. You ——————— not very polite. The well ——————— deep. We ——————— sitting in the sun.

5. Use each of these verbs in turn: *grow, know, wear, throw, bring.*
   The boy was interested only in cars, but the girl——————— flowers.

STANDARD ENGLISH IS OFFICE ENGLISH.

STANDARD ENGLISH IS SCHOOL ENGLISH.

STANDARD ENGLISH IS MEDIA ENGLISH.

Shift from nonstandard to standard pronoun forms.

Nonstandard usage differs from the standard use of two kinds of pronouns. The first is the "pointing" kind—the **demonstrative** pronouns. Standard English uses *this* and *these* (*this* car, *these* cars) and *that* and *those* (*that* building, *those* buildings).

The second is the "pointing back" kind—the **reflexive** pronouns: *myself, himself, themselves.* In each of the following examples, can you find what the *–self* pronoun points back to?

Do it yourself.
Every man for himself!
I'll do it myself.
Help the handicapped to help themselves.

Learn to recognize the nonstandard uses listed below. If any of these are part of your everyday speech, learn to shift to the standard forms.

them books, them people	*Them* does not appear in standard English as a demonstrative pronoun. If the pronoun *points to* the noun that follows it, use *these* or *those.*
	Standard: *Those* books. *These* people. *Those* crazy schemes. *These* pipes. Bring me some of *those* tacks. He checked all *those* figures for me. *These* fancy gadgets never work. Give me some of *those* nice cupcakes. Here are the labels for *those* boxes.
this here book, that there shelf	The *here* after *this* and the *there* after *that* are omitted in standard English.
	Standard: *This* book. *That* shelf. I found *this* article. I looked it up in *that* dictionary. *Take* a look at *this* battery. He was sitting on *that* bench. Don't touch *that* plant.
hisself, theirself	The standard forms are *himself* and *themselves.*
	Standard: He did it by *himself.* The boy had cut *himself.* The accused *himself* did not testify. He always looked out for *himself.* They considered *themselves* superior. The girls were sitting by *themselves.* The boys had bought *themselves* huge Mexican hats.

ourself, yourself | The standard forms use *–selves* when the pronoun refers to more than one.

> Standard: We asked *ourselves* several questions. We built the cabin *ourselves*. He asked use to identify *ourselves*. Please put back your chairs *yourselves*. You could have had *yourselves* arrested. Protect *yourselves* against thieves.

the man, he; my mother, she | Standard English omits the *he*, *she*, or *they* after the noun in sentences like "my mother, *she* loves to cook" or "the principal, *he* told me to leave." Either the pronoun is omitted or the reflexive pronoun (*himself*, *herself*, *themselves*) is put in its place for emphasis.

> Standard: My mother loves to cook. My mother *herself* did very little cooking. The principal told me to leave. The principal *himself* told me to leave. The workers took their time. The workers *themselves* had not been told.

yourn, hisn, hern, ourn | The standard forms are *yours*, *his*, *hers*, *ours*, and *theirs*.

> Standard: This letter is *yours*. The gray coat is *hers*. He had forgotten to bring *ours*. Most of it is *his*. They considered the land *theirs*. We received *yours* but not mine. Are these gloves *yours* or *hers*? This house used to be *ours*. The yellow car is *his*.

For Oral Practice: Read the following sentences over several times, paying special attention to the italicized words. ALL THE FORMS USED ARE STANDARD ENGLISH.

He blamed *himself* for the accident. His aunt disliked *those* new-fangled electric ovens. The responsibility is *his*. They congratulated *themselves* on their achievements. The last door on the left is *ours*. We should call *ourselves* something different. They admitted it *themselves*. Your team is better than *ours*. My aim is better than *his*. The superintendent *himself* was not in. I told all my friends and she told *hers*. I can see you enjoyed *yourselves*. Put down *those* packages. She sent me *this* note. We watched all *those* birds circle over the pier. He reminded *himself* to stay calm. The driver *himself* was not hurt.

THE WAY PEOPLE
TALK

HOW THEY TALKED IN NORTH CAROLINA

Charles Waddell Chestnutt was a writer from North Carolina. His tales show us how old-timers used to talk in the "Tar Heel State." Some of the people talking in the following examples are former slaves. Some are poor white "sandhillers." What are they talking about? Can you translate what they are saying into standard English? Point out several features of folk speech that we can still hear today.

1. Well, suh, you is a stranger ter me, en I is a stranger ter you, en we is bofe strangers ter one anudder, but 'f I 'uz in yo' place, I would n' buy dis vimya'd. . . . I dunno whe'r you b'lieves in conj'in er not—some er de w'ite folks don't, er says dey don't—but de truf er de matter is dat dis yer ole vimy'd is goophered.[1]

2. Some o' the gals snickered, and one or two o' the boys lafft out. But Tom wa'n't a bad lookin' feller, and was a good dancer; there was nothin' agin 'im, 'ceptin' his bein' pore and no 'count, so the gals wa'n't sorry to see 'im. An' as he would fight when he got his dander up, the boys was afeared to laff much. When the music started up ag'in, Tom mixed in with the crowd and got to talkin' an' 'dancin', and had almost forgot he wa'n't ax' to the dancin', when the old man Dunkin, who had'n' forgot it, come in to call em to supper.

3. I'm gittin' monst'us ti'ed er dish yer gwine roun' so much. Here I is lent ter Mars Jeems dis mont', en I got ter do so-en-so; en ter Mars Archie de nex' mont', en I got ter do so-en-so; den I got ter go ter Miss Jinnie's: en hit's Sandy dis en Sandy dat, en Sandy yer en Sandy dere, tel it 'pears ter me I ain't got no home, ner no marster, ner no mistiss, nor no nuffin.

[1] goopher—conjure, put under a spell.

—courtesy of Mrs. Sylvia Render, North Carolina College

Find out for *yourselves*. They *themselves* stayed behind the scenes. Our cafeteria was larger than *theirs*. Someone tangled *those* wires. The fault is neither *yours* nor *ours*. They should have removed *these* barriers. Stay clear of *that* hook. We brought it on *ourselves*.

ACTIVITY

Pronouns change as the words they point to change. Thus we say "*I* cut *myself*" but "*he* cut *himself*." We say "*this* book" but "*these* books." Fill in the blanks in the following sentences, changing the pronoun as necessary to fit in with the changes earlier in the sentence. USE ONLY STANDARD FORMS.

Use this activity first for oral practice. Then write down the forms called for by the instructions. Write on a separate sheet of paper.

1. I thoroughly enjoyed *myself.*
   Alice, did you enjoy ——————?
   Jim said he had enjoyed ——————.
   Alice said she was enjoying ——————.
   We were enjoying ——————.
   Did you enjoy ——————, children?
   My friends said that they had enjoyed ——————.

2. I knew the fault was *mine.*
   Do you admit, Fred, that the fault was ——————?
   Fred admitted that the fault was ——————.
   Jean admitted that the fault was ——————.
   We freely admitted that the fault was ——————.
   Why can't you admit, boys, that the fault was ——————?
   The boys admitted that the fault was ——————.

3. I went to the door *myself.*
   Fred, please go to the door ——————.
   The mother had come to the door ——————.
   The host and hostess came to door ——————.
   The father opened the door ——————.
   We decided to go to the door ——————.
   Why didn't you two go to the door ——————?

4. The long-sleeved coat is *mine.*
   The lady claimed the coat was ——————.
   Are these books ——————, Diane?
   He was sure the prize would be ——————.
   How could these people sell land that was not ——————?
   We took only what was ——————.
   Do you two remember which one was ——————?

5. I finished the work by *myself.*
   Tim finished the work by ——————.

The boys had decided the matter by —————.
Mary went home by —————.
We settled the problem among —————.
You two brought all this on —————.
You brought all this on —————, Jim.

margin: U1c / A Checklist of Other Forms

Learn to avoid nonstandard expressions.

Some nonstandard expressions are common only in some regions of the country, like the *reckon* in "I *reckon* I'll just have to be late." Others have more general currency. If you use any of those listed below, learn to shift to the standard ways of saying the same thing.

being as, being that   Not used in standard English to introduce a *reason* in sentences like *"being as* he was a close friend of mine . . ."* or *"being that* the store was closed. . . ."* The standard connective is *because.*

Standard: *Because* he was a friend, I lent him the money. *Because* the store was closed, we had to go to a restaurant. *Because* we were all tired, we stopped.

didn't say nothing   In expressions like "I didn't say nothing" and "I couldn't find none," the *nothing* or *none* repeats the *not* that is already contained in *didn't* and *couldn't.* This **double negative** is avoided in standard English. Use one or the other but not both—*not* or *nothing, not* or *none.*

Standard: I *didn't* say anything. I said *nothing.* I *couldn't* find any. I could find *none.* He *couldn't* ever sit still. He could *never* sit still. I *didn't* see anybody. I saw *nobody.* We *didn't* go anywhere. We went *nowhere.* I *don't* tell you any stories. I tell you *no* stories.

irregardless   *Regardless* already means *"without* regard to." Standard English omits the *ir—* that would duplicate the *without.*

Standard: *Regardless* of your age. *Regardless* of his protests.

learned me to   In standard English, a teacher *teaches* something to the student. The student *learns* something from the teacher.

> Standard: My father *taught* me how to swim. I *learned* Spanish. I *taught* Rover to sit up. Rover was *learning* many new tricks. Your mother should have *taught* you manners. The children had never *learned* to sit still. Mr. Brown was *teaching* us grammar. We *learned* the parts of speech. The accident *taught* me a lesson. Fred *learned* his lesson well.

nowheres, nohow

The standard expressions are *nowhere* and *not at all*.

> Standard: I could find it *nowhere*. He was *not* fit for the job *at all*.

off of

Standard English omits the *of* in expressions like "he took it *off of* his income tax." It substitutes *from* for *off of* in expressions like "he borrowed ten dollars *off of* his brother-in-law."

> Standard: He took everything *off* the table. He borrowed money *from* his brother. The girl tried to jump *off* the bridge. He would have sold the clothes *off* his back to help his family.

seeing as how

Seeing as how is replaced in standard English by *because*.

> Standard: *Because* you are a good friend of mine, I am going to make an exception.

**without,
on account of**

Without and *on account of* are used in standard English as prepositions introducing a noun (*without* your help; *on account of* our friendship). Do not use them as a connective introducing a clause with its own subject and predicate (*without* we pay the rent; *on account of* I knew him in Kansas). Replace them with *unless* and *because*.

> Standard: He will sue *unless* we pay the rent. I trust him *because* I knew him in Kansas. I cannot go out with you *unless* you apologize.

For Oral Practice: Read the following sentences over several times, paying special attention to the italicized words. ALL THE FORMS USED ARE STANDARD ENGLISH.

The club *didn't* pay us *anything*. The club paid us *nothing*. The club *never* paid us anything. I cannot admit you *without* a ticket. Warren never went anywhere *without* his uncle's approval. Warren never went anywhere *unless* his uncle approved. The game was canceled *on account of* the rain. The game was canceled *because* it rained. The first year I *didn't* know *anybody*. The first year I knew *nobody*. She had left the lid *off* the jar. She took the jar *off* the shelf. He borrowed the mower *from* a neighbor. He bought the bicycle *from* a friend. Miss Brown *taught* us how to make jewelry. We *learned* how to enamel metal. He did not *teach* me very much. I *learned* very little. We had invited him *regardless* of his attitude. We went out *regardless* of the rain. My aunt did *not* take us *anywhere*. My aunt took us *nowhere*. My aunt *never* took us *anywhere*.

ACTIVITY

In each of the following pairs, which sentence is standard English and which is nonstandard? Put the letter for the *standard* sentence after the number of the pair. Write on a separate sheet of paper.

Example: a. We set out on the trip irregardless of the rain.
             b. We set out on the trip regardless of the rain.
(Answer)   *b*

1. a. He went out into the rain without his coat.
   b. Don't go out without you put your coat on.

2. a. Some people can't never get anything straight.
   b. Some people can't ever get anything straight.

3. a. Being that I was his brother, I understood how he felt.
   b. Because I was his brother, I understood how he felt.

4. a. We postponed the trip on account of the weather.
   b. We postponed the trip on account of it rained.

5. a. We couldn't persuade nobody that we were right.
   b. We couldn't persuade anybody that we were right.

6. a. We cannot proceed without you sign the contract.
   b. We cannot proceed unless you sign the contract.

7. a. I had learned all the algebra I know from Mr. Brown.
   b. Mr. Brown learned me all the algebra I know.

8. a. Al had bought the car off of a good friend.
   b. Al had bought the car from a good friend.

9. a. She was so hoarse she couldn't say nothing.
   b. She was so hoarse she couldn't say anything.

10. a. My father never gave anything to anybody.
    b. My father never gave nothing to nobody.

REVIEW ACTIVITY

You can turn each of the following sentences into standard English by substituting *one single word* for a nonstandard expression in the original. Write the standard form after the number of the sentence. Write on a separate sheet of paper.

Example: He should have wrote to say he was not coming.
(Answer)   *written*

1. We should have protected ourself by buying insurance.
2. The afternoon train don't stop here anymore.
3. We missed the speech on account of the bus was late.
4. My brothers ran because they was afraid of the dark.
5. You should have went home right after the talk.
6. The ranger couldn't tell us nothing new.
7. My uncle used to call hisself a self-made man.
8. My family always distrusted them city lawyers.
9. The accused really done nothing wrong.
10. That kind of person don't impress me.
11. They had already ate when we arrived.
12. Everyone there knowed that his story wasn't true.
13. We ought to complete this here project first.
14. The men refused to identify theirself.
15. I thought the car in the driveway was yourn.

Be able to use formal and informal standard English.

We all recognize degrees of formality in dress and manners. We expect a business executive to wear sports clothes at a picnic. We expect the same executive to wear business clothes in the office. If we see a girl in a bathing suit, we expect her to be heading for the beach. We expect her to wear something more formal to class. There are similar differences in our use of language. We talk one way at a picnic and another way at a council meeting. We talk casually and write more deliberately.

U2
FORMAL AND
INFORMAL

Among themselves, many students speak extremely **informal** English. They use more **formal** English when participating in class or when writing a paper. They shift from the informal English we might use with a friend to the more formal English we use in public.

Informal English is conversational English. It employs such shortened forms as *bike* for *bicycle* or *mike* for *microphone*. It makes free use of contractions: *don't* for *do not*, *doesn't* for *does not*, *can't* for *cannot*, *won't* for *will not*. Other telltale signs are the "Well . . ." and the "Why . . ." we use at the beginning of a sentence when we are still thinking about what to say. In the following sentences, informal words or expressions appear in italics:

> *They're* always *kidding* me about my Boston accent.
> *Most* everybody went out of *their* way to make me welcome.
> At first the *kids* in my class *joshed* me *a lot.*
> *Why,* you *wouldn't* do such a thing to a *pal!*
> *Well,* the sale *wasn't* exactly a *whopping* success.

Over the years, American English has become more informal. Much advertising is deliberately made to sound chatty and casual. Political speakers try hard not to sound like "stuffed shirts." But people still naturally shift to a more serious, more formal kind of English when they "mean business." Informal English will serve you well in informal conversation or in a personal letter. But be able to use more formal English in an oral report to the class, in a discussion of serious issues, or in a paper that treats a serious subject.

U2a
Informal Word Choice

Learn to recognize words with a distinctly informal flavor.

Many dictionaries label informal words **colloquial.** *Colloquial* has nothing to do with "local." It means "chatty, suited for informal conversation." The most extremely colloquial words are often labeled **slang.** Slang is colorful; it gives us a chance to play games with language. But it is so informal that it can turn a polite reply into one that sounds insulting. It can turn a serious statement into a joke. When the same slang expression is repeated over and over again, people get tired of it.

Do you agree that the first sentence in each of the following pairs sounds more informal than the second?

> Informal: One visitor *swiped* a 16th-century snuffbox.
> Formal: One visitor *stole* a 16th-century snuffbox.

INFORMAL ENGLISH FOR INFORMAL TALK

Informal: Your new friend is too *pushy*.
Formal: Your new friend is too *aggressive*.

Here are some other informal words with more formal words
to take their places:

Informal	Formal
flunk	fail
goof	blunder
gripe	complain
kid	child, youngster
skinny	thin
stump	baffle
swap	trade

Many informal expressions consist of *more than one word*:

Informal: We asked everyone to *chip in*.
Formal: We asked everyone to *contribute*.

Informal: They were unable to *come up with* the answer.
Formal: They were unable to *find* the answer.

Informal: Mr. Brown asked Jim to *cut it out*.
Formal: Mr. Brown asked Jim to *stop*.

FORMAL AND INFORMAL
A BIRD'S-EYE VIEW

There are two major kinds of standard English. *Informal* English is conversational English. We use it in chatting with old acquaintances, or in writing a letter to a close friend. In your written work you will usually use *formal* English. Formal English is the language of serious discussion. We use it in giving a talk to a group or writing a paper on a topic of general interest.

Here are the most clear-cut features of *informal speech*:

Word Choice:	faze; swipe; flunk; swap; ornery; chip in; come up with
Pronoun Forms:	that's him; it's her; me and John did; between you and I; who did you ask
Adverb Forms:	ran good; was hurt bad; real good; awful fast; sure was a pleasure
Verb Forms:	if I was you; don't just set there; I want to lay down
Miscellaneous:	like I said; everybody left theirs; these kind; those kind; most anybody

Formal words are not always "big words" that someone just found in his dictionary. Often they are short and simple, familiar to everyone. The main difference is that they sound more serious, more businesslike than "shirtsleeve English."

Your Turn: How good is your ear for informal English? Which of the words in the following list sound clearly informal to you? What would be a more formal substitute for each informal word?

snooze	scram	peeved
enthused	interview	tedious
complain	crackpot	middleman
splurge	convict	knuckle under
disappointed	ex-con	right on the button
boo-boo	wise up	shindig

A TRIP TO THE JAZZ AGE

Much new American slang became widely known in the twenties—the era of jazz and prohibition. Do you know what a "flapper" was? When is the last time you have heard someone use expressions like "kiddo" and "whoopee"? Do you know the meaning of the jazz-age slang expressions listed below? (Write the letter for the right meaning after the number of the sentence.) Explain how some of these slang expressions got their meaning. Write on a separate sheet of paper.

1. She thought he was *the cat's meow.*
   a. something wonderful
   b. something worthless
   c. something amusing

2. Uncle Jim met a *gold digger* on the beach in Miami.
   a. a confidence man
   b. a man selling worthless oil stocks
   c. a girl who is after a wealthy man for his money

3. His cousin was always seen with his *torpedoes.*
   a. expensive Cuban cigars
   b. hired gunmen
   c. white shoes

4. She was *stuck on* a boy who had gone to the same high school.
   a. stuck with
   b. infatuated with
   c. angry with

5. My cousin took us to a *ritzy* restaurant.
   a. elegant
   b. cheap
   c. Chinese-American

6. The agents discovered the *hooch* in Fred's garage.
   a. bootleg liquor
   b. forged banknotes
   c. stolen goods

Bonus Question: How many of the following slang expressions from the twenties are still current with your friends today? What does each mean? *the main drag, hand someone a line, gyp, fall guy, have a crush on, bunk, big cheese, bump off, hokum*

ACTIVITY 1

Put a *more formal* word or expression in place of the italicized one. Write on a separate sheet of paper.

Example: My friends always *joshed* me.
(Answer)   *teased*

1. The club members used to *swap* coins and stamps.
2. Jean had always been a *skinny* girl.
3. My brother asked us to *cut out* the noise.
4. Fred always came back with *gripes* about the food.
5. The problem *stumped* even the best students.
6. Everyone had *ganged up* on the sole boy in the class.
7. We decided not to let his attitude *faze* us.
8. The boy who had written the notices had *goofed*.
9. His pain seemed too real to be *faked*.
10. Ralph was afraid he would *flunk* algebra.
11. All the *kids* in the class wanted a part in the play.
12. We cannot buy the gift unless everyone *chips in*.
13. Uncle Mike never *came up with* the brilliant invention we expected.
14. The group had left the meeting room in a terrible *mess*.
15. Mr. Smith *had it in for* anyone from California.

ACTIVITY 2

Which is the more formal of the two words or expressions in each pair? Put the letter for the *more formal expression* after the number of the pair. Be prepared to compare and discuss your own conclusions with those of other members of your class.

Example: a. faze; b. discourage
(Answer)   *b*

1. a. put up with   b. tolerate
2. a. have a fit   b. become very angry
3. a. monkey business   b. foolishness
4. a. bankrupt   b. broke
5. a. cheat   b. gyp
6. a. barge in   b. intrude
7. a. put the heat on   b. put pressure on
8. a. dream up   b. imagine
9. a. obtain   b. latch on to
10. a. shape up   b. take shape

11. a. fold   b. go bankrupt
12. a. pick on   b. criticize
13. a. butter up   b. flatter
14. a. go over big   b. be successful
15. a. crack down on   b. be strict with

For Branching Out: Much of the material in *newspaper columns* is intended for casual reading and entertainment. The following is a very informal newspaper account of a topic that might be treated more seriously in a science textbook. Point out any features of this selection that might make its language too informal for the typical high school textbook.

Your teacher may ask you to *rewrite* the selection in a more formal, more businesslike style.

THE ELEPHANT SEALS OF CALIFORNIA

Every spring a large herd of elephant seals shows up on an island off the California coast. The elephant seal's rear paddles are useless for walking purposes and just drag along on land like a partially filled sack of oatmeal. In spite of his apparent limitations, the elephant seal gets where he wants to go. He will drag himself up 30 or 40 feet out of the water over the most impossible looking rocks and then hurl himself back into the surf in a gleeful belly flop which ought to spread barrels of his blubber all over the place but never fazes him. The sleeping end of the business is where the elephant seal is tops. He can crawl out onto a beach with a thousand or so of his pals and be asleep in no time. However, all it takes to get things moving again is a loud-mouthed sea lion who gets panicked over something and starts yelling as though the crack of doom was at hand. There are always a bunch of sea lions scattered among the snoozing seals. The sea lions then go off to the water, barking bloody murder and flooping all over the seals. Before the seals are fully awake, they are caught in the howling rush for the sea, joining the mob of bulls and cows thrashing about in the cold water.

Recognize pronoun uses that are typical of informal English.

The personal pronouns like *I, you, he, she,* and *they* are "noun substitutes." Depending on the function of the pronoun in a sentence, we change it from *I* to *me,* from *he* to *him,* from *she* to *her,* from *we* to *us,* from *they* to *them.* The first form in each pair is

U2b
Informal Pronoun
Forms

the **subject form.** We use it when the pronoun is the *subject* of the sentence:

I	wrote home for money.
He	answered our letter.
They	refused the offer.

The second form in each pair is the **object form.** We use it when the pronoun is the *object* of a verb:

The story interested	*me.*	
His friends expected	*him.*	
The company sent	*them*	a brochure.

The object form is also used when the pronoun is the object of a preposition:

Was there any mail	for *me?*
Fred talked it over	with *him.*
The majority voted	against *them.*

Look at the following inventory of informal uses of pronouns. Practice the formal choices until you use them naturally.

me and Jim knew — If there are *several subjects* for the same verb, use the form that would fit if there were only *one* subject. Do not use "*me* and Jim knew" because we would not say "*me* knew." Do not use "Sue and *him* turned back" because we would not say "*him* turned back."

> Formal: *I* knew. Jim *and I* knew. *He* turned back. Sue *and he* turned back. *I* notified the others. My brother *and I* notified the others. *He* was late. *He and* the others were late. *She* declined. *She and* her friends declined. Tell me when *he* calls. Tell me when *he and* his friends come.

asked Jim and I — If there are *several objects* for the same verb, use the form that would fit if there were only *one* object. Do not use "she asked Jim and *I*" because you would not say "she asked *I.*" Do not use "we invited *he* and his girlfriend" because you would not say "we invited *he.*"

> Formal: She asked *me.* She asked Jim *and me.* We invited *him.* We invited *him* and his

HOW PRONOUNS FIT INTO A SENTENCE

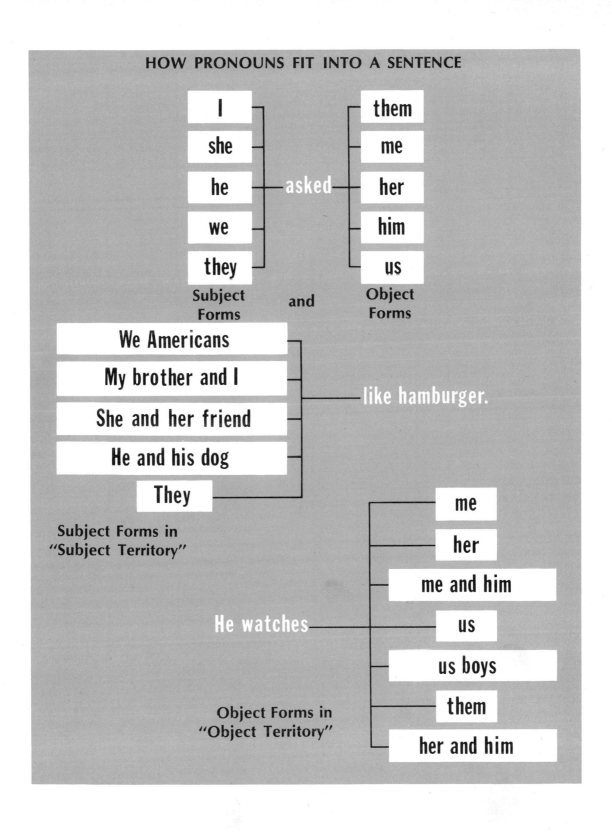

girlfriend. He refused to lend *me* the money. He refused to lend you *and me* the money.

between you and I   If there are *several objects* for the same preposition, use the form that would fit in if there were only *one* object. Do not use "a letter for you and *I*" because you would not say "a letter for *I*."

Formal: This is strictly between you *and me*. Here is a letter for you *and me*. I chatted with her mother *and her*. I had to choose between you *and them*. I know you are prejudiced against his wife *and him*.

us boys did   Use the subject form when a combination like "we Americans" or "we boy scouts" appears as a subject. Use the object form ("us Americans," "us boy scouts") when the combination appears as the object of a verb or preposition.

Formal: *We Americans* believe in justice. He always criticized *us Americans. We boy scouts* support good causes. He had bad news for *us boy scouts*. We girls dislike rudeness. I knew he disliked *us girls*.

that's her   *Is (was, has been*, etc.) is a linking verb and does not take an object. After the linking verb formal English requires the subject form. In formal usage, avoid *it's him, that's her, it's us, it's them.*

Formal: It is always *he* who is asked first. The only girls still waiting were *she* and her friend.

better than me   Fill in the *missing part* of a comparison to decide whether the subject form or object form is appropriate.

Formal: He speaks Spanish better than *I* (do). That style suits her better than (it does) *me*. I am almost as tall as *he* (is). We pay you almost as much as (we pay)

WHO	*DO YOU THINK WILL WIN?*
I THINK **HE**	*WILL.*
WHOM	*DO YOU EXPECT TO WIN?*
I EXPECT **HIM**	*TO WIN.*
I CALLED **HIM.**	
WHOM	*DID YOU CALL?*
HE	*CALLED.*
WHO	*CALLED?*

him. Her brother left earlier than *she* (did). I met her brother earlier than (I met) *her.* I come there more often than *they* (do). I see you more often than (I do) *them.*

who did you ask   *Who* asks a question about the subject. It is used when *he* or *they* are possible answers. *Whom* asks a question about the object of a verb or preposition. It is used when *him* or *them* are possible answers.

Formal: *Who* told you? (*He* did.) *Whom* did you tell? (I told *him.*) Who wrote that? (*He* did.) To *whom* did you write? (I wrote to *him*.) *Who* had helped them? (*He* had.) *Whom* had he helped? (He had helped *them*.) *Who* was George Washington's wife? (*She* was.) *Whom* did George Washington marry? (He married *her*.)

the person who I asked

Who as a relative pronoun is the *subject* of the modifying clause. *Whom* is the *object* of a verb or preposition in the modifying clause.

Formal: I had never seen the man/*who* asked me. (*He* asked me.) I had never seen the man/*whom* I asked. (I asked *him*.) I had never seen the man/for *whom* she worked. (She worked for *him*.)

NOTE: Some informal uses of pronouns are so much a part of everyday speech that the formal choices have come to sound awkward. For instance, "it's me" is so generally accepted that "it is I" is almost never heard.

For Oral Practice: Read the following sentences over several times, paying special attention to the italicized words. All FORMS ARE ACCEPTABLE IN FORMAL ENGLISH.

Who baked the cake? Sue *and I* did. *We girls* did. It was *she* who suggested it. *Whom* did they invite? They invited Sue *and me*. They invited *us girls*. They sent an invitation for you *and me*. *Who* broke the window? Was it *he* who broke the window? Jack *and he* were the ones. *We boys* are always blamed. With *whom* did he work? He worked with Jack *and me*. He worked with *us committee members*. He worked faster than *we*. He worked as fast as *we*. I like Fred better than *him*. I like Fred as much as *him*. Jim is the man *who* hired me. Jim is the man *whom* I hired. Jim is the man with *whom* I work. He looked for a girl *who* knew how to ski. She looked for a girl with *whom* she could play tennis. *Who* expected you? *Whom* did you expect? Fred *and I* did the dishes. Sue *and he* were the winners. Ann *and she* are old friends. All cheered when *we players* marched in. He insulted *us voters*. This is between you *and me*. I told the news to her father *and her*. *Who* told you? *Whom* did you tell? Her sister was more cooperative than *she*. We asked him more questions than *her*.

ACTIVITY

Choose the form appropriate to *formal usage*. Write the form you have chosen after the number of the sentence. Write on a separate sheet of paper.

Example: He had news for you and *I/me*.
(Answer)   *me*

1. Fred and *I/me* went for a walk.
2. *Who/whom* left this package?
3. *We sophomores/us sophomores* are not eligible.
4. This is strictly between you and *I/me*.
5. The girl *who/whom* came to the door wore a red dress.
6. My sister types much faster than *I/me*.
7. By *who/whom* was the paper signed?
8. She always aimed pointed remarks at Herbert and *I/me*. ✓
9. *He/him* and his brother have impossible manners.
10. It was *he/him* who first asked me my name.
11. We intended the present for both her sister and *she/her*.
12. My grandmother read fairy tales to *we children/us children*.
13. The man *who/whom* he pointed out was six feet tall.
14. *Who/whom* should we ask for advice?
15. You should have asked Jim and *I/me* for advice.
16. Few of my friends work as hard as *I/me*.

Recognize adverb forms that are typical of informal English.

U2c
Informal Adverb Forms

Adjectives are words like *generous*, *real*, *smart*, and *lucky*. Adverbs are words like *generously*, *really*, *smartly*, and *luckily*. Adjectives modify nouns. They tell us "which one?" or "what kind?" Adverbs modify verbs. They tell how, when, or where something is done.

Adjective: The *happy girl* played the piano.
  Adverb: The usually glum girl *happily played* the piano.

Adjective: My *generous uncle* helped all his relatives.
  Adverb: My stingy uncle *generously gave* me a dime for the phone.

Informal English often uses adverb forms that are *the same* as the adjective. Formal English uses the *separate* adverb form to "show how."

Usage

Remember that adjectives follow a linking verb that pins a label on the subject. Adverbs modify action verbs, typically telling us *where, when,* or *how* an action takes place.

Adjective Following a Linking Verb

> The train was *slow.*
> The music sounded *loud.*
> His reply seemed *quick.*

Informal Adverb with Action Verb

> We told him to drive *slow.*
> He talks *loud.*
> Come *quick!*

Formal Adverb with Action Verb

> We told him to drive *slowly.*
> He talks *loudly.*
> Come *quickly!*

One-syllable words like *slow, loud,* and *quick* are so generally used as adverbs that they are seldom criticized as too informal. But avoid the following uses of informal adverbs in serious discussion and writing:

clean it good   The formal adverb is *well.* We use it when we express approval *of the way something is done.*

Formal: Clean it *well.* He plays *well.* His daughter read very *well.* His grandfather does not see *well.* Jim speaks Spanish *well.* They have done it *well.* The work was done *well.* The sash had not been fastened *well.*

was hurt bad   Use *bad* after linking verbs (it is *bad;* I feel *bad;* it sounds *bad*). Use *badly* with action verbs.

Formal: He was hurt *badly.* She plays the piano *badly.* The trip started *badly.* His hand had been cut *badly.*

he worked steady   Use the form with −*ly* as the adverb for words with two or more syllables.

Formal: He worked *steadily.* We suffered *terribly.* The situation had improved *considerably.* He swore *dreadfully.*

real heavy,
awful fast

Use the form with *-ly* not only to modify action verbs but also to modify *adjectives and other adverbs* (*truly* sorry; *really* shocked). When *real* and *awful* simply indicate degree, substitute *very* or *extremely*.

Formal: He was a *very* good talker. The package was *extremely* heavy. The car was going *very* fast. He bought a *very* flashy car.

sure was lucky

Use *surely* or *certainly* as an adverb that applies to a statement as a whole.

Formal: You can *surely* do better than that. I *certainly* miss you. He *certainly* made a mistake.

NOTE: Do not simply start adding *-ly* to *all* words that seem to be used as adverbs. Do not use *thusly* instead of *thus,* or *muchly* instead of *much.* Like *fast* and *well, thus* and *much* are used as adverbs even though they do not have the *-ly* ending.

For Oral Practice: Read over the following sentences several times, paying special attention to the italicized words. All FORMS ARE ACCEPTABLE IN FORMAL ENGLISH.

The cake was *good.* She baked it *well.* The tune sounded *good.* The band played it *well.* His eyesight was *good.* He could see *well.* The results were *bad.* His foot hurt *badly.* The news sounded *bad.* He told the story *badly.* John was a *real* athlete. John was a *truly* dedicated athlete. The confusion was *awful.* Order was restored *very* fast. We were not *sure.* We *surely* were lucky. Lucky was a *sure* winner. You *certainly* picked a winner. The poem was very *good.* Jim read it very *well.* The paper was very *bad.* Jim read it very *badly.* The soup did not taste *good.* She did not know how to make soup very *well.* John has always been a *real* friend to me. The neighbors have always been *very* friendly. The accident looked *awful.* The police arrived *very* fast.

ACTIVITY

Use this exercise first for oral practice. Then write down the forms called for by the instruction. USE ONLY FORMS ACCEPTABLE IN FORMAL ENGLISH.

1. Fill in *good* or *well:*
   a. Mary writes _____.
   b. The new halfback was very _____.

REVISING THE INFORMAL ADVERB

In each of the following, one word should be changed from an adjective to an adverb form. Write the adverb form after the number of the sentence.

1. His father treated him very bad.
2. The crisis developed very gradual.
3. Voters should listen very careful to a candidate.
4. They became real good friends after their horse won the big race.
5. She dressed very neat but used awful language.
6. He picked up the injured dog very gentle.
7. The President spoke calm as he announced the end of the war.
8. The United States teams do good in most sports events.
9. The accident would never have happened if the man had driven less reckless.
10. Pollution is a real serious problem in our country.

    c. The offer sounded —————.
    d. The meat had not been cooked very —————.
    e. The choir sang —————.

2. Fill in *bad* or *badly:*
    a. Attendance had been —————.
    b. Her injury hurt the team —————.
    c. I feel ————— about the accident.
    d. The weather had been very —————.
    e. He needed a haircut —————.

3. Fill in the appropriate form of the word in parentheses:
    a. It was raining —————. (steady)
    b. Our losses have been —————. (considerable)
    c. He rewarded us —————. (noble)
    d. The thunder sounded —————. (terrible)
    e. Her escort embarrassed us —————. (terrible)

4. Fill in the appropriate form of the word in parentheses:
    a. We were ————— that he was wrong. (sure)
    b. You are ————— wrong. (sure)
    c. The records should ————— be examined. (certain)
    d. This time we have ————— been disappointed. (real)
    e. No one had thought that the bear would be —————. (real)

U2d
A Checklist of Other
Forms

Recognize informal expressions that are often criticized.

Some expressions are criticized only by a strict listener or reader. For instance, *the reason is because* (instead of *the reason is that*) appears in public statements of educated and successful people. Other expressions, though used informally by some educated people, are still widely considered unacceptable. Look at the following informal expressions. In each case, the formal alternative is the *safe* form to use in serious speaking and writing.

couldn't hardly

Formal English omits the shortened *not* before *hardly* or *barely* in expressions like "I couldn't hardly" and "I couldn't barely."

Formal: I *could hardly* keep from laughing. We *could barely* see the sky. I *had scarcely* spoken to him.

everybody took theirs

In formal English *everybody* (and *everyone*), *anybody* (and *anyone*), *somebody* (and *someone*), *nobody* (and *no one*) are treated as singulars. A pronoun that points back to any of these is then also singular. Use *he* and *his*, or *she* and *her*, rather than *they* and *their*.

Formal: Everybody took *hers*. Someone had left *his* coat. No one raised *his* hand. If you fail to invite somebody, you cannot blame *her* for feeling left out. We did not find anybody who had finished *his* work. Everyone should have minded *his* own business.

if I was you

After *if* and *as if*, use *were* instead of *was* if you are talking about something that is impossible or not now true.

Formal: If I *were* you, I might go. If he *were* your brother, he could come along. If she *were* more polite, she would have less trouble. The dog jumped as if it *were* a monkey. He acts as if it *were* all my fault.

I want to lay down

In formal speech and writing, the words that mean "recline" and "stretch out" are *lie* and *lie down*, with *lay* and *lay down* used as the past

tense. When *lay* is used in the present, it typically means "to *place* something somewhere."

Formal: He always *lies down* after supper.
           Books were *lying* on the floor. I want
           to *lie down*. When I come home, *I lie
           down*. When I came home, I *lay*
           down. Usually the forms *lie* on this
           shelf. The broken cable was *lying*
           on the ground. I now *lay* my cards
           on the table. Yesterday he *laid* his
           plans before us.

like I said   Formal written English uses *like* as a preposi-
                  tion (*like* my mother) but not as a connective
                  introducing a clause (*like* my mother said). Sub-
                  stitute *as* or *as if*.

Formal: I look *like* my mother. I do *as* my
           mother says. It looks *like* rain. It
           looks *as if* it will rain. *Like* me, you
           should practice. *As* I said, you
           should practice. This machine does
           not work *like* the old one. This ma-
           chine does not work *as* it should.

most everybody   Formal speech and writing uses *almost* or
                     nearly.

Formal: *Almost* everybody was there. *Almost*
           anything was welcome.

set down   In formal English, we set *something* down. A
               person who is seated or takes a seat *sits* (or *sits
               down*) and, in the past, *sat* (or *sat down*).

Formal: *Sit down*, Fred. He was *sitting* at the
           table. Today, I *sit* here. Yesterday, I
           sat here. *Sit* still. Grandfather used
           to *sit* there. He *sat* there all day. *Set
           down* that vase. He *set* his glass
           down before he got up.

these kind, those kind   Formal English uses *this kind* and *that kind*
                             (singular) or *these kinds* and *those kinds*
                             (plural).

Formal: I have never liked *this kind* of car. Fred is fascinated by *that kind* of girl. *This kind* of argument leads nowhere. I have never tried *this kind* of apple. Everyone was eager to try out for *that kind* of play. Have you tried all *these* different *kinds*?

We just sit (or lie). But we set (or lay) something.

Today I <u>sit</u> in the sun.   Today I <u>set something</u> up.
Yesterday I <u>sat</u> in the sun.   Yesterday I <u>set something</u> down.
I <u>have sat</u> there before.   I <u>have set up an appointment</u>.
I love <u>sitting</u> in the sun.   She hates <u>setting the table</u>.

Today I <u>lie</u> in the sun.   Today I <u>lay my cards</u> on the table.
Yesterday I <u>lay</u> in the sun.   Yesterday I <u>laid tile</u>.
I <u>have lain</u> in the sun too long. I <u>have laid something</u> on the shelf.
I should stop <u>lying</u> in the sun. He was <u>laying bricks</u>.

FOR REVIEW

AROUND THE WORLD IN THE NATIONAL GEOGRAPHIC

Of the two choices given in each of the following sentences, which would be the clearly appropriate one in *formal written English?* Write the form you choose after the number of the sentence. Write on a separate sheet of paper.

Example: My aunt looked exactly *as/like* my mother.
(Answer)   *like*

1. Some boys act *like/as if* there were no magazines besides *Popular Mechanics*.
2. Any reading that is not about cars or planes *stumps/baffles* them.
3. The sweetest sound for these *kids/youngsters* is the hum of a well-tuned engine.
4. Fred used to be one of *this/these* kind of readers.

5. He would give my sister and *I/me* long lectures about brakes and transmissions.

6. There was little for *we two/us two* to do except listen.

7. However, last year someone mentioned *his/their* favorite magazine to Fred.

8. This person was *very/real* excited about the *National Geographic*.

9. The magazine is intended for people *who/whom* love to travel.

10. While you are *setting/sitting* in your chair, the lead article will take you to Egypt.

11. You will see tall modern buildings, *as/like* you would in Chicago or Detroit.

12. You will see peasants for *who/whom* the motor car is still a mystery.

13. My only *gripe/complaint* is that there are not enough pictures.

14. The photographers always do their job *good/well*.

15. *Who/whom* would not like more pictures of the Nile or the Pyramids?

16. Fred liked the magazine even better than my sister and *I/me* did.

17. If you *was/were* one of Fred's friends, this change would surprise you.

18. Fred is not usually *awful/extremely* eager to read anything.

19. Now everybody who has *his/their* own favorite magazine has to tell Fred about it.

20. That is *he/him* over there, reading the *National Geographic*.

For Oral Practice: Read over the following sentences several times, paying special attention to the italicized words. ALL FORMS ARE ACCEPTABLE IN FORMAL ENGLISH.

Somebody had parked *his* car in the driveway. Everyone turned in *his* paper. No one wanted to give up *her* seat. *Lie down. Lay down* your books. *Sit* still. *Set* it down in the corner. Do *as* I tell you. It was *as* she had said. She glared at me *as if* it had been my fault. *Almost* everybody came. *Almost* anybody would have known. *This kind* of cloth. *This kind* of tree. *That kind* of word. If I *were* you, I would leave. If he *were* faster, he would make a good halfback. He acted as if he *were* a millionaire. If it really *was* his car, he should have said so. If it *were* his car, he would not drive this way. Fred did not act *like* a dutiful son. Fred did not act *as* a son should. She wanted to be a carpenter *like* her father. She was a carpenter, *as* her father had wished. I now *sit* where he *sat* yesterday. She *sets* the table today, because I *set* it yesterday. Only the shells now *lie* where eggs *lay* this morning. No one *lays* bricks today the way my father *laid* bricks. I *could hardly* wait to see him. I'm so tired I *can hardly* walk. He *could barely* hold up his head.

ACTIVITY

Use this activity first for oral practice. Then write down the forms called for by the instructions. USE ONLY FORMS ACCEPTABLE IN FORMAL ENGLISH.

1. Fill in *his* or *their:*
   Everybody wants fair value for _____ money.
   Some people never receive fair credit for _____ work.
   Nobody likes to have _____ feelings hurt.
   I did not expect anyone to raise _____ hand.
   She did not allow students to park _____ bicycles there.

2. Fill in *was* or *were:*
   You should not treat him as if he _____ a slave.
   If she _____ your friend, she would lend you the books.
   If he _____ really hungry, he should have asked for food.
   If Fred _____ in charge, this could never happen.
   Merton always acts as if the house _____ his rather than mine.

3. Fill in *like* or *as:*
   Much modern furniture does not look _____ furniture.
   The paper will print it _____ we wrote it.
   _____ I said before, his story is incredible.
   For once he acted _____ a gentleman should act.
   Salespersons _____ Jim know how to calm a customer.

4. Fill in *sit, set,* or *sat:*
   The last time I went, the dog _____ on the sofa.
   If it gets dark, we can _____ by the window.
   Who wants to _____ in the back?
   _____ the bowl down gently, please.
   Eager students usually do not _____ in the back row.

5. Fill in *lie, lay,* or *laid:*
   He asked the prisoners to _____ down their weapons.

When the days grow hot, the animals ——————— in the shade.
Let sleeping dogs ———————.
I ——————— the letter on the table in front of him.
There was not enough room for the prisoners to ———————
down.

REVIEW ACTIVITY

Change each of the following sentences to make it acceptable
in formal written English.

1. His new kidney was working real good.
2. It was always him who was blamed.
3. He ate like he had gone without food for a week.
4. Nobody kept their desk in better order than Jim did.
5. None of the planes had been hit real bad.
6. She spends money like my name was Rockefeller.
7. Between you and I, I think we goofed.
8. Much longer runways will be required for these kind of planes.
9. Most everybody in town had heard rumors about the incident.
10. When I was a kid, walking to school didn't faze me.
11. Someone carved their name into the tree.
12. As our dog got older, it just liked to lay in the sun.
13. The teacher had it in for students who left things in a mess.
14. Me and Gerald had planned the trip for months.
15. He never told me who he was going to ask.

Know how to handle basic relationships in a sentence.

U3
BASIC
RELATIONSHIPS

Written sentences are more carefully built than spoken sentences. When we speak, we may abandon a half-finished sentence and start all over. If someone gives us a blank look, we can repeat or explain what we just said. A written sentence is more like a finished product. It must speak for itself. Remember:

—A sentence can deliver its message only *if it is clear*. When we speak, we may use sentences like the following:

Give me that.
They told me so yesterday.
Cleaning the garage, the shelf collapsed.

If the person we speak to does not know what "that" is, we can point to it. If the person does not know who "they" are, or who cleaned the garage, he or she can ask. A written sentence must carry that information with it if it is to be clear.

—A well-built written sentence must follow the *conventions of written English*. We follow **convention** when we do things the way they are usually done. When we see people *disregard* convention, we may be distracted from more important things and become annoyed. At the dinner table, we find it hard to follow the conversation if our neighbor is trying to cut meat with a spoon. A reader used to the conventions of written English may be annoyed or distracted if your sentences do not follow those conventions.

In working out basic relationships in a sentence, pay attention to three things:

(1) *Agreement between a subject and its verb.* Whenever for some reason there is not simply a single subject *immediately preceding* a single verb, make sure that the verb agrees with its true subject:

> The *bitterness* of the attacks *was* a surprise.
> There *are* now *a freshman and two sophomores* on the team.

(2) *The relationship between a pronoun and its antecedent.* What a pronoun points to should not be left to guesswork. To prevent confusion, make sure that a pronoun points clearly to one thing rather than to another, to something *clearly stated* rather than merely implied:

> *Donna* lent *her* bicycle to Jean.
> The assembly passed *the bill,* but the governor vetoed *it.*

(3) *The relationship between a modifier and what it modifies.* If a word or a phrase modifies something that is merely implied, the modifier is left *dangling.* If a modifier appears in the *wrong position,* it may seem to modify the wrong part of the sentence. To prevent confusing double takes, place a modifier in clear relation to what it modifies:

> He looked at the frame he *had pried* apart *with his knife.*
> *Smiling sadly,* the *old man* continued his story.

U3a
Checking Agreement

Check agreement between a verb and its subject.

Most English nouns have one form to show *one* of a kind **(singular).** They have a different form to show *several* of a kind **(plural).** Most plural nouns have the –*s* ending, but –*en* and a few others also occur: one *boy*/several *boys,* one *car*/several *cars,* one *building*/several *buildings,* one *child*/several *children,* one *crisis*/several *crises.*

Many sentences show this difference between singular and plural more than once. The verb, too, may show that the subject is one of a kind rather than several. Here the *–s* ending is used in the *opposite* way: The form with *–s* is the singular of the verb. The form without the *–s* is the plural. Notice that in the following pairs *the verb and its subject change together.* We say that the verb **agrees** with the subject:

Singular:	The boy *mows* the lawn.
Plural:	The boys *mow* the lawn.
Singular:	This little pig *goes* to market.
Plural:	These little pigs *go* to market.
Singular:	A small child *learns* a new language easily.
Plural:	Small children *learn* a new language easily.
Singular:	One platoon *has* already left.
Plural:	Two platoons *have* already left.

The change in the verb occurs only in the present tense (in reference to something happening *now*) or in forms where we have a choice between *is* and *are, was* and *were, has* and *have:*

Change	No Change
he speaks	he spoke
they speak	they spoke
he *is* speaking	he will speak
they *are* speaking	they will speak
he *was* speaking	he can speak
they *were* speaking	they can speak
he *has* spoken	he had spoken
they *have* spoken	they had spoken

Notice that this change does *not* take place in the verb when we talk about ourselves, using *I* or *we* ("first person"). Nor does it take place when we talk *to* someone, using *you* ("second person"). The singular *–s* appears after the verb only when we talk *about* someone or something ("third person"). The *–s* form is the form for "one single third party, action now."

	Singular	Plural
(first person)	I speak	we speak
(second person)	you speak	you speak
(third person)	he speaks	they speak
	she speaks	

Agreement problems come about in two ways. When the subject does not stand *directly in front of* the verb, we may lose sight of it and fail to make the verb agree. Or, when the subject is singular in form, it may yet have the idea of "more than one" as part of its meaning. Here is how such agreement problems are solved in formal written English:

one of these is

When you single out *one* thing among several, or talk about one quality shared by several things, *a plural noun may come between the subject and its verb*. Make the verb agree, *not* with the intervening plural, but with its true subject:

Formal: *One* of my friends *was* late (one was late). *The gist* of these remarks *is* clear (the gist is clear). *The attitude* of the students *has* improved (the attitude has improved). *The accuracy* of his shots *is* amazing (the accuracy is amazing). Only *one* of my teachers *appreciates* me (one appreciates).

pulling weeds is hard work

When a verbal noun points to *one action* that affects *several things*, it may carry with it a plural object. Make the verb agree, *not* with the intervening plural, but with the verbal noun:

Formal: *Finding* enough parking spaces *was* a problem (*finding* something was a problem). *Understanding* your own problems *helps* (*understanding* helps). *Admitting* your own mistakes *is* difficult (*admitting* something is difficult).

there are several left

In informal English, we often start a sentence with *there is* or *there was* regardless of whether what "is there" will turn out to be singular or plural. In formal English, the verb after *there* agrees with the *postponed* subject:

Formal: There *were* several *sandwiches* left (several *were* left). There *are* a *store and a gas station* at the corner (both *are* at the corner). There *are hundreds* of refugees living here (hundreds *are* living here). There *were* an *American, a French Canadian, and an Eskimo* on our team (all three *were* on the team).

STOP THE SPACE CAB—I WANT TO GET OFF

Check for agreement of subject and verb in the following capsule plots from the strange world of science fiction. After the number of the sentence, write the choice that would fit best in written English.

1. Radioactivity from nuclear engines *is/are* turning the crew into lizardlike creatures.
2. Passengers who have boarded the spacecraft on Mars *is/are* trying to take over the bodies of the Earth crew.
3. Nuclear tests at the North Pole *shift/shifts* the Earth's orbit.
4. A number of mysterious explosions *breaks/break* up the polar ice cap.
5. Strange creatures with many limbs and multiple eyes *enter/enters* the Miss Universe contest.
6. A female astronaut is one of the scientists who *is/are* exploring the inside of a mysterious hollow moon.
7. A human captain or a computer *is/are* going to take over command of a damaged spaceship.
8. Space-age gladiators on a highly developed planet *battles/battle* to the death before a holiday crowd.
9. There *is/are* only three pressurized space suits in a space cab carrying five passengers.
10. Discovering new planets *becomes/become* necessary as a new ice age destroys life on Earth.

each of them is, either is

When you mention "each one" or "either one," you *mean* several people. But you are taking up each *one* of them individually:

Formal: Each of the players *was* mentioned individually. Either of the choices *is* acceptable.

pork and beans is good for you

When the same verb has two subjects joined by *and*, the resulting **compound subject** is treated as a plural. However, treat it as a *singular* when the whole combination describes *one single thing or person*:

Formal: Ham and eggs *is* my favorite breakfast (this particular dish *is*). My friend and partner *was* not yet there (*one person*, at the same time a friend and a partner, *was* not yet there). The Stars and Stripes *flies* from the flagpole (*the flag* bearing that name *flies*). *Bread and Wine* is the name of a famous novel (*the title* of a single book *is* singular).

Fred or Jim is, Fred as well as Jim is

Or may give us a choice between two singular subjects. *As well as, together with,* and *in addition to* leave a single subject singular. (They merely show that what is said about the subject *applies* to something else as well):

Formal: The janitor or a teacher *locks* the doors. The result as well as the cause *was* studied. Uncle Ted together with his two brothers *lives* in a cabin.

the team is, the team are

Collective nouns, such as *team, class, police, committee,* and *jury,* are treated as singular when we think of the whole group together. They are treated as plural when we visualize the individual members:

Formal: The team *is* leaving tomorrow (the whole group). The team *were* changing their clothes (the separate individuals). The class *was* studying myths (the whole group). The police *were* disappointed (several officers). The committee *votes* on each item separately (the whole group).

two dollars is enough

A plural noun is treated as a singular when the statement concerns *a whole amount* rather than separate units:

Formal: Two-thirds *is* too much. Thirty dollars *was* a good price.

For Oral Practice: Read the sentences in each pair, paying special attention to the italicized words. Make sure you can explain *why* the form of the verb is different in the second sentence in each pair. ALL FORMS ARE ACCEPTABLE IN FORMAL ENGLISH.

1. Each of the applicants *was* interviewed.
   All of the applicants *were* interviewed.

2. Pork and beans *is* my favorite dish.
   Pork and veal *are* my favorite kinds of meat.

3. There *is* a tunnel after the turn in the road.
   There *are* few lights in the tunnel.

4. His phone calls *annoy* me.
   Receiving his phone calls *annoys* me.

5. The mines *have* been kept secret.
   The location of the mines *has* been kept secret.

6. Jim and his brother *deserve* credit.
   Jim as well as his brother *deserves* credit.

7. His family *was* opposed to the marriage.
   His family *were* seated around the table.

8. Five dollar bills *were* lying on the counter.
   Five dollars *was* far too much.

9. The rancher and one of the hands *patrol* the fences.
   The rancher together with one of the hands *patrols* the fences.

10. There *was* only one coin left.
    There *were* only a dime and a nickel left.

ACTIVITY

Of the two choices given in each of the following sentences, which would be appropriate in *formal written English?* Write the form you choose after the number of the sentence. Write on a separate sheet of paper.

Example: There *is/are* regional differences in American English.
(Answer)   *are*

1. The language of other people sometimes *differ/differs* from our own.
2. There *is/are* different ways of pronouncing the same word.
3. Sometimes the word itself as well as the pronunciation *seem/seems* strange.
4. Perhaps one of your friends *is/are* from a different state.
5. *Is/Are* there unfamiliar words in his everyday speech?
6. *Does/Do* either of you call a faucet a spigot?
7. Perhaps hot cakes and syrup *is/are* your favorite breakfast.
8. There *is/are* people who say "griddle cakes" or "flannel cakes" instead.
9. Studying such words *teach/teaches* us something about our country.
10. Different regions of the country *has/have* their own dialects.
11. Dialects developed before there *was/were* radio and television.
12. The speech of New Englanders *was/were* different from that of Southerners.

13. There *was/were* at least three major dialect areas.
14. The study of these dialects *has/have* kept investigators busy.
15. The older people in a community *know/knows* the local dialect best.
16. The speech of younger Americans *is/are* often more standardized.
17. The reasons for this change *is/are* obvious.
18. Radio together with television *has/have* created a nationwide audience.
19. There *is/are* few obvious differences in the speech of announcers and entertainers.
20. The influence of local dialects *is/are* decreasing all the time.

U3b
Checking Pronoun
Reference

Check reference of pronouns.

Pronouns are pointing words. *He* may point to Charles or Paul, *she* to Sue or to Jean. *This* points to an object over here, *that* to an object over there. When you speak, a nod of the head can show which of two men you mean if you say "*He* is the one." A pointing finger can show which of several cars you mean when you say "*this* car." When you write, there is no nod and no pointing finger to help the pronoun do its job. In writing, pronouns must point clearly to the people or things they refer to.

Sometimes a reader cannot tell which of two people a pronoun like *he* or *she* points to. Such a pronoun is **ambiguous.** It has an unintended double meaning. The following sentences contain ambiguous pronouns:

Ambiguous: Bill talked to Mr. Smith about *his* illness.
              (Who was ill? Bill or Smith?)

Ambiguous: Mary dislikes my sister because *she* is a tomboy.
              (Who is a tomboy? Mary or your sister?)

When a pronoun might confuse your reader, take the following precautions:

(1) *What the pronoun points to should be clearly stated,* not merely hinted at or implied:

Confusing: His hands were chained, but *they* were removed at the
              door.   (the hands?)
Clear: His hand were in *chains,* but *these* were removed at the
              door.

(2) If there are two things for the pronoun to point to, *try shifting one of them* to a different part of the sentence:

Confusing: *Bill* talked to *Mr. Smith* about *his* illness.
Clear: *Bill* talked about *his* illness to *Mr. Smith*.

(3) If necessary, *drop the pronoun* and fill in what you are pointing to:

Confusing: Take the *wrapping* off the *present* and burn *it*.   (the present?)
Clear: Unwrap the present and burn the *wrapper*.

The noun that a pronoun points back to is called its **antecedent** —literally "what comes before." Make a pronoun point clearly to its antecedent. Watch for the following:

informal *they*   Informally, we say "In New York, *they* have humid summers" and "In this magazine, *they* print many good articles." In formal English, we state directly who "they" are:

Clear: *New Yorkers* have humid summers. The *editors* of this magazine print many good articles.

orphaned *it*   The *it* has lost its antecedent in sentences like "Because my father is a teacher, I am also choosing *it* as my profession," or "We used to sing songs in the dormitory, but *it* was against regulations." In formal English, *state the idea that is here merely implied:*

Clear: Because my father is a teacher, I am also choosing *teaching* as my profession (*it* cannot refer to "teacher"). We used to sing songs in the dormitory, but *singing* was against regulations (*it* cannot refer to "songs").

vague *this*   When *this* points back to *the whole idea* expressed in what goes before, it is often ambiguous: "I have stopped practicing on the violin; *this* bothers my father" (does the *practicing* bother him, or the fact that you have *stopped* practicing?). *Fill in the necessary explanation:*

Clear: I have stopped practicing on the violin; *this* kind of noise bothers my father.

vague *which*   *Which* also is often ambiguous when it points back to the general idea of a sentence rather than to a *specific noun:* "She gave up playing tennis, *which* was bad for her health" (*playing* tennis, or *giving it up?*). *Rework the whole sentence*:

Clear: *Giving up tennis* was bad for her health.

informal you   In formal English, use *you* to mean "you, the reader" rather than somebody not clearly specified: "When *you* wear high heels, beware of holes in the road" (what if the reader is a boy?). "In the Middle Ages, *you* had to be a nobleman to achieve wealth and status" (in the Middle Ages, the present reader had not yet been born). Substitute a specific reference, or the more general pronoun *one:*

Clear: When *a girl* wears high heels, *she* should beware of holes in the road; in the Middle Ages, *one* had to be a nobleman to achieve wealth and status.

Pronoun reference seldom seems a problem to the *writer* who usually knows what his or her pronouns stand for. The writer has to ask, "Does the *reader* know? Would this pronoun be clear to the *reader?*"

ACTIVITY

Examine pronoun reference in each of the following pairs. Which sentence might confuse or distract a reader because of a pronoun used informally, without clear and specific reference? Which sentence is clear? *Put the letter of the clear sentence after the number of the pair.* Be prepared to explain the difference between the two sentences in each pair.

Example: a. In my hometown, they are tearing down the old city hall.
b. In my hometown, the old city hall is being torn down.
(Answer)   *b*

1. a. After Dutton fought Olivera, he retired.
   b. Dutton retired after he fought Olivera.

2. a. When a meeting is scheduled during school hours, I have to miss it.
   b. When a meeting is at the same time as a class, I have to miss it.

3. a. My sister stays away from Susan, because she hates blondes.
   b. Because Susan hates blondes, my sister stays away from her.

4. a. Though my uncles were sailors, I did not follow their example.
   b. Though my uncles were sailors, it has never appealed to me.

5. a. Eileen locked out the dog, which annoys me.
   b. Eileen's locking out the dog annoys me.

6. a. We found that in Quebec many people speak French.
   b. We found that in Quebec they speak mostly French.

7. a. We were appalled by the dirt, but this will change.
   b. We were appalled by the dirt and decided to clean up.

8. a. He sent me the announcement of his wedding, which surprised me.
   b. I was surprised·that he sent me the wedding announcement.

9. a. In the old West, you had to look out for roving Indians.
   b. People living in the old West had to guard their possessions carefully.

10. a. When teenagers talk to older people, they should be polite.
    b. When a teenager talks to older people, he should be polite.

Pay careful attention to where modifiers are placed in a sentence.

Modifiers change or narrow down the meaning of *some other part* of a sentence. In other words, modifiers modify *something*. It must be clear to the reader what that something is. When a speaker uses a confusing modifier, he can often clarify its meaning by pausing at the right point or changing his tone of voice. A written sentence must make its way without this kind of help.

There are two major kinds of confusing modifiers:

(1) A **dangling modifier** appears in a sentence without anything for the modifier to modify. What the modifier is supposed to modify is not stated but merely implied. To eliminate confusion, *state directly* what the modifier goes with. If necessary, rework the whole sentence.

Dangling: *Cleaning the garage,* the shelf collapsed.
            (Who was cleaning the garage? Not the shelf.)
Clear: *Cleaning the garage,* I made the shelf collapse.
Clear: When I was cleaning the garage, the shelf collapsed.

Dangling: *Driving across the range,* some buffalo came into view.
            (Who was driving? Not the buffalo.)
Clear: *Driving across the range,* the visitors saw some buffalo.

Clear: As the visitors were driving across the range, some buf-
          falo came into view.

(2) A **misplaced modifier** appears where it might seem to
modify the *wrong* part of a sentence. To eliminate confusion, *shift
the modifier into a better place.* Or, shift the confusing sentence
part away from the modifier.

Misplaced: We have bicycles for boys *with adjustable seats.*
              (What had adjustable seats? Not the boys.)
Clear: For boys, we have bicycles *with adjustable seats.*

Misplaced: Many people who attend church *through the week* for-
              get their Sunday vows.
              (They do not attend church through the week; rather,
              they forget their vows through the week.)
Clear: Many people who attend church forget their Sunday
              vows *during the week.*

Here are some kinds of modifiers that may cause a confusing
double take. (Check the chapter on "Sentences" for a more complete description of these.)

—Adverbs like *only, just,* and *almost* are often confusing when
they are not placed close to what they modify:

Poor: I *only* looked at the cake.
         ("only looked" or "only at the cake"?)
Clear: I looked at the cake *only.*

—Prepositional phrases are easily movable and confuse the
reader when they appear in the wrong place:

Poor: She wrote the note for the boy *with trembling hands.*
         (Whose hands trmebled—hers or the boy's?)
Clear: *With trembling hands,* she wrote the note for the boy.

—Appositives should fit in clearly with the noun they rename:

Poor: We have one vacancy, *a cashier.*
         (The cashier, a person, is not "a vacancy.")
Clear: We have a vacancy for one person, *a cashier.*

—Participial phrases, easily left dangling, are also easily misplaced:

Poor: He hit the man *driving the jeep.*
         (Who was driving—he or the man?)
Clear: *Driving the jeep,* he hit the man.

SOME HUMOR IS UNINTENTIONAL.

Cleaning the garage, the shelf collapsed.

Driving across the range, some buffalo came into view.

Dogs should walk the streets with their master on a leash.

—The *who*, *which*, or *that* at the beginning of a relative clause should point clearly to what the clause modifies:

Poor: I read a book on insects *that I had picked up.*
(What had you picked up—the insects or the book?)
Clear: The book *that I had picked up* was about insects.

NOTE: Some modifiers that are technically danglers are acceptable in formal English. We say, *"Considering the price,* the quality is satisfactory." Or, *"Generally speaking,* dress should conform to community standards." These phrases carry with them an implied *I* or *we* ("When we consider the price . . ."). They clarify the attitude or intention of the speaker or writer.

ACTIVITY 1

Examine the *position of modifiers* in each of the following pairs. Which sentence might confuse a reader because of a dangling or misplaced modifier? Which sentence is clear? Write the letter of the *clear* sentence after the number of the pair. Be prepared to explain the difference between the two sentences in each pair.

Example: a. I heard a lecture on problem children by a Harvard professor.
b. I heard a Harvard professor lecture on problem children.

(Answer)   *b*

1. a. Visiting the Capitol, the legislature was in session.
   b. Visiting the Capitol, we attended a session of the legislature.

2. a. Being a freshman, Shakespeare meant little to me.
   b. Being a freshman, I had little interest in Shakespeare.

3. a. He is the tenant with the poodle that likes to sing popular songs.
   b. He is the tenant that has a poodle and likes to sing popular songs.

4. a. After she married, I called her Miss Brown by mistake.
   b. I called her Miss Brown after she married by mistake.

5. a. He carried a list of the students who played instruments in his pocket.
   b. He carried in his pocket a list of the students who played instruments.

6. a. Having bought a second car, our garage was too small.
   b. After we bought a second car, our garage was too small.

7. a. We paid the doctor by mail for the operation she had performed.
   b. We paid the doctor for the operation she had performed by mail.

8. a. Sharks are a danger when vacationing in tropical waters.
   b. Sharks are a danger when vacationers swim in tropical waters.

9. a. Being an unruly child, the principal often admonished me.
   b. Being an unruly child, I was often admonished by the principal.

10. a. Having finished my meal, I looked for the waiter.
    b. Having finished my meal, the waiter brought the check.

ACTIVITY 2

Each of the following sentences contains a dangling or confusing modifier. What was the meaning the writer originally intended? *Rewrite each sentence so that it clearly states the most plausible possible meaning.* Be prepared to explain why other possible meanings are unlikely or absurd.

1. He slit open the fish he had caught with his knife.
2. At the age of seven, Grandmother came to live with our family.
3. Coming around a bend in the road, the camp appeared among the trees.
4. My brother squirted the water on people who walked by on purpose.
5. Dogs will be allowed on the city streets only with their master on a leash.
6. Reading the newspaper, the dog suddenly barked.
7. Many boys are involved in offenses that are not arrested.
8. Listening to stereophonic sound, the orchestra seems to be in front of me.
9. We received tickets for a concert, the Philadelphia Orchestra.
10. Labeled a failure by the critics, the audiences stayed away from the play.

REVIEW ACTIVITY

What is the problem in each of the following sentences? After the number of each sentence, write the appropriate code: *A* for trouble with agreement; *P* for trouble with pronoun reference; *M* for trouble with modifiers; *N* for no trouble.

Be prepared to explain how you would revise the problem sentences.

1. When newspapers write about student misconduct, parents are appalled by this.
2. At the school I attend, they have an annual drama festival.
3. In ancient Rome, you were born either as a patrician or as a plebeian.
4. Each of his arguments seems to have some flaw.
5. Father knows that I am doing poorly, (which) makes me nervous.
6. Considering the danger, you should have stayed behind.
7. We learned that the tyrant had died with great relief.
8. He bought a watch for his sister-in-law, a cheap-looking thing.
9. There was a restaurant and a fire station at the top of the hill.
10. The usefulness of these devices are questionable.
11. Using a telephoto lens, a photographer can get excellent pictures from far away.
12. Jane told Margery that her clothes did not fit her anymore.
13. We looked for shirts for boys that do not shrink.
14. Either the boy or his friend are to blame.

U4
WRITING EFFECTIVE
SENTENCES

Write sentences that do their work smoothly and effectively.

To do a job effectively means to do something more than the bare minimum. Some people work awkwardly, with a great deal of strain. Just watching them tires us out. Other people work easily and naturally, with just the right amount of energy at the right time. Watching them is a pleasure.

Similarly, some sentences are awkward or strained. They clank along with much unnecessary machinery. Other sentences are a pleasure to read because they move along smoothly, with each part falling naturally and easily into place.

The rules of thumb in the following sections will help you keep your sentences moving along smoothly. They will help you keep unnecessary sentence machinery out of the way of the reader. They will help you keep a sentence free of unexpected twists and turns.

U4a
Unnecessary
Duplication

Avoid unnecessary duplication of words and ideas.

Repetition is effective when we use it to make sure we are heard. When we say "Never! Never again!" we repeat the word *never* intentionally, for greater emphasis. *Un*intentional repetition merely clutters up our sentences, making a paragraph or a paper hard to read.

In revising a paragraph or a theme, check for the following kinds of unintentional repetition:

(1) Words that *unintentionally restate the same idea* are called <u>**redundant.**</u> "At three A.M. in the morning" is redundant, because three A.M. has *got* to be in the morning. Can you explain what makes the following sentences redundant?

> Space travel will be commonplace in the future to come.
> As a rule, the gate is usually locked.
> In my opinion, I think the law ought to be changed.
> We should return the package back to its owner.

(2) In hasty writing, the *predicate of a sentence may repeat all or part of the subject.* When someone says, "The *value* of the lot *was worth* very little," the idea of value, or worth, appears both in the subject and the predicate:

> Redundant: The *choice* of our new car *was selected* by my mother.
> Revised: Our new car *was selected* by my mother.

> Redundant: The *attendance* at the meeting *was overcrowded.*
> Revised: The meeting *was overcrowded.*

> THERE'S A PAPER SHORTAGE. AVOID UNNECESSARY DUPLICATION.

(3) In hasty writing, *parts of the sentence machinery* may appear twice: prepositions like *to* or *with,* connectives like *that.* The *–er* and *–est* used with adjectives in comparisons may be duplicated by *more* or *most.* Eliminate such needless duplication:

> Faulty: He said *that* if we agreed *that* he would reconsider.
> Revised: He said *that* he would reconsider if we agreed.

> Faulty: I need a car *on* which I can depend *on.*
> Revised: I need a car *on* which I can depend.

> Faulty: This is a *more* fast*er* plane than any previous model.
> Revised: This is a fast*er* plane than any previous model.

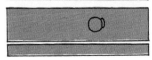

Sometimes, we go *too far* in omitting elements that seem to duplicate some other part of a sentence. When a similar idea is expressed by two *different* prepositions, or by two *different* verb forms, both should be preserved:

> Faulty: He acted both jealous and superior *to* the other boys.
>   (Jealous *to* the other boys?)

> Revised: He acted both jealous *of* and superior *to* the other boys.

THE STRANGE WAYS OF WORDS

In each of the following paragraphs, *one* sentence needs some adjustments in the sentence machinery. Either the same idea is duplicated, making the sentence carry unnecessary freight, or a form nearly identical with something else in the sentence has been left out, leaving the sentence incomplete. Find the sentence that is out of kilter. Explain how you would revise it.

Words often come into our language in strange ways, frequently. The word *curfew* is derived from the French words meaning "cover the fire." Originally, the curfew was the time to cover the fire for the night.

Boycott originally was the name of a person. When he tried to collect rent, the tenants refused to pay. The purpose of a boycott is designed to change someone's mind. An organization may boycott a company until it meets certain demands.

Newspapers sometimes report that someone went "berserk." The word originally referred to a bearskin shirt. Such a shirt was worn by a famous Scandinavian warrior. Before battle, he worked himself into the kind of violent rage to which the word has come to refer to.

Everyone who watches television Westerns knows what a posse is. Often, when we turn on the set, the sheriff's posse either just has or shortly will apprehend the badman. The word *posse* was at first a legal term. It is derived from a Latin word meaning "ability" or "power."

Faulty: He *has* not and *will* not surrender the keys.
(*Has surrender?*)
Revised: He *has* not *surrendered* and *will* not *surrender* the keys.

ACTIVITY

In which of the following sentences is there *unnecessary repetition*? Put *D* for duplication after the number of each such sentence. In which sentences has a necessary preposition or verb form been omitted? Put *O* for omission after the number of each such sentence. Put *S* for satisfactory after the number of each sentence that is acceptable as it is. If your teacher tells you to, rewrite each unsatisfactory sentence.

Example: He wanted a friend to whom he could write to.
(Answer)   D

1. The purpose of the meeting was intended to discuss our proposal.
2. They never have and never will keep their promises.
3. Jim sent us a postcard from almost every city that he visited.
4. We should take note of but not interfere with their activities.
5. We found that if we hurried that we could get there in twenty minutes.
6. His machine was similar but inferior to most rival products.
7. As far as I know, the road is safe, to the best of my knowledge.
8. The group can and will go ahead with the project.
9. Tourists tend to act spoiled when traveling in foreign countries abroad.
10. Your friend forgot to leave an address to which we could write to.
11. We have supported him in the past and will support him in the future.
12. The purpose of the meeting was to introduce the candidates to the voters.
13. No one knew when he was going to return back to his quarters.
14. John wanted us to be proud and loyal to our school.

Do not confuse two different ways of saying the same thing.

U4b
Mixed Construction

When we speak, we often start a sentence one way. Then we shift to what seems a better way. One reason we *revise* our written sentences is to make sure that we catch such shifts. We look for sentences that confuse two different ways of expressing the same thought.

To revise such garbled sentences, disentangle the two possibilities that have become confused. Can you see how two different patterns became mixed in each of the following garbled sentences?

Mixed: *Any new fad* Jack had to follow *it.*
Clear: Whenever there was a new fad, Jack had to follow it.
Clear: Jack had to follow any new fad.

Mixed: He showed me a model plane *of which* he was proud *to have built.*
Clear: He showed me a model plane of which he was proud.
Clear: He showed me a model plane that he was proud to have built.

Mixed: *In case of* fire *should be reported* to the office immediately.
Clear: In case of fire, report to the office immediately.
Clear: Fire should be reported to the office immediately.

Mixed: We discussed the city and the *fascination* I held *for it.*
Clear: We discussed the city and the admiration I held for it.
Clear: We discussed the city and the fascination it had for me.

Some mixed constructions are common in informal speech but are often criticized when they appear in writing. *When* and *because* usually introduce *adverbial* clauses. They show the time or the reason for whatever happens in the main clause. Avoid a *when* clause after *is* in definitions where the *when* clause would take the place of a noun:

Informal: Insurrection *is when* people rise against the government.
Formal: An insurrection *is a revolt* against the government.
Formal: An insurrection *occurs when* people rise against the government.

Informal: Combustion *is when* you ignite inflammable materials.
Formal: Combustion *takes place when* someone ignites inflammable materials.
Formal: Combustion *is the process* of burning.

Avoid a *because* clause that replaces the subject of the main clause:

Informal: *Because you say so* doesn't make it right.
Formal: *Your saying so* does not make it right.
Formal: It is not right merely *because you say so.*

Informal: *Just because he objects* is no reason to change.
Formal: *His objection* is no reason to change.
Formal: We need not change merely *because he objects.*

ACTIVITY 1

In each of the following sentences, two ways of saying the same thing have become mixed. *Write two versions of each sentence.* Each time bring out *one* of the possibilities that the writer probably had in mind when he wrote the original sentence.

1. The influence of society on its young people must assume responsibility for their goals.
2. The lecture was canceled because of not enough people came.
3. He sent us an insufficient amount of money than he had promised.
4. John's fever has disappeared and is getting along much better.

5. The principal rejected him to be one of the candidates.

6. The divorce rate for couples marrying after twenty generally have more success in marriage.

7. It is difficult for a social science teacher to stay out of politics than, say, someone who teaches chemistry.

8. I have formed my own conclusions about race prejudice and are not based on any particular instance.

9. If children reading comic books know right and wrong will do relatively little damage.

10. We have a tree that in the fall all the leaves turn a gorgeous red and yellow.

Watch out for confusing shifts in point of view.

U4c
Shifts in Perspective

Writers have to be aware of how they look at people and events. For instance, they may describe everything as though it were happening *now*. Or they may describe everything as *past* and done with. If they keep shifting back and forth between past and present, they will confuse the reader. A sentence is "consistent" if it stays in the same pattern.

Watch out for three kinds of shifts:

(1) *Shifts in tense.* The tense forms of verbs show the relationship of events in time. The **present** tense makes us visualize events as happening now. The **past** tense makes us see events during a period that has come to an end:

Present: When I *see* him, I *laugh.*
  Past: When I *saw* him, I *laughed.*

Present: In modern wars, computers *help* fight battles.
  Past: In World War II, airdrops *helped* underground fighters.

Guard against shifting *from the past to the present* when some event becomes particularly vivid in your memory:

Shift: As we *sang* around the fire, I suddenly *notice* a big
              brown snake.
Consistent: As we *sang* around the fire, I suddenly *noticed* a big
              brown snake.

The **perfect** tense, formed with *have* (or *has*), points to an event that has happened in the *past* but that has a bearing on the present:

Perfect: I profit (now) from what I *have learned.*
Perfect: During this decade, many new techniques *have developed*
              (and are now being used).

The **past perfect,** formed with *had,* takes us back into a time *before* some other events in the past took place:

Past Perfect: I profited from what I *had learned.*
Past Perfect: By 1920, many new techniques *had been developed.*

Guard against *treating events as simultaneous* if one actually happened before the other:

Shift: My grade *was* disappointing, because I *studied* hard.
Consistent: My grade *was* disappointing, because I *had studied* hard.
(The studying took place *before* the receipt of the grade.)

Shift: Joan's husband *said* that he *was* a confirmed bachelor.
Consistent: Joan's husband *said* that he *had been* a confirmed bachelor.
(He was a bachelor *before* he became a husband.)

(2) *Shifts to the passive.* The **passive** reverses the "actor-action" pattern of the typical **active** sentence. It makes the target or result of the action the subject of the sentence. We use the passive when who *did* something is less important than who *was* *affected* by it:

Active: The queen *admired* the exhibits.
Passive: The queen *was admired* by her subjects.

Active: Jim *had* accidentally *hurt* one of the players.
Passive: Jim *had been hurt* in a football game.

Guard against shifting from the active to the passive when *the same person (or thing) is still the active element* in the sentence:

Shift: If the tourist *drinks* unboiled water, typhoid *may be contracted.*   (by whom?)
Consistent: If the tourist *drinks* unboiled water, he *may contract* typhoid.

Shift: I *hosed* down the driveway, and later the garage *was swept.*
Consistent: I *hosed* down the driveway and later *swept* the garage.

(3) *Shifts in reference.* A writer has different ways of referring to himself, to his reader, and to people in general. Once you choose one of these ways, carry it through consistently. Guard against starting with *one* or *a person* and then shifting to the more personal *you:*

THE CASE OF THE FRUSTRATED GOURMET

Which of the sentences in the following paragraph show an *unnecessary shift* in perspective? Write down the number of each such sentence. Be prepared to explain what kind of shift it illustrates and how it could be revised.

(1) When one studies my Uncle Pierre, a perfect case of the frustrated gourmet may be observed. (2) A person is a gourmet if he loves good food and drink. (3) Uncle Pierre claims that the art of fine cooking is dead. (4) One can find very few restaurants where your food is cooked the day you eat it. (5) Few young brides nowadays know the difference between "braise" and "sauté." (6) The prospect of delicious home-cooked food is no longer an incentive for the bachelor who wants to get married. (7) Most families are used to TV dinners, and food is eaten for nourishment rather than enjoyment. (8) I remember the meals that Uncle Pierre used to enjoy at my grandmother's house. (9) After the women started to cook, my uncle rushes to the kitchen to watch the preparations. (10) Each part of the finished meal was served without hurry. (11) When my uncle had eaten his ample share, a cigar was lighted and every detail of the meal was discussed. (12) At this time, my grandmother heard many compliments and a few polite criticisms of the meal she cooked. (13) Most of my uncle's conversation deals with meals he has recently eaten. (14) I doubt that I will ever be as demanding about food as Uncle Pierre. (15) However, I am not going to marry a girl that buys you your dinner ready-made in a can.

Shift: *A person* can travel abroad even if *you* have little money.

Consistent: *A person* can travel abroad even if *he* has little money.

Shift: *One* never knows what will become of *your* children.

Consistent: *One* never knows what will become of *his* children.

Avoid shifting from a reference to yourself to reference to people in general:

Shift: If *I* were an actress, *I* would shun reporters who pry into *your* private life.

Consistent: If *I* were an actress, *I* would shun reporters who pry into *my* private life.

ACTIVITY

Each of the following sentences shows a confusing shift in perspective. After the number of the sentence, write *T* for shift in time, *P* for shift to the passive, *R* for shift in reference. Your teacher may ask you to revise several or all of these sentences.

1. I went to five different schools before my Dad decided to settle in Oregon.
2. In comparing these two models, one finds that the smaller car gives you more for your money.
3. When you are losing someone you love, a person tends to become selfish.
4. One must remember that success comes to you only if you work for it.
5. As the first Indians climbed over the walls, the U.S. Cavalry appears on the horizon.
6. After we had finished the roast, dessert was eaten and stories were told.
7. I am tired of fighting a system that will never let you win.
8. The last person out should turn off the light, and the door should be locked carefully.
9. Jim told us that he was a very sickly baby.
10. The boys swept up the leaves, and the car was washed later in the afternoon.

U4d
Parallel Structure

Line up similar elements in a sentence in parallel form.

When a vehicle has four wheels, we align the wheels so that they will run parallel. When a sentence has several similar parts, we make them "parallel" to help keep the sentence on its track. A sentence may have more than one subject or more than one verb. An action verb may show the same action directed at several targets. To keep the sentence on its track, the repeated parts should fit the same category. Can you see that in each of the following sentences the italicized parts are the same kind of word?

The visitors *worked* and *played.*
The hikers were *weary* but *happy.*
The island was famous for its *mountains, forests,* and *beaches.*
He called the speech *vague, repetitious,* and *insincere.*

Sentence parts joined by *and, or,* or *but* trip up the reader if they do not stay within a consistent pattern. A noun should be linked to a noun (or its equivalent). An adjective should be linked to an adjective. When an *and* or a *but* links parts from different categories, the sentence seems off balance.

Note how each of the following sentences has been revised by changing one of its parts from one kind of word to another:

Nonparallel: His new car was *economical* and *a beauty*.
               (adjective and noun)
   Parallel: His new car was *economical* and *beautiful*.
               (two adjectives)

Nonparallel: He liked *to swim* and *relaxing* in the sun.
               (infinitive and verbal noun)
   Parallel: He liked *to swim* and *relax* in the sun.
               (two infinitives)

Nonparallel: I asked him *for money* and *if he could give me advice*.
               (prepositional phrase and dependent clause)
   Parallel: I asked him for *money* and *advice*.
               (two nouns)

Nonparallel: She liked *the country* and *to walk* in the fields.
               (noun and infinitive)
   Parallel: She liked *the country* and long *walks* in the fields.
               (two nouns)

Sometimes, you may have to *add* something to the sentence to make it parallel. Or you may have to take out the *and* altogether and put the sentence together a different way:

Nonparallel: High school students want to be *popular* and *leaders*.
               (adjective and noun)
   Parallel: High school students want *to be* popular and *become* leaders.
               (second infinitive added)

PARALLEL PARTS

Nonparallel: The landlord was *a retired admiral* and *who had seen much of the world*.
               (noun and relative clause)
   Parallel: The landlord was a retired admiral who had seen much of the world.
               (*and* removed)

NONPARALLEL PARTS

Parallel structure is especially important when an *and* or an *or* links together a **series,** that is, *three or more* parts serving the same function. Sometimes the first two parts of a series are parallel while the third upsets the pattern. Sometimes each part of a faulty series is from a different grammatical category:

Faulty Series: He liked *to swim, to relax,* and *the country atmosphere.*
                 (two infinitives and a noun)

Parallel: He liked *to swim, relax,* and *enjoy* the country atmosphere.
(three infinitives)

Faulty Series: He told me *about his illness, that he was planning to leave,* and *other personal stories.*
(prepositional phrase, dependent clause, and noun)

Parallel: He told me about *his illness, his plans* for leaving, and *other personal matters.*
(three nouns)

FOR REVISION
PRACTICE

EDITOR FOR A DAY

Assume that you are editing the following text for inclusion in a collection of student writing. Limit your editing to the writer's handling of *basic relationships* (agreement, pronoun reference, modifiers) and to problems of *sentence structure and effectiveness* (duplication, mixed construction, shifts, lack of parallel structure).

On a separate sheet of paper, note the line (or lines) where a problem occurs. Then explain what the problem is and how the passage should be revised.

```
           Deer Hunting in Michigan

 1       While deer hunting in Michigan,
 2  I became attached and very familiar with
 3  the enchanting forests that are
 4  plentiful there.
 5       As in other states, they limit the
 6  time when different kinds of game may be
 7  hunted.  Deer season is in the winter
 8  months when there is usually snow on
 9  the ground.  A snowfall in the forest is
10  very beautiful, very quiet, and has a
11  certain kind of excitement about it.
12       A typical first day of a deer
13  hunting season is always full of sus-
14  pense.  Imagine yourself very early in
15  the morning as you proceed to your
16  stand.  At the stand you wait for a
17  possible chance to get a shot at a deer.
```

```
18 While on your stand, the noise horns
19 are blowing.  You can hear the shouts of
20 hunters over the unmistakable noise of
21 cars moving slowly down forest trails.
22      At just about daylight the woods
23 grow quiet again as the hunters wait
24 for a deer to approach.
25      At the first sound of a deer ap-
26 proaching, your heartbeat begins to
27 beat faster.  To your surprise, the deer
28 appears much closer than you expect,
29 since a deer can move very quietly
30 through the forest.  You strain your
31 eyes to make out horns on the deer.
32 At last, you get a good look at his
33 head, and a clear outline of a nice
34 set of horns is seen.  The excitement
35 overtakes you, and you throw your rifle
36 to your shoulder and fire.  The next
37 instant you look and the deer has dis-
38 appeared.  Your thoughts wander as you
39 approach the spot where the deer had
40 stood.
41      In the clear white snow lay the
42 still body of a deer.  You relax a
43 little, and all of a sudden you feel
44 very small.  You ask yourself, "What
45 right have I to take this creature's
46 life?"
```

ACTIVITY 1

Revise each of the following sentences to correct a *lack of parallel structure*. Rewrite each sentence so that parts linked by *and, but,* or *or* will be parallel.

1. Though she seems gay and carefree, Jean can be very serious and a real spoilsport.
2. The city overwhelmed me with its rushing cars, great bridges, and because of the people everywhere.
3. He told me about his Austrian parents and that he was an orphan.
4. The receiver is small, compact, and runs on batteries.
5. She asked me about my plans for a job and where I was going to live.

6. The defenders were prepared for the worst and to sell their lives dearly.
7. The best way to teach children is not by threatening them but to explain things to them patiently.
8. The new coach is relaxed, experienced, and makes you feel confident.
9. The book explained how to build a gun cabinet and the various steps in gluing furniture.
10. Anna was reliable and a hard worker.

ACTIVITY 2

Check the following sentences for parallel structure. Write down the number of each sentence that is *unsatisfactory*. Be prepared to explain in class which sentence parts are parallel and which are not. Be prepared to explain how the unsatisfactory sentences could be revised.

1. He called for her punctually, helped her with her wrap, and escorted her to his car.
2. In choosing the ideal girl, a boy should consider her education, her religion, and is she able to tolerate differences of opinion.
3. My uncle's ambition was to retire and living as a gentleman of leisure.
4. Not everyone can be a model scholar or a star athlete.
5. Grandfather told us about his trip to Norway and other travel stories.
6. Foreign travel extends one's knowledge and broadens one's horizons.
7. You should try to study more regularly and getting enough sleep.
8. Football gives a student a chance to build up his muscles and to get some fresh air.
9. My friend drives a car built in Italy and which resembles a pumpkin.
10. As the daughter of an immigrant and meeting many foreign visitors, Gretchen had learned to respect people from other countries.

REVIEW ACTIVITY

Which of the sentences in the following paragraph illustrate *common sources of awkwardness or confusion*? Write down the number of each sentence that is *unsatisfactory*. Be prepared to explain how the sentence went wrong and how it could be revised.

(1) Once a person has learned how to write, you are likely to take the written word for granted. (2) Actually, our way of writing has a long and complicated history. (3) About 6000 years ago, man started not to rely on memory but keeping written records. (4) The first writer looked at an object, and a simplified picture was drawn of what he saw. (5) A triangle standing on its head and looking like the letter *V* might represent the head of an ox. (6) A triangle resting on its base might stand for a tent. (7) Gradually the picture of a tent acquired additional meanings. (8) Three tents together might stand for a trip taking three days and which required the traveler to pitch his tent three times. (9) The big change in writing was from picture writing to the use of an alphabet. (10) Picture writing is when each written symbol stands for an idea. (11) In an alphabet, each written symbol stands for a sound. (12) A combination of these symbols is then combined to stand for an idea. (13) In our own alphabet, the same symbol may stand for several different sounds. (14) Some words contain letters for sounds that have not been pronounced in English for many centuries. (15) In my opinion, I feel that our system of writing should be brought up to date.

HOW PEOPLE USE LANGUAGE

Everyone has many opportunities to observe the *variety* of language—the differences in the way people use our common language. Everyone has opportunities to study the *reactions* of listeners and readers to such differences. The following assignments will help you make use of some of these opportunities.

Assignment 1: Some of the characters in a play or novel may speak *nonstandard English*. The following scene is from Lorraine Hansberry's *A Raisin in the Sun*, a play about a black family in Chicago. Study the scene carefully and then answer the following questions:

1. What features of nonstandard English appear here?

2. Does this selection show anything about the use of *different* kinds of language on different occasions?

3. What kind of people are these—how are they presented by the author? How does this selection *confirm* your ideas about speakers of nonstandard English? How does it *change* them?

Walter: I want so many things that they are driving me kind of crazy . . . Mama—look at me.

Mama: I'm looking at you. You a good-looking boy. You got a job, a nice wife, a fine boy and—

Walter: A job. *(Looks at her)* Mama, a job? I open and close car doors all day long. I drive a man around in his limousine and I say, "Yes, sir; no, sir; very good, sir; shall I take the Drive, sir?" Mama, that ain't no kind of job . . . that ain't nothing at all. *(Very quietly)* Mama, I don't know if I can make you understand.

Mama: Understand what, baby?

Walter (Quietly): Sometimes it's like I can see the future stretched out in front of me—just plain as day. The future, Mama. Hanging over there at the edge of my days. Just waiting for me—a big, looming blank space—full of *nothing.* Just waiting for *me.* (*Pause*) Mama—sometimes when I'm downtown and I pass them cool, quiet-looking restaurants where them white boys are sitting back and talking 'bout things . . . sitting there turning deals worth millions of dollars . . . sometimes I see guys don't look much older than me—

Mama: Son—how come you talk so much 'bout money?

Walter (With immense passion): Because it is life, Mama.

Mama (Quietly): Oh—*(Very quietly)* So now it's life. Money is life. Once upon a time freedom used to be life—now it's money. I guess the world really do change . . .

Walter: No—it was always money, Mama. We just didn't know about it.

Mama: No . . . something has changed. *(She looks at him)* You something new, boy. In my time we was worried about not being lynched and getting to the North if we could and how to stay alive and still have a pinch of dignity too . . . Now here come you and Beneatha—talking 'bout things we ain't never even thought about hardly, me and your daddy. You ain't satisfied or proud of nothing we done. I mean that you had a home; that we kept you out of trouble till you was grown; that you don't have to ride to work on the back of nobody's streetcar—You my children—but how different we done become.

Assignment 2: Almost everyone has at some time been criticized for not using "good English." The following survey will give you a chance to study the *attitudes and reactions* of people when they make such judgments. Copy the following sentences on a sheet of paper and show them to the people you want to interview during this survey. Interview at least half a dozen people. Make sure they do not all have the same occupation or background. After they read the sentences, ask them the questions provided below.

Sentence One: *How come* you are late?
Sentence Two: I *used to could* lift it with one arm.
Sentence Three: I am *right* pleased to see you.
Sentence Four: *Don't nobody* live there anymore.
Sentence Five: Do *like* I said.

Questions: 1. Do you ever use this expression yourself? When, for instance?
            2. Do you object to it when other people use it? Why?
            3. What kind of people do you think use this expression? Where would you expect to hear it?

Take notes on the answers you obtain. Then compare the different reactions. Are they all nearly the same? If they are different, how do you explain the differences? Write a report that sums up what you have found out.

Assignment 3: People doing roughly the same kind of work may vary considerably in the *formality* of the language they employ. Select three such people that you have the opportunity to hear regularly—for instance, three radio disc jockeys or three sports announcers. Study the way they use language and rate them on a scale of formality. Which of them is the most formal? Which most informal? Which in between?

Prepare a report in which you present your findings. For each speaker, give examples of specific words and expressions that made you rate her or him the way you did.

Assignment 4: Can you locate two or three real "old-timers"? Try to get them to talk about *old-time words and expressions* that hardly anybody uses anymore. Try to get them to talk about subjects dealing with times gone by: vanished modes of transportation, work on the farm or in an old-style family business, life in a large old-style family. Prepare a report on the language of yesteryear.

Assignment 5: How good are you at reading *regulations* printed in small type? How good are you at filling in *questionnaires* that ask fifty-five questions? For years, people have complained that the language used by bureaucrats is unnecessarily complicated and obscure. Are they right? Do your own study of the language government offices use in dealing with the public. Obtain some letters, regulations, or questionnaires from a welfare office or the like. Prepare a brief guide to the language of government.

CHAPTER
6

Mechanics: Words on a Page

Pay attention to how words appear on a page.

The external appearance of your written work is the first thing to strike your readers. It helps to put them in a receptive mood. Once readers start grumbling over a missing comma or a word you failed to capitalize, they are being distracted from what is most important. Spelling and punctuation are similar to grooming. We would rather be judged by our character than by the way we comb our hair. But it is hard to get credit for the important things unless we pay attention to the little things that also count.

Handwriting, spelling, and punctuation are part of the **mechanics** of written English. They are the machinery we need to convey a message to the reader. In your study of mechanics, watch three important relationships:

—*The relationship between writing and meaning.* Marks and symbols are easiest to remember when they convey one definite meaning or perhaps several closely related ones. For instance, the colon typically means "as follows":

There were three candidates: Frank, John, and Tom.

—*The relationship between writing and sound.* In English, this relationship is incomplete. Many marks and symbols do *not* stand for one definite sound. The last sound in all the following words is the same, but it is spelled in many different ways: *be*, *bee*, *tea*, *Leigh*. Many of our words are spelled the way they were pronounced many centuries ago.

—*The relationship between writing and convention.* Convention is the way things are *usually* done. Much of our writing machinery is a matter of custom. There is no particular *reason* why businessmen wear a tie rather than a scarf. It is simply customary. Often when we ask, "Why is there a comma here?" the answer is simply, "That is the way it is usually done."

Keep working on your spelling.

Your spelling is the most external thing about your writing. But at the same time it is the most obvious. Correct spelling is important because many people treat it as a *token:* If you spell poorly, many people will jump to the conclusion that you also write poorly or think poorly.

In English correct spelling means *customary* spelling. Many modern English words were first written down when they were pronounced differently. When writers first put the *gh* in words like *light* and *night,* there actually was a sound there, related to the *y* in *year* or *yarn.* Over the centuries, the sounds in many such words changed, but the spelling stayed the same. Often, the spelling of a group of related words will follow a predictable pattern or observe a common rule. But many other spellings have to be memorized *one by one,* the way we memorize telephone numbers or the last name of new acquaintances.

Since there are thousands of words to memorize, you should have a definite system for keeping your spelling up to par. Do the three following things *regularly:*

(1) *Pay close attention to the words most likely to cause trouble.* Some of these are very *common* words. Every English teacher has a list of 100 or 150 words that have been misspelled over and over by generations of students. Section **M1a** gives you a chance to work your way through such a list so that you can see which of these cause trouble in your own writing. Other words that may cause spelling problems are *new* words that you encounter in your study and reading. Make sure to copy down and take a close look at words like *psychology* and *anesthetic.* When you read a play or a novel, study the spelling of important names.

Keep a spelling record or *spelling notebook* and record your spelling devils, old and new. Work on it at least once a week.

SPELLING CHANGES VERY LITTLE

(2) *Make it a habit to look up words in your dictionary.* If you know the word you want to use but are not sure how it is spelled, look it up. Never substitute a word that is only half right but that you happen to know how to spell.

(3) *Work out a system for committing words to memory.* Merely looking up a word without a definite effort to memorize it is a waste of time. Most people are poor rememberers and good forgetters. There are four ways you can help your memory retain the spelling of a word:

—*Sight:* Run your eyes over the word several times. First pay attention to each individual letter and then to the shape of the word as a whole. Some people have to *visualize* a word before they can spell it correctly. If you are a "visualizer," look at a word again and again until it is firmly printed in your mind.

—*Sound:* Read the word aloud. Then spell out each letter individually: *R-E-C-E-I-V-E.* Some people remember things if they can *hear* them in their minds. If your memory is hearing oriented, pronounce the letters several times until they are firmly recorded.

—*Motion:* Trace the word in large letters. Some people remember things better when their nerves and muscles are brought into play. Give your memory a chance to remember what it *feels like* to write the word.

SOUNDS AND LETTERS

Sometimes you will not find a word where you think it would alphabetically appear in the dictionary. When this happens, remember that *most English sounds may be spelled several different ways.* The following list will help you remember some of the more important possibilities:

a (as in *vane*)	also *ai:*	vain, constrain, maid
	ei:	vein, sleigh, weigh
	ay:	bray, clay, stray
	ey:	they, whey
	ea:	break, steak
e (as in *equal*)	also *ee:*	deed, creed, tureen
	ea:	beam, team
	ei:	receive, ceiling
	ie:	believe, retrieve
f (as in *father*)	also *ph:*	phone, phrase, emphatic
	gh:	laugh, cough
g (as in *go*)	also *gh:*	ghost, ghastly, burgher
	gu:	guess, guest, brogue
h (as in *hot*)	also *wh:*	whole, who
i (as in *hit*)	also *y:*	hymn, gymnasium, cryptic
	ui:	build, guild
i (as in *hide*)	also *ai:*	aisle
	ei:	height, stein
	ey:	eye
	uy:	buy, guy
	y:	sky, rye, defy

—*Association:* Most people remember things that are part of a pattern better than things that stand by themselves. Whenever you can, memorize the kind of jingle or nonsense sentence that ties a spelling word in with something else: "There's IRON in the environment." "The VILLAIN had a VILLA." The following section of this chapter will provide some of these.

Use all of these methods. Concentrate on the method that seems to work best. Remember: No one learns to spell quickly. If you want real improvement, you have to work for it.

j (as in *jam*)	also *g*:	gypsy, oxygen, logic
	dg:	budget, knowledge, grudge
k (as in *kin*)	also *c*:	castle, account
	ch:	chemist, chlorinate, chrome
	qu:	clique, oblique
n (as in *noon*)	also *gn*:	gnat, gnarled, gnash
	kn:	knife, knave, knight
	pn:	pneumonia, pneumatic
o (as in *tone*)	also *oa*:	toad, shoal, foal
	ou:	soul, though
	ow:	low, crow, stow
	ew:	sew
r (as in *run*)	also *rh*:	rhythm, rhapsody, rhubarb
	wr:	wrong, wrangle, wry
s (as in *sit*)	also *c*:	cent, decide, decimate
	sc:	scent, descent, science
	ps:	psychology, psalm, pseudonym
sh (as in *shine*)	also *ce*:	ocean
	ch:	machine
	ci:	special, vicious
	si:	impression, possession, tension
	ti:	notion, imagination
	sci:	conscious, conscience
u (as in *use*)	also *eu*:	feud, queue
	ew:	few, curfew, dew
	ue:	cue
	iew:	view, review
z (as in *zero*)	also *x*:	xylophone, xerox

M1a
Spelling Words

Avoid common spelling errors.

Some spelling errors occur over and over in student writing. Make sure you have mastered the words in the following three groups:

Group One

accept

When you *accept* an invitation or *accept* a ride, you are using a quite different word from the one that takes people *out of* a group: "everyone *except* you and me." REMEMBER: The boy with the *accent accepted* the blame for the *accident*.

all right

Two separate words. REMEMBER: *All right* means ALL is RIGHT.

a lot

Two separate words, shown by the fact that we can say "a *whole* lot." REMEMBER: a lump, a little, *a lot*.

beginning

Begin has a single *n*; *beginning* has a double *n*.
There is an INNING in beginning.

believe

One of the most frequently misspelled words in the language. Use *ie* in *believe* and *belief*. REMEMBER: EVE and STEVE belie*ve*.

business

The *i* in *business* is not pronounced but must be written. REMEMBER: Put an *i* in business.

choose

We *now* choose something (with a double *o*); in the *past*, we chose something (with a single *o*). REMEMBER: Choose rhymes with OOZE; chose rhymes with HOSE.

AS YOU STUDY DIFFERENT SUBJECTS, LEARN HOW TO SPELL THE WORDS

HISTORY	SCIENCE	Law

Empire
Kingdom
Defeat
Foreign
Governor
Conquer
Disaster
Traitor

Carbon
Liquid
Quantity
Theory
Poison

Burglar
Custom
Identity
Property
Punish
Witness

coming	Never double the *m* in co*m*ing.
conscience	Someone who has been badly hurt may still be *conscious* when the doctor gets there; someone who has stolen a wallet may be bothered by his *conscience*. Both words have the *sc*.
definite	The problem is the *i* in the *–ite* ending. Compare this word with related words like defin*i*tion and infin*i*te. REMEMBER: Spell ITE as in KITE to get defin*ite* right.
disastrous	The *e* drops out of the word *disaster* when we change it to *disastrous*.
friend	Make sure you have *ie*. REMEMBER: His best *friend* was a FIEND.
government	Preserve the *n* at the end when you change *govern* to *government*. REMEMBER: People who GOVERN are a *government*.
hoping	When you have hope, you are *hoping* (with a single *p*); when you hop about on one foot, you are *hopping* (with a double *p*). REMEMBER: *Hoping* rhymes with MOPING; *hopping* rhymes with STOPPING.

THIS IS MY BEST FRIEND, A. FIEND.

Group Two

its	*Its* is a pronoun and points back to a noun: "The *horse* bared *its* teeth." *It's*, with the apostrophe, shows that something has been *omitted*; the complete version is *it is*. Never use the apostrophe unless you can substitute *it is*: "*It's* (it is) a shame that you had to miss the party."
library	Notice the *r* that follows the *b*. REMEMBER: The liBRarians BRought BRicks for the BRanch liBRary.
lose	When you have a losing streak, you lose all the time (single *o*). When a car door rattles, something has come loose (double *o*). REMEMBER: *Lose* rhymes with WHOSE; *loose* rhymes with GOOSE.
necessary	First a *c*, then double *ss*. REMEMBER: The reCESS was neCESSary.
occasion	Watch for the double *c* and the *s*. REMEMBER: oCCur, oCCupy, oCCasion; invasion, occasion
occurred	Single *r* in *occur* and *occurs*; double *r* in *occurred* and *occurring*. REMEMBER: Double *r* occurred in occurred.

SOME EMBARASSING MISPELLINGS

In each of the following sentences, one word is mis-spelled. Write the correct spelling of the word after the number of the sentence.

1. We had planed our strategy in advance.
2. Each anniversary of my father's death, my sister and I visit the cemetary to put flowers on his grave.
3. The house looked as though every new tenent over the years had painted over the old paint.
4. The test was conducted at a special labratory.
5. With extream caution, the boy approached the house.
6. The possition he took on dress codes was extraordinary.
7. The only embarassed face in the group was that of his little brother.
8. I tried to get my point acrost, but he was too dull to under-stand.
9. She would then fall down on her knees and prey.
10. When we finally got to the house, nobody was their.

FOR PROOFREADING PRACTICE

prejudice	People with prejudices have made *judgments* *pre*maturely; they *pre*judge people and ideas without giving them a fair hearing.
principle	A basic idea or basic rule is a princi*ple* (with *ple* at the end); the person who runs a school is a princi*pal* (with *pal* at the end). REMEMBER: He paid us triPLE on princi*ple*.
privilege	There is a second *i* in the middle, and a simple *g* toward the end. REMEMBER: sacrIleGe, privilege
quantity	Make sure to put in the first *t*. REMEMBER: enTity, quantity
quite	The word with *ite* means "entirely" (you are *quite* right). The word with *iet* means "silent" (keep *quiet*). REMEMBER: *Quite* rhymes with KITE; *quiet* rhymes with DIET.
receive	One of the three or four most common spelling problems. It's *e* after *c*. REMEMBER: CEIling, deCEIve, receive
	Double *m*. REMEMBER: Double *m* is recoMMended in recommend.

WORDS FREQUENTLY MISSPELLED

ATHLETE   answer   Library   elevator   SURPRISE   SUCCESS   receive   SENSE   Individual

Group Three

referred
: Single *r* in *refer* and *refers;* double *r* in *referred* and *referring.* REMEMBER: Refer spells like HER; referring spells like HERRING.

separate
: Another all-time misspelling champion. It's *ate* at the end. REMEMBER: Spell ATE as in KATE to get separ*ate* straight.

similar
: Concentrate on the −*lar* ending. REMEMBER: circuLAR, popuLAR, simi*lar*

studying
: The *y* in *study* is kept in *studying.* REMEMBER: Stud*y*ing is done in a STUDY.

succeed
: Double *c* in su*cc*eed and su*cc*ess. REMEMBER: Accelerate if you want to su*cc*eed.

surprise
: The first syllable is *sur−.* REMEMBER: When the SURfer SURfaced we were *sur*prised.

than
: Use the *a* in comparisons (brighter *than*). Use the *e* in talking about time (now and *then*).

there
: Use the *eir* spelling only when you talk about what *they* do or what belongs to them (*their* car, *their* behavior). Use the *ere* spelling when pointing to a place (over *there*) and in the *there is/there are* combination (*there* is time). Use *they're* only when you can substitute *they are.* REMEMBER: Th*eir* car was not th*ere*.

to
: *To* indicates direction (*to* church, *to* school) and occurs in the *to* form of the verb (He started *to* run). *Too* shows that there is *too* much of something, but then it means "also," *too.* REMEMBER: *Too* late, he *too* came *to* school *to* learn.

together	When people g*a*ther (with *a*), they are tog*e*ther (with *e*).
tries	It's *y* in *try*, but *ie* in *tries* and *tried*. REMEMBER: cr*y*, fl*y*, tr*y*; cr*ies*, fl*ies*, tr*ies*
villain	The *a* is first, then the *i*. REMEMBER: The vill*ai*n went to SPAIN.
whose	"Who*se* house?" means "belonging to whom?" Use *who's* only if you can substitute *who is*. REMEMBER: Who's the girl wh*ose* book you found?
women	It's one wom*a*n (with *a*), but several wom*e*n (with *e*).
writing	Single *t* in wri*t*e and wri*t*ing, double *t* in wri*tt*en. REMEMBER: Wri*t*ing rhymes with BITING; wri*tt*en rhymes with BITTEN.

ACTIVITY 1

After studying the words in this section carefully, have someone dictate them to you. (Where two words sound the same, the person will have to indicate *which* of the two you are supposed to spell—for instance, *whose* as in "whose car.") Make a list of the words you misspelled and give this list special attention.

ACTIVITY 2

Here is an additional list of *common spelling problems*. Follow the same instructions as in Activity 1. As you make up the list of words you misspelled, write a brief note on each to show where the problem lies. If you can, make up a memory aid—a brief sentence or jingle. You may want to compare or exchange some of these aids with those of your classmates.

accommodate	basically	criticize
achievement	beautiful	
acquire	benefited	decision
already		describe
among	category	description
apology	children	different
apparent	clothes	disappoint
argument	competition	discipline
athlete	completely	disgusted
attitude	controversy	dissatisfied
available	convenient	dropped

eliminate	listener	relieve
embarrass		religion
enough	maintenance	repetition
enterprise	marriage	
entertainment	meant	scene
entrance	medicine	sense
environment		several
equipment	noble	shining
exaggerate		sincerely
existence	opinion	straight
experience	opportunity	strength
explanation	oppose	strict
extremely		suppose
	persuade	suspense
fascinate	planned	swimming
finally	possible	
	practical	temperament
height	practice	tendency
	prepare	thorough
	primitive	tragedy
incidentally	pursue	
independent		undoubtedly
intelligent		useful
interest	really	
	recognize	
license		

M1b
Spelling Rules **Know the spelling rules for words that follow a common pattern.**

Some groups of words follow a common pattern. The rule that applies to them will usually have its exceptions, but it will help you memorize many words that you would otherwise have to learn one by one.

—I before E.

In some words the *ee* sound is spelled *ie,* in others *ei.* When you sort out these words, you get the following pattern:

ie: believe, achieve, grief, niece, piece (of pie)
cei: receive, ceiling, conceited, receipt, deceive

In the second group, the *ei* is always preceded by *c.* remember: It is *i* before *e except* after *c.* Exceptions:

ei: either, neither, leisure, seize, weird
cie: financier, species

—Doubled consonant.

In many words the final consonant is doubled before the verb endings *—ed* and *—ing* or the adjective endings *—er* and *—est*. This doubling happens after two conditions are met:

(1) A single final consonant follows a *single vowel: plan, hop, run.* The vowel cannot be a combination (**diphthong**) signaled by a double letter (*load, sleep, read*) or have a silent *e* at the end (kit*e*, hop*e*, hat*e*). The spelling reflects the difference in pronunciation in the following pairs:

plan—plan*n*ed	plane—plan*ed*
hop—ho*pp*ing	hope—ho*p*ing
scrap—scra*pp*ed	scrape—scra*p*ed

(2) The syllable with the doubled consonant must be *stressed* when you pronounce the word. If the stress shifts away from the syllable, doubling does *not* take place:

Doubling	*No Doubling*
adMIT, adMITTed	BENefit, BENefited
overLAP, overLAPPing	deVELop, deVELoping
reGRET, reGRETTed	exHIBit, exHIBited
beGIN, beGINNing	WEAKen, WEAKening

—Y as a vowel.

Y appears as a *single* final vowel in words like *dry* and *try, hurry* and *carry.* This *y* changes to *ie* before *s* and to *i* before all other endings. The *y* remains *un*changed, however, before *ing.*

ie: try—tries, dry—dries, family—families, quantity—quantities, carry—carries, hurry—hurries

i: easy—easily, beauty—beautiful, happy—happiness, dry—drier, copy—copied

y: carrying, studying, copying, hurrying

When it follows another vowel, the *y* usually remains unchanged: *played, joys, delays, valleys, grayness.* Exceptions: *day—daily, pay—paid, say—said, gay—gaily, lay—laid.*

—Final e.

A silent *e* appears at the end of words like *hate, love, like.* This final *e* drops out before an ending that starts with a vowel. It stays in before an ending that starts with a consonant.

	Vowel	*Consonant*
hate	hating	hateful
like	likable	likely
bore	boring	boredom

Exceptions: *argue—argument, true—truly, due—duly, mile—mileage, whole—wholly.* Notice also that this rule does not apply to the *e* that accounts for the *dge* sound in chang*e*able, courag*e*ous, outrag*e*ous or the *ss* sound in notic*e*able.

—Changed plurals.

A number of common words change their spelling when we go from one to several, from singular to plural:

Singular *o:*	hero	potato	tomato	veto	Negro
Plural *oes:*	heroes	potatoes	tomatoes	vetoes	Negroes
Singular *man:*	man	woman	freshman	postman	fireman
Plural *men:*	men	women	freshmen	postmen	firemen
Singular *f (fe):*	life	knife	calf	wife	half
Plural *ves:*	lives	knives	calves	wives	halves

Some of the less common words ending in *o* or *f* do not change their spelling in the plural: *solo—solos, soprano—sopranos.* Check the word in your dictionary when you are in doubt.

ACTIVITY 1

On a separate sheet of paper, write down the words called for in the following instructions.

1. Fill in *ei* or *ie*: bel--ve, dec--ve, rec--ving, rel--f, l--sure, c--ling, n--ce, s--ze, conc--ted, ach--vement.
2. Write the *plural* of the following words: family, Negro, freshman, quantity, knife, woman, hero, soprano, veto, half, valley, potato, fly, postman, calf.
3. Write the *past* form of the following verbs: regret, rob, prohibit, prefer, stop, float, hope, bat, admit, rivet, try, play, copy, say, delay.
4. Add *—ing* to the following words: regret, study, love, prefer, stop, carry, bore, forget, develop, concentrate, run, hurry, hunt, drop, try.
5. Add *—er* to the following words: sad, lovely, carry, hot, great, white, grim, fancy, swim, float.
6. Add *—able* to the following words: change, regret, prefer, notice, envy, inhabit, enjoy, exchange, break, forgive.

ACTIVITY 2

Of the two italicized words in each sentence, write down the one that *fits the context.*

1. The commission *barred/bared* him from fighting in New Jersey.
2. The bird was *hoping/hopping* around in a circle.
3. The singers were *robed/robbed* in white.
4. My grandmother *canned/caned* her own vegetables.
5. When a board was too rough, the carpenter *planned/planed* it.
6. A stranger stepped up to him and *taped/tapped* him on the shoulder.
7. The butcher was *scraping/scrapping* the meat from the bones.
8. The pilot *gripped/griped* the controls firmly.

Know how to tell confusing words apart.

M1c
Confusing Pairs

Learn to distinguish the words in three major types of confusing pairs.

(1) The *same root word* in different uses:

courteous ... but courtesy
curious ... but curiosity
describe ... but description
four, fourteen ... but forty
generous ... but generosity
nine, ninety ... but ninth
pronounce ... but pronunciation
speaking ... but speech
till ... but until

Watch for the following:

We advise you to try.   (verb)
She gave us advice.   (noun)

We passed the turnoff.   (verb)
Let us forget the past.   (noun)

We found very little prejudice.   (noun)
They are extremely prejudiced.   (adjective)

We use cardboard and colored tape.   (present)
We used to meet in the hall.   (past)

(2) Words that *sound similar* or alike:

capital   Paris is the capital of France: a bank needs capital; the name was printed in capital letters

capitol   the Capitol is the building where the legislature meets

cite   the soldier was cited for bravery; (his name appeared in a citation)

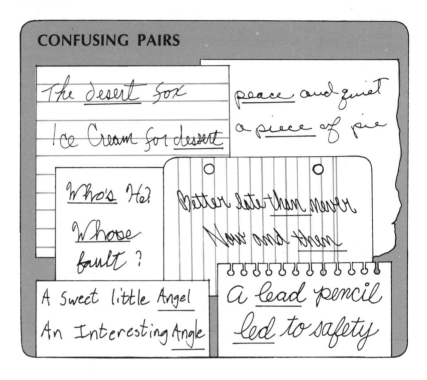

CONFUSING PAIRS

The *desert* fox

Ice Cream for *dessert*

peace and quiet

a *piece* of pie

Who's He?

Whose fault ?

Better *late* than never

Now *and* then

A Sweet little *Angel*

An Interesting *Angle*

a *lead* pencil

led to safety

site   we visited the *site* of the new high school (where it is going to be *situated*)

counsel   the coun*sel*ing staff coun*sels* or gives advice (its members are coun*sel*ors)

council   a governing board or committee is sometimes called a coun*cil*, as in city coun*cil* (its members are coun*cil*ors)

desert   we drove through the de*sert*; he de*sert*ed his friends; he got his just de*sert*s

dessert   we had pie for de*ssert* (put the double *s* only in what you *eat*)

personal   he always interfered in my perso*nal* affairs

personnel   the manager hired additional perso*nnel*

presents   he brought us presen*ts* (gifts)

presence   your presen*ce* is essential (opposite of absen*ce*)

(3) Words *with parts that sound similar* or alike:

–able	acceptable, indispensable (as in dispensary)
–ible	possible (also possibility,) irresistible
–ance	attendance, performance
–ence	experience, existence, excellence
–ant	attendant, brilliant
–ent	excellent, independent
–cede	precede, secede
–ceed	succeed, proceed (but procedure)

Make sure to spell out the *have* that sounds like a shortened *of* in the following combinations:

could *have* come	(never *could of*)
should *have* stayed	(never *should of*)
would *have* written	(never *would of*)
might *have* worked	(never *might of*)

ACTIVITY 1

Of the two words in each pair, write the one that *fits into the sample sentence.*

1. (*counsel/counsel*) Advisors —————— the students.
2. (*use/used*) We —————— to live in Kansas.
3. (*personal/personnel*) We insured our —————— belongings.
4. (*presents/presence*) He gave testimony in the —————— of a lawyer.
5. (*desert/dessert*) The children were waiting for ——————.
6. (*have/of*) The work could —————— been finished earlier.
7. (*passed/past*) The truck —————— us at high speed.
8. (*advise/advice*) Jim asked us for ——————.

ACTIVITY 2

After the number of each sentence, write the letter or letters missing at the space indicated. If no letter is missing, write *No*.

1. The new *princip*—————— visited our classroom.
2. Austrians consume great *quan*——————*ities* of whipped cream.
3. *Prejudice*—————— is not easy to overcome.
4. Take the books back to the *lib*——————*ary*.
5. Mr. Greene never gave us a *defin*——————*te* answer.
6. The class is *begi*——————*ing* to plan the spring picnic.

7. Mr. Fields *use*————*to* chat with us after class.
8. I could never find enough time for *stud*————*ing.*
9. His stories were often hard to *bel*————*ve.*
10. He refused to grant anyone special *privile*————*es.*
11. The late rain had been *disast*————*rous* for our farmers.
12. The Italian government signed a *separ*————*te* peace.
13. A plaque marked the spot where the accident had *occ*————*ed.*
14. After some confusion, the ceremony *proc*————*ded* as planned.

Learn how to use capital letters, apostrophes, and hyphens.

When we transfer spoken words to the written page, we use not only the ordinary alphabet but also capital letters and special marks. These marks often do not have an exact equivalent in speech—they are not "pronounced" in a way that would clearly signal when to put them in. We therefore have to study and practice the several uses to which each of these devices is put.

Capitalize the first word of a sentence and proper names.

A capital letter appears at the beginning of each new sentence. The pronoun *I* is always capitalized. In addition, we use a capital at the beginning of a **proper name**—a name used to set one person or thing apart from other members of the same group. Capital letters *single out;* we use them typically for one of a kind.

Remember the three kinds of names that should be capitalized:

(1) *Single words,* such as the names of people, places, ships, days of the week, months (but not seasons), religions: *John, Mary, Chicago, Russia, California, S.S. Independence, Tuesday, May, Hinduism.* We capitalize not only the proper name itself but also words *derived* from it:

England	English grammar
Brazil	Brazilian coffee
France	French pastry

When people forget that a word was derived from a proper name, the lowercase letter replaces the capital as the generally acceptable spelling:

Pasteur (a French scientist)	. . . but	pasteurized milk
India (a country)	. . . but	india ink

ETHNIC IS MY MIDDLE NAME

After the number of each sentence, write down (and *capitalize*) each word that should start with a capital letter.

Example: His brother came to our high school from oakland junior high.

(Answer)   *Oakland Junior High*

1. My parents came to pennsylvania from germany.
2. My grandfather had been a captain in the german army.
3. He had fought in france and russia in world war I.
4. He expected father to join the army and become at least a general.
5. My father had no ambition to become general braun or even major braun.
6. He wanted to study english and french and see the world.
7. In high school, he read books about africa, south america, and the far east.
8. He still loves books with titles like *around the world on a raft.*
9. For father's day, the family buys him a book like *life among the headhunters.*
10. Actually, he could write a book himself called *my travels.*
11. After the last war, he emigrated to canada.
12. He still takes us there during the summer, usually in july or august.
13. He went back to germany to marry my mother.
14. She was born in holland but then worked as a secretary near hamburg.
15. Now she talks dutch only when she is very angry.
16. They came to this country and first settled in the south.
17. Then they moved to the middle west.
18. They are lutheran and usually vote democratic.
19. They like swiss cheese, french pastry, and viennese waltzes.
20. If my father had not liked to travel, I would not be at glendale high school.

Some words are used two different ways: They serve as a *general* term, used to describe different examples of the same thing; or they serve as a proper name that picks out *one* example among all the others.

Ancient Greece developed *democratic* institutions.   (examples of a type)

She voted for the *Democratic* party.   (name of *one* party)

Several of our *presidents* have been assassinated.   (persons holding the same office)

The *President* held a press conference.   (identifies *one* person)

"A president," "a queen," or "a pope" means "one of several." "The President," "the Queen," or "the Pope" means "the only one"; we use the capitalized forms the same way we would use "President Harding," "Queen Elizabeth II," or "Pope Pius." This difference also explains why we write "my *mother*" but "Yes, Mother"; "his *father*" but "I knew Father was right." We use the lowercase letter when we rely on *my* or *his* to single out one mother or father; we capitalize the word when we use it like a proper name, instead of *Jim* or *Jean*.

(2) Combinations in which a general term *combines with a proper name*. We then capitalize not only the proper name but also the word that indicates a title, rank, a type of institution, and the like:

a mayor	. . . but	Mayor Brown
a general	. . . but	General Wainwright
a high school	. . . but	Oakdale High School

(3) *Names of books, titles of articles, names of paintings* and other works of art. When these consist of more than one word, we capitalize the *first* word and all other words *except* articles (*a, an, the*), prepositions (*at, with, for, of*) and connectives (*and, but, when, if*). We capitalize even the prepositions and connectives when they have *five* or more letters (*through, without, about, around, because*):

The Night They Burned the Mountain
Welcome to the Monkey House
Much Ado About Nothing

Capitalize words this way when you write the title of your *own* theme and when you mention a book or article *in* your theme. The titles you mention, but not the title of your own theme, should also be *italicized*. (See **M 6b.**)

Building the Habit: Use the following activity for habit building. Read it several times, paying special attention to pairs where the same word is used once with and once without a capital letter.

a city in Kansas, Oklahoma City, Dearborn Township, a small town, Washtenaw County; the Atlantic, Lake Huron, an island in the Pacific, Long Island, a rocky trail, the Rocky Mountains; our postman, the Postmaster General, Professor Smith, an English teacher, the Reverend Brown, Councilor Wakefield; a Ford convertible, the Ford Motor Company, General Motors, General Electric appliances; a side street, Main Street, the Ambassador Hotel, the Good Samaritan Hospital, a business college; the U.S. Army, the Senate, Senator Brown, the Congressional Record; *The New York Times,* the Merryvale *News; Gone with the Wind, The Bridge of San Luis Rey, Brave New World, A Midsummer Night's Dream;* the Greek gods, God Almighty, Christ and His disciples, the Mosaic law; Mother's Day, Easter, last spring, Christmas Eve, the last Saturday in November, the Middle Ages, a middle-aged man; the Civil War, a civil war; the Democratic ticket, the Negro voter, the Inaugural Ball, the Fourth of July, the Declaration of Independence, the Bill of Rights

ACTIVITY

Of the two possibilities, write down the one that fits the sample sentence. Write on a separate sheet of paper.

1. *(south/South)*   He had spent the year in the —————— of France.
2. *(queen/Queen)*   When we visited London, the —————— was abroad.
3. *(democratic/Democratic)*   The country had never had a ————— form of government.
4. *(southerner/Southerner)*   Helen had married a ——————.
5. *(president/President)*   The senator decided to run for —————.
6. *(india/India)*   He asked us to use —————— ink.
7. *(mother/Mother)*   We told ————— about the accident.
8. *(father/Father)*   His ————— picked him up at the airport.

Use the apostrophe as a sign of omission and as the sign of the possessive.   M2b
The Apostrophe

There are three major uses of the apostrophe:

(1) The apostrophe is used in **contractions.** In *informal* English, we often shorten words by leaving out some of the sounds

THE USES OF THE APOSTROPHE

or letters. The apostrophe indicates *where* the omission has taken place:

| you are | *You're* right. |
| we would | *We'd* call. |

Many contractions contain a shortened form of *not*. Take care not to misspell these, especially *doesn't* (*does* not):

cannot	I *can't* tell.
have not	We *haven't* heard.
is not	It *isn't* true.
will not	He *won't* believe you.
do not	They *don't* like to.
does not	It *doesn't* count.

Some contractions sound exactly like other forms that have quite different uses. Make sure you *spell* them differently:

| *It's* means *it is:* | *It's* too early. |
| *Its* means *of it:* | The ship kept *its* course. |

Who's means *who is:*	*Who's* your friend?
Whose means *of whom:*	*Whose* car did you ride in?
They're means *they are:*	*They're* my cousins.
Their means *of them:*	We found *their* cabin.

Use contractions mainly when accurately reporting a conversation. An occasional *don't* or *it's* may appear in a serious article, but many readers consider contractions too informal for serious discussion. Avoid them in formal reports, research papers, letters of application.

(2) The apostrophe is used to mark the **possessive.** The possessive shows where something belongs, what it is a part of, and other close relationships. We produce the possessive form when instead of putting an *of* between two nouns we put the *second noun* first. This noun is then usually followed by the apostrophe plus *s:*

the purse of my *sister*	my *sister's* purse
the garage of Mr. *Brown*	Mr. *Brown's* garage
the model planes of *John*	*John's* model planes
the rodeo of the *firemen*	the *firemen's* rodeo

The same form is used in many common expressions dealing with time and price:

a *day's* work	a *week's* pay
a *moment's* notice	a *dollar's* worth

Most *plural forms* already have the plural −s. Do not add a second s to these:

Singular:	the girl	the *girl's* dress
Plural:	the girls	the *girls'* pool
Singular:	one week	one *week's* pay
Plural:	two weeks	two *weeks'* pay

Use the apostrophe plus *s* for the possessive of the so-called **indefinite pronouns:** *one, everybody (everyone), somebody (someone), anybody (anyone), nobody (no one).* But never use the apostrophe for the possessive forms of **personal pronouns.** Never use an apostrophe in *his, hers, its, ours, yours, theirs.* Contrast the sentences in each of the following pairs:

The story aroused *everyone's* curiosity.
The bird shook *its* tail feathers.

The car must be *somebody's*.
The car must be *hers*.

(3) The apostrophe is used to separate the plural *s* from the *name of a letter or of a number*, or from a *word discussed as a word* (as for instance in a discussion of grammar):

His record showed many C's and a few B's.
There were three 7's in the number.
His speech contained many if's and but's.

Building the Habit: Use the following activity for habit building. Read it over several times, paying special attention to pairs where the same word is used in different ways.

an hour's wait, two hours' wait, waited two hours; a friend's house, good friends, the children's hour, the boys' bicycles, the principal's day off, the secretary's desk, the teachers' salaries, the nurse's uniform, the students' lockers; they're out, their report cards; don't panic, doesn't work, whose towel, who's there; A's and B's, p's and q's, two 3's and one 9; the sergeant's report, the jury's duties, the judge's instructions, the spectators' reactions; for goodness' sake, without a moment's hesitation, after several moments of silence; child's play, man's work, a dog's life, a mother's love, women's clubs; it's a shame, changed its position, can't tell, haven't seen him; doctor's orders, in accordance with her parents' wishes, the bride's farewell.

ACTIVITY

Of the two possibilities, write down the one that *fits the sample sentence*. Write on a separate sheet of paper.

1. a. *(students/student's)*   He checked every _____ notebook.

   b. *(student's/students')*   He knew all the _____ families.

2. a. *(It's/Its)*   _____ too late for another game.

   b. *(it's/its)*   The church had lost _____ steeple.

3. a. *(families/family's)*   Jim contributed to the _____ income.

   b. *(families/families')*   Two new _____ had moved in.

4. a. *(who's/whose)*   I wonder _____ fault it was.

   b. *(who's/whose)*   I wonder _____ to blame.

5. a. *(weeks'/week's)*   You owe me three _____ pay.

   b. *(weeks'/week's)*   He asked for one _____ rent.

6. a. (*years/years'*)   Two _____ had been wasted.
   b. (*years/years'*)   Two _____ work had been wasted.
7. a. (*they're/their*)   I am tired of _____ complaints.
   b. (*they're/their*)   Now _____ living in Texas.
8. a. (*boys/boy's*)   Who are this _____ parents?
   b. (*boy's/boys'*)   Who are these _____ parents?

Use the hyphen in compound words that have not yet merged into a single word.

M2c
The Hyphen

The hyphen is conventionally used in compound numbers from *twenty-one* up to *ninety-nine*. In addition, the hyphen is used in three major ways to tie together words or parts of words:

(1) When *two or more words form a single unit*, they are called **compound words.** Many of these are both pronounced and spelled as single words—without a break or a hyphen. Contrast the members of the following pairs:

a black bird (black BIRD)   a blackbird (BLACKbird)
a dark room (dark ROOM)   a darkroom (DARKroom)

THE HYPHEN IS THE TIE THAT BINDS

However, other words pronounced the same way are still spelled with the parts separated:

a high price (high PRICE)   a high school (HIGH school)

Still other words are at the halfway stage, with a hyphen used to tie the parts together. Many words that used to be hyphenated are now written solidly. Others are used either way. When you are in doubt, use the word the way it is listed in your dictionary. Remember some of the more common words in each major category:

One Word: bellboy, bridesmaid, gunman, headache, highway, newspaper, stepmother

Two (or More) Words: bus boy, commander in chief, goose flesh

Hyphen: able-bodied, bitter-sweet, bull's-eye, cave-in, court-martial, great-grandfather, gun-shy, merry-go-round, mother-in-law

Make sure to get the following right:

One Word: today, tomorrow, nevertheless, nowadays
Two Words: all right, a lot (of time), be able, no one

(2) *A part of a word that can be put in front of many different words* is called a **prefix.** Most prefixes combine with the word that follows into a single unit. Put a hyphen after the prefix in the following situations:

—After *all–, ex–* (when it means "former"), and *self–:*

all-knowing, all-powerful; ex-champion, ex-president; self-conscious, self-respect

—Before a *capital* letter:

all-American, pro-British, anti-German, non-Catholic

—Between two *identical vowels:*

anti-intellectual, semi-independent

(3) Several words that are normally kept separate may combine to form a **group modifier** that is put *in front of a noun.* Use hyphens whenever such a group of words takes the place of a single adjective:

Separate: He described the process *step by step.*
Hyphens: We wanted a *step-by-step* account.

Separate: The meal was *well balanced.*
Hyphens: She served a *well-balanced* meal.

Do not use hyphens when one part of the group modifier is an adverb ending in *–ly:* a *rapidly growing* city, a *carefully prepared* demonstration.

Building the Habit: Some words appear both with and without the hyphen. With many other words, however, the use of the hyphen is well established. *Read over the following activity several times in order to fix in your mind words and expressions in which the hyphen is definitely expected.*

> stepfather, grandfather, great-grandfather, in-laws, brother-in-law, great-uncle, bride-to-be; ex-fiancée, self-confidence, ex-senator, un-American, all-embracing; drive-in, walkie-talkie, first-class mail, first-rate; four-wheel drive, high-grade ore, a play-by-play account, a devil-may-care attitude; self-styled, ex-governor; thirty-three, forty-six, nineteen, eighty-four; a man-eating tiger, a hard-driving employer, bloodthirsty enemies, a strictly personal question; drive in the middle of the road, middle-of-the-road policies; stretched from wall to wall, wall-to-wall carpets; a heart-to-heart talk, a world-shaking event, a person-to-person call, a run-of-the-mill performance.

IT'S ABOUT TIME YOU ATE A WELL-BALANCED MEAL!

ACTIVITY

In each of the following sentences, find the combination that needs one or more hyphens. *Write down the hyphenated word or expression on a separate sheet of paper.*

1. His brother in law had gone to the same high school.
2. The labor unions of the country had been pro American.
3. The ex governor discussed the charges point by point.
4. She made a person to person call to her cousin in Maine.
5. The governor ran a first class campaign.
6. My stepfather took us all to a drive in restaurant.
7. My brother took me aside for a man to man talk.

REVIEW ACTIVITY

In each of the following sentences, one word (or group of words) needs a *capital letter, an apostrophe, or a hyphen.* Write the revised word after the number of the sentence.

1. The mayor was known for middle of the road policies.

   2. An honor guard greeted the president when he returned to the capital.
   3. Honored guest at the groundbreaking was mayor Brown.
   4. When the plant closed down, each worker received two weeks pay.
   5. My father doesnt like telephone soliciting.
   6. The form asked for my mothers birthplace.
   7. Her mother had been an episcopalian all her life.
   8. In the distance I could hear my parents voices.
   9. All you need is more selfconfidence.
   10. I was getting tremendously annoyed by his wait and see attitude.
   11. The living room was littered with childrens toys.
   12. The company was building a new factory in georgia.
   13. On Sundays we usually went to the drivein theater.
   14. His arrogance soon got on everyones nerves.

Use end punctuation to show that an utterance is complete.

When speaking, we use different kinds of breaks and changes in the tone of voice. These help signal what words go together. When we pause briefly, *the way* we pause shows whether we have completed a statement or whether we are only halfway through a sentence. When we say "This is John" the normal way, it means one thing. When our voice goes up at the end in a questioning way ("This is John?"), the same words mean something else. The rising and falling in the tone of voice is called **pitch.** Changes in pitch and the different kinds of breaks in the flow of speech are part of English **intonation.**

When we shift from speech to writing, *punctuation marks take over some of the work done by intonation in spoken English.* They can indicate what belongs together and what should be kept apart. They can show what is important and what is unimportant. They can prepare us for what follows.

The most basic punctuation marks are those that bring an utterance to a complete stop. The exclamation point, the question mark, and the period are the basic stop-and-go signals regulating traffic on the page. We use them to indicate that a group of words, or sometimes just one single word, stands by itself—that it is complete and self-contained.

Use the exclamation point or question mark after single words and groups of words.

The **exclamation point** adds emphasis. Use it for shouts, orders, expressions of strong emotion. Use it to signal anger, surprise, indignation:

THEY DID IT AGAIN!

YOU'RE RIGHT!

I'VE BEEN BILKED!

GREAT!

The **question mark** follows an utterance that asks for a reply. It also turns a simple statement or observation into a question the way the rising tone of voice does in speech:

Who was it?	Yes?
Did you see him?	You mean they get *paid*?

Make sure not to forget the question mark after *questions that are long or involved:*

Which team had the largest number of consecutive losses in the history of major-league baseball?
Why is gambling legal in one state but illegal in another?

Use the following procedure with *questions that only look like questions:*

(1) Use the question mark after **rhetorical questions.** These do not really give the listener a choice. What the right answer is supposed to be is already strongly hinted in the question itself:

Are you implying that I am dishonest?
Do you want millions to die in a needless war?

(2) Feel free to use either the question mark or a period after requests that are worded as questions for the sake of *politeness:*

Will you please pass the information on to your friends?
Will you please pass the information on to your friends.

EXCLAMATION MARKS ARE FOR PEOPLE WHO COME ON STRONG.

ACTIVITY

Each of the following utterances is punctuated three ways. To show the different effects, *explain orally* who might use each version that way and when or why.

1. Peanuts!
   Peanuts?
   Peanuts.

2. No classes on Monday.
   No classes on Monday!
   No classes on Monday?

3. You are Jim's brother.
   You are Jim's brother!
   You are Jim's brother?

4. Jean won a scholarship!
   Jean won a scholarship.
   Jean won a scholarship?

M3b
Sentences and Fragments

Use the period at the end of complete sentences.

The **period** separates one complete sentence from the other. To be complete, the normal sentence must have its own subject and predicate. It must not be subordinated to another sentence by a word like *when, if,* or *because.* In speech, we often start up again after a complete sentence and add an afterthought that does not have its own subject and predicate. When such afterthoughts are kept separate from the preceding sentence by a period, we call them **sentence fragments.**

Typically, what is missing from a fragment is *all or part of the verb.* Often, both the verb and a possible subject are lacking:

Fragment: We had an unexpected visitor. *My uncle.*
Complete: We had an unexpected visitor. My uncle *came.*

Fragment: We heard the new neighbor. *Mowing the lawn.*
Complete: We heard the new neighbor. *He was* mowing the lawn.

Avoid the sentence fragment in serious writing. The first step in learning to avoid it is to take a look at the sentence parts that cause fragments when left to stand alone:

Appositives

He drove an old battered car. *A Ford.*
She invited only one boy. *My brother.*

Adjectives, Adverbs

She had bought a new dress. *Beautiful but expensive.*
Ask him to return it. *Immediately.*

Prepositional Phrases

Jim had gone swimming. *With his friends.*
The bandit left the store. *In a hurry.*

Verbals

My friends were outside. *Loafing in the sun.*
He had gone to Detroit. *To visit relatives.*

Dependent Clauses

The plan was dropped. *Because the mayor objected.*
The letter was from Baltimore. *Which is my hometown.*

Which of these causes the sentence fragment in each of the following examples?

He was a perpetual candidate. Running for office in every election.
Friends are very important. Especially for a boy around that age.
The coach was a Mr. Kelley. An intelligent man in his early thirties.
We had two weeks to prove our ability. Because thirty boys were
    signed up with only room for twenty on the team.

Learn how to tie such fragments to the preceding sentence. Remember the *four major ways* an afterthought may be punctuated as part of a complete sentence:

(1) Many afterthoughts can become part of the preceding sentence without any break in speech and *without any punctuation* in writing. Most adverbs and prepositional phrases and many verbals should be tied into the preceding sentence without any comma or other mark:

Ask him to return it *immediately.*
Jim had gone swimming *with his friends.*
He had gone to Detroit *to visit relatives.*

(2) Most appositives and many verbals and dependent clauses can be joined to the preceding sentence by a slight break in speech and a **comma** in writing.

He drove an old battered car, *a Ford.*
She invited only one boy, *my brother.*
My friends were outside, *loafing in the sun.*
The letter was from Baltimore, *which is my hometown.*

Use the comma before a fragment when it adds examples to a more general statement after *such as, especially, for example, for instance,* and *namely.* (A *second* comma is used in much formal writing after the last three of these.)

Jim loved science subjects, *such as chemistry.*
My uncle disliked folksingers, *especially girls.*
All the children studied a foreign language, *for instance, Spanish.*

(3) The **colon** serves to tie a detailed *list, description, or explanation* to the more general statement that comes before:

There were two outstanding players: Jane and Lois.
Breakfast was always the same: *fruit, oatmeal, and coffee.*
The players lacked one important thing: *talent.*

(4) The **dash** actually *keeps an afterthought apart* as something that we add after a definite break. Like other marks that call special attention to something we say, the dash easily loses its effect when overused.

There was our home in ruins—*a sad sight.*
They had worked long and hard—*for nothing.*

Sometimes it is impossible to relate a fragment to the preceding sentence in one of these four ways. Turn such a fragment into a *complete separate sentence:*

Fragment: We tried to lift the car. *Being a futile effort.*
Complete: We tried to lift the car. *The effort was futile.*

NOTE: **Permissible fragments** occur in writing when the writer deliberately reproduces grammatically incomplete units that are part of the natural flow of speech or thought. You are likely to find such permissible fragments in reading the following:

(1) Written records of *conversation,* the *dialogue* of a play, *answers* to questions:

IT'S COLD ON JUPITER TONIGHT

Most of the following sentences are punctuated correctly. Put *C* for correct after the number of each such sentence. Be prepared to explain in class *why* the sentence was punctuated the way it was. A few of the sentences in this exercise are followed by *sentence fragments*. Put *F* for fragment after the number of each such sentence. Be prepared to explain how the fragment could be revised.

Example: She returned his Christmas gift: a baby alligator.
(Answer)   *C*

1. Space travelers can be sure of only one thing: danger.
2. The Earth is utterly different from other planets, for instance, Jupiter.
3. Its atmosphere is thick and lethal—a soup of poisonous gases.
4. Hydrogen is mixed with other gases: methane and ammonia.
5. The days are short and ice-cold. The nights are even colder.
6. The surface is a soggy quicksand. Offering no support to a spaceship.
7. Other conditions also differ, such as the pull of gravity.
8. More than double our gravity would weigh down everything. Men and equipment.
9. Something else would add to this weight—the dense atmosphere.
10. A spacecraft would need tremendous thrust. To return from this giant planet.
11. There are more hospitable planets, namely, Venus or Mars.
12. Here a spacecraft can actually land. On solid ground.

That's Jim Chase. *A fine boy. Not very talkative,* though. *Too bad. Better leave now.* What did we gain? *Nothing.*

(2) *Descriptive passages* that register impressions the way they would pass through the mind of the observer:

We looked out over the valley stretching at our feet. *An immense blue sky. Mountain peaks in the distance. Cars moving along the highways like toys.*

(3) *Narrative passages* reproducing the effect of random, naturally moving thoughts:

> Jim dropped in. *An old friend. Must be about forty now. Still living in the hills.*

You yourself may use such permissible fragments when reporting a conversation or writing a story. Avoid them when writing a paper devoted to serious argument or research.

Building the Habit: Each of the sentences in the following paragraph illustrates one way of avoiding a possible sentence fragment. *Read this passage over several times* so that the punctuation rules it illustrates will become completely familiar to you. Be prepared to explain in class what way of avoiding a fragment each sentence illustrates and why it is appropriate to the meaning of the sentence.

Today we talk over long distances without difficulty. The human voice is carried by efficient technical devices, such as radio or telephone. Written messages can be sent just as fast—by telegraph or teletype. These systems depend on a fairly recent discovery: electricity. People managed without electric current for many centuries. People with a message often had only one choice, namely, to send a messenger. Here and there other means of communication were developed, for example, the smoke signals of the American Indian. The receiver of the signal had to be within eye range—on a clear day. Africans developed another similar device: the talking drums. These carried news from village to village, for instance, warnings of enemy attack. The South Sea islanders used hollowed-out trees sounding like huge gongs. Each such signaling system needs two major elements: a medium and a code. The medium is the physical device for conveying the message. The code is needed to turn words into signals. Each signal must mean the same to the drummer and to the listener—to the transmitter and to the receiver.

ACTIVITY 1

Which of the following groups of words should be punctuated as two complete sentences, *separated by a period?* Which can be combined into a single sentence, without a break in speech and *without punctuation* in writing? Sort these groups of words out into these two categories. Rewrite them, *using the appropriate punctuation.* Punctuate a group of words as a separate sentence only if it has its own subject and predicate. (Do not add or delete any words; do not change word forms or word order.)

CODES TRANSMIT LANGUAGE

"England expects that every

man will do his duty"

THE MORSE CODE

A	● —	I	● ●	R	● — ●
B	— ● ● ●	J	● — — —	S	● ● ●
C	— ● — ●	K	— ● —	T	—
D	— ● ●	L	● — ● ●	U	● ● —
E	●	M	— —	V	● ● ● —
F	● ● — ●	N	— ●	W	● — —
G	— — ●	O	— — —	X	— ● ● —
H	● ● ● ●	P	● — — ●	Y	— ● — —
		Q	— — ● —	Z	— — ● ●

THE DEAF-MUTE ALPHABET

Spell out a simple word or simple message, using these hand signals. (See if your classmates get the message.)

Example: The spectators left   in a hurry
(Answer)   *The spectators left in a hurry.*

1. The band stopped playing   the crowd began to leave
2. There were hundreds of swallows   circling around the tower
3. Fred went on a hike   with his friends
4. We walked cautiously   the ice was treacherous
5. One of the boys had left   to look for help
6. The beach looked deserted   the boardwalk was empty
7. Maria had been fishing all day   without much success
8. Seagulls were everywhere   gliding swiftly above the water
9. The visitors had left the park   the guard locked the gate
10. The flood took everyone by surprise   houses were swept away
11. We pitched camp late at night   in a sheltered spot
12. Our group moved down the steep path   slowly but surely

ACTIVITY 2

Most of the following sentences are punctuated correctly. Put *C* after the number of each such sentence. In the remaining sentences, punctuation needs to be revised. Put *R* after the number of each of these. Be prepared to explain in class *why* each correct sentence is punctuated the way it is and why the remaining ones need to be revised.

1. All week he served the same lunch: pork and beans.
2. We never reached our goal. The car broke down.
3. They were taking business courses. For instance, typing.
4. My brother had left school to join the navy.
5. Why are older sisters always criticizing their younger brothers.
6. The dentist was on vacation—what luck!
7. The fugitives abandoned the stolen car. A battered station wagon.
8. Why should the innocent suffer with the guilty?
9. Rachel always did well in science subjects, such as chemistry.
10. Silence! How can anyone study with all this noise?
11. My uncle George loved to travel. Especially by plane.
12. How do you expect me to remember all these details.

M4
LINKING
PUNCTUATION

Know when to put the semicolon or the comma between two clauses.

Often, two statements combine, each becoming a "subsentence" in the larger combined sentence. We call such subsentences

---

LINKING PUNCTUATION

A SUMMARY

SEMICOLON

Use the semicolon when two closely related clauses appear without a connective or with an adverbial connective *(therefore, however, besides):*

> Fred adores Gwendolen; she hates him.
> Fred adores Gwendolen; however, she hates him.

COMMA

The comma is typical with a coordinator *(and, but, or)* or with a nonrestrictive dependent clause. When a dependent clause *precedes* the main clause, a comma shows where the main clause starts:

> Fred adores Gwendolen, but she hates him.
> Fred adores Gwendolen, though she hates him.
> Though Fred adores Gwendolen, she hates him.
> Fred adores Gwendolen, who hates him.

NO PUNCTUATION

Use no punctuation when a subordinator *(if, when, unless)* or a relative pronoun *(who, which, that)* introduces a restrictive clause. Use no punctuation with noun clauses, which typically start with *that* (used as a special connective), or with question words like *why, how,* and *when:*

> Gwendolen hated Fred when he adored her.
> Fred hated the boys who adored Gwendolen.
> Fred knew that Gwendolen hated him.
> Fred wondered why Gwendolen hated him.

---

clauses. Each of the following sentences is a combination of *two* clauses. Each clause has its own subject and verb:

> *The house seemed* empty; *the car was* gone.
> *The doorbell rang,* but *nobody answered.*
> *No one was* near the car, though *the motor was running.*
> *I read* the letter that *Fred had written.*

Remember that a request is still a complete sentence even though the subject is omitted (or "understood"). A clause may also be in the request form and thus *lack a subject:*

The *lights are* still on; *turn* them off.
You may go now, but *be* careful.

How do we punctuate such combined clauses? The first question to ask is: "Is there a connective between two clauses, or are they simply *placed next to each other?*" The second question is: "If there is a connective, *what kind of connective* is it?"

Use the semicolon or comma between independent clauses.

Independent clauses are linked very loosely. They could easily be unhitched again and go their separate ways. There are *three ways* two or more independent clauses can come together:

(1) Often two statements go together even though there is *no connective* to tie them together. A **semicolon** may then replace the period. In this case, the first word of the second statement is *not* capitalized. When the semicolon is used this way, it could be called a "semiperiod."

In the following pairs, can you find a subject and a verb on *both* sides of the semicolon?

The windows were closed; the curtains had been drawn.
Fred is a junior; his sister is in college.
Some people like cats; others hate them.

In informal writing, a comma at times replaces the semicolon between two independent clauses. The result is called a **comma splice** or a **run-on** sentence. *Avoid this use of the comma in your own writing.* The safe practice is to use the comma only when *three* or more clauses are closely parallel in the way they are put together:

He came, he saw, he conquered.
Fred beat the drum, George blew the trumpet, I played the flute.

(2) Often two statements are related to each other by an *adverbial connective.* This category includes *however, therefore, nevertheless, besides, moreover, furthermore, accordingly,* and *in fact.* Again the **semicolon** may replace the period between the two clauses:

WHERE THE SEMICOLON GOES

Look at the following sentences. Each combines two closely related statements that should be joined by a semicolon. After the number of each sentence, put the *last* word of the first statement. Then put the semicolon after it.

Example: The birds cried small animals scattered.
(Answer)   *cried;*

1. Grandma was artistic Grandpa was practical.
2. He saw himself in the mirror he wasn't tired anymore.
3. The mother couldn't teach her to drive the father was too busy.
4. People are people we cannot predict their reactions.
5. He offered me two dollars an hour I could hardly refuse.
6. His insults were not limited to members he treated employees and outsiders all the same.
7. I heard a crash everything went black.
8. My parents would talk to me in Chinese however I would answer in English.
9. I ran off the road this caused the car to turn over several times.
10. We sat drinking Coke we were playing cards too.

BUILDING THE HABIT

The weather improved; *therefore,* we changed our plans.
I am short of cash; *besides,* the store is closed.
He likes to fish; *in fact,* he does little else.

Remember that this kind of connective may *shift its place in the second clause.* The semicolon stays at the point where the two clauses join:

P.E. is required; *therefore,* the students have no choice.
P.E. is required; the students, *therefore,* have no choice.
P.E. is required; the students have no choice, *therefore.*

A terrible accident occurred; *nevertheless,* the race went on.
A terrible accident occurred; the race, *nevertheless,* went on.
A terrible accident occurred; the race went on, *nevertheless.*

In formal writing, as in all of these examples, a **comma** usually keeps the adverbial connective apart from the rest of the second clause. If the connective appears in the middle of the second clause, *two* commas are needed. The commas used for this purpose are *optional*.

(3) Often two statements are joined by a *coordinator*. There are only seven words in this group: *and, but, for, so, yet, or,* and *nor*. The **comma** is the most typical punctuation when one of these words joins two complete clauses:

> The walls shook, *and* the mirror dropped from the wall.
> The sky was cloudy, *but* the hikers were in a good mood.
> We worked hard, *for* we had been promised a reward.
> It rained all day, *so* we ate inside.
> He was only thirty, *yet* his hair was gray.
> Help with the work, *or* leave the shop.
> He does not speak English, *nor* does his wife.

This kind of connective *cannot* shift its place in the second clause. Nor can the clause it introduces shift to the beginning of the sentence. All the words in this group have *other* uses (that often require no punctuation).

REMEMBER: In your own writing, observe the following basic rule for joining independent clauses: *semicolon with no connective or with an adverbial connective; comma with a coordinating connective*. In your reading, however, you will also encounter the following possibilities:

—Both adverbial and coordinating connectives leave the two clauses independent. It is therefore possible to use the **period** with either type of connective for a more definite break:

> The floodwaters were still rising. *Therefore,* the town had to be evacuated.
> There is no need to apologize. *Besides,* they left hours ago.
> I called his home. *But* nobody answered.

—A **semicolon** is possible with all coordinating connectives, especially if the two clauses are *long or complicated:*

> Napoleon was a national hero to the French; *but* he was hated and feared in many other European countries, such as Austria and England.

—*And, but,* and *or* sometimes appear *without punctuation* between clauses that are very short:

> He talked *and* we listened.
> Fred agreed *but* George balked.

Building the Habit: Each of the sentences in the following paragraph illustrates typical punctuation between independent clauses. *Read this passage over several times* so that the punctuation rules it illustrates will become completely familiar to you. Be prepared to explain in class why each sentence was punctuated the way it was.

Writing has a long history, for people early needed written records. Cattle drovers needed a rough record of ownership; traders needed lists of goods. Merchants deal with number and quantity; therefore, the first written signs included numbers. People scratched such numbers into tablets of wet clay, and the clay then baked hard in the sun. These signs could not be erased; in fact, forgers must have had a hard time. The tablet could be kept as a record, or it could be sent with a shipment of goods. Such record-keeping may seem clumsy, but other forms of writing were even more unwieldy. Ancient Egypt had little timber, so palaces and temples were built of stone. Egyptian writing was slow and precise, for it was carved into the stone walls. These stone carvings told about gods and heroes; however, an easier kind of writing was available for everyday use. The Egyptians wove together the fibers of a reed; the result was a primitive kind of paper. The reed was called papyrus; our own word for paper derives from its name. This paper was not very smooth; nevertheless, it took ink very well. Records were now much lighter; besides, they could be rolled up for storage. The Egyptians had solved the problem; other countries, however, could not obtain the right kind of reed.

ACTIVITY

What would be the *most typical punctuation* at the break indicated in the following sentences? Put one of the following abbreviations after the number of each sentence: *S* (for semicolon) if there are two clauses related by no connective or an adverbial connective; *C* (for comma) if two clauses are joined by a coordinating connective; *No* (for "no punctuation") when the second part of a sentence is not really a separate clause.

Use *No* when a coordinating connective does not introduce a second clause but merely adds *a word or a phrase* to the first part of the sentence.

Example: Many people keep pets ⎯⎯⎯ their neighbors often
                       disapprove.
(Answer)   *S*

1. Some people love animals ⎯⎯⎯ others can do without them.
2. Cars are mechanical gadgets ⎯⎯⎯ but animals are alive.

3. A dog may obey its master ———— however, it also has a mind of its own.
4. Birds are full of life ———— moreover, they remind us of life outside the cities.
5. Children love cuddly kittens ———— and almost any kind of pet.
6. Girls keep parakeets ———— and boys bring home snakes and beetles.
7. Not all parents approve ———— for animals can also be a nuisance.
8. Pets must be fed right ———— besides, they must be kept clean.
9. Dogs tear up lawns ———— neighbors, therefore, disapprove of them.
10. Cats serenade each other at night ———— and wake up the neighborhood.
11. Many cities have ordinances about pets ———— nevertheless, many pet owners disregard the rights of others.
12. Bad feeling often results ———— one angry neighbor recently killed a dog with his shovel.
13. Many people sympathized ———— the court, however, took the side of the dog.
14. In many cities pigeons flutter over the public squares ———— and dirty the passersby.
15. A single hit can ruin a suit ———— furthermore, these birds carry diseases.
16. Pigeon lovers do not know these facts ———— or simply ignore them.
17. Sometimes a city decides on war ———— so poisoned bait is spread in the parks.
18. Soon angry letters are written to the city officials ———— and indignant editorials appear in the newspapers.
19. Few dead pigeons are ever found ———— in fact, the city pigeon seems indestructible.
20. Soon the campaign is called off ———— and public squares remain as dirty as ever.

M4b
Adverbial Clauses

Use the comma to set off nonrestrictive adverbial clauses.

Subordinating connectives do not merely join a second clause loosely to the first. They subordinate it. They turn it into a *dependent clause*, which normally cannot stand by itself. These connectives typically introduce **adverbial clauses.** Such clauses tell us something about the time, place, reasons, or conditions of the main action or event.

To make sure you have a subordinator, try putting the adverbial clause *in front of* the main clause. This test does not work with the other two major types of connectives:

Normal: We started the fire *when the sun went down.*
Reversed: *When the sun went down,* we started the fire.

Normal: The hike will be canceled *if the rain continues.*
Reversed: *If the rain continues,* the hike will be canceled.

Some adverbial clauses require *no punctuation;* others are *set off by a comma.* Remember three major possibilities:

(1) *Use no punctuation when you add a restrictive clause to the main clause.* Many subordinators deal with time, place, or conditions: *when, while, before, after, since, if, unless.* The clause they introduce often makes *all the difference.* "You may drive the car" means one thing. "You may drive the car *when you grow up*" means another. "When you grow up" *restricts* the meaning of the main clause in an important way. It is called a **restrictive** clause.

Can you see how the added clause in each of the following pairs *restricts* the original meaning?

His dog always growls.
His dog always growls *when a stranger goes by.*

NO COMMAS FOR ESSENTIAL DEPENDENT CLAUSES

> The road is safe.
> The road is safe *after the snow is gone.*

(2) *Set off nonrestrictive clauses.* Some subordinators set up a contrast: *though, although,* and *whereas;* also the combinations *no matter what* and *no matter how.* The clause each introduces is **nonrestrictive.** It does not change the meaning of the main clause. It merely points out that *something else is also true:*

> We enjoyed the trip (true), *though* the roads were bad. (also true)

Use a **comma** when you add a nonrestrictive clause to the main clause. This comma corresponds to a characteristic break in the *spoken* sentence. Can you hear the break in the following examples?

> Jim knows no Spanish, *although* he was born in Spain.
> The boys liked Westerns, *whereas* the girls preferred comedies.
> The schedule cannot be changed, *no matter what* you say.

(3) When the *dependent clause comes first,* you need not decide whether it is restrictive or nonrestrictive. Use a **comma** to indicate where the main clause starts:

> *When the thunder started to roll,* we headed for the shore.
> *If he ordered the record,* he should pay for it.
> *Unless you exercise,* eating less will do little good.

NOTE: A few subordinators introduce *either a restrictive or a nonrestrictive* clause, depending on the meaning of the whole sentence. With *because* and *so that,* use *no punctuation* if the major point of the sentence follows the connective. Use the **comma** if the major point is in the main clause—with the adverbial clause merely giving additional information or explanation.

Can you see the difference in meaning, and can you *hear* the break signaled by the comma in the following pairs?

> Why are you leaving? I am leaving *because I have to study.*
> What are you doing? *I am leaving,* because I have to study.

> Why did you leave? I left *so that he could study.*
> What did you do? *I left,* so that he could study.

ACTIVITY

What would be the *most typical punctuation* at the break indicated in the following sentences? In which sentences should the two clauses be separated by a comma? Put C after the number of each such sentence. In which sentences should there be no punctuation? Put *No* after the number of each such sentence.

1. When humans invented picture writing ——————— they used symbols.
2. They used symbols ——————— because many things cannot be drawn.
3. We cannot draw a day ——————— although we can draw the sun.
4. We call an object a symbol ——————— when it stands for something else.
5. The sun is a symbol ——————— if it means "day."
6. Though symbols stand for something else ——————— their meaning is often obvious.
7. Other symbols are obscure ——————— so that we must use our imagination.
8. The Indians used picture writing ——————— before white men came to America.
9. The Indian symbols still make sense ——————— no matter how different the language of their users may have been from ours.
10. A simple circle may represent life ——————— whereas a shaded circle represents death.
11. Arrows mean war ——————— when they point in opposite directions.
12. If an arrow is broken ——————— it means peace.
13. Short wavy lines on a map may occur ——————— where someone had found water.
14. The same lines mean dryness ——————— if crossed lines cancel them out.
15. Very short upright lines show the young grass ——————— after it sprouts in the spring.
16. Scouts often learn these symbols ——————— so that they can write Indian letters to their friends.

Use the comma to set off nonrestrictive relative clauses.

Learn how to punctuate two special kinds of dependent clauses. The relative pronouns (*who, whom, whose, which, that*) start a **relative clause.** Relative clauses fill in information about one of the nouns in the main clause:

Bart owned a plane, *which took mail to the islands.*
The boy *who had borrowed my bicycle* had disappeared.
The team *that had won the game* celebrated its victory.
We could not find the house *to which we had been invited.*

M4c
Relative and Noun
Clauses

That and question words like *why, how, where,* and *when* are used as special connectives starting a **noun clause.** A noun clause takes the place of one of the nouns in the main part of the sentence:

The manager admitted *the truth.*
The manager admitted *that the price had changed.*

The principal asked *a question.*
The principal asked *why the door was locked.*

Remember three points:

(1) Use *no* comma with *who (whom, whose)* and *which* when the relative clause is **restrictive.** A restrictive clause is essential *to identify somebody* or something. It helps us single out *one* among many. It becomes an essential part of the sentence and is not set apart by any punctuation. But when somebody has already been identified (for instance, we know his name), the relative clause merely adds further information. It is **nonrestrictive**—not an essential part of the main statement. The nonrestrictive clause is set off by a **comma.**

Can you tell the difference in meaning, and can you *hear* the break with the nonrestrictive clause, in the following pairs?

Restrictive: We traced the man *who had ordered the tickets.*
                        (tells us *which one*)
Nonrestrictive: We asked Jim Brown, *who had ordered the tickets.*
                        (tells us something more about Jim Brown)

Restrictive: We looked for an actor *who could play Hamlet.*
                        (answers the question, *what kind* of actor?)
Nonrestrictive: She complimented my brother, *who had played Hamlet.*
                        (answers the question, *what about him?*)

When a nonrestrictive clause is inserted into the main clause, *two* commas are needed. Make sure to use both of these:

Our guide, *who spoke Spanish,* questioned the villagers.
B Company, *to which he had been assigned,* had already left.

(2) When *that* is used as a relative pronoun, the clause is restrictive and receives *no punctuation:*

We studied the specimens *that the class had collected.*
The car *that blocked the driveway* was towed away.
This is the house *that Jack built.*

I GREW UP IN THE NATION'S CAPITAL

What would be the *most typical punctuation* between the two clauses in each of the following sentences? After the number of each sentence, put the right abbreviation: *S* for semicolon; *C* for comma; *No* for no punctuation.

1. When I was a boy in Washington _____ the city seemed a place of endless delight.
2. The city then had open streetcars _____ few people drove automobiles.
3. I remember the taste of dust _____ when we went to the polo field near the Lincoln Memorial.
4. The streetcars are gone now _____ and the polo field is a divided parkway.
5. The monuments are the same _____ nevertheless, the city has changed.
6. Tourists still file up to the statue of Lincoln _____ who sits in a classically simple shrine.
7. They look at the Declaration of Independence _____ which is exhibited at the National Archives.
8. Thousands come for the Cherry Blossom Festival _____ however, the weather is unpredictable.
9. One year there was sleet _____ therefore, the tourist should bring an umbrella.
10. I never went to the marble halls _____ unless my family had visitors.
11. My mother felt _____ that I should accompany my sightseeing relatives.
12. I spent long hours in the lines of people _____ who were waiting for a tour of the White House.

That is often *omitted* in such sentences. Punctuation remains unchanged:

I counted the money *I had left.*
We studied the specimens *the class had collected.*
This is the house *Jack built.*

(3) Use *no punctuation* when *that* or question words like *why, how, where,* and *when* introduce a noun clause:

John announced *that he would run.*
The coach explained *how our performance could be improved.*

REMEMBER: Use the comma with *who* and *which* when they follow something that has already been singled out. Never use the comma with *that*, no matter what kind of clause it introduces.

Building the Habit: Each of the sentences in the following passage illustrates typical punctuation of relative and noun clauses. *Read this paragraph over several times* so that the punctuation rules it illustrates will become completely familiar to you. Be prepared to explain in class why each sentence was punctuated the way it was.

Rome, which was once the capital of a great empire, is still a world center. Americans who visit the city wander through its famous ruins. The Romans, who conquered half of the known world, loved monumental architecture. A huge arch of triumph honors an emperor who gained a great victory. The inscription tells us when the campaign took place. The arch shows that the Romans admired military strength. The pictures on the walls show the prisoners they took. We see the crowds that cheered the victorious general. The huge stadium that the Romans built for their spectacles is called the Colosseum. The gladiators, who were carefully trained for their profession, fought to the death here. Most of the structures the Romans built now lie in ruins. One exception is the Pantheon, which was once a pagan temple. The people who came there could worship many different gods. Tourists know that thousands of homeless cats live around this building. No one can say why the cats picked this spot. Some people claim that there were Egyptian cat gods among the gods in the ancient Pantheon.

ACTIVITY

In each of the following pairs, one sentence contains a non-restrictive clause that should be *set off by a comma*. The other sentence contains a restrictive clause and requires *no punctuation*. After the number of each pair, put the letter for the sentence that requires a comma.

Example: a. He was looking for George _____ who had the key.
             b. He was looking for the boy _____ who had the key.
(Answer)   *a*

1. a. The letter was for Uncle Jim _____ who lives up the street.
   b. The letter was for the people _____ who live upstairs.

2. a. Paolo admires Americans —————— who speak Portuguese.
   b. We met Paolo —————— who speaks Portuguese.

3. a. Jim is frank with people —————— whom he trusts.
   b. Jim is frank with his older sister —————— whom he trusts.

4. a. The police had condemned the building —————— that collapsed.
   b. A gust of wind struck our tent —————— which collapsed.

5. a. I talked to our student body president —————— who dislikes controversy.
   b. We elected a student body president —————— who dislikes controversy.

6. a. The school had a principal —————— who stressed achievement.
   b. The idea appealed to the principal —————— who stressed achievement.

7. a. Sue avoided Henry —————— who liked to tease her.
   b. Sue hates boys —————— who act tough.

8. a. The bill pleased the President —————— who had supported it from the start.
   b. The country needs a president —————— who can provide strong leadership.

Know when to use commas or other inside punctuation.

No punctuation is required *within* a single clause as long as it contains only the most basic elements. We do not put a comma between a subject and its verb or between a verb and its object. Nor do we use a comma when we proceed from these basic elements and add phrases that state circumstances, reasons, or conditions:

Philip	ate	his breakfast	in a hurry.
His father	had been	a sergeant	during the war.
Jim	left	school	to find a job.

"Inside" punctuation becomes necessary when we insert things that make such a simple sentence more complicated. A simple sentence proceeds smoothly, without a break. A more complicated sentence may contain signals that make us slow down, or stop temporarily, or even take a short detour.

COMMAS FOR INSIDE PUNCTUATION

A SUMMARY

The *comma* used for inside punctuation appears with the following sentence elements:

(1) *nonrestrictive modifiers*—modifiers *not used* to single out one or one of a kind:

> The Lincoln Memorial, *a magnificent structure*, was next.

(2) *sentence modifiers*—modifiers that seem to apply to the sentence as a whole rather than to any one part:

> *To keep out the deer*, we built a wooden fence.

(3) *series* of three or more elements of the same kind:

> We talked about *art, music, and poetry.*

(4) *dates, addresses, and measurements* with two or more parts:

> The family had moved to *Lincoln, Nebraska.*

(5) *interchangeable adjectives* modifying the same noun:

> The settlers discovered a *cool, moist* valley.

(6) *names, questions, and comments* added to a sentence:

> Your application, *John*, has been approved.

(7) *alternatives* inserted for contrast after *not* or *never:*

> I wanted the hoe, *not the spade.*

M5a
How to Punctuate
Modifiers

Use commas to set off nonrestrictive modifiers.

The basic elements in a sentence are often accompanied by modifiers that clarify or in some way limit their meaning. Learn to recognize the basic situations where a modifier might require a comma:

(1) *Modifiers may follow a noun.* Sometimes such a modifier helps us single out one thing among several or one kind of thing among several kinds. It narrows the possibilities; it helps us identify something. Such a modifier is **restrictive** and requires *no punctuation:*

COMMAS MAKE A DIFFERENCE

What difference do commas make in each of the following pairs?

I hear somebody calling Tom.
I hear somebody calling, Tom.

The teacher stopped giving me angry looks.
The teacher stopped, giving me angry looks.

Jim, my hamster, died.
Jim, my hamster died.

When eating, chickens make a clucking noise.
When eating chickens, make a clucking noise.

Donald Duck!
Donald, duck!

Smiling, Jack left town.
Smiling Jack left town.

While eating, the natives drink freely,
While eating the natives, drink freely.

During the evening, prayer meetings were held.
During the evening prayer, meetings were held.

RESTRICTED

Only Employees
With
Identity Cards
Are Allowed
Beyond
This Point.

Your friend *with the red cap* borrowed my book.
(Which friend? The one *with the red cap*)

We talked to the men *guarding the gate*.
(Which men? Those *guarding the gate*)

When something has already been clearly identified, the modifier merely adds further information. It does not single something out; it just tells us more about it. Such a modifier is **nonrestrictive** and is typically set off by a **comma**. If the sentence continues after the modifier, two commas are required:

I talked to Mr. Greene, *the new coach*.
(After a proper name, the modifier gives further information)

Jim, *dressed in a pink shirt*, stood outside the door.
(The modifier tells us more about Jim)

His new Buick, *parked illegally*, had been towed away.
(The modifier gives further details)

NON-RESTRICTED

All Employees
Full-time or
Part-time, Are
Allowed
In This Area.

BUILDING THE
HABIT

GERMAN PRINTER INVENTS MOVABLE TYPE

Each of the sentences in the following passage illustrates typical punctuation of modifiers. *Read this paragraph over several times* so that the punctuation rules it illustrates will become completely familiar to you. Be prepared to explain in class why each sentence was punctuated the way it was.

For several thousand years, books were handwritten. To make a single copy of a book, a scribe worked for many months. Using expensive parchment, the copyist copied each word with his pen. Chaucer, the first great English poet, was worried about mistakes made by these scribes. The Chinese, using old rags, first made good cheap paper. Wooden seals, carved by hand, stamped designs on playing cards. Imitating the Chinese, some European printers carved the text for a whole page into a wooden block. A printer using these blocks could produce several copies of a book at the same time. This method, unfortunately, still took much time. The men making the blocks carved separately every letter of every page. Gutenberg, the famous German printer, perfected a better method. Using metal instead of wood, a printer could make many copies of each letter from a single die. These letters, used over and over again, could be assembled in a page-size frame. One of the first books printed this new way was the Bible. The same basic method, improved over the years, is still used today.

Can you hear the slight break (or breaks) that set off these nonrestrictive modifiers when you read these sentences out loud?

(2) *Modifiers may apply to the sentence as a whole.* Such sentence modifiers are set off by one or more **commas** when they are stressed enough to stand out in speech, separated from the rest by a slight break. Always use this comma when a verbal or verbal phrase comes at the beginning of a sentence. Also, set off any verbal or verbal phrase that comes later in the sentence but seems to apply to the sentence as a whole:

To start the motor, turn the ignition key.
Smiling, she dropped his manuscript into the fire.

The price is not bad, *considering the location.*
Billie Jean King, *to name only one,* is a first-rate athlete.

With modifiers other than verbals this use of the comma is optional. As a rule of thumb, use the comma with any *introductory modifier of more than three words:*

> *After much fruitless talk,* the conference was adjourned.
> *With a twinkle in his eye,* Father took me out to the garage.

Set off expressions like *after all, of course, unfortunately, on the whole, as a rule, certainly,* and *on the other hand:*

> You will put everything back in order, *of course.*
> No one, *unfortunately,* had any matches.
> *On the whole,* we are satisfied with the results.

ACTIVITY 1

In each of the following pairs, one sentence contains a non-restrictive modifier that should be *set off* by one or more commas. The other sentence contains a restrictive modifier and requires *no punctuation.* After the number of each pair, put the letter for the sentence that *requires one or more commas.*

Example: a. Gutenberg ———— the German printer ————
             used metal type.
         b. The printers ———— using metal type ————
             learned from Gutenberg.

(Answer)   *a*

1. a. President Truman ———— known for his blunt language ———— made a speech.
   b. A president ———— known for blunt language ———— may offend voters.

2. a. I looked for the guard ———— assigned to the gate.
   b. I looked for Jim ———— my best friend.

3. a. Tourists ———— leaving the country ———— need passports.
   b. Her father ———— planning a trip abroad ———— needed a passport.

4. a. The boy ———— driving the car ———— wore a hat.
   b. The driver was Jim ———— wearing his new hat.

5. a. High schools ———— located in rural districts ———— offered few science courses.
   b. Roosevelt High School ———— located in a rural district ———— offered few science courses.

6. a. Mr. Thorpe _____ the new principal _____ announced the awards.
   b. The man _____ announcing the awards _____ is our new principal.

7. a. We lived in a town _____ hidden in a small valley.
   b. We moved to Seattle _____ a much larger town.

8. a. His oldest sister _____ a junior _____ joined our group.
   b. Girls _____ joining the group _____ must be juniors.

ACTIVITY 2

Which of the following sentences *need a comma* at the space indicated? Put *C* after the number of each such sentence. Put *No* after the number of a sentence if no punctuation is required. Be prepared to explain in class why you would punctuate each sentence the way you did.

1. Irene, a bright and lively girl _____was envied by her friends.
2. The restaurant barred women _____ wearing jeans.
3. Considering his lack of experience _____ he did well.
4. A school, after all _____ is not a private club.
5. Our swimming team _____ determined to win, worked hard all summer.
6. I never liked the man _____ to tell you the truth.
7. The man sitting on the porch _____ seemed very old.
8. The class studied magazine articles _____ concerned with foreign policy.
9. He was chatting with Dr. Reagan _____ the school physician.
10. Swerving violently _____ the truck went off the road.
11. My brother is never talkative _____ early in the morning.
12. To start the day right _____ he exercised for half an hour.
13. John memorized statistics _____ about baseball players.
14. His record, on the whole _____ was satisfactory.

M5b
How to Punctuate Equal
Parts

Use commas where several elements of the same kind appear in a sentence.

In the typical sentence, several equal parts may work together. The same verb may have several subjects. The same noun may have several modifiers. When we have several parts of the same kind, there is often a connective like *and* or *or* to **coordinate** them; that is, to tie them together. Often there are punctuation marks *in addition to* or *in place of* such a connective.

Notice how several items of the same kind take the place of a single sentence part in each of the following examples:

Jeremy helped us pack.
Tim, Ed, and Jeremy helped us pack.

Today is *Friday.*
Today is *Friday, September 4.*

The teacher gave us a *difficult* assignment.
The teacher gave us a *long, difficult* assignment.

Learn to recognize the situations where such coordinated elements might require commas or other punctuation:

(1) *Three or more elements of the same kind* are called a **series.** In the most common kind of series, **commas** appear between the elements of a series, with the last comma followed by a connective that ties the whole group together. Study this "*A, B,* and *C*" pattern in each of the following examples:

Jean, Betty, and *Mary* went swimming together.
Fred had *a dog, a cat,* and *a pet raccoon.*
He *smiled, shook* hands, and *asked* us in.
The valley floor was *rocky, arid,* and *hot.*

The slots in such a series may be filled by whole clauses, each with its own subject and predicate:

The *earth shook,* the *walls trembled,* and *pictures crashed* to the floor.

The last comma in a series is *optional.* Use it in your own writing, because it is never wrong:

The speaker discussed *voting rights, farm income,* and *foreign aid.*

Sometimes the separate parts of a series *already contain commas.* We then use **semicolons** instead of additional commas to show the major breaks:

Three other people were in the car with him: Elinor, his older sister; Jim, a cousin from Georgia; and Albert, his best friend.

(2) *Dates, addresses, page references,* and similar information often consist of two or more parts. Use **commas** between the dif-

ferent elements with another comma *after the whole group,* unless the last word is at the same time the last word of the sentence:

The date was *Monday, August 9, 1965.*
Monday, August 9, 1965, was a memorable day.

Send our mail to *34 Pine Street, Dearborn, Michigan.*
Lakeside Township, Illinois, is near Chicago.

Look at *Chapter 5, page 43.*
Chapter 3, Volume II, deals with regional history.

2031 Market Street, St. Louis, Mo.

DETROIT, MICHIGAN

SUNDAY, FEBRUARY 4, 1976

1808 BROADWAY, NEW YORK

WINDSOR, ONTARIO

Commas also separate the different parts of *measurements* that use more than one unit of measurement. Here no additional comma is used after the last item:

Her uncle was *six feet, two inches* tall.
Nine pounds, three ounces is heavy for this kind of fish.

(3) *Two or more adjectives* may modify the same noun. Sometimes these come in different layers. For instance, we first call someone a *public servant* and then say what kind: a *loyal public servant. Loyal* and *public* are not interchangeable (a *public loyal servant* would not make sense). When two adjectives *are* inter-

changeable, they may be coordinated by *and* or, instead, by a
comma:

a dirty *and* shaggy dog
a *dirty, shaggy* dog

a long *and* difficult assignment
a *long, difficult* assignment

happy *and* carefree crowds
happy, carefree crowds

Use the *and*-test to decide whether to put in this comma:

a delicious hot dog   (**NOT:** a delicious *and* hot dog)
a dry, hot summer   (**COULD BE:** a dry *and* hot summer)

ACTIVITY

Which of the following sentences *need a comma* at the space
indicated? Put *C* after the number of each such sentence. Put *No*
after the number of the sentence if no punctuation is required.
Be prepared to explain in class why you would punctuate each sentence the way you marked it.

1. The company had an office on Independence Square _____
    Philadelphia.
2. Mr. Greene was a popular _____ friendly teacher.
3. The smallest pony stood exactly three feet _____ two inches
    high.
4. The picnic was set for Sunday _____ May 1.
5. He had moved from Dayton, Ohio _____ to Lubbock, Texas.
6. Six pounds, three ounces _____ is about an average weight.
7. Tom Paine was a courageous _____ passionate, and uncom-
    promising writer.
8. Paine was an eyewitness of the violent _____ French Revo-
    lution.
9. The passage was taken from Chapter 3 _____ page 65.
10. Taro root is cooked _____ pounded, and kneaded to make
    poi.
11. The Northwest has beautiful mountains _____ and lakes.
12. We now live at 584 Board Street _____ Boise, Idaho.
13. Our vacation started on a foggy _____ chilly day.
14. We resumed our familiar _____ daily routine.

CITIZEN TOM PAINE

Each of the sentences in the following paragraph illustrates typical punctuation of coordinated elements. *Read this paragraph several times* so that the punctuation rules it illustrates will become completely familiar to you. Be prepared to explain in class why each sentence was punctuated the way it was.

Thomas Paine served the cause of revolution in England, America, and France. He had been a sailor, a tax collector, and a teacher. He was an eager, tireless student of books and ideas. He helped hungry, discontented workers petition for higher wages. In 1774 Tom Paine came from Lewes, England, to Philadelphia, Pennsylvania. Benjamin Franklin had met him in London, recognized his talents, and recommended him as a worthy young man. In America Paine wrote newspaper articles, pamphlets, and books. His most famous article appeared on January 10, 1776. It denounced King George, called Britain an open enemy, and asked for a "Declaration for Independence." Paine's pamphlets on "The American Crisis" appeared between December 19, 1776, and December 9, 1783. These writings built up the fighting spirit of Washington's ragged, demoralized army. Paine attacked the summer soldier, the sunshine patriot, and the secret traitor. He always offered the reader "simple facts, plain arguments, and common sense." The strength of his writing lay in his fiery, passionate idealism and his courageous, indomitable spirit.

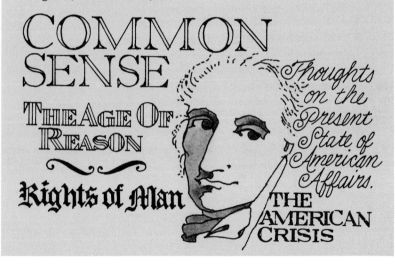

Use commas or other marks to set off interrupting elements.

Especially in conversation, we often *interrupt* a sentence. We interrupt what we are saying in order to address the listener by name. When we explain something, we stop to insert some information that we forgot to mention. There are three major ways of setting off such "interrupters" from the rest of the sentence:

(1) *Light interrupters* blend into the sentence with only a slight break. They are set off by **commas**. They need two commas when they appear in the middle of a sentence. They need only one comma when they are moved to the beginning or the end. Use the commas that go with light interrupters when you

—*address the listener or reader:*

> This, *Jim,* will be your room.
> The decision, *my friends,* cannot be postponed.

—*show how true something is, or who thought so:*

> The damage, *I am sure,* will be repaired.
> He is not coming, *it seems.*

—*start a sentence with* yes, no, well, *or* why:

> *Yes,* we heard about the accident.
> *Well,* boys will be boys.
> *Why,* I don't even know that man!

—*tack on a short question addressed to the listener:*

> You are my friend, *aren't you?*
> So he backed out, *did he?*

—*insert something for contrast after* not *or* never:

> The parents, *not the children,* were to blame.
> The club meets Mondays, *never on Tuesday.*

(2) *Heavy interrupters* cause a definite break in speech and are set off in writing by **dashes**. Overuse of the dash makes for jerky, disconnected writing. Use the dashes that go with heavy interrupters when you

—*stop in order to insert a complete sentence:*

> Police officers—*I know several personally*—are quite average people.
> In Tulsa—*we moved there in June*—I found many friends.

ON THE SET WITH BUSTER KEATON

The following sentences illustrate conventional punctuation in the English sentence. Study these examples of how things are done right. Be prepared to explain *why* each sentence was punctuated the way it was.

1. Between 1925 and 1930, hundreds of people were injured in film production in California.
2. Over fifty people—mostly stunt men and women—died.
3. To the stunt performer, any stunt is a "gag."
4. In Hollywood, California, falls used to be called "Brodies."
5. They were named after Steve Brodie, who jumped from the Brooklyn Bridge and lived.
6. A car driven by Lewis Jackson, who regularly drove in car stunts, left the road, killed two onlookers, and cut down the cameraman.
7. When the camera was found unharmed, the director used the film.
8. Buster Keaton, a great actor, was also a great stunt comic.
9. In his movies, trap doors open, cannons swivel, and bombs explode.
10. In one of Keaton's movies, a house crumples in a cyclone, and the entire front wall falls over him.
11. Buster is left untouched, because he stands in the gap left by the window.
12. Harold Lloyd was a famous comedian who wore a straw hat, horn-rimmed glasses, and a shy smile.
13. He performed many terrifying stunts, but he was nearly killed on a movie set in 1919.
14. Two fingers were blown off, one eye was severely damaged, and his face was lacerated.
15. Lloyd would dangle dangerously from a building over a crowded street; however, he always made it to safety.

—*insert a modifier that already contains commas:*

The new teacher—*a tall, handsome man*—looked at us with a smile.
My friends—*Bip, Shnorkel, and Bop*—were waiting outside.

—*make something stand out for an especially strong effect:*

He walked through the prison gates—*a free man.*
The poor, the crippled, the blind—these were the objects of his love and care.

(3) *Unimportant information* is often given in a lower tone of voice and appears in writing in **parentheses.** Use parentheses instead of dashes when you

—*insert a complete sentence as an aside:*

> Police officers *(I know several personally)* are quite average people.
> In Tulsa *(we moved there in June)* I found many new friends.

—*insert page references, dates, and the like as supplementary information:*

> The author's summary *(p. 45)* was badly needed.
> Her birthday *(June 2)* is still several months off.
> MacDonald *(sometimes spelled Macdonald)* is a common family name.

When a whole sentence appears *separately* in parentheses, it carries its own end punctuation with it:

> We gave him our telephone number. *(He never called.)*

ACTIVITY 1

Each of the sentences in the following paragraph illustrates typical punctuation of interrupters. *Read this paragraph over several times* so that the punctuation rules it illustrates will become completely familiar to you. Be prepared to explain in class why each sentence was punctuated the way it was.

> Today, dear John, I am going to discuss manners. Much of this, I am sure, will be familiar to you. Many sources—newspapers, magazines, and books—provide guidance on our social customs. Introductions (once a very formal matter) are now quite simple and natural. It is now entirely proper, most people feel, to introduce oneself. Asking another person's name—this takes a little more courage—is also quite all right. We usually introduce a man to a woman, not the woman to the man. The names, you will agree, should not be mumbled. The manner should be natural, not stiff. "Mrs. Burke, this is Bill Jones." Young people (you, for example) introduce their friends to their parents. "Mother, this is Joan." The man being introduced is expected to stand, isn't he? Women, I think, may remain seated. In other countries—in Europe, especially—women are expected to shake hands. Gentlemen of the old school (not many of them are left) will kiss the lady's hand. The lady must have the presence of mind to extend her hand the right way (at chest level, palm dawn). She must also avoid a stunned look and give the right response—a gracious smile.

ACTIVITY 2

In each of the following pairs, one word or group of words is used in two different ways. In one sentence, it is used as an interrupter, causing a slight break. It then needs to be *set off* by one or more commas. In the other sentence, it is used as part of the grammatical structure of the sentence, with no break in speech. It then requires *no punctuation.* After the number of each pair, put the letter of the sentence that *requires one or more commas.*

Example:　a. Jim ——————— please close the windows for me.

　　　　　　b. Jim ——————— finally closed the windows for me.

(Answer)　*a*

1. a. The new clerk was always early ——————— never too late.
   b. All year the new clerk was ——————— never too late.

2. a. I am sure ——————— of her honesty and devotion.
   b. The results ——————— I am sure ——————— will be favorable.

3. a. Jim showed ——————— Mrs. Brown ——————— the new design.
   b. Jim will show you the new design ——————— Mrs. Brown.

4. a. You are the new treasurer ——————— aren't you?
   b. Aren't you ——————— glad you were elected?

5. a. The figures ——————— it seems ——————— were inaccurate.
   b. It seems ——————— that the figures were inaccurate.

6. a. Why ——————— I never said such a thing.
   b. Why ——————— in the world did you tell him?

7. a. He was writing letters to ——————— dear friends.
   b. The need ——————— dear friends ——————— is desperate.

8. a. The class was intended for sophomores ——————— not juniors.
   b. Several students in the class were ——————— not juniors.

REVIEW ACTIVITY

Most of the sentences in this exercise illustrate *typical inside punctuation.* Put *S* for satisfactory after the number of each such sentence. The remaining sentences illustrate unsatisfactory inside punctuation. Put *U* after the number of each such sentence. Look especially for the following: (1) commas missing with material that is clearly nonrestrictive; (2) commas *used* with material that is clearly restrictive; (3) commas missing with coordinated and interrupting elements; (4) only one comma used where *two* are needed to set off an element in the middle of a sentence.

(Your teacher may ask you to revise unsatisfactory sentences. Be prepared to explain what was wrong with each sentence and why you revised it the way you did.)

1. The Stone Age, Bronze Age, and Iron Age have gone into history.
2. Now we are embarked on the most interesting of all—the calorie age!
3. Americans it seems, have become weight conscious.
4. We used to aim at being the mightiest nation not the thinnest.
5. Fat people were expected to be happy, friendly individuals.
6. Now we expect them to be disappointed disillusioned and neurotic.
7. Manufacturers, producing food, label every product "low in calories."
8. These words jump at the shopper from every can, box, and bottle in the store.
9. To judge from my own experience, teenagers are especially diet prone.
10. My own doctor, concerned about the teenager's health, counsels against fad diets.
11. My oldest sister, always eager to lose weight, tries them all.
12. Results unfortunately, are not guaranteed.
13. A person, eating everything in sight, may still stay thin.
14. People starving themselves still gain weight.
15. But there is no harm in trying, is there?
16. Pushing away the layer cake, let us reach for the Rye-Krisp.

Know how to work quoted material into your text.

**M6
QUOTATION**

Writers have to be able to show when they are repeating words and ideas not their own. They have to show by punctuation and other means that they are recording what somebody else said or copying what somebody else wrote.

Use quotation marks to set off someone's exact words.

**M6a
Direct Quotation**

When you repeat someone's exact words, you are using **direct** quotation. Though you may repeat only a part of what someone said or wrote, the part you do repeat must be *verbatim*—word for word the way it was first said. Material quoted word for word is enclosed in **quotation marks.** Usually, a **comma** separates the quotation from the introductory statement—the credit tag that identifies its source:

> The girl replied, "You told me all this before."
> "I know I can trust you," my father said.

The comma is used regardless of whether the credit tag appears at the beginning or at the end. If the credit tag *splits a complete sentence*, you need two commas:

> "The cauliflower," Mark Twain said, "is only a cabbage with a college education."
> "When I read Homer," he said, "all men look like giants."

If the credit tag separates two complete sentences, you need a comma before it and *a period* after it:

> "Let them charge again," the general replied. "Men cannot live forever."

When a quotation ends or is interrupted, commas and periods stay *within* the quotation. They come *before* the final quotation mark, as in all the above examples. Semicolons go outside the quotation; they follow the final quotation mark:

> He said, "We have done all we can"; nevertheless, the work went on.

Question marks go inside the quotation if the quoted part asks a question. They go outside if you are asking a question *about the quotation*. Exclamation points go inside if the quoted part was shouted or had strong stress on it. They go outside if you are making a strong point *about the quotation:*

> Everyone asked us, "What can we do to help?"
> Was it Napoleon who said, "There shall be no Alps"?
>
> Fred kept shouting, "They are gaining on us!"
> Don't ever say to me, "No one told me"!

You will encounter a few important variations:

(1) *Short quotations* often appear without a comma to set them off, especially when they are part of a longer sentence:

> He always said "Good morning."
> Saying "I told you so" only makes matters worse.

No comma is used *after* a quotation ending with a question mark or exclamation point.

> "What happened?" my brother asked.

WHAT THE SHIPWRECKED SAILOR SAID

Many humorous stories hinge on a clever answer or unexpected reply. Look at the way quotations are handled in each of the following examples. Can you explain why each sentence was punctuated the way it was?

The men on the stormy beach said, "Do you see that sailor holding on to the piece of wood?"

"We are coming out to rescue you!" they shouted to the shipwrecked man.

He called back across the water, "What country is this?"

He heard voices shouting "New Jersey" across the waves.

"Maybe," he shouted back, "I'll float a little farther."

Did you hear about the 94-year-old man who said: "I've been smoking four packs a day since I was twelve years old"?

A tobacco company executive told him, "We need you! We are filming some television commercials," he told the old fellow. "Let us put your story on film for a thousand dollars."

"When do you want me?" the old-timer asked.

"Come to the office marked 'Public Relations' at nine in the morning."

"That's too early," the old man replied. "I don't stop coughing until noon."

Bonus: Find a conversation that ends in a clever answer or unexpected reply. Write it down using quotation marks as needed for the different bits of dialogue.

(2) *Long quotations* are often introduced by a **colon** rather than by a comma:

The line ran: "We are strangers here; the world is from of old."

Long quotations running to more than ten lines of prose or more than one full line of poetry are usually treated as **block quotations.** They are *not* enclosed in quotation marks but instead indented and, in a typed paper, single-spaced.

(3) *Quotations within a quotation* would be confusing if simply indicated by a second set of the usual double quotation marks. Use **single quotation marks** to show that the person you are quoting is in turn quoting somebody else:

In the words of Senator Clarke, "Let us always remember the dictator who said, 'If I were to grant freedom of the press, my power would not last three days.' "

(4) *Omissions* from a quotation are shown by three spaced periods, called an **ellipsis.** Use four periods if the omission includes the period at the end of a complete sentence:

> Plato said, "All good poets . . . write their verses when inspired or possessed."

(5) *Comments or corrections* added to a quotation are inserted between **square brackets:**

> The report said: "On Monday, October 3 [actually October 4], we set out across the ice for the mainland."

Notice that in all the examples in this section the first word of a quotation is *capitalized.* This is done whenever it would have been capitalized anyway if the quotation were written down separately, without being quoted in your text.

ACTIVITY 1

The sentences in each of the following groups illustrate different ways of punctuating quotations. *Read them over several times* so that the punctuation rules they illustrate will become completely familiar to you. Be prepared to explain in class how each example differs from the others in the same group.

1. Ambrose said, "A coward thinks with his legs."
   "A coward thinks with his legs," Ambrose said.
   "A coward," Ambrose said, "thinks with his legs."
   "Jim is a coward," Ambrose said. "He thinks with his legs."

2. The author wrote: "Love is a temporary insanity curable by marriage."
   The author wrote, "Love is . . . curable by marriage."
   Who said, "Love is curable by marriage"?
   He said, "Love is curable by marriage"!

3. Jim asked, "What does *platitude* mean?"
   Who said, "A platitude is a thought that snores"?
   He always said "How true!" when someone uttered a platitude.
   Fred announced, "Webster's [the collegiate edition] defines a platitude as a weak, trite saying."

4. "There's a unicorn in the garden," the man said to his wife.
   "The unicorn," his wife replied, "is a mythical beast."

"I saw a unicorn," the husband said. "It ate a lily."
"It's true," she told the police. "He said, 'I saw a unicorn.' "

5. "Did you know McGann?" my friend asked.
I replied, "No, I didn't know McGann"; nevertheless, he went on.
"He was a great practical joker," my friend said. "He was always stretching string across passageways or putting snakes in people's boots."
"Dear me!" I said. "What a humorist!"

ACTIVITY 2

At the space indicated in each of the following sentences, a quotation mark is required, usually followed or preceded by one other mark. In one or two cases, more than two marks are required. Write the missing marks (in the right order) after the number of each sentence.

Example: "He plays the piano _____ I said.
(Answer)   ,"

1. "What did you learn today _____ my father said.
2. "The performance," the critic wrote _____ exceeded all expectations."
3. "There's a man at the door _____ he observed casually.
4. "It's too late," Jim said _____ All the stores are closed."
5. He shouted, "Don't ever come back again _____
6. Who said, "Hunger never saw bad bread _____
7. The last sentence read: "May future generations say of him, 'He kept us out of war _____
8. "When the well is dry," Benjamin Franklin said _____ we know the worth of water."
9. Why did you tell him, "Things will get worse _____
10. Mumbling "I am sorry _____ cannot make up for what you did.
11. He asked everyone in turn, "Is it true _____
12. "Hope and fear _____ the author said, "are inseparable."
13. "I weep for you _____ the walrus said. "I deeply sympathize."
14. "Don't give yourself airs _____ he shouted.

Use no punctuation with indirect quotations, but set off phrases quoted verbatim.

We do not always reproduce the exact wording of what someone said. Instead we translate what the person said into our own

M6b
Indirect Quotation and
Words Set Off

words. This way of quoting someone is called **indirect** quotation. Typically, indirect quotations are joined to the introductory statement by the special connective *that* or question words like *how, why, what,* and *where.* Such indirect quotations fit into the sentence *without punctuation*—no comma, no quotation marks:

Someone announced *that the plane would be late.*
Fred asked *how we could help.*

A direct quotation looks at things from the point of view of the *speaker*, at the time the speaker was talking. An indirect quotation looks at things from the point of view of the person who *quotes*, at the time the quoter is quoting. Notice how references to persons and to time change in the following pairs:

Direct: Fred asked, "How *can I* help *you?*"
Indirect: Fred asked how *he could* help *us.*

Direct: The manager told her, "*Your* hours *will* be changed."
Indirect: The manager told her that *her* hours *would* be changed.

Even in indirect quotations, you may want to show that you have preserved *some of the original words*—because they are striking, or typical of the speaker, or especially important. Enclose such words and phrases (but not the rest of the quotation) in **quotation marks**:

Emerson said that pictures should not be "too picturesque."
The speaker kept saying that we needed a "constructive approach."
The chief claimed that "professional agitators" caused the riot.

In addition to such directly quoted words and phrases, the following are usually set off from the writer's own text:

(1) *Technical or unusual terms* are put in **quotation marks** to show that they are new or deserve special attention:

The engine had an "afterburner" especially designed for this plane.

(2) *Words discussed as words,* as in a discussion of word meanings, are indicated by **italics** (or by underlining in typed and handwritten papers):

The word *imply* means to hint or give to understand.

(3) *Words borrowed from foreign languages* and still considered foreign, like many legal and scientific terms, are indicated by **italics**:

Poison sumac (*Rhus vernix*) has spoiled many a vacation trip.

(4) *Titles of complete publications*—such as books and magazines—are indicated by **italics.** Titles for *separate parts* of a publication—such as a chapter of a book, an article in a magazine, a poem in a collection—are enclosed in quotation marks:

He wrote a chapter called "Greek Music" for the *Music Guide.*

Students often use quotation marks to set off words (often slang terms) for humorous effect. This practice is much overdone.

ACTIVITY

The following passages illustrate different ways of *setting off individual words and phrases.* Explain why each word or phrase was set off the way it was.

1. Winston Churchill was the first to say that an "iron curtain" separated Russia from the West.
2. The word *ersatz* is German for a cheap substitute.
3. The passenger pigeon *(Ectopistes migratorius)* is now extinct.
4. The instruction sheet mentioned a "reactivating lever."
5. Jim said that we should "hang our heads in shame."
6. An *aficionado* is a fan or devotee.
7. His first book was called *How to Tell Your Friends from the Apes.*
8. Tennyson's "Ulysses" was included in *Adventures in Poetry.*
9. Be sure to read "The Plight of the Schools" in the current *Atlantic.*
10. Mr. Green assigned Chapter 3, "Reptiles I Have Known," in the *Handbook of Zoology.*

REVIEW ACTIVITY

After the number of each sentence, write down the punctuation marks missing at the space indicated. Write *No* if no punctuation is required.

1. The hero asked, "Where did you put my boots ——   ——
2. Jim was fond of unoriginal sayings, like ———— Age before beauty."
3. "Humor," the writer said ———— is the highest product of civilization."
4. The officer told us ———— that the roads were covered with ice.
5. "My father," the stranger said, "used to quote Ben Franklin: 'He that lies down with dogs shall rise up with fleas ————
6. Was it Mark Twain who said, "Training is everything ————

7. The teacher asked me —————— why I was always late.

8. "Why are you always late —————— the teacher said.

9. "I hate you —————— Linda shouted at her startled escort.

10. Mrs. Post called such remarks conversational —————— door slammers."

11. Her "Dinner is served —————— was the signal for a wild scramble to the dining room.

12. "The waiter —————— Jim reported, "looked at the dime as though it were an insect."

13. Her uncle was fond of saying —————— that age does not guarantee wisdom.

14. "You are early," my uncle said —————— The fair starts next week."

M7
MANUSCRIPT FORM

Hand in neat and legible copy observing standard form.

The outward appearance of your paper shows what you think of your reader. It shows whether you care about your reader's convenience, eyesight, standards of neatness.

M7a
Preparing Copy

Write or type your papers neatly, legibly, and in standard form.

Pleasing, legible **handwriting** is the result of effort and practice. Keep the loops open in letters like *e*. Keep the dots right over each *i* and cross your *t*'s. Do not run together combinations like *mm, mn, ing, tion*. Avoid excessive slanting and excessive crowding; use letters of the exact standard size and proportion. Flourishes and squiggles do not impress the reader; they annoy the reader. If your teacher does not require any special type of theme paper, use paper of *standard size,* ruled in *wide* lines.

Competent **typing** is a skill that a student can hardly do without. Type the original copy on *nontransparent* paper—unlined, of standard size. Semitransparent sheets (onionskin) are for carbon copies.

(1) *Double-space* all material except block quotations and footnotes. Leave two spaces after a period or other end punctuation. Use two hyphens—with no space on either side—to make a dash.

(2) *Leave adequate margins.* Leave about an inch and a half on the left and at the top. Leave about an inch on the right and at the bottom. *Indent* the first line of a paragraph—about an inch in longhand, or five spaces in typed copy.

PRINT CARRIES THE MESSAGE.

THE GAZETTE

☆ ☆ ☆

HORSEMEAT BOOM

IMPRESSIVE
CONCERT

SALES INDICATE A RETURN
TO THE PONY EXPRESS

Tie Rally
Salvages

CATALOG

DESIGNED
FOR PEOPLE

(3) *Capitalize words in the title* of your paper as you would in a title you merely mention (see **M 2a**). Observe the three *don'ts* for the title you give to your own theme: Do *not* underline or italicize it; do *not* enclose it in quotation marks (unless it is indeed a quotation); do *not* put a period at the end (but use a question mark or exclamation point where needed).

> How to Become Extinct
> Is War Inevitable?
> Help Prevent Crime!

(4) *Proofread a first draft carefully* for hasty misspellings or typographical errors. The following last-minute **corrections** are permissible on the final copy if they are neat and few in number:

—Draw a line through words or phrases you want to *omit*. Do *not* use parentheses or square brackets for this purpose.

—To *correct* a word, draw a line through it and write the corrected word in the space immediately above. Do *not* cross out or insert individual letters.

```
                    quickly
          He  quiely changed his tune.
```

—To *add* a missing word, insert a caret (∧) and write the word immediately above.

```
                 had
          We been waiting for a long time.
             ∧
```

—To change the *paragraphing* of a paper, insert the symbol ¶ to indicate an additional paragraph break. Insert *no*¶ in the margin to indicate that an existing paragraph break should be ignored.

```
....was finished. ¶The second part of the program.....
```

(5) *Divide words as recommended by your dictionary.* Most dictionaries use centered dots to show the possible breaks (com·pli·ment). Divide words only if otherwise you would have an extremely uneven right margin. Remember the following points:

—Do not set off *single letters,* as for instance in *about, alone, many, via.* Do not set off the *–ed* ending in words like *asked* and *complained.*

—When a word is clearly a *combination* of other meaningful parts, divide at the point where the original parts are joined: *blue·bird, harm·ful.*

—Divide *hyphenated words* only at the point where the hyphen occurs, for instance in *un-American* or *sister-in-law.*

—Do not divide the *last word* on a page.

(6) *Underline,* or italicize, *for emphasis,* but use this device only rarely, when clearly appropriate:

> The teacher was expected to present the evaluation to the parent *in person.*

Use abbreviations and figures only where they are appropriate.

Abbreviations and figures save much time and space. In ordinary writing, however, avoid excessive shortcuts. The following **abbreviations** are *generally acceptable* in ordinary writing:

(1) Before or after *names,* the titles *Mr., Mrs., Ms., Dr., St.* (Saint); the abbreviations *Jr.* and *Sr.;* degrees like *M.D.* and *Ph.D.:*

> We were introduced to Mr. and Mrs. Jones.
> The sign identified him as John E. Gielgud, Jr., M.D.

(2) Before or after *numerals,* the abbreviations *No.,* A.D. and B.C., A.M. and P.M. (or *a.m.* and *p.m.*); and the symbol $:

> The battle of Actium was fought in 31 B.C.
> The plane leaves at 9:25 A.M.

(3) *Initials* standing for the name of agencies, business firms, technical processes and the like, providing these initials are in common use:

> Mr. Smith had been an agent for the FBI.
> We studied an article about UNESCO.

(4) *Latin abbreviations* such as *e.g.* (for example), *etc.* (and so on), *i.e.* (that is), though the modern tendency is to use the corresponding English expressions instead:

> The writer ignored important new resources, e.g. nuclear energy.

Other abbreviations are acceptable in addresses, business records, and the like but are *spelled out* in ordinary writing:

(1) Names of *countries, states, streets,* and the like (with a few exceptions: *U.S.S.R.; Washington, D.C.*):

> His first stop in the United States was Buffalo, New York.
> Her office was on Union Street in Pittsburgh, Pennsylvania.

(2) *Units of measurement* like *lb.* (pound), *oz.* (ounce), *ft.* (foot), with the exception of *mph* and *rpm:*

> The first fish he caught weighed three pounds, two ounces.

Figures are *generally acceptable* in references to dates and years, street numbers and page numbers, exact sums and technical measurement, especially those referring to percentages or including decimal points:

He was born on May 13, 1922.
They lived at 1078 Washington Avenue.
The town had 23,456 inhabitants.
The rate had gone up 17.5 percent.

The following are usually *spelled out:* numbers from one to ten; round numbers requiring no more than two words; a number at the beginning of a sentence. Notice that, when they are spelled out, compound numbers from 21 to 99 are hyphenated.

The first issue of our paper sold about three hundred copies.
Twenty-five years ago he was not even born.
The nursery school was for children from two to six years old.

ACTIVITY

Most of the sentences in the following exercise use *abbreviations and numbers* in a way that would be satisfactory in ordinary writing. Put *S* after the number of each such sentence. The remaining sentences need to be revised. Put *R* after the number of each such sentence. Be prepared to explain why and how each of these should be revised. (Your instructor may ask you to write down the revised versions.)

1. Jim announced that exactly $14.87 remained in the treasury.
2. 23 of the students had never bought a hard-cover book.
3. The directory listed them as Dr. and Mrs. Mark Hunt, Jr.
4. The PTA invited a representative of the AFL-CIO.
5. Jr. always practiced on the violin in the A.M.
6. The auditorium had room for roughly two thousand people.
7. His card file listed 2350 names.
8. The firm was located at Terre Haute, Ind.
9. The shelf was about two feet and three inches long.
10. According to the guide, the tree was 100 years old.
11. They had moved from Acorn, Illinois, to Washington, D.C.
12. The fullback weighed one hundred and twenty-six lbs.
13. Plato was born in 428 B.C.
14. The library closes at 9:30 P.M.

WORDS IN PRINT

In the mechanics of writing, we are expected to follow certain basic conventions. But at the same time we have some freedom of choice. The following assignments for further study give you a chance to explore some of the variations and complications encountered by the attentive reader of the printed page.

Assignment 1: The following words may cause spelling problems for you as you extend your range of study and reading. Look up the unfamiliar ones in your dictionary. For each word, do the following: (1) Make sure you know the meaning. (2) Make sure you know something about the uses or the history of the word that will help you remember it. (3) Make sure you have mastered the spelling of the word.

alleviate	financier	miniature
apparatus	hypocrisy	optimism
conscientious	initiative	parallel
dilemma	intellect	philosophy
discrimination	interference	propaganda
disillusioned	laboratory	psychology
escapade	maneuver	reminisce
fallacy	mathematics	sociology
fantasy	medieval	tyranny
fictitious	melancholy	vacuum

Assignment 2: What is the *difference* in meaning and in use between the two members of each pair? What is the *connection* between the two members of each pair?

catholic—Catholic; evangelical—Evangelical; highlands—Highlands; liberal—Liberal; orthodox—Orthodox; republican—Republican; socialist—Socialist

Assignment 3: The use of the *hyphen* is one of the least stable features of English spelling. Many words once kept separate are now hyphenated; many words once hyphenated are now written solid. In current issues of newspapers and magazines, find fifteen to twenty examples of hyphenated words. Which of them seem to fit in with the conventions described in this chapter? Are there any general observations you can make?

Assignment 4: Examine the use of *punctuation between clauses* in the following passage. Does it conform to the conventions outlined in this chapter? Are there any complications? Ask the same questions about other aspects of the mechanics of writing—punctuation as well as use of capitals, hyphens, apostrophes, figures.

Star Gazing in the Desert

When night fell on the desert, I understood at once the ancient Arabs' proficiency in astronomy. By day the featureless blue sky held little to tell him, but now the black sky was ablaze with stars. The Milky Way shone with a soft radiance, and its dark bays and indentations were as clearly demarcated as a coast on a nautical chart. First-magnitude stars glowed like lamps, and the constellations were brilliantly outlined. Small wonder that the Arab wanderer of the desert should become adept at finding his way by the stars.

During the Dark Ages, it was the Arabs who kept alight the lamp of knowledge lighted by the Greeks. Of the 57 stars chosen by international agreement for navigation purposes, 38 have names of Arab origin, and some of the commonest words used by navigators come from the Arabic: azimuth, zenith, nadir, alidade, almanac.

—Luis Marden, "The Other Side of Jordan," *National Geographic*

Assignment 5: Most newspapers and some magazines use *open punctuation*—a style that omits some of the commas expected in more formal writing. Study the following typical newspaper report. Where are commas used in accordance with the conventions you have studied? Where are there commas missing that would follow the conventions of a more formal style?

Ireland, oasis for Britain's criminals, will close its doors to fugitives from British justice. Under a new extradition treaty police will begin rounding up an estimated 70 men wanted for crimes in Britain. Some have turned over a new leaf, married and become respectable. Most of the men are petty thieves, wife-beaters and runaway husbands. Some of the fugitives are lawyers from Northern Ireland, the British-ruled part of the country. They are accused of fleeing across the border with their clients' money. There has been a rumor that a luxury yacht lies offshore near Baltimore, County Cork, ready to take off a load of villains.

CHAPTER 7

Resources: Letters, Dictionaries, Libraries

R1
WRITING A LETTER

Write letters that serve their purpose.

A letter is your representative; know how to make it welcome. If you are busy or angry when you are writing it, remember that the letter will actually do its job at a time when your busy or angry moments have already passed.

R1a
The Friendly Letter

Make a friendly letter as personal as a personal visit.

The friendly letter might be called "the conversational letter" or "the visiting letter" or "the personal letter" since it is essentially a "visit" on paper.

Use plain white stationery and blue or black ink for a friendly letter. Until recently, it was considered too businesslike and cold to typewrite a personal letter, but most people now appreciate the legibility of print and do not object to receiving a typewritten friendly letter.

The form of a friendly letter is simple. The heading (sender's address and the date) is often written to the right of center near the top of the page. Leaving some space, the salutation (Dear _____) is written at the left-hand margin. Then, leaving a little space again, the body of the letter is written in paragraph form. The closing is at the right under the sender's address and date. *Sincerely, Sincerely yours, With love,* or *With fond regards* are often used as closings. The signature must be handwritten even if the letter itself is typed.

The envelope should be addressed as shown below. A return address should always appear, preferably in the upper left-hand corner.

```
Shiela Kelly
43 Hempstead Road
Dayton, Ohio   45445
```

```
                  Miss Marilyn Koch
                  445 Goodhue Drive
                  Northfield, Minnesota   55057
```

A comma always separates city from state (Tacoma, Washington) or city from country (Paris, France). A comma separates day from year (May 1, 1967). A period follows any abbreviation.

A comma or colon follows the salutation, and a comma follows the closing.

ACTIVITY

Pretend you have a good friend who went to the hospital for a grave operation, or who went traveling on a serious secret mission, or who was unjustly imprisoned. Tell about your life since your friend went away.

Use a business letter to secure action, information, or merchandise.

R1b
The Business Letter

Use white, single sheets of *standard-sized typewriter paper* (or printed letterhead paper). Envelopes should also be plain in either 6½ or 9½ inch width. If it is at all feasible, typewrite a business letter. A handwritten letter is acceptable, but the typewritten letter is preferred.

Make a carbon copy of every business letter you send. You will then have a record of your request or order. *Onionskin* paper is ideal for carbon copies. It is sometimes good to make an extra carbon copy to send to a third party who is concerned in the transaction; this is a simple way of keeping him informed of what you are doing about the situation.

The heading (address and date) is written at either the right- or the left-hand upper corner unless letterhead paper is used, in which case only the date is necessary. Leaving some space, the entire address of the letter's recipient, just as it will appear on the envelope, is written at the left-hand margin. Two typewriter lines below that is the salutation, which is "Dear Mr. _____," "Dear Mrs. (Miss) (Ms.) _____," or the formal "Dear Sir," "Dear Madam," or "Gentlemen."

Two lines below the salutation begins the body of the letter. Two lines below the body appears the closing, the formal "Yours truly," or "Yours very truly" or the more common "Sincerely" or "Sincerely yours."

Under the closing is the signature, which must be handwritten even if the letter is typed. It is helpful to type one's name below the signature, and a woman may put "Miss," "Mrs.," or "Ms." in parentheses before her name. The representative of a group should write her or his position and the name of the group after the signature.

Resources

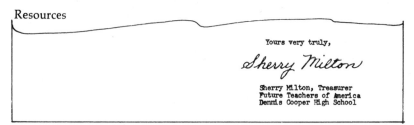

Yours very truly,

Sherry Milton

Sherry Milton, Treasurer
Future Teachers of America
Dennis Cooper High School

The envelope should be addressed just as the heading. The return address should be in the upper left-hand corner.

NOTE: Commas are placed between city and state or city and country, between day and year, and before Inc. (incorporated). If a title is used on the same line as a proper name, a comma comes between the name and the title:

Charles Pattus, Secretary
Student Council

A colon (not a comma) comes after the salutation and a comma after the closing. All abbreviations are followed by periods.

ACTIVITY

Is there something you have always wanted but never had the money for? Pretend you have suddenly inherited enough money for your "dream." Write to an appropriate business or institution telling them what you want.

R1c
The Social Note

Send a note containing a single message.

A note may be written on regular stationery or on correspondence cards or small folders called notepaper that are often decorated. The content keeps to one subject and requires no answer.

(1) *The thank-you note:* If a close relative, such as your grandfather, sends you a present, write a full-length letter to him covering matters in addition to your appreciation. But, if someone who is not a close relative sends you a gift, a thank-you note is appropriate. The note should mention the item and express appreciation for it and the thoughtfulness of the sender. If you have special use for the gift, the donor will be pleased to hear about it.

(2) *The bread-and-butter note:* A thank-you letter is in order after you have enjoyed someone's hospitality. If you spend the night with a school friend who is apt to spend the night at your house before long, a verbal expression of appreciation is enough. But if you are a guest for several days, or if you take a trip as the guest of a friend, write to thank the parents. It is good to mention an outstanding treat or aspect of the visit.

170 Northland Ave.
Buffalo, New York 14228
June 28 1975

Dear Dr. and Mrs. Buckner,

Thank you for letting Joe take me along when you went camping last week. It was fun in spite of the rain, or perhaps it was more fun because of the rain. So far I haven't been down with the pneumonia Dr. Buckner said we'd all get, and I hope none of you has either. The fact is I think I gained a couple of pounds from all the good food Mrs. Buckner cooked. I had a wonderful time. Thank you for taking me along.

Sincerely,
David

8210 Lawrence St.
Sioux Falls, S. Dak.
January 11, 1975

Dear Amy,

I was very sorry to hear about your father. I can imagine what a shock his death was to your whole family. He was always so nice to me when I came to your house that I am going to miss him, too.

I hope you will soon be back to school. I am taking complete history and biology notes, which I will type up for you. If I can help in any other way, let me know.

With love,
Helen

50 Fairway Street
Wilmington, Delaware 19707
March 22, 1975

Dear Mrs. King:

I was thrilled with the stamp album you sent me for confirmation. I didn't expect anyone to remember that I collect stamps, and I was planning to buy the type of album you sent me. Now I will have extra money for stamps with which to start this book. Thank you for a wonderful gift.

Sincerely yours,
Bruce Carroll

(3) *The sympathy note:* Send condolences to a person who has lost a near relative or dear friend through death. There are printed cards to do this duty, but a personal note is a finer expression of sympathy.

ACTIVITIES

Using appropriate materials and form:

1. Write a note of thanks either for a gift or for hospitality.

2. Write a note of sympathy. Choose one of the following: Write to the family of a prominent person whose death has been recent news. Or, write to the family of a historical or fictional character as if you were the deceased's contemporary.

R2
THE DICTIONARY

Learn to use the resources of different kinds of dictionaries.

People are forever creating new combinations of sounds to stand for new concepts, and dropping those for which the concepts have disappeared. Therefore, a dictionary is never finished once and for all. The technical name for dictionary making is *lexicography*:

> **lex·i·cog·ra·pher** \\,lek-sə-'käg-rə-fər\\ *n* : an author or compiler of a dictionary
> **lex·i·cog·ra·phy** \\-fē\\ *n* **1** : the editing or making of a dictionary **2** : the principles and practices of dictionary making — **lex·i·co·graph·ic** \\-kō-'graf-ik\\ *or* **lex·i·co·graph·i·cal** \\-'graf-i-kəl\\ *adj* — **lex·i·co·graph·i·cal·ly** \\-i-k(ə-)lē\\ *adv*
>
> *—Webster's New Students Dictionary*

R2a
General Dictionaries

Study the full range of information provided in general dictionaries.

Unabridged dictionaries are huge, heavy, and expensive. They are usually found on pedestals in libraries, and very few people buy them for personal use. An *abridged* dictionary is a smaller, less complete list of words with only the more common definitions. Although there are pocket-sized and pamphlet-form abridged dictionaries, most students find the college-size edition best for their needs. Some dictionaries of this size are:

Webster's New Collegiate Dictionary (Merriam-Webster)
The American Heritage Dictionary
Webster's New World Dictionary of the American Language
The Random House Dictionary, College Edition
Funk and Wagnalls Standard College Dictionary
Webster's New Students Dictionary
Thorndike Barnhart High School Dictionary

Each word discussed in a dictionary is called an entry. Entries are arranged in columns in alphabetical order. The two words **at** the top of each page are the first and last entries found on that page and serve as a guide for the rapid finding of the word sought.

A dictionary offers the following information about every entry:

(1) SPELLING: Some words have *more than one* correct spelling. Example: *caddie* or *caddy*. The plural of *ski* is given as *"skis or ski also skiis,"* meaning that *ski* or *skis* is equally common but that *skiis* is less often used. Different spellings may be listed as separate entries. For example, in *The American College Dictionary* we find:

> **ee·rie** (ĭr′ĭ), *adj.,* **-rier, -riest.** **1.** inspiring fear; weird, strange, or uncanny. **2.** affected with superstitious fear. [ME *eri,* d. var. of obs. *argh,* OE *earg* cowardly, c. G *arg* bad] —ee′ri·ly, *adv.* —ee′ri·noss, *n.* —**Syn. 1.** See **weird.**
> **ee·ry** (ĭr′ĭ), *adj.,* **-rier, -riest.** eerie.

(2) PRONUNCIATION: There is *no one standard system* for representing sounds. Each major dictionary uses its own makeshift way of indicating English pronunciation. The symbols used are explained, with examples, at the beginning of the book, and usually at the bottom of every page. Pronunciation is often indicated in parentheses, as follows:

(ˌlek-sɔ-ˈkäg-rɔ-fē) or (lĕk′ sɔ kŏg′ rɔ fi).

(3) PART OF SPEECH: The grammatical status of a word usually appears in abbreviated form after its pronunciation: n. (noun); v. or vb (verb); v.t. (transitive verb); v.i. (intransitive verb); adj. (adjective); adv. (adverb); conj (conjunction, or connective); prep. (preposition); pron. (pronoun); interj. (interjection—words like *Ah* and *Oh*).

Often a word can be used in more than one way. *Like,* for example, can be a *vi,* a *vit,* a *n,* an *adj,* an *adv,* a *prep,* or a *conj.* It may appear as a separate entry in each of these capacities, or one entry may have many definitions, each introduced by the appropriate part of speech.

(4) CHANGING FORMS:

—*Plurals* If the plural of a word is unusual it will be listed after the letters *pl.* Example: *"moose* (mo͞os) n. pl. moose."

—*Past tense and participles* If a verb is regular, that is, if it adds –*ed* for its past tense and past participle *(walk, walked, had walked, walking*), these forms are usually not listed. If it is irregular, the dictionary gives the variations; for example, "*take* (tāk), v., *took, taken, taking.*" Sometimes there is more than one past tense; for example, "*hang* (hang) v. *hung* or (esp. for capital punishment and suicide) *hanged; hanging.*"

—*Comparative or superlative* No forms are given for adjectives and adverbs that are regularly compared (*small, smaller, smallest,* or *hostile, more hostile, most hostile*). However, if the adjective or adverb is irregular, the comparative and superlative are given in the dictionary; for example, "*little, less, least.*"

—*Other forms* Adjectives and adverbs that logically evolve from nouns in spelling and meaning may be put at the end of the noun entry. For example, if you look for the word *sarcastically,* you may find *sarcasm* as an entry. At the end of that entry may be *sarcastic* and *sarcastically.* Nouns directly formed from an adjective may be put at the end of the adjective entry. For example, under the entry *inseparable,* we find *inseparability* and *inseparableness,* as well as the adverb *inseparably.* While some words beginning with *in–* or *un–* and having a negative meaning are alphabetically included in the entries, others whose meanings are directly opposite to their root words are listed in columns either under *in–* and *un–* or at the bottom of several pages of *in–* or *un–* words.

(5) DEFINITION. Most words have several meanings and, when used with other words, become expressions with still other meanings. The word *take* used as a transitive verb may have nineteen numbered definitions; as an intransitive verb, eight more. Then there will be expressions using *take* as a part of a verb phrase, such as *take account of, take heart, take place,* etc. A definition with several meanings may give the oldest one first—the original sense of the word—and then others chronologically. Or it may give the most common meaning first. At times the arrangement is at random. The important thing is to find the sense of the word that fits the context in which you are using it.

(6) STATUS LABELS: Be alert for italicized words or abbreviations before definitions. Some of the common ones are:

Obs.   Obsolete. Has not been standard usage for at least 200 years.

Archaic   Old-fashioned. Sometimes used now but not current modern usage.

Slang	Extremely informal. Not acceptable for serious speech or writing.
Substand. or Nonstand.	Not acceptable in standard use.
Dial.	Dialect. Regional (sometimes with part of country given).
Poetic or Literary	Not used in ordinary conversation or writing.
Colloq.	Informal, everyday speech and writing.

(7) ETYMOLOGY: Dictionaries give the derivation of words—they tell us where words came from and how they grew. The entry for *eerie* in the *New Collegiate* adds in square brackets: [ME *eri*, fr OE *earg* cowardly, wretched]. ME stands for *Middle English*, fr means *from*, and OE is *Old English*. An Old English word *earg* evolved into a Middle English word *eri* and then into our modern word *eerie*. Along with spelling change came meaning change, since the word no longer has the meaning of *cowardly*.

(8) SYNONYMS AND ANTONYMS: At the end of an entry you may find the abbreviation *Syn*. For example, after the word *center* we find "*Syn. 1. See middle.*" This means that *middle* is like *center* in some, but not necessarily all, of its meanings. After *Syn.* there may be the abbreviation *Ant*. An antonym is a word that means the opposite or almost the opposite of the entry. For example, in the entry *large* we find "*Ant. 1. small.*"

(9) ADDITIONAL INFORMATION: Trademarks, biography, mythical characters, historical events, geographical names, medical terms, and scientific names of plants and animals are often found in the main part of the collegiate-sized dictionary so that the dictionary can be used as an encyclopedia if only minimal information is sought. Most collegiate-sized dictionaries have, in addition, information at the front or back of the book. First and most important, there is always information on that particular dictionary and how to use it. There may be as well:

a guide to punctuation
abbreviations (sometimes included in main part)
signs and symbols (mathematics, music, etc.)
proofreaders' marks
biographical names
a gazetteer (with pronunciation)
forms of address

given names (with meanings)
rhymes
colleges and universities with location
weights and measures
foreign alphabets

ACTIVITY 1

Look up the following words for spelling, part of speech, pronunciation, plural (for nouns), definition, and derivation. Be sure to note whether there is more than one spelling and/or more than one way of saying the word:

Caribbean	doomsday	develop
cerebrum	general	carp
harass	eclectic	gee

ACTIVITY 2

Look up *sinister*. How many senses (meanings) of the word are given? Which do you suppose was the earliest? Why? In what order does your dictionary give the definitions—chronological? common usage? at random? Which words are formed from *sinister*? Which ones share the entry? Which are separate entries? Are there any synonyms or antonyms?

R2b
Specialized Dictionaries

Learn to use specialized dictionaries limited to words and expressions on one subject.

Familiarize yourself with one or more of the following:

—*The thesaurus:* A thesaurus is a dictionary of synonyms and antonyms. The best-known and most widely used is *Roget's International Thesaurus.* In this book, words are grouped by subject and must be located by means of an index which is heavily cross-referenced. Each subject covers a considerable range of meanings so that one must be alert to guard against going "off the track" when searching for ways to express an idea. Pertinent quotations are printed at the bottom of each page. There are paperbacks serving the same purpose, which are less complete but easier to use, as well as *Funk and Wagnalls Standard Handbook of Synonyms, Antonyms and Prepositions* and *Webster's Dictionary of Synonyms.*

—*Special-purpose dictionaries:* Lists of words with their meanings peculiar to professions and special interests are almost endless.

Some specialized dictionaries are as follows. (Their names indicate their content.)

A Practical Dictionary of Rhymes
Abbreviations Dictionary
Harper's Bible Dictionary
The American Political Dictionary
The McGraw-Hill Dictionary of Modern Economics
2001 Business Terms and What They Mean
The Barnhart Dictionary of New English Since 1963

ACTIVITY 1

Study one of the following entries in *Roget's Thesaurus*. Prepare a report on everything you learned:

chance   untruth   freedom

ACTIVITY 2

Find a specialized dictionary related to one of your hobbies or special interests. Prepare a brief report.

Learn how to find information in a library.

The library is the resource area of the school, a depository of information that we consult to expand upon and enrich the work of the classroom. The library is to the humanities what the laboratory is to the sciences.

R3
THE LIBRARY

Become familiar with the overall plan of your library.

Although there is a general plan of arrangement that holds true for all libraries, you must become familiar with the organization of the room that houses your school library.

The printed material in a library's collection is broken down into definite categories. Books, for example, are divided into the categories of *fiction* and *nonfiction*. There are further classifications within these two categories. Periodicals and magazines are also considered separately. Nonprinted materials, such as records, tapes, microfilm, and possibly motion picture films, are separated from the printed items. A typical library's collection will be organized as follows:

(1) One section of the shelves will be devoted to fiction, that is, novel-length stories. They will be arranged alphabetically, ac-

R3a

The Arrangement of a
Library

cording to the first letter of the author's last name. Several books by the same author will be arranged alphabetically according to the first letter of the title. (The articles *a, an,* and *the* appearing at the beginning of a title are not considered for purposes of alphabetical listing.)

(2) Frequently, collections of short stories are separated from novels, although they are sometimes kept on the same shelves. When such stories are kept in a separate place, they will be arranged on the shelves in the same way as the novels, according to the alphabetical order of the author's or editor's last name.

(3) Periodicals and magazines are usually kept on racks in a separate section of the library. These are usually arranged alphabetically according to the *title* of the magazine or periodical. (Sometimes they are arranged according to subject matter.)

(4) Nonfiction or *factual books* are arranged numerically rather than alphabetically. The **Dewey Decimal system** is one classification system. Melvil Dewey classified nonfiction into ten major categories and assigned a numerical designation to each:

000–099	general reference works: dictionaries, encyclopedias, etc. These are almost always kept apart from the other nonfiction books.
100–199	philosophy, psychology, ethics
200–299	religion (including mythology)
300–399	social sciences: immigration, economics, government, education, folklore

Within these hundreds, each group of ten sketches out a subdivision of the large area. For instance, 970–979 is North American history; 980–989 is South American history. Each digit within these groups of tens subdivides further: For instance, 972 covers the history of Mexico; 973 the history of the United States. A decimal added after these three numbers helps divide American history into periods: Colonial history is 973.2. Even further subdivision may be necessary, each with a reason of its own. A book dealing with the French and Indian wars during colonial times may be classified as 973.26.

The **Library of Congress system** divides books into categories identified by letters of the alphabet. It then uses additional letters and numerals to subdivide each main category. For instance, the call number of a book on religion would start with a capital *B;* the call number of a book on education starts with a capital *L.*

NOTE: Magazines do not have a "call number." They are simply identified by name, number of the volume (if any), and date of the issue. A "volume" of a magazine usually includes all the issues appearing in one calendar or academic year. After they have been collected, the issues for one or more volumes are usually bound together.

ACTIVITY

Can you find all the following books in your library?

The World Almanac published by *New York World Telegram and Sun*
A Farewell to Arms by Ernest Hemingway
The Epic of Man by the editors of *Life* magazine
All the King's Men by Robert Penn Warren
My Cousin Rachel by Daphne du Maurier
Othello by William Shakespeare
Profiles in Courage by John F. Kennedy
Mythology by Edith Hamilton

Learn to use the card catalog.

R3b
The Card Catalog

While some libraries use only one card catalog, others have a main catalog plus auxiliaries for special books or reference materials such as microfilms.

(1) The main card catalog will be a cabinet of little drawers containing 3 × 5 cards, arranged in alphabetical order. Generally, these cards are bought from the Library of Congress and come with the books when they are purchased. There are ordinarily *three cards* for every book: a card on which the *author's name* appears at the top and which is filed by the last name of the author; a *title card*, on which the book's name appears at the top and which is filed by the first word of the title; and a *subject card*, on which a brief description of what the book is about is at the top and which is filed by the first word of that description.

(2) There may be a *short story catalog* separate from the main set of drawers. This will list short stories, telling in which book or books of collected stories each appears. Suppose a teacher has assigned "The Outcasts of Poker Flat" by Bret Harte. You would go to the short story card catalog, find *Harte, Bret*, turn your attention to the titles of his stories and locate "Outcasts," which would be in alphabetical position under *O*. You would see that it

AUTHOR CARD

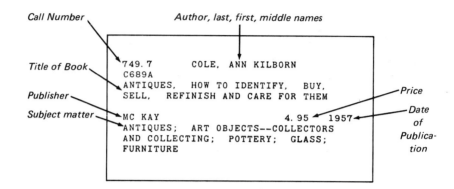

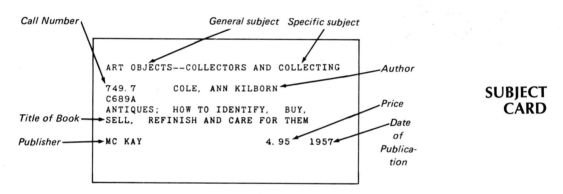

SUBJECT CARD

could be found in several different collections. After copying down the names of editors and their books, you would go to the SC (story collections) part of the stacks and find one of the collections containing the story. The book's index would tell you on what page your story appears.

(3) Catalog cards for *records, filmstrips,* and *microfilm* may be mixed in with the book cards, or they may be in a portable file somewhere in the library. Records ordinarily have four cards each: composer, title, performer, and type of selection or album.

(4) The *vertical file* is a fancy name for a very plain device. Every library accumulates many nonbooks, that is, pamphlets and papers that cannot be put on the shelves. There is often valuable, up-to-date information in those awkward publications. The solution is to file them by subject matter, putting articles on the same topic into manila folders, labeling the folders, and alphabetizing. If you are assigned a research project, look into the vertical file; you may find recent and pertinent material on your subject.

ACTIVITY 1

How is a *nom de plume* handled in the card catalog? Take Mark Twain or George Eliot as examples unless you can think of some double-named authors yourself.

ACTIVITY 2

Examine catalog cards on the following subjects:

animals   electricity   United States

Make a few notes on the divisions within these large subjects. You need not copy them all.

ACTIVITY 3

Guess how many cards are in your library's card catalog under "United States." Was it necessary for your librarian to break down the subject with guide tabs? Would it be necessary to know specifically what aspect of the United States you wanted in order to find an appropriate book?

ACTIVITY 4

In how many different collections in your library can one find:

1. "The Outcasts of Poker Flat" by Bret Harte
2. "The Ransom of Red Chief" by O. Henry
3. "To Build a Fire" by Jack London

Learn to use the Readers' Guide to Periodical Literature.

     R3c
     The Readers' Guide

The *Guide* is itself a magazine that comes out twice a month ten months of the year but only once in July and August. The contents of these issues are combined every two years and published as hard-cover books. There are other indexes to periodical literature, but most high schools subscribe to the *Readers' Guide* only.

(1) While the *Readers' Guide* lists articles from over 100 magazines, it may not cover all the periodicals received by your library. Conversely, your library is unlikely to stock all the magazines with which *Readers' Guide* deals.

(2) Listings for magazine articles are by author and subject, not by title. Listings for stories are by title and author, not by subject. Items come one after the other down the page in alphabetical order, authors and subjects intermingled. The order of the author entry is as follows:

AUTHOR (last name first)
Article title (without quotation marks) ; magazine (often abbreviated—key is found in the front of guide) ; volume; pages; date of issue.

ROSS, Arnold
Natural world of the post office. Natur Hist
77:28-31 Ja '68

The subject entry order is:

SUBJECT:
Article title; author; magazine; volume; pages; date of issue.
Other articles may follow.

POSTAGE stamps
Natural world of the post office; natural history theme on stamps.   A. Ross.   ii   Natur Hist 77:28-31 Ja '68

The subjects POEMS and DRAMA list all poems and plays in the participating magazines. Poems and dramas are also listed by author.

There is a great deal of cross-referencing, so, if you cannot find a specific subject, think of other ways the same concept might be expressed and look again.

ACTIVITY 1

(A) List three magazines mentioned in the *Readers' Guide* that are *not* carried in your school library.

(B) List any magazines received by your library that are not mentioned in the *Readers' Guide*.

ACTIVITY 2

Can you find any poems by or articles about Robert Frost listed in the *Readers' Guide* for 1965–67? How many of each?

R3d
Reference Books

Learn to use reference books as sources of factual information.

Ordinarily reference books cannot be taken out of the library.

(1) Almanacs and yearbooks: *Consult an almanac for a quick answer to a definite question.* An almanac is a "yearly calendar." Books of dubious predictions about the weather and world events used to be published under the name of "farmers' almanac." Today, the word refers to a book of accurate information, largely statistical, about what has happened in the preceding year and years past. From an almanac a person can quickly find out which was the first, the biggest, the last, or the best of just about anything.

—Popular almanacs:

> *The World Almanac and Book of Facts*
> *Information Please*
> *Statesman's Yearbook*
> *Reader's Digest Almanac*

(2) Encyclopedias: *Consult an encyclopedia for a bird's-eye view of a subject.* Encyclopedias go beyond the statistical treatment of the almanac to tell why and how as well as who, where, and when. They give a convenient *survey* of a subject. *Topics* are usually, but not always, arranged alphabetically with the last volume containing an *index* of all references to any subject throughout the volumes. Most, but not all, encyclopedia publishing houses print *yearly supplements* to keep the sets up to date between editions. Periodically, major revisions are made and entirely new editions appear. *Encyclopaedia Britannica,* for example, was totally overhauled for its 1974 publication.

—Some general encyclopedias:

Encyclopaedia Britannica	Very complete: pictures, charts, innovative format
Encyclopedia Americana	Index contains illustrated chronology of last five years
Colliers Encyclopedia	Many pictures, index volume contains bibliography on many subjects

—Some specialized encyclopedias (titles indicate subject matter):

> *Encyclopedia of World Art*
> *Scribner Music Library*
> *McGraw-Hill Encyclopedia of Science and Technology*
> *The Harper Encyclopedia of Science*
> *The Book of Popular Science*
> *Worldmark Encyclopedia of the Nations* (including the United Nations)
> *Lands and Peoples*

(3) Biographical reference books: *Consult a biographical reference book when you want to know factual details about a person.* Biographical reference books do not judge a person's contribution, nor do they try to explain his or her character as a full biography would do. The more specialized they are in scope, the more detail they are likely to give. Most biographical reference books are specialized as to nationality, profession, or era, with overlapping categories.

—Some biographical reference books limited by *nationality:*

> *Dictionary of American Biography*
> *Who's Who in America*
> *Who Was Who in America*
> *Who's Who of American Women*
> *Who's Who in France* (or other countries)
> *Concise Dictionary of National Biography*

—Some biographical reference books limited by *profession:*

> *American Men of Science*
> *Groves Dictionary of Music and Musicians*
> *Twentieth Century Authors*
> *Contemporary Authors*

(4) Reference books on literature: By using the proper reference book, you can find out if there has ever been a book written on a certain subject, the exact words of a quotation, or where to find a copy of any poem or story. You can also read a brief review of any book.

—Some general books on literature:

> *The Concise Encyclopedia of Modern World Literature*
> *Reader's Encyclopedia of American Literature*
> *Cassell's Encyclopedia of World Literature*

—Two books of quotations:

> *Home Book of Quotations*   Arranged by subject
> *Bartlett's Familiar Quotations*   Arranged chronologically; alphabetically by key word

—Some indexes (titles indicate contents):

> *Books in Print*   Three volumes: author, title, and subject; a book is found as in the card catalog
> *Cumulative Book Index*
> *Book Review Digest*   Printed yearly with a cumulative index every few years

ACTIVITY

Find the following information. After each answer write the name of the reference book in which you found it.

1. Which actor, actress, and picture won the motion picture academy awards in 1964?
2. Give three pertinent facts about the manufacture of glass.
3. What are the dates of Thomas Edison's birth and death? Where was he born? Where did he live most of his life?
4. What is known about the earliest inhabitants of the American continent?

ILLUSTRATION CREDITS

(listed clockwise from upper left)

Cover art: Jack Weaver. Title Page: Lee Lorenz. Page vi: Big Sky, Montana. viii: Michal Heron. ix: Haas/Magnum. x: Jane Latta. xi: Rice/Monkmeyer; Burri/Magnum. xii: Bailey/Stock Boston. xiii, xiv: Joel Gordon. 2: Lee Lorenz. 5: B. Bölstad/Peter Arnold; Rice/Monkmeyer; Big Sky, Montana; Michal Heron. 6: Amos/Photo Researchers; Steve Eagle; Bailey/Stock Boston. 7: B. Bölstad/Peter Arnold; Jane Latta; Siteman/Stock Boston; Franken/Stock Boston. 10: Jack Weaver. 13. Rogers/Monkmeyer; Joel Gordon; Franken/Stock Boston; Franken/Stock Boston. 14: Robert Capece; Michal Heron; Jane Latta. 15: Franken/Stock Boston; Michal Heron; Bettina Cirone; Steve Eagle. 16, 25, 30, 37, 45, 50, 51, 55, 57, 58: Jack Weaver. 61: Wood/Photo Researchers. 62, 65, 66: Jack Weaver. 82: Lee Lorenz. 91, 96, 104, 107, 115, 119, 120, 121, 130: Jack Weaver. 134: Michal Heron. 137, 143, 144, 145, 156, 157: Jack Weaver. 160: The Bettmann Archive. 163: Jack Weaver. 165: Krasemann/Peter Arnold; Hays/Monkmeyer; Janion/Monkmeyer; Merrim/Monkmeyer. 166: Jack Weaver. 171: Peter Buckley. 175: Rue/Monkmeyer. 184: Lee Lorenz. 197, 207, 211: Jack Weaver. 214: Sapieha/Stock Boston; B. Bölstad/Peter Arnold; B. Bölstad/Peter Arnold; Michal Heron. 221: Jack Weaver. 235: Stradanus/The Bettmann Archive. 240, 252: Jack Weaver. 257, 258, 259: Eisenstaedt/Time Picture Agency. 262: Jack Weaver. 273: Bill Binzen. 274: Avery/Stock Boston. 275: Lanks/Monkmeyer; Erwitt/Magnum. 284: Haas/Magnum. 285: Burri/Magnum. 286: Jack Weaver. 294: Gahan Wilson/(c) 1973 by Mercury Press, Inc. Reprinted from *The Magazine of Fantasy and Science Fiction*. 299: Pinney/Monkmeyer; Herbert Noxon; Joel Gordon; Joel Gordon; Robert Capece. 303: Jack Weaver. 321: Metropolitan Opera Association, Inc., Press Department. 324: Robert Capece/Jack Guaghan, *Analog*, (c) 1974 by Mercury Press, Inc. Reprinted from *The Magazine of Fantasy and Science Fiction*; *Fantastic Science Fiction and Fantasy Stories*; *Galaxy*. 326: Lee Lorenz. 330, 331: Jack Weaver. 350: Library of Congress; Wide World Photos; Franklin D. Roosevelt Library. 354: Lee Lorenz. 355, 356, 365, 375, 377: Jack Weaver. 381, 383: Vantage Art. 387, 399, 407, 411, 419: Jack Weaver. 428: Lee Lorenz. 430, 433, 434, 435, 442, 448, 451, 453: Jack Weaver. 456: (c) 1974 United Feature Syndicate, Inc. 461: Vantage Art. 465, 469, 477, 484, 497, 505, 506, 507: Jack Weaver.

ACKNOWLEDGMENTS

We are indebted to the following for permission to reprint copyrighted material:

Mrs. Frederick Lewis Allen for permission to reprint an excerpt from "Horatio Alger, Jr." which appeared in *Saturday Review*.

The American Heritage Division of McGraw-Hill, Inc. for permission to reprint excerpts from "The Great American Game" by Bruce Catton.

American Mercury for permission to reprint excerpts from "Our Enemy, the Cat" by Alan Devoe; and from "Juvenile Delinquency and Its Cure" by Billy Graham. Both reprinted from *American Mercury*, P. O. Box 1306, Torrance, CA 90505.

Atheneum Publishers, Inc. for permission to reprint "Alarm Clock," "Umbilical," "Markings: Exclamation," and "Markings: Semicolon" by Eve Merriam from *Finding a Poem*. Copyright © 1970 by Eve Merriam; and for an excerpt from "Out Loud Out Loud Out Loud" by Eve Merriam. Copyright © 1973 by Eve Merriam. All used by permission of Atheneum Publishers, Inc.

Dr. Sylvia Lyons Render, at the Library of Congress, for permission to reprint selected excerpts by Charles Waddell Chesnutt, and for her definition of *goopher*.

G. Robert Carlsen and the NCTE for permission to reprint short reviews by G. Robert Carlsen of *His Enemy, His Friend, A Teacup of Roses,* and *Soul Catchers,* which appeared in the February, 1974, *English Journal.*

Loretta Clarke and the NCTE for permission to reprint "*The Pigman:* A Novel of Adolescence" by Loretta Clarke, which appeared in the November, 1972, *English Journal.*

Raymond D. Crisp for permission to reprint an excerpt from "Last Man on Earth" which appeared in *Cumflaging Together.*

Dodd, Mead and Company for permission to reprint an excerpt from *Winnowed Wisdom* by Stephen Leacock.

Doubleday & Company, Inc., for permission to reprint an excerpt from *The Indian and the White Man,* edited by Wilcomb E. Washburn, copyright © 1964.

Farrar, Straus & Giroux, Inc. for permission to reprint an excerpt from *Lives Around Us* by Alan Devoe.

Beverly Haley and the NCTE for permission to reprint short reviews by Beverly Haley of *I'll Get There: It Better Be Worth the Trip* and *Up a Road Slowly,* which appeared in the February, 1974, *English Journal.*

Harcourt Brace Jovanovich, Inc. for permission to reprint excerpts from *Abinger Harvest* by E. M. Forster, copyright 1936, 1964 by E. M. Forster; from *A Walker in the City,* copyright 1951, by Alfred Kazin; and "Wilderness" from *Cornhuskers* by Carl Sandburg, copyright 1918, by Holt, Rinehart and Winston, Inc., renewed 1946 by Carl Sandburg. All reprinted by permission of Harcourt Brace Jovanovich, Inc.

Harper & Row, Publishers, Inc. for permission to reprint excerpts from *Going Into Space* by Arthur C. Clarke, copyright 1954 by Harper & Row; from *A Choice of Weapons* (pages 1–2) by Gordon Parks, copyright © 1966 by Harper & Row; and from *One Man's Meat* (page 333) by E. B. White, copyright 1944 by Harper & Row.

Hawthorn Books, Inc. for permission to reprint an excerpt from *Short Grass Country* by Stanley Vestal. Copyright 1941 by Stanley Vestal. By permission of Hawthorn Books, Inc. All rights reserved.

G. & C. Merriam Company for permission to reprint entries from *Webster's New Collegiate Dictionary,* as follows: "Salk vaccine," "sapodilla," "scherzo," "schizophrenia," "schnozzle," "shortstop," "*sic passim,*" "Sigurd," "Simon," "Sirius," "smearcase," "sonnet," "spoils system," and "surrealism." Copyright © 1974 by G. & C. Merriam Company, publishers of the Merriam-Webster Dictionaries; and from *Webster's Third New International Dictionary,* as follows: "sky coach," "pants," "patagonian," and "physique." Copyright © 1971 by G. & C. Merriam Company, publishers of the Merriam-Webster Dictionaries. All reprinted with permission.

Holt, Rinehart and Winston, Inc. for permission to reprint an excerpt from *Brave Men* by Ernie Pyle.

Ebony Magazine for permission to reprint an excerpt from "Joe Dorgan's Strange Will" by Chuck Offenburger; and for an advertisement featuring Leontyne Price, both from the March, 1974, issue of *Ebony*. Copyright © 1974 by Johnson Publishing Company, Inc.

Macmillan Publishing Company, Inc. for permission to reprint an excerpt from *Sixpence in Her Shoe* by Phyllis McGinley. Copyright © 1960, 1962, 1963, 1964 by Phyllis McGinley.

Harold Matson Company, Inc. for permission to reprint an excerpt from *Martian Chronicles*—"August 2026" by Ray Bradbury. Copyright 1946, 1948, 1949, 1950, 1958 by Ray Bradbury. Reprinted by permission of Harold Matson Company, Inc.

McIntosh and Otis, Inc. for permission to reprint excerpts from "How to Tell Good Guys From Bad Guys" by John Steinbeck. Appeared originally in *The Reporter*. Reprinted by permission of McIntosh and Otis, Inc.

Scott Meredith Literary Agency, Inc. for permission to reprint an excerpt from *Night Wings* by Robert Silverberg. Copyright © 1968, 1969 by Galaxy Publishing Company, Inc. Reprinted by permission of the author and his agents, Scott Meredith Literary Agency, Inc., 580 Fifth Avenue, New York, NY 10036.

National Geographic Society for permission to reprint an excerpt from "The Other Side of Jordan" by Luis Marden.

The New York Times for permission to reprint excerpts from "Kennedy Is Killed by Sniper as He Rides in Car in Dallas; Johnson Sworn in on Plane" of November 23, 1963; and from "Grandma Moses" by Harold Schonberg of *The New York Times Magazine*, 1959. Copyright © 1963/1959 by The New York Times Company. Reprinted by permission.

Organization of American States for permission to reprint an excerpt from "Mexico's Model Children" by H. Allen Smith which appeared in the November, 1957, issue of *Américas*.

Oxford University Press for permission to reprint excerpts from *The Sea Around Us* by Rachel L. Carson. Copyright © 1950, 1951, 1960 by Rachel L. Carson. Reprinted by permission of Oxford University Press, Inc.

A. D. Peters and Company for permission to reprint an excerpt from *Journey Down a Rainbow* by J. B. Priestley. Reprinted by permission of A. D. Peters and Company.

Frederik Pohl for permission to reprint an excerpt from *Some Joys Under the Star* by Frederik Pohl. Copyright © 1973 by Frederik Pohl. Reprinted by permission of the author.

Prentice-Hall, Inc. for permission to reprint an excerpt from *A History of the English Language* by Albert C. Baugh, Second Edition, © 1957. Reprinted by permission of Prentice-Hall, Inc., Englewood Cliffs, NJ.

Rand McNally & Company for permission to reprint an excerpt from *Kon-Tiki* by Thor Heyerdahl. Copyright 1950 by Thor Heyerdahl. Published in the United States by Rand McNally & Company.

Random House, Inc. for permission to reprint excerpts from *The American College Dictionary*, the entry "eerie," copyright © 1960 by Random House; from *I Know Why the Caged Bird Sings* by Maya Angelou, copyright © 1969 by Maya Angelou; from *The Immense Journey* by Loren Eiseley, copyright © 1957 by Loren Eiseley; from *The Natural History of Nonsense* by Bergen Evans, copyright 1946 by Bergen Evans; from "The Bear" from *Go Down, Moses* by William Faulkner, copyright 1942, renewed 1970 by Estelle Faulkner and Jill Faulkner Summers; from *A Raisin in the Sun* by Lorraine Hansberry, copyright © 1959 by Lorraine Hansberry; from *Farewell to Sport* by Paul Gallico, copyright 1937, 1938 by Paul Gallico; from "To Sleep, Perchance to Steam" by S. J. Perelman from *The Best of S. J. Perelman*, copyright 1942 by S. J. Perelman; from *Of Whales and Men* by R. B. Robertson, copyright 1954 by R. B. Robertson. All reprinted by permission of Random House, Inc

Sylvia Render for permission to reprint excerpts by Charles Waddell Chesnutt.

William Saroyan for permission to reprint an excerpt from "Romance," which appeared in *Peace, It's Wonderful* by William Saroyan, copyright 1939.

Saturday Review for permission to reprint excerpts from "Television: The Splitting Image" by Marya Mannes; and from "The Rhinoceros" by Henry Morgan.

Scott, Foresman and Company for permission to reprint the entry "fancy" from the Thorndike-Barnhart Advanced Dictionary by E. L. Thorndike and Clarence L. Barnhart. Copyright © 1973 by Scott, Foresman and Company. Reprinted by permission of the publisher.

Irving Shepard for permission to reprint an excerpt from *The Call of the Wild* by Jack London.

United Publishing Corporation for permission to reprint an excerpt from "I Have a Dream," a speech delivered by Martin Luther King, Jr., at Washington, D. C. on August 28, 1963, reprinted in *The Journal of Negro History*.

The Viking Press, Inc. for permission to reprint excerpts from *The Overloaded Ark* by Gerald M. Durrell. Copyright 1953 by Gerald M. Durrell. Reprinted by permission of The Viking Press, Inc.

Wadsworth Publishing Company, Inc. for permission to reprint excerpts from *Communications in Business* by Walter Wells. Copyright © 1968 by Wadsworth Publishing Company, Inc., Belmont, CA 94002. Reprinted by permission of the publisher.

The Washington Post for permission to reprint an excerpt from a July 21, 1969, article on the first manned lunar landing.

INDEX